MW01001430

VIOLIN-MAKING
A HISTORICAL AND PRACTICAL GUIDE

Edward Heron-Allen

Tone quality, sound post 150
Bridge 159 —
Maggini, double purfling 163, f hole 73
Ground 118, 294
Gamboge 294
Varnish 295
Fingerboard, pry off 297
Wood clips to true the Bridge 161-162
Oil, linseed 176-177

DOVER PUBLICATIONS, INC.
Mineola, New York

Bibliographical Note

This Dover edition, first published in 2005, is an unabridged republication of the second edition of *Violin-making, as it was and is,* originally published by Ward, Lock and Company, London, in 1885. Three fold-out charts of violin moulds have been reduced to fit this edition and can be found on pages 369–371.

International Standard Book Number: 0-486-44356-6

Manufactured in the United States of America
Dover Publications, Inc., 31 East 2nd Street, Mineola, N.Y. 11501

VIOLIN-MAKING
A HISTORICAL AND
PRACTICAL GUIDE

"Forewords."

"For herde yt ys a man toe attayne
"Toe make a thynge perfytte atte first syghte :
"But wan yt ys rede, ande wel ouer seyne
"Fautes maye bee founde thatte neuer cam toe lyghte,
"Though ye makere doe hys dyligence and myghte.
"Prayeing theym toe take yt as J haue entendyd,
"Ande toe forgiue mee, yf thatte J haue offendyd."

E. H.-A.

VIOLIN-MAKING,

AS IT WAS AND IS;

BEING A

Historical, Theoretical, and Practical Treatise

ON THE

SCIENCE AND ART OF VIOLIN–MAKING,

FOR THE USE OF

VIOLIN MAKERS AND PLAYERS,

AMATEUR AND PROFESSIONAL.

BY

ED. HERON-ALLEN,

AUTHOR OF "THE ANCESTRY OF THE VIOLIN," "THE HISTORY OF A GREAT VIOLIN CASE,"
"THE ROMANCE OF A STRADIVARI," ETC., ETC.

WITH UPWARDS OF 200 ILLUSTRATIONS BY THE AUTHOR.

Viva fui insylvis, sum durâ occisa securi,
Dum vixi tacui, mortua dulce cano.

PRECEDED BY

An Essay on the Violin and its Position as a Musical Instrument.

From a Photograph by Van der Weyde.

Always most sincerely Yours

Ed Heron Allen

Music ! O Thou who in the eternal past,
Awful, divine, inexorable, grave,
Broodedst, as did the Spirit of the Lord,
Upon the water's face, we come to Thee.

Great Soul of Life ! Stern Judge ; Sweet Comforter ;
Magnificent, severe, and heavenly high
Yet tender as a mother to her babe,
Though she pluck kisses eagerly, and while
Impassioned as a lover's rhapsody,
Still melting as the pleading of a child
We bless Thy holy name for evermore.

In such poor ways as we are masters of,
We sing Thy praises : and this small sweet thing.
Devised in love, and fashioned cunningly
Of wood and strings, shall weave the harmonies
Thy Spirit sways ; until we know Thee nigh,
Who, now afar yet shining in some eyes,
Speakest eternal Life in changeless Love,
And whisperest of things unspeakable.

PERCY REEVE.

PREFACE TO THE SECOND EDITION.

As many of my Readers are doubtless already aware, much of the substance of the Theoretical and Practical parts of the following treatise appeared originally in the pages of *Amateur Work Illustrated* (vols. i., ii., iii., 1882-3-4). The work has profited largely by this preliminary publication in serial form, for, as chapter after chapter appeared, many valuable letters were received from readers of the Magazine who were interested in Violin-making, both professionally and *en amateur*, containing information on doubtful points, hints and suggestions as to the desiderata of fiddle-makers, and pointing out where my work was to the casual reader unintelligible, or seemingly incorrect. All such corrections and additions as were thus suggested have now been added to the original text, greatly, of course, to its advantage, for it is hardly necessary to point out that there must always be much in a work which may seem clear as the noonday to the writer, but which may be incomprehensible to the reader who cannot follow what was the Author's chain of thought as he committed his sentences to paper. In the same way, since the appearance of the first edition at the end of the year 1884, I have received many valuable suggestions from readers, suggestions by which I have gratefully profited, and I seize this opportunity to record my indebtedness in this respect to Mr. John Bishop (of Cheltenham), with whose kindly and careful assistance I have been enabled to add many touches where they have been seriously needed, and also to elucidate many points which have appeared vague in the text.

Written originally for the pages of an exclusively practical Magazine, the work in its serial form was of an exclusively practical nature, but now that space is no longer an object of so much consideration as it is in a periodical, whose pages are carefully allotted amongst its contributors, I have thought it of interest and advantage to the work to add an Introductory Essay, and the Historical chapters, to the somewhat bald dogmata which it was necessary to lay down in a string without any comment upon them, when describing the actual steps to be taken in the solution of the problem :—" *Given*, a log of wood ; *make*, a fiddle." These chapters are the tabulated results of many years of assiduous study of the history of Stringed Instruments, and of constant research among more or less forgotten authors for passages which might assist me in forming an idea of the estimation in which "the king of instruments " has been held throughout the centuries which have elapsed since the introduction of bow instruments in their present forms, and I have been most careful to give the fullest references to every author I have consulted, so that my work may have a bibliographical as well as an historical value.

Written originally for Amateurs, I trust that the data I have given, with all the minuteness resulting from a long experience of Violin-making, may prove of much practical value to those whose *metier* it is to give life and song to the dull wood, which is destined to become " that wonder of music, the violin."[1]

Until recently most works which have been published on the Violin, whether practical or otherwise, have been written by Amateurs, who have had but little or no actual experience of the practical processes of Violin-making, and, therefore, the only books which have been of any great value to the luthier have been those written under the direction of, if not dictated by, some practical fiddle-maker. Thus that scarce little work " La Chelonomie," by the Abbé Sibire,[2] was, we know, practically in its entirety the work of the celebrated maker Nicolas Lupot ; again, the anonymous " Luthomonographie,"[3] written

---

[1] " To perfect that wonder of travel—the locomotive—has perhaps not required the expenditure of more mental strength and application, than to perfect that wonder of music—the violin."—*W. E. Gladstone.*

[2] " La Chelonomie, ou le Parfait Luthier," par M. l'Abbé Sibire (Paris: Millet, 1806), reprinted in J. Gallay's " Les Luthiers Italiens, aux xvii⁰ et xviii⁰ siècles ; Nouvelle edition du Parfait Luthier de l'Abbé Sibire " (Paris, 1869).

[3] "Luthomonographie Historique et Raisonnée," etc., par un Amateur (Frankfort s/m : Ch. Jugel, 1856).

by the Russian prince Youssoupow (or Jousoupof), is so full of strange mistakes as to be of but little value apart from its bibliographical rarity ; and there is no doubt that Sandys and Forster's " History of the Violin "[1] owes its popularity and value entirely to the fact that to the charming style and cultivated research of Mr. Sandys, F.S.A., was added the practical knowledge of the great Simon Andrew Forster. Thus it is that, though many works are annually produced in various languages on the subject of the Violin, until very recently there has existed really no practical guide to the actual manufacture of Violins in any language, save the somewhat meagre " Manuel Roret " of MM. Maugin et Maigne.[2] It was urged by this terrible consideration that I determined to write the present work, so that Amateurs need no longer say in despair, " I should *like* to make a fiddle, but cannot find directions anywhere *how* to set to work," so that violinists may at last really know something about how their instruments are made, and so that those who would learn how fiddles are built can do so without going through the tedious and expensive course of tuition which I, and all other fiddle-makers, have had to endure. Thus, to the Theory which has been my constant study ever since I first touched a violin, I have brought the Practice which has been the fascinating amusement of late years, and I think I am right in saying that now for the first time the History, Theory, and Practice of Violin-making have been combined in a single volume.

With a view to reducing to a minimum the historical part of my work (so as to make it as much as possible a practice-book), I have confined such part to my Introduction and a few preliminary chapters, so separated from the rest of the work that those who are not interested in the instrument, beyond the actual principles and practice of its construction, need not necessarily read them to understand the rest of the treatise, but I can hardly imagine that " there breathes the man with soul so dead " as not to feel any curiosity in the evolution, and in the incidents

[1] " The History of the Violin, and other Instruments played on with the bow,' etc., by William Sandys and Simon Andrew Forster (London : Smith, 1864).

[2] Manuels Roret, " Nouveau Manuel Complet du Luthier," etc., par MM. J. C. Maugin et W. Maigne (Paris : Roret, 1869).

of existence, of the instrument which he watches growing beneath his hands into the very incarnation of MUSIC. Such theories as I have quoted from other works, I have supported by the authority from whence they came, so as not to make myself responsible for the errors of others, which I have stigmatized as such whilst presenting them to my readers; and such particulars as have been by their nature or volume inadmissible as foot-notes, I have set out as appendices.

Finally, I beg to lay a tribute of the warmest gratitude at the feet of those members of the violin-trade who have at all times placed their valuable time, experience, and treasures at my absolute disposal, with a courteous generosity which I had neither a right to expect nor the temerity to demand. Especially I desire to thank *Mons. Georges Chanot*, whose pupil in the art of violin-making it has been my privilege to be, for the pains with which he has answered my minutest inquiries, and has put his stores of knowledge, skill, and experience at my disposal; and finally *Mr. William Ebsworth Hill*, and his two sons, whose enormous experience of the trade, and whose enthusiasm and energy in all matters connected with the instrument, have made the friend-ship they have uniformly extended to me of incalculable value in the composition and revision of the following pages, and to the many readers of this work who have applied to them for information and instruction, that circumstances have prevented me from supplying them with personally.

With this prefatory excursion, which I have deemed necessary to prefix to the second edition of my work for the purpose of explanation and introduction (if not of apology), I take leave of my Gentle Readers, many of whom I know are already old friends, to whose criticisms and suggestions anent my work when it appeared in *Amateur Work*, and upon its first appearance in volume form, I owe much of such commendation as may reward my efforts to initiate them in the fascinating mysteries of the Science and Art of Violin-making.

ED. HERON-ALLEN.

ST. JOHN'S, PUTNEY HILL,
LONDON, S.W., *September*, 1885.

CONTENTS.

PART I.—Historical.

CHAPTER I.

THE ANCESTRY OF THE VIOLIN.

CHAPTER II.

THE WELSH CRWTH.

CONTENTS.

CHAPTER III.

BIOGRAPHICAL.

CHAPTER IV.

THE BOW.

CHAPTER V.

THE VIOLIN, ITS VAGARIES AND ITS VARIEGATORS.

PART II.—Theoretical.

CHAPTER VI.

THE WOOD—THE MODEL.

CHAPTER VII.

THE BACK, BELLY, AND SIDES.

CHAPTER VIII.

THE INTERIOR OF THE VIOLIN.

CHAPTER IX.

THE EXTERIOR OF THE VIOLIN.

CHAPTER X.

THE VARNISH.

CHAPTER XI.

FITTINGS AND APPLIANCES.

CHAPTER XVIII.

THE BELLY.

CHAPTER XIX.

PURFLING AND FINISHING THE BODY.

CHAPTER XX.

THE NECK AND SCROLL.

CHAPTER XXI.

THE GUARNERIUS MODEL, WITH WHOLE TABLES ON AN INSIDE MOULD.

CHAPTER XXII.

VARNISHING AND FITTING UP.

CHAPTER XXIII.

REPAIRS.

Appendices.

"Poems."

LIST OF ILLUSTRATIONS.

LIST OF WOOD-CUTS.

The Instrument on which he played
Was in Cremona's workshops made,
By a great master of the past,
Ere yet was lost the art divine.
Fashioned of maple and of pine,
That in Tyrolean forests vast
Had rocked and wrestled with the blast:
Exquisite was it in design,
Perfect in each minutest part,
A marvel of the lutist's art;
And in the hollow chamber, thus
The maker from whose hands it came
Had written his unrivalled name,—
"ANTONIUS STRADIUARIUS."

H. W. LONGFELLOW,
"Tales of a Wayside Inn.

Introduction

"Echoes."

Tutta la notte in sogno mi venite
Ditemi, bella mia, perchè lo fate
Echi viene da voi quando dormite.—STORNELLO TOSCAN

Where is the scent of the Flowers we gathered
　When your rose-garden was all aglow,
And the air too heavy, almost, with sweetness?
　—Vanished, as surely as last year's snow.
Masses of yellow and cream and crimson,
　Deepest golden and faintest pink;—
But the scent of one blood-red bud you gave me
　I shall never forget, I think.

Where is the sound of the Songs you sang then?
　(You on the terrace and I within.)
How fair you looked, with the sky behind you,
　Idly touching your Violin,—
Not classic, no; but your voice was tender,
　(Tears sounded through, though your songs were gay)—
As though you stretched out your hand and touched me,
　It had such a passionate, pleading way.
Soft old Lieder recalling the pine woods,
　Snatches of tinkling serenade;
But one keen sweet phrase in an old Stornello,
　All these years in my soul has stayed.

Surely one day—be it Yule or Summer,
　Rain or sunshine,—by land or sea—
The faint rich fragrance of those dead roses
　Their soul, that still lives, may steal back to me.
And one day, may-be, in some warm still weather,
　Whilst a pale light stays in a tender sky,
I shall hear the notes of your old Stornello
　Wandering back from the hours gone by.

R. A.

July, 1879.

"Hey diddle diddle
The Cat & the Fiddle"

Randolph Caldecott

VIOLIN-MAKING: AS IT WAS AND IS.

Hei didulum ! atque iterum didulum ! Felisque ! Fidesque !
Vacca super Lunæ cornua prosiluit :
Spectatum admissus risit sine fine Catellus,
Et subito rapuit lanx cochleare fuga !

INTRODUCTION.

THERE are but few of us who can look upon the above delightful drawing of Mr. Randolph Caldecott's,[1] and deny that the
Violin was one of the first impressions of our childhood. To
me it has always been a most significant fact, that so many of
the Nursery Rhymes with which we amuse our children are in

---

[1] I have to thank Mr. Caldecott for the above reduction from the frontispiece
of his well-known work, " Bye Baby Bunting " (London, 1882), which he has
kindly adapted and subscribed in his autograph for me.

some way connected with the fiddle. The one trait of Old King Cole's character which to my juvenile mind proved he was not wholly vile (as his pipe and bowl would indicate!) was his love of music and *penchant* for the violin,[1] and I remember a doggerel for which I always had a great affection, was that one beginning :—

> ' 'Cock a doodle doo, my Dame has lost her shoe,
> My Master's lost his fiddling stick, and don't know what to do!
> Cock a doodle doo, what *is* my Dame to do?—
> Till Master finds his fiddling stick, she'll dance without her shoe!"

That man was always my ideal of blank despair. Nor is the rhyme I have quoted above the only one in which a cat figures as a violinist : Halliwell (*vide* note) gives two rhymes in which this phenomenon occurs, viz.:—

> " A cat came fiddling out of a barn,
> With a pair of bag-pipes under her arm,"—

a wondrous performance truly, which made up for her want of vocal attainments, for—

> " She could sing nothing but ' Fiddle cum fee,
> The mouse has married the humble-bee ; ' "

and he also quotes one of still greater antiquity, where the

---

[1] " Old King Cole was a merry old soul, and a merry old soul was he,
    He called for his pipe and he called for his bowl, and he called for his
        fiddlers three,
    Every fiddler he had a fiddle, and a very fine fiddle had he
        (Twee, tweedledee, tweedledee went the fiddlers).
    Oh ! there's none so rare as can compare
    With King Cole and his fiddlers three."

The traditional nursery rhymes of Great Britain commence with a legendary satire on King Cole. who reigned in Britain, as the old chronicles inform us, in the third century after Christ. According to Robert of Gloucester, he was the father of St. Helena, and if so, Butler must be wrong in ascribing an obscure origin to the celebrated mother of Constantine. King Cole was a brave and popular man in his day, and ascended the throne of Britain on the death of Asclepiod amidst the acclamations of the people, or, as Robert of Gloucester expresses himself, "the folc was tho of this lond y-paid wel y-now." At Colchester there is a large earth-work, supposed to have been a Roman amphitheatre, which goes popularly by the name of " King Cole's Kitchen." According to Jeffrey of Monmouth, King Cole's daughter was well skilled in music, but we unfortunately have no evidence to show that her father was attached to that science further than what is contained in the foregoing lines, which are of doubtful antiquity.—*Vide* J. O. Halliwell, " The Nursery Rhymes of England " (London, 1844: J. R. Smith).
    In Lewis' "History of Great Britain " (London, 1729) three monarchs rejoicing in the name of " King Cole " are mentioned.

word "crowd" is substituted for fiddle.[1] But in riper years my affection for all these has waned in favour of "John," whose affection for his violin far exceeded that for his wife, for it runs :—

"John, come sell thy fiddle, and buy thy wife a gown."
" No, I'll not sell my fiddle for any wife in town ! "

(truly a most ungallant and sensible man !)
It is from such songs as these that most of us become first acquainted with the fiddle, and become inspired with a love of the instrument which draws a wide gulf between us and the " Clerke " mentioned in the Prologue to Chaucer's " Canteroury Tales." [2]
It hardly seems natural or possible to us to-day, who are wont to hear the violin played by members of all classes, from a Royal Duke downwards, that it could ever have been considered that " fiddler " was a term of the greatest reproach, and " fiddling " a synonym for dishonesty ; and yet such was the case; indeed, it is comparatively recently that Lord Chesterfield told his son that " fiddling puts a *gentleman* in a very frivolous and contemptible light, and brings him into a good deal of bad company, and takes a good deal of time which might be much better employed ; " [3] an opinion, I grieve to say, largely shared

---

[1] " Come dance a jig, to my granny's pig,
And pussy-cat shall crowdy."

Messrs. Sandys and Forster ("History of the Violin," etc. London, 1864 : J. R. Smith) give the following interesting note on this subject of the cat and fiddle :—"Middleton in his play of *The Witch* (1778), in one of the scenes of conjuring or enchantment, introduces a cat playing on the fiddle, but the well-known nursery rhyme is older than this, and the fact of equal authenticity in both. We have a curious old French print, where there is a cat playing on the fiddle, and a dog with a fool's cap dancing ; a pantaloon is also playing a guitare. . . . Pussy's fiddle is of the viol character, with four strings and no frets. The print is called, " Le Diuertisement de Mardy Gras." Among the lines at the bottom are the following :—

" La grotesque rejouissance
Du chat jouant du Violon
Et du chien qui dance, en cadence
De la Guitare à pantalon."

[2] "A Clerke there was of Oxenforde alsoe.
      .   .   .
For him was lever han at his beddes hed,
A Twenty Bokys clothyd in blacke or rede,
Of Aristotel and hys philosophie,
Than robys riche or *fidel* or sautrie. "

G. CHAUCER, " Canterbury Tales :" Prologue, " The Clerke of Oxenforde."

[3] " Lord Chesterfield's Letters to his Son, Philip Stanhope, together with several other Pieces on various subjects " (London, 1774), 4to, 2 vols.

by many "parents and guardians" of our own days. It seems
to have been rather a mania with Lord Chesterfield to consider
fiddling disreputable, and the word a synonym for disreputa-
bility; for he says in another place: [1] "And I heard some
persons assert that King James was sung and fiddled out of
the kingdom by the Protestant tune of 'Lillybullero,' and
that SOMEBODY else would have been fiddled into it again,"
etc. This abuse of "fiddlers" has not, however, been confined to any one period, as the following instances will show.
Parke tells a story of Miss Brent, who as Dr. Arne's
favourite pupil was a source of considerable revenue to him till
she married Pinto, the great violin-player of the time.   On
some one mentioning her, Dr. Arne is said to have exclaimed,
"Oh, sir, *pray* don't name her, she's married a *fiddler !* " [2]

Anthony à Wood tells us that "before the Restoration, gentlemen played three, four, and five parts with viols.   They
esteemed a violin to be an instrument only belonging to
a common fidler, and could not endure that it should come
among them for feare of making their meetings to be vaine
and frivolous, but before the Restoration of King Charles II.,
and especially after, viols began to be out of fashion, and
only violins used as treble violin, tenor, or bass violin,
and the King, according to the French mode, would have
twenty-four violins playing before him whilst he was at meals,
as being more airie and brisk than viols." [3]   The enemies of
Roger L'Estrange used to vent their spleen by calling him
" Roger the Fidler," and published notably a celebrated squib,
entitled " The Loyal Observator: or Historical Memoirs of the
Life and Actions of Roger the Fidler; *alias* the Observator "
(London, 1683: 4to, 12 pp.) [4]   The following interesting note
is appended :—" The subject of this libellous pasquinade was
Sir Roger L'Estrange, who was nicknamed " Cromwell's
Fidler," from his having been heard playing in a concert where
the Usurper was present.   Of this affair he speaks in his " Truth
and Loyalty Vindicated " [5] thus :—" Concerning the story of

[1] " Miscellaneous Works of the late Philip Dormer Stanhope, Earl of Chesterfield " (Dublin, 1777), vol. ii., p. 97.   " Miscellaneous Pieces, No. XVIII.,"
being a letter in *Common Sense or the Englishman's Journal*, October 14th,
1738 (London, 1739), vol. ii., p. 213.
    [2] Parke's " Musical Memoirs " (London, 1830), vol. i., p. 150.
    [3] A. Wood's Life, in MS. in the Ashmolean Library, Oxford ; written 1653,
and published at Oxford in 1772.
    [4] Reprinted in the " Harleian Miscellany ; A Collection of Scarce, Curious, and
Entertaining Pamphlets and Tracts, etc." (London : White & Co., 1810), vol.
vi., p. 65.
    [5] " Truth and Loyalty Vindicated from the Reproaches and Clamours of
Mr. E. Bagshawe," etc. (London, 1662, 4to).

the fiddle, this, I suppose, might be the rise of it ; being in St. James's Park, I heard an organ touched in a little low room of one Mr. Henckson's ; I went in, and found a private company of some five or six persons. They desired me to take a viol and bear a part. I did so, and that part, too, not much advance to the reputation of my cunning. By-and-by, without the least colour of design or expectation, in comes Cromwell. He found us playing, and so he left us." " The Observator " was a paper set up by Sir Roger after the dissolution of Charles II.' Parliament in 1679 ; the design of which was to vindicate the measures of the Court, and the character of the King from the charge of being popishly affected. To the above pasquinade and others he wrote in reply, " The Observator defended by the author of the Observators in a full Answer to several Scandals cast upon him," etc., etc. (London, 1685).

Thus it will be seen that to be a violinist required in the days of our forefathers some courage on the part of an amateur, just as a few years ago it required considerable nerve for a lady to play the violin in public. Parke, the genial and discursive, was not free from this foible ; for he says (under date February 19th, 1790), whilst discussing the performance of oratorios (notably the *Messiah*) at Covent Garden :—" The concertos were by Clementi on the pianoforte, and Madame Gautherot on the violin. It is said by fabulous writers that Minerva, happening to look into the stream whilst playing her favourite instrument (the flute), and perceiving the distortion of countenance that it occasioned, was so much disgusted that she cast it away and dashed it in pieces. Although I would not recommend any lady playing on a valuable Cremona fiddle to follow the example of the goddess, yet it strikes me that, if she is desirous of enrapturing her audience, she should display her talent in a situation where there is only just light enough 'to make darkness visible.' " [1] It occurs to me that if the society of the present day entertained any such horrible ideas, a very large amount of worldly pleasure would be lost to the devotees of music in general, and of the violin in particular.

Dubourg [2] tells us that Queen Elizabeth was a violinist, and his statement seems to be carried out by the wonderful fiddle, now exhibited in the South Kensington Museum, which is made of boxwood, beautifully carved " with woodland scenes," and which is said to have been given by Queen Elizabeth to the

---

[1] W. Parke, " Musical Memoirs " (London, 1830), vol. i., p. 129.
[2] G. Dubourg, " The Violin," etc. (London, 1st Edition, 1836 ; 2nd Edition, n.d [1837] ; 3rd Edition, n.d. [1850] ; 4th Edition, 1852 ; 5th Edition, enlarged by John Bishop, 1878). 1st Edition, p. 224 ; 5th Edition. p. 254.

Earl of Leicester.[1] The best known instance of a lady amateur of the last century is that of Signora Maddalena Lombardini, to whom Tartini wrote his celebrated "Lettera alla Signora Maddalena Lombardini, inserviente ad una importante lezione per i suonatori di Violino," which was published a few months after his death in "Europa Litteraria" (tome v., 1770, pt. ii., p. 74).[2] As Hullah justly remarks[3] :— "The blank and stupid astonishment with which the apparition —nay the very mention—of a female violinist was once received amongst us, is happily a thing of the past, and the instrument which Fiesole has so often put into the hands of his angels, and Raphael of his saints, is no longer regarded as unbecoming to 'the sex' nor in any hands ungraceful. But 'everything in this world,' said Metastasio, 'is habit; even virtue itself!' There is an Oxford tradition that at an amateur concert about the year 1827, the performance of the first male pianist that had been seen in that university was rewarded with a storm of hisses. The pianoforte was then regarded as essentially a woman's instrument!" Fortunately *nous avons changé tout cela;* but the fact remains that till comparatively recently the "fiddle" was essentially the instrument of what "Democritus Junior" (R. Burton) calls "circumforean rogues and vagabonds;" and Francis Bacon was only using the language of his era when he tells us that Themistocles, "desired at a feast to touch a lute, he said he 'could not *fiddle,* but yet he could make a small town a great city';[4] and he goes on to say, 'And certainly those

[1] This instrument is illustrated and fully described in Sir John Hawkins' "History of Music" (London, 1776), vol. iv., p. 342, and also in Carl Engel's "Descriptive Catalogue of the Musical Instruments in the South Kensington Museum" (London, 1874), p. 287, in which latter place its full history may be found. It is also mentioned in Dr. Burney's "General History of Music" (London, 1776). *Vide* p. 109.

[2] This letter was published separately with a translation on the opposite pages by Dr. Burney thus intituled :—"Lettera del defonto Signor Giuseppe Tartini alla Signora Maddalena Lombardini," etc. (Londra, 1771), and the translated title page (opposite) runs, "A letter from the late Signor Tartini to Signora Maddalena Lombardini (now Signora Sirmen), published as an important lesson to performers on the violin, translated by Dr. Burney (London, 1771). A second edition appeared in 1779, and a German translation entitled "Brief au Magdalen Lombardini, enthaltend eine wichtige Lection für die Violinspieler" (Hanover, 1786). This translation had before appeared in Hiller's "Lebensbeschreibungen berühmter Musikgelehrten und Tonkünstler," etc. (1784), p. 278. An English translation appears at p. 257 of Dubourg's work (*vide* note [2], p. 5), 5th edition.

[3] J. Hullah, "Music in the House" (London, 1877), p. 30.

[4] "The Works of Francis Bacon," by J. Spedding and others (London, 1858) vol. v., p. 79. The passage he refers to about Themistocles is that one found in PLUTARCH:—ΠΛΥΤΑΡΧΟΥ ΒΙΟΙ: ΘΕΜΙΣΤΟΚΛΗΣ II (δ),˝Οθεν ὕστερον ἐν ταῖς ἐλευθερίαις καὶ ἀστείαις διατριβαῖς ὑπὸ τῶν πεπαιδεῦσθαι δοκούντων χλευαζόμενος ἠναγκάζετο φορτικώτερον ἀμύνεσθαι λέγων, ὅτι λύραν μὲν ἁρμόσασθαι καὶ μετα-

degenerate arts and shifts, whereby many councillors and
governors gain both favour with their masters and estimation
with the vulgar, deserve no better name than *fiddling!*'"
Now, however, the violin finds its votaries, as I have said, alike
among princes and peasants. England has been peculiarly
fortunate in numbering members of its Royal families among
amateur players.[1] In Parke's "Musical Memoirs," above quoted,
we find, under date January 14th, 1787, an account of a Sunday
concert at Lord Hampden's, concerning which he says :—" In
one of the overtures the Prince of Wales and the Dukes
of Gloucester and Cumberland performed ; the two former
on the violoncello, and the latter on the violin." King
Charles I., we are told by Messrs. Sandys and Forster (*vide*
note [1], p. 3), was not only a great patron of music, but also
a fine player on the bass-viol or viol da gamba himself,
especially in " those incomparable phantasies of Mr. Coperario
to the organ," which had an accompaniment for one violin and
a bass-viol.[2] And to come down to to-day, the brotherhood of
amateur violinists is led by His Royal Highness Alfred Duke
of Edinburgh ; so that the ancient stigma attaching to the
instrument we may now consider to be a thing of the past, and
when it crops up we can look upon it as a relic of barbarism!
   Whilst on the subject of amateurs, it must be noted that the
term amateur is *not* the highest compliment that a player can
be paid, for it is, and always has been, almost equivalent to an
accusation of mediocrity when one is asked, " How does So-and-so
play ? " to reply, " Oh, *en amateur.*" In the last century it
was the custom to distinguish amateurs from professionals by
calling the former " gentlemen players ; " and a story is told,
dating from 1791 (Parke's " Musical Memoirs," vol. i., p. 142)
of a gentleman who, being asked how Lord C—— (who was a
very indifferent violinist) played, replied : " His Lordship, I
can assure you, sir, plays in a very *gentleman-like.* manner."
Perhaps one of the most genial and eccentric of amateur violinists was Franz Anton Weber (father of the celebrated composer), who was on this account a great favourite at the court

χειρίσασθαι ψαλτήριον οὐκ ἐπίσταται, πόλιν δὲ μικρὰν καὶ ἄδοξον παραλαβὼν
ἔνδοξον καὶ μεγάλην ἀπεργάσασθαι. Bacon translates λύραν μὲν ἁρμόσασθαι καὶ
μεταχειρίσασθαι ψαλτήριον by " fiddle ! "

[1] " Others import yet nobler arts from France,
    Teach kings to *fiddle*, and make senates dance ! "
          A. POPE, " The Dunciad," Book IV., line 598.

[2] " Coperario " was the Italianized name of one John " Cooper," a composer
for, and performer on, the lute and viol da gamba. He was the master of the
children of King James I., and died during the Protectorate of Cromwell, leaving
behind him many compositions evidently done " to order."

of Karl Theodor, Elector of the Palatinate, about the middle of the eighteenth century. " He played the violin remarkably well, and used to astonish the good people of Hildesheim during his walks in the neighbourhood by wonderful flights of fancy on his favourite instrument. He afterwards degenerated into ' Stadt Musikant,' or fiddler at balls, weddings, and the like." [1]

Charles IX. of France was an amateur violinist, [2] a fact, however, which did not prevent Goudimel (instructor of Palestrina) from being killed in the massacre of St. Bartholomew's day. Poisot says he has seen the instrument this monarch played on in the Bibliothèque de Cluny (Saône et Loire). [3] I need not quote the time-honoured but idiotic legend that Nero fiddled whilst Rome burned, but the above anecdote reminds me of it. Cyprien Desmarais [4] tells us that Charles IV., Duke of Lorraine and Bar, was a great patron of violin-making, and that it was under his auspices that one of Amati's workmen, named Medar, was established in France, and commanded to make a set of bow instruments for the State concerts ; that these instruments were illuminated (like those of Amati, vide note [2]) with the ducal arms. [5]

Some of the best amateurs who have left their marks on the rolls of fame have been clergymen, from the monks of the middle ages to the musical " clericos " of to-day. [6]

---

[1] " The Great Musicians," edited by Francis Hueffer. " Weber," by Sir Julius Benedict (London, 1881).

[2] It was for Charles IX. that Andreas Amati made the celebrated instruments known as " Charles IX. Amatis." These were twenty-four violins (twelve large and twelve small pattern), six violas and eight violoncellos. The workmanship was exquisite, and the colour a rich red-brown. They were illuminated with the arms of France, and the motto " Pietate et Justitia." One of them is represented in the Photographs, Plates II. and III. (vide page 73).

[3] C. E. Poisot, " Histoire de la Musique en France depuis les temps les plus reculés jusqu'à nos jours " (Paris, 1860 : Dentu).

[4] Cyprien Desmarais, " Archéologie du Violon. Description d'un Violon Historique et Monumental." (Paris, 1836 : vide note [1], p. 20.)

[5] The same writer goes on to say : " Louis XIV. fut le premier prince qui adopta pour sa chapelle et pour le service divin, l'usage des instruments à cordes et à archet, tels que violons, altos, basses, et contre basses. Ce fut Lully, surintendant de la musique du roi, qui fut chargé de s'en procurer. Ils furent fabriqués et fournis par Médar, luthier à Nancy : les violons furent peints d'une couleur rouge, moins foncée cependant que celle des violons de Stradivarius. Ils furent armoriés aux armes de France et de Navarre, avec cette devise du grand roi : Nec pluribus impar. Tous les rois de l'Europe s'empressèrent de suivre l'exemple de Louis XIV. en adoptant pour leur musique l'usage des instruments à cordes et à archet."

[6] As I write the above my thoughts naturally wander to that eccentric enthusiast and exquisite writer on all subjects connected with music and the violin, the Rev. H. R. Haweis, of whom, and of whose wonderful execution in the old days at Cambridge, wonderful stories are still told by eye-witnesses and hearers. To all who are interested in the violin, what can be more fascinating than the large section of his recent work, " My Musical Life " (London, 1884`. Book iii., pp. 215-388, " The Violin."

Sandys and Forster (*vide* note [1], p. 3) relate that the eminent preacher Bourdelot was a performer on the violin, and quote the following anecdote: "He was appointed to preach on Good Friday, and the proper officer to attend him to church having arrived at his house, was directed to go to the study for him. As he approached he heard the sound of a violin, and, the door being open a little way, he saw Bourdelot stripped to his cassock, playing a brisk tune on the instrument, and dancing about the room. He was much surprised, and knocked at the door, when the distinguished divine laid down his instrument, and putting on his gown, told the officer with his usual composed look that he was ready to attend him. On their way his companion expressed his surprise at what he had seen to Bourdelot, who replied, that he might be, unless made acquainted with his practice on these occasions. On thinking over the intended subject of his discourse, he found that he was too depressed to treat it as he ought, and, therefore, had recourse to his usual method—some music and a little bodily exercise,—and thus put himself into a proper frame of mind to enable him to go with pleasure to what would otherwise have been a work of pain and labour to him." Truly, an instance of a "dancing parson," which reminds us of the gay young clergyman of the time of Edward II., of whom we are told that when he goes out:—

"He putteth in his pawtener a kerchief and a comb,
A skewer and a coyf to bind with hijs locks
And ratyl in the rowbyble,[1] and in non other books.
                                        Ne mos!"

So much for the amateurs who have gone before us. It is to be presumed that the term "amateur" must continue to be in some way a term of contempt until the sex, which is by a strange misnomer termed "the weaker," shall have wiped away this reproach. In conclusion, I can only say that many is the time when I have devoutly wished that amateurs would bear in mind the words of Stephens,[2] who remarks with much dry humour and sound sense, "A fiddler is, when he plays well, a delight only for them that have their hearing, but is, when he plays ill, a delight only for those who have not their hearing."

Even to-day the word "fiddle" has many opprobrious significa-tions, relics of the days when "a fiddler" was a synonym for a rogue or useless fellow, and the French, as we know, have even now the phrase "mettre au violon," meaning "to imprison or

[1] Rowbyble, rubible, rubebe, rebec ; terms synonymous, *vide* chap. i.
[2] J. Stephens, "Essayes and Characters, Ironical and Instructive" (London, "The Second Impression," 1615).

lock up." About the origin of this use of the word *violon* there
have been many discussions among philologists and etymologists ;
a writer in *Notes and Queries*, in 1864,[1] tells us that in the
time of Louis XI. the " Salle des Pas Peradus " (? Perdus)
was so much frequented by spadassins, turbulent clerks and
students, that a bailiff of the palace, to put an end to their
disturbances, adopted the plan of shutting them up in a lower
room of the conciergerie whilst the courts were sitting, but, as
they were not guilty of any punishable offence he allowed them
a *violin* to amuse themselves with during their temporary cap-
tivity. Hence the word " violon " came to be applied to places
where persons under provisional arrest were confined.[2] However this may be, it is anything but complimentary to the instrument which, as a writer in the *Daily Telegraph*[3] justly remarks,
" is pre-eminently the instrument of peace and contentment, of
gentle suasion and harmony among mankind," for, indeed, as
Captain Macheath says in his pretty compliment alike to woman
and the violin[4]—

> " If the heart of a man is depressed with cares,
> The mist is dispelled when a woman appears ;
> Like the notes of a fiddle she sweetly, sweetly
> Raises the spirits and charms our ears,"—

and Tom Hood spoke from the bottom of his heart when he
rather descriptively put it : " Heaven reward the man who first
hit upon the very original notion of sawing the inside of a cat

[1] *Notes and Queries*, third series, vol. vi., p. 496 (December 17th, 1864).
[2] The above appeared originally in *Galignani*. On January 21st, 1865, another
writer in *Notes and Queries* (vol. vii.), referring to the above recited article,
says, *à propos* of this subject : [*translation*] " The following explanation by the
eminent French philologist Génin, is more to the purpose. 1 took note of it
from a series of papers he furnished some years ago to the *Journal d'Illustration*, but it is to be found with many other curious things in his ' Récréations
Philologiques ' : ' METTRE AU VIOLON.—It is well known that in the middle
ages they said, instead of " mettre au violon," " mettre au psaltérion." Psaltérion, saltérion, sautérion, are all identical with the Latin word " psalterium,"
these being Gallicized forms. Throughout the middle ages the seven penitential
psalms were as much used as " l'oraison dominicale " itself. By degrees it
became a habit to say casually " time to say a *sept-pseaumes*," as now we say
" time to recite a *pater*." " Mettre au psaltérion " meant, therefore, to be set
down to one's psalter, to be set down to a penance, to meditate over one's follies,
to repent of them, and to recite the seven penitential psalms (une *sept-pseaumes*)
without fear of interruption. But the " psaltérion " was also a musical instrument, and the populace took advantage of the equivoque, and, seeing that the
psalterium was antiquated, substituted for it the violin, which had asserted itself
as the king of instruments. Instead of saying " mettre au psaltérion " we say
" mettre au violon," and the play upon words is kept up.' "
[3] February 13th, 1882.
[4] J. Gay, " *The Beggar's Opera* " (London, 1727), act ii., sc. 1.

with the tail of a horse!"[1] The vanity which fiddling was supposed by our forefathers to be, is amply proved by their many writings in its disparagement. Dr. Barnes (chaplain to King Henry VIII.) distinguishes fiddling as a reprehensible trade in his "What the Church is,"[2] etc.; and Dryden's lines,—

> "Stiff in opinions, always in the wrong,
> Was everything by turns, but nothing long,
> But in the course of one revolving moon
> Was chymist, *fiddler*, statesman, and buffoon,"[3]—

are too well known to require quotation.

"Fiddle-faddle," as an expression denoting frivolity, is of very great antiquity, and is obviously derived from the old idea of the vanity and frivolity of the instrument; thus Ford says,[4] "Ye may as easely outrun a cloud driven by the northern blast, as *fiddle-faddle* so;" and Samuel Butler uses the word in his celebrated "A Ballad on the Parliament" (verse 1), which begins :—

> "As close as a goose sat the Parliament House, hatching the Royal Gull ;
> After much *fiddle-faddle* the egg proved addle, and Oliver came from the North."

It seems to have been an expression much in use about this time, doubtless because the fiddle had just been introduced by the Stuarts, and was looked upon as one of the many follies of those sovereigns. Beaumont and Fletcher, in their play *The Humorous Lieutenant* (London, 1620), act i., sc. 1, say :—

> "And that sweet tilting war with eyes and kisses,
> Th' alarms of soft vows and sighs and *fiddle-faddle*, spoils all our trade."[5]

And even in our day the expression (which is now antiquated) has appeared on title-pages and the like.[6] So much, therefore,

---

[1] This is a description which reminds me of the Irishman who on returning home from a fair where he had heard a violin played, described it to his wondering circle thus : "It was the shape of a turkey and the size of a goose, and he turned it over on its back and rubbed its belly wid a stick, and och ! St. Patrick, how it did squale ! "

[2] London, *circa* 1530. "Whether they be Jew or Greeke, free or bounde, friar or fiddler."

[3] J. Dryden, "Absalom and Achitophel," part i., line 547.

[4] J. Ford, " *The Broken Heart*," A Tragedy (London, 1633), act i., sc. 3.

[5] "The Works of Beaumont and Fletcher," edited by Geo. Darley (London, 1840), p. 236.

[6] As, for instance, "Fiddle-faddle's Sentimental Tour in Search of the Amusing, Picturesque, and Agreeable " (London, 1845 : G. Virtue : illustrated by " Phiz "), and that delightful squib on the dress of the dandies of a former generation, " The Fiddle-faddle, Fashion Book, and Beau Monde à la Française, enriched with numerous highly coloured figures of Lady-like Gentlemen," edited by the Author of the "Comic Latin Grammar." The costumes and other illustrations by John Leech. (London : n.d. [1840].)

for the opinions of our forefathers concerning the violin, **and the** meaning, in their estimation, of the word " fiddle." [1]

However small may have been, in days gone by, the esteem in which the violin was held, there is no doubt about its high position nowadays, both socially and commercially,[2] now that our daughters are being taught the violin instead of the piano, and that violins fetch sums of money which are simply out of all reason. As regards the former of these " signs of the times," a writer in *Cassell's Family Magazine* justly remarked a short time ago :[3] "The rage for teaching girls the violin, which at present exists in England, is little more than a fashion, and, unless it is directed with more knowledge and care on the part of parents than most of them now show, it will die like one. And we are not quite clear that, if this care is withheld, a more suitable and salutary end could overtake it. A new terror would be added to society were every budding " Miss," no better instructed in the art than under the present *régime* she is likely to be, were permitted or required to compel the silence of the drawing-room whilst she scraped out one of Bellini's airs with variations." This is quite true *en bloc,* but there is no doubt that when the first rage consequent on the perfect technique of such lady-players as Normann-Neruda,

[1] Before I go further I would say a word on my constant use of the word "fiddle" instead of " violin ;" it is a prejudice of mine. I always prefer to say "fiddle," " tenor," " bass," and " double bass," rather than use the Italian words " violin," " viola," " violoncello," and " violono," or the French " violon," " alto," " basse," and " contre-basse." We should not much like it if we were made to use the Polish "skrzpcé," " altowka," " basetla," and " kontrabas ;" so why cannot we use English words when we have them to use ? People have often asked me (in absolute good faith and innocence), " What is the difference between a fiddle and a violin ?" a question which always reminds me of a story told by Mr. A. Chasemore, in his " History and Associations of the Old Bridge at Fulham and Putney " (London, 1875, 8vo), of an old waterman at Putney, who, in describing the glories of a certain band known as " Brook's Band," which played on the occasions of the old Fulham watermen's Regatta, stated that it consisted of " a big drum, a clarionet, two fiddles and a *violin !* "

[2] Whilst I write the above there comes into my mind a little book which was sent me the other day, and which by its recent date shows that the antique prejudice against the fiddle is not absolutely extinct even now. This little booklet, which is fortunately anonymous, is entitled, " The singular life and surprising adventures of Joseph Thompson, known by the name of Fiddlei Thompson of Halifax, with an account of the various hardships he endured ; the wickedness of common Fiddlers and Fiddling ; his practice as a Horse-rider and Juggler ; narrow escape from death ; his being a Fiddler on a cruise in a Privateer ; his cruelty as a husband, father, &c., and his subsequent con-version and devotedness to God." (Wakefield : W. Nicholson, n.d. [1880]). It is extraordinary to me, how in these days of enlightenment such a philippic could have been published.

[3] Vide *The Musical Standard,* August 5th. 1882. and the *Orchestra and Choir* September 1882.

Teresina Tua, de Pommereul, and other well-known violinistes, has cooled down, the ladies who continue to play the violin will raise (as I have said before) the name of "Amateur Violinist" from the slough of despond in which it is at present sunk ; for it is obvious that the greater perseverance, delicacy, and spirit of emulation, of the fair sex, to say nothing of the greater time at their disposal, must soon raise them far beyond the standard attained by nineteen out of every twenty male bipeds who "play the fiddle a little, you know."

The present is neither a suitable place nor an appropriate occasion for an exposition of the failings of the ordinary amateur; but there are two principal ones which deserve a passing notice : these are, excessive tuning and "showing off." There seem to be many amateur fiddlers who think it shows self-confidence, skill, or nonchalance to tune with unnecessary vigour and at unnecessary length, not reflecting that to the experienced musician such a proceeding is a certain indication of executory inaptitude.[2] The passion for "showing off" is apparently an incurable disease, for one hears even advanced players running scales up and down the finger-board and playing bravura passages whenever they can get a suitable or unsuitable opportunity. It is a maddeningly contemptible habit. What is more distressing to the musical ear than the discordant *quart-d'heure* that precedes the overture in most of our theatres? If one listens carefully, one can often distinguish whole exercises by well-known masters being "run through" by individual fiddlers. It is related of Cramer, that when on his way to England he was engaged to play a concerto on the violin at the "Concert-Spirituel" in Paris. On entering the orchestra he was struck with amazement at seeing

[1] Francis Beaumont, "*The Knight of the Burning Pestle*," Comedy, first played in 1611.
[2] Philip Massinger was also impressed with this idea, when fiddles first came over to England, for he says :—

> "Wire-string and cat-gut men, and strong-breathed hoboys,
> For the credit of your calling have not your instruments
> To tune when you strike up."
>
> *The Guardian*, a comedy (London, 1655).

And I can always feel for, and sympathise with, the Court in the old story of the Eastern potentate for whose delectation a band was sent forth to his domains. Before their first (proposed) performance they began to tune their instruments, an operation which produced on the Court the same kind of effect that stepping on a red-hot shovel produced on Mark Twain's contemplative spider. (He first expressed a wild astonishment and then shrivelled up !) *Obstupuerunt, steteruntque comæ*—and the miserable fiddlers were sent home as fast as possible by the king, who refused to hear another note of their music, fearing it might be "up to sample !"

the second, and inferior violin players playing for their own (?) amusement the most difficult bravura passages at the top of the finger-board. " If," thought he, " the French subordinate fiddle-players possess such uncommon powers of execution, I can have little chance of pleasing a Parisian audience.' However, he went through his concerto and was accorded a whirl-wind of applause ; next day, on his mentioning the matter to an eminent French musician, the latter replied, " Oh ! confound them, they only practise such monkey-tricks, and can play nothing else." Such a player as this was the celebrated Lolli,[1] who seems to have been a trick-player of marvellous force, *et præterea nihil !* Indeed Parke in his " Musical Memoirs " (vol i., p. 52) says of him: —" His execution was astonishing, and the tricks he played in various parts of his concerto excited the risibility more than the admiration of his auditors." [2] The only person of our day (as far as I know) who has made a practice of this kind of charlatanry is a certain eccentric professional, who has recently made his appearance at music-halls and other entertainments of a similar nature under the hideously suggestive title of " Paganini Redivivus." My readers (who have not *seen* him) will judge of him and his merits when I say

[1] Antonio Lolli was a native of Bergamo, born in 1730, whom Sir George Grove in his " Dictionary of Music and Musicians " (London, 1880—1884) describes as "a most extraordinary performer, but also the type of an unmusical, empty-headed virtuoso, and in addition a complete fool ; " and this opinion of him is unanimously that of all his biographers.

[2] Mr. H. C. Lunn, in his " Suggestions for a Musical *Amphitheatre* " in " Musings of a Musician " (London, 2nd Edn., 1849, p. 200), gives a delight-ful item in an imaginary programme, being a hit at the sickening way in which inferior players pander to the popular taste by these "exhibitions " of " musical pyrotechnics." He says :—" Mr. LUCIUS GRAHAM WALKER, the Miraculous Violinist (justly surnamed the *One-stringed Prodigy*) will afterwards go through the whole of his much admired performances UPON A SINGLE STRING. In order that there may be *no deception* in this, the violin will be brought before the audience and three strings *broken* in their presence. After this feat he will exhibit some of his new effects for the instrument which have been received on each representation with SHOUTS of LAUGHTER and THUNDERS of APPLAUSE. Amongst the most prominent of these will be a *peculiar sound* got by gently *tapping* the string, whilst the wood of the bow is placed close to the bridge and suddenly drawn up and down the string with *great force*. The *portamento* too, so much used by singers and lately by violinists, which consists of gliding one note into the other instead of separating them *as they are marked upon the paper*, will, on this occasion, be *carried to an extreme*. He will perform a portion of a well-known concerto, in which, by simply using the means above mentioned, he will make the most lovely andante appear a series of *the most extraordinary wails* ever listened to, and transform a beautiful composition into a *correct* representation of *a concert of cats*. This feat has always been received with the utmost LAUGHTER and APPLAUSE,"—and, in truth, this just describes many of the wonderful exhibitions of musical gymnastics forced upon wondering ears by hundreds of charlatans, amateur and professional, in the drawing-room, on the platform—and in the circus.

he appears, a ghastly object, "made up" to resemble the corpse
of Nicolo Paganini according to the weirdest likenesses of him,
on a darkened stage and to slow music, after which he plays
one or two of the "tours-de-force" which are associated with
the name of the arch-charlatan and virtuoso, the king of
violinists, Paganini. I simply *must* reproduce an advertisement
of his which appeared in the *Times* of the 2nd March, 1883,
and which runs thus :—

> PAGANINI REDIVIVUS begs to make known, in
> reply to numerous inquiries, that he seldom
> performs Beethoven's Concerto, Mendelssohn's
> Concerto, Tartini's Devil's-Sonata, Bach's "Cha-
> conne," or the other stereotyped pieces of the
> inevitable so-called classical répertoire. Paganini
> Redivivus has heard them so frequently hackneyed
> about by little conservatoire pupils on the Conti-
> nent, that they have lost their importance for him.
> However, although from a violinistic point of view
> *they are worse than trivial*, still as musical com-
> positions they are very admirable. Therefore later
> on Paganini Redivivus *may be induced* to give a
> SPECIAL RECITAL of the above stated pieces, *in
> order to show the London public how they should be
> played.*

No comment of mine is needed to point the moral of the
above edifying paragraph. True, he was a marvellous executant,
but from an artistic point of view—bah ![1] It is this terrible
temptation to charlatanry which spoils the playing of so many
amateurs, for in their love of exciting wonder and applause,
they lose sight entirely of the glories of purity of tone and
expression, which *must* be the substratum to which all ornaments of style are purely incidental, so that people may say in
the words of Edmund Gosse,[2]—

> . . . . "And when I stand
> To watch the fingers of a master's hand,
> And taste the rich arpeggios, and ablaze
> With florid chords, hear how the fire is fanned,
>
> I throb with joy; and as I look I learn."

Of course the great thing which stands in the way of
amateurs is want of practice. Boys cannot or will not give the
requisite time to the instrument which is the inevitable pathway
to proficiency; they cannot realize the powers of the "Niebelungenlied" Volker, who is described as wielding the fiddle-bow
as dexterously as the sword; they can very seldom even be
persuaded to follow the example of dear old Samuel Pepys, who

---

[1] Any one who feels an interest in this nineteenth century Lolli should refer
to the pages of the *Musical Standard* for March 10th and 24th, 1883.
[2] E. W. Gosse, "On Viol and Lute" (London, 1873), "Ad auditorem," p. 1.

tells us (December 3rd, 1660) :—" Rose by candle, and spent my morning in fiddling till time to go to the office ; " and it is urged that the pursuits of boys and men unfit the hands for the delicate touch necessary to a perfect intonation. or the suppleness requisite for a proper technique upon the finger-board : [1] this is why I hail the time when women shall play the violin to us, when the execrable amateur fiddler, whom we have all endured and anathematized, shall be a thing of the past, and when it will be counted a shame and a disgrace to play the violin either like a marvellous piece of mechanism or a trained animal.[2] Of coure it is out of the question to suppose that amateurs (even ladies!) will ever emulate the phenomenal application which is reported of Paganini, of whom we have handed down to us terrible stories of ten and twelve hours a day uninterrupted practice,[3] or that they will practice till their fingers bleed, like the pupils of the genius Fossegrin ; [4]

[1] " Nothing could possibly add to the charm and variety of Music in the House like a general increase of skill in violin-playing. And if this increase is to be made, it must be made for the present at least through female aid. An exclusive devotion, through the growing years of boyhood, to cricket and boating, however directly conducive to ' the promotion of piety and good literature, leaves little time for the acquisition of skill on a musical instrument, not to say that hands stiffened by the bat and oar are little likely to make much of the bow or finger-board."—*J. Hullah,* " Music in the House " (London, 1877).

[2] Speaking of trained animals reminds me of a most interesting note which I find in " Knight's " American Mechanical Dictionary " (New York, 1875, 3 vols., articles " Fiddle " and " Violin "), which points out the fact that though grasshoppers, crickets, and the like are frequently spoken of as " singing," yet " they do not sing, they fiddle. By rubbing legs and wings together—each in the manner peculiar to the species—these insects produce the sounds which characterize them. Locusts are fiddlers. Their hind legs are the bows, and the projecting veins of their wing-covers the strings. On each side the body, in the first segment of the abdomen, just above and a little behind the thighs, is a deep cavity closed by a thin piece of skin stretched tightly across it like a banjo-cover. When a locust begins to play he bends the shank of one hind leg beneath the thigh, where it is lodged in a furrow designed to receive it, and then draws the leg briskly up and down several times against the projecting lateral edge and veins of the wing-cover." Shortly after reading the above, I was lying in the blazing sun on one of the southern slopes of the Pyrenees, and an enormous field-cricket or grasshopper, unaware of my presence, came and sat down a few inches from my head, and gave me a concert. I watched him very carefully, and the operation was exactly as above described ; his tone was full and round, and formed a pleasing contrast to that of a lady field-cricket who was fiddling about a yard away, with whom my soloist seemed to be conversing. Her tone was comparatively thin and weak, and presently ceased altogether, whereupon my gallant insect skidded away to make inquiries.

[3] F. J. Fétis, " Notice Biographique sur Nicolo Paganini," etc. (Paris, 1851), translated into English by Wellington Guernsey :—" Biographical notice of Nicolo Paganini," etc. (London : Schott, n.d.) Second edition, anonymous (London, n.d. [1876]).

[4] In Norway the genius Fossegrin teaches the violin on the night of Holy Thursday to any person who sacrifices to him a white goat,and throws it into a cascade flowing northward, taking care to turn away his head. The genius

but the forbearance of their relations will surely allow them to give more time than (as a rule) they do, and it is certainly time that the people who can afford most for tuition should produce the best results. Another fault of amateurs is their *constancy;* an amateur will go on playing snatches of tunes, "somehow like this," in what Mr. Corney Grain calls "the there or thereabouts style," till one longs to be afflicted with a thickening of the tympanum. I once knew an amateur who would go on worrying his fiddle by the hour together for my edification, out of pure vanity of his own powers. He reminded me of a French virtuoso, named Alday, who played on his first appearance in England (at Coleman's Theatre in 1792) a concerto on "God save the King" with variations. After some seventeen or eighteen variations some wag in the gallery called out, "Are you going to play all night, Mr. All-day?" This started a laugh, which, turning into a hiss, drove the discomfited soloist from the platform.

There is no doubt about it, that to have *learnt* the violin has often been the first musical training of the greatest composers. We all have heard the well-known story of Mozart, who when he was quite a child taught himself to play the violin ; the story is told by Hogarth[1] as follows :—"When the family returned to Salzburg in 1762 Mozart (being then six years old) brought with him a small violin with which he amused himself. An able violin-player of the name of Wenzl called one day on his father to ask his opinion of six trios he had just composed. They proceeded to try them, Wenzl himself playing the first violin, Mozart's father the bass, and a performer of the name of Schachtner[2] the second violin. Young Mozart begged hard to be allowed to play this last part, but his father angrily refused his request, naturally conceiving it to be a childish whim. At last, however, on the good-humoured intercession of Schachtner, the

then seizes the right hand of his pupil, and moves it over the strings of the fiddle till the blood comes out under the nails. The apprentice is thenceforward a master, and his enchanted violin will make trees dance and rivers stay their course !—*Music and the Drama,* March 10th, 1883.

[1] G. Hogarth, "Musical History, Biography, and Criticism," etc. (London, 1835), ch. xiii., p. 240 (2nd edition, 1838, vol. ii., ch. i., p. 3).

[2] Johann Andreas Schachtner held the post of Court Trumpeter at Salzburg, and was an intimate friend of the Mozart family. All these particulars of the childhood of Mozart (as well as many others) are taken from a letter written by Schachtner, after Mozart's death, to his (Mozart's) sister, under date April 24th, 1792. The original is in the possession of Herr Aloys Fuchs, and is to be found at length in Otto Jahn's "Life of Mozart," translated from the German by Pauline Townshend (London, 1882, Novello), 3 vols., vol. i., p. 21. ("W. A. Mozart" : Leipzig, 1826-59 ; Breitkopf, 4 vols. 8vo). It is also to be found in G. R. de Nissen's "Biographie W. A. Mozarts" (Leipzig, 1828), and in A. H. F. Schlichtegroll's "Nekrolog der Deutschen" (Gotha, 1790-1806).

child was allowed to play along with him on his little violin, and cautioned by his father to make little noise. In a few minutes, nodding to his companions, Schachtner laid down his instrument, and Mozart went on alone, playing his part with the utmost accuracy and steadiness, to the admiration and astonishment of the party."[1]

Again, Sebastian Bach (born at Eisenach, in Thuringia, March 31st,[2] 1685) was in his youth his father's pupil on the violin, and it was his proficiency on this instrument (joined to his fine treble voice) which got him into the " Matin " choir at the Michaëlis Schule at Lueneberg ; and when his voice cracked he held for some months the post of violinist in the band of Prince Johann Ernst of Weimar.[3] Schubert also, we are told,[4] was his father's pupil on the violin at the age of eight. In 1808 he became one of the Imperial Chapel Choir, and a pupil of the Stadtconvict, where he soon became leader of the school orchestra.[5]

CREMONA! It would almost seem unnecessary to ask whether there breathes any one who has never heard of a " Cremona Violin," but it is not so ; often when talking of violins some one has said naïvely, " And then,—what is a ' Cremona ? ' " indeed, the name which is more than a household word to all violinists is by no means understood in its full signification by οἱ πολλοί ; even the well-informed Parke says (vol. i., p. 301) : " As the appellation of ' Cremona fiddles ' may not be generally understood I will take this opportunity to explain it. These instruments were made by two Italians, named Amati and Stradivarius at

---

[1] He was fond of playing on Schachtner's violin on account of the sweetness of its tone, and Schachtner used to tune it and leave it with him. One day when Schachtner came to visit his father, Mozart remarked to him that the last time he tuned his violin he had not kept it at its former pitch. " It is half a quarter of a tone," said he, " lower than this one of mine." They at first laughed at this extreme exactness ; but the father, who had often observed the extraordinary delicacy of his son's ear and his memory for sounds, desired him to bring Schachtner's violin, and it actually proved to be half a quarter of a tone below the other.

[2] Many biographers state that he was born on the *twenty*-first, and they also are right, for Bach was born on the 21st (old style) and 31st (new style) of March, 1685.

[3] R. L. Poole, " Sebastian Bach " (London, 1882). (" The Great Musicians," edited by F. Hueffer.)

[4] H. F. Frost, " Schubert " (London, 1881). (Same series.)

[5] As an instance of his delicacy of ear, parallel to that of Mozart (*vide* note [1]), we are told that at home, when the family played quartetts (he playing the viola, his father the bass, and his brothers the violins), he would detect the smallest blunder. In the instance of one of his brothers he did not scruple to rebuke by word or look ; but if his father played a wrong note or made a false entry, he would ignore the mistake once, and if it occurred again, he would say with hesitation, " Father, I fear there is a mistake somewhere ! " The viola has been the favourite instrument of more than one great composer. Besides Schubert, both Mozart and Mendelssohn were tenor-players.

Cremona, in the Milanese ; and, like the well-known ' Sedan chairs,' originally made in France, go by the name of the town in which they were first manufactured " (!). This is a terrible statement for a musical historian to make, but it shows us what was the opinion in musical circles in 1830. That Cremona violins have always enjoyed a high reputation in this country is shown by the following entry in the Enrolments of the Audit Office in the reign of Charles II., 1662, vol. vi., No. 359: " These are to require you to pay, or cause to be paid to *John Bannester*, one of his Maties musicians in ordinary, the some of fourty poundes for two Cremona violins by him bought and delivered for his Maties service, as may appeare by the bill annexed ; and also tenn poundes for stringes for two years ending 24th June, 1662. And this shall be your Warrant. Given under my hand this 24th day of October, 1662, in the fourteenth yeare of his Majesty's reign : (signed) E. Manchester. To Sir Edward Griffin, K^{nt,} Treasurer of his Maties chamber." [1] The position of Cremona violins in the present day is, perhaps, a trifle anomalous : as Charles Reade very justly says : [2] " The fiddles of Cremona gained their reputation by superior tone, but they hold it now mainly by their beauty. For thirty years past violins have been made equal in model to the *chef-d'œuvres* of Cremona, and stronger in wood than Stradivarius, and more scientific than Guarnerius in the thicknesses."

This is an argument which, though obviously true to all connected with violins, is very difficult to hammer into the heads of amateurs and others, who either possess or *crave* for the possession of a masterpiece of Cremona. No one who has seen the magnificent new instruments of Chanot, of Hill, of Boullangier, of Simoutre, of Gand and Bernardel, and of many other living makers, can possibly deny that these instruments will be, when a little matured by age, far sweeter and finer than any of the time-withered, tampered-with, over-repaired, and dilapidated instruments which flood the market under the names

[1] Communicated to *Notes and Queries*, vol. vii. (first series), p. 36, by Peter Cunningham.
[2] C. Reade, " A Lost Art Revived : Cremona Violins, Four Letters descriptive of those exhibited in 1873 (*sic*) at the South Kensington Museum ; also giving the Data for producing the True Varnishes used by the Great Cremona Makers," reprinted from the *Pall Mall Gazette*, by G. H. M. Muntz (Gloucester, 1873). This is a pamphlet of considerable rarity and bibliographical value, got up in a style *de luxe*, and consisting of four letters written by Charles Reade in the *Pall Mall Gazette* of the 19th, 24th, 27th, and 31st August, 1872, descriptive of the violins exhibited at the special Exhibition of Ancient Musical Instruments at South Kensington in 1872 (not 1873, as stated on the title-page of the brochure in question). *Vide* note [1], p. 24.

of Stradivari, of Guarneri, of Amati, of Ruggerius, of Stainer, of Bergonzi, and a hundred lesser names. People hear masters like Joachim, Wilhelmj, Sainton, or Sarasate play on a gem from some Cremonese workshop, and make up their minds that the exquisite purity of tone comes from the instrument (and not from the player !), and not so much from the instrument as from its age ! It reminds one of the old story about Giardini, whose taste and purity of tone were simply exquisite. Parke says of him : " Giardini when in his zenith produced on the violin a tone more powerful and clear than any of his contemporaries. This knack, if I may be allowed the expression, proved very profitable to Giardini, enabling him to sell his inferior instruments for a large price to gentlemen who in his hands admired their powerful tone, though they found afterwards, to their great surprise, that they could draw forth very little, apparently not aware that the tone came from the skill used, and not from the fiddle." People have even written books (or rather, pamphlets) to impress this on the devotees and collectors of the violin, which though too often simply written as advertisements of a particular make, are really absolutely correct, and if properly studied (apart from their " puff" element) would conduce to a more liberal patronage of contemporary work, and I have, personally, no doubt that a hundred pounds spent *now* in bran new instruments would more than increase tenfold in the space of fifty to eighty years, for, as a writer in one of the above-mentioned pamphlets wisely remarks, the supply of Italian master-violins is necessarily limited, and in a comparatively short time players will be *obliged* to turn to modern makers for their instruments.[1] I have played on bran

---

[1] The works which I have in my mind as I write this are particularly a delightfully conceited work by George Gemünder, the violin-maker of Astoria, New York, entitled " George Gemünder's progress in Violin-making," etc. (Astoria, N.Y., 1881, 8vo), which for cast-iron self-glorification far surpasses the most eloquent lucubrations of the historic Pharisee ! Another opusculum of the same kind is Mr. J. Broadhouse's " Facts about Fiddles, Violins Old and New," a brochure which has seen two editions (London, n. d., [1879 and 1882]), and is devoted entirely to the advertising of the instruments of an amateur maker named Mr. John Day. A third, which has recently made its appearance, is a work called " Aux Amateurs du Violon. Historique, Construction, Reparation et Conservation de cet Instrument "(Bâle, 1883), and written by M. C. Simoutre, of whose fiddles it is in fact a great advertising puff. And to go back to the beginning of the century, we have the well-known work by Jacob Augustus Otto, " Ueber den Bau der Bogen-instru-mente," etc., 1st edition (Halle und Leipsic, 1817); 2nd edition (Jena, 1828), which has been translated into English by T. Fardely, " Treatise on the Construction,etc., of the Violin, etc." (London and Leeds, 1883); and by John Bishop, of Cheltenham, "A Treatise on the Structure, etc., of the Violin, etc." (London, 1st edition 1848 ; 2nd edition 1860 ; 3rd edition 1875) ; and the very scarce, if not unattainable pamphlet of M. Cyprien Desmarais, " Description d'un Violon

new violins—violins the varnish of which has been absolutely
"sticky," and their tone has been perfect (that is, of course, it
has given *great* promise), and no doubt after the transition period
will be quite as fine, if not finer, in tone than those wonderful
violins bearing talismanic names which raise their prices into
the hundreds of pounds. It is perhaps not generally known
that it is only in what I have called "the transition period" that a
well-made violin is hideously rough and discordant, that its tone
is described as "new," and that players avoid it as they would
the Evil One. When a violin is *first* made, and the wood is
soft and sappy, and the varnish sticky and elastic, the tone is
muffled in a manner which gives an idea of softness and sweetness which is very deceptive to an inexperienced player; it is
when the fiddle has been played on for a month or two, and the
fibres of the wood are beginning to answer to the sound-waves,
that the tone becomes harsh and *musard*. At this point many a
good fiddle is permanently spoilt by having the sound-post and
bass-bar shifted about and the wood scooped out, but as this
belongs to another part of the work, I must not air this griev-
ance in this place. Often when I have been playing my own
fiddles "into condition" friends have said : "Well, old fellow,
it seems unkind to say so to you who made it, but that's a beastly
fiddle." I always reply, "Tout vient à celui qui sait attendre,"
and, indeed, it is after a month or two of this "cracked-voice"
condition that the instrument settles down gradually into a full,
sweet tone (or the reverse). I have expatiated thus at length
on the subject of *age*, because it is a matter so little understood
even by violinists themselves, and it simply reduces itself to this :
If a violin is well made, its tone from the beginning will either
be good in itself, or indicate future sweetness, and it will
gradually improve with *use* and *age*; but if a fiddle is originally
inferior, *no* amount of playing upon it, and no length of time,
will make it more than it is, "a squeaking crowde," fit only for
the orchestra, or, worse still, for the peripatetic fiddler, who
extracts rather than coaxes pennies from the passer-by. Dr.
Oliver Wendell Holmes, in his "Autocrat at the Breakfast
Table,"[1] discusses this question most beautifully, saying :
"Certain things are good for nothing till they have been kept

Historique et Monumental " (Paris, 1836), which is a description of a violin
made by the *wife* of the late M. Georges Chanot, of Paris, and a puff of her
husband's works. All these, as will be seen, are merely written by way of
advertisement, but they are all valuable additions to the literature of the violin.
because they point out the possibility of excellence in new fiddles, which
excellence is, of course, destined to increase as time and *use* mellow the
instruments.

[1] Appeared originally in the *Atlantic Monthly* in November. 1857.

a long while, and some are good for nothing till they have been
long kept and used . . . Of those which must be kept long
and *used* I will name . . . violins . . . the sweet old Amati,
the divine Stradivarius.   Played on by ancient masters till
the bow-hand lost its power and the flying fingers stiffened ;
bequeathed to the passionate young enthusiast, who made it
whisper his hidden love, and cry in inarticulate longings, and
scream his untold agonies, and wail his monotonous despair ;
passed from his dying hand to the cold virtuoso, who let it
slumber in its case for a generation, until, when his hoard was
broken up, it came forth once more and rode the stormy
symphonies of royal orchestras beneath the rushing bow of
their lord and leader ; into lonely prisons with improvident
artists ; into convents, from which arose day and night the holy
hymns with which its tones were blended ; and back again to
orgies in which it learned to howl and laugh as if a legion of
devils were shut up in it ; then again to the gentle dilettante,
who calmed it down with easy melodies until it answered him
softly as in the days of the old maestros, and so given into our
hands its pores all full of music, stained through and through
with the concentrated sweetness of all the harmonies which have
kindled and faded on its strings . . . Now you know very well
that there are no less than fifty-eight (*sic*) different pieces in a
violin.   These pieces are strangers to each other, and it takes a
century, more or less, to make them *thoroughly* acquainted.   At
last they learn to vibrate in harmony, and the instrument becomes
an organic whole, as if it were a great seed capsule which had
grown from a garden bed in Cremona.   Besides, the wood is
juicy and full of sap for fifty years or so, but at the end of fifty
or a hundred more gets tolerably dry and comparatively re-
sonant." What more beautiful explanation of the matter can
we want? What I have said concerning this matter of new
violins (or, as the writer in *The Orchestra and Choir*[1] says,
" modern examples ") introduces the next portion of this subject,
and that is the *Collection* of violins.

Concerning Collections of Violins much has been said in favour
of them and much against them.   The first record I have found
of such a collection is in Parke's " Musical Memoirs," where
we find (vol. i., p. 301), " Mr. E. Stephenson, the banker, had
perhaps the best and most valuable collection of Cremona
violins of any private gentleman in England. I am, however,
inclined to think that these are frequently more estimated on
account of their scarcity (like strawberries in January) than

their valuable qualities." (He then goes on with the remarks quoted on p. 18.) I do not know if any collection has been recorded before this date (1802), if so, I have never come across it. As to the ethics of violin collecting, there seem to be three opinions. First, that violin collecting is in every way to be deplored, as thereby magnificent fiddles are shut away out of sight and never heard ; this is the opinion of Mr. J. M. Fleming,[1] and he suggests that the owners of collections ought to give them to players, or else to trustees, to lend to students ; a practice simple enough to propound, but slightly utopian, to use no stronger expression. Second, that violin collecting is a most praiseworthy and expedient pursuit, as it tends to preserve old violins much longer than they could otherwise last, and that thereby the masterpieces of the old makers become handed down from generation to generation, with occasional periods of rest, which prevent their dying out altogether. And third, that every man has a perfect right to do what he likes with his own, and that it is nobody's business to say that a man ought not to keep instruments which he has bought and paid for. The latter is principally my opinion. Of course, there is no doubt that it is a pity that the exquisite tones of these stored violins should never be heard ;—this is the basis of the controversy which is got up at intervals about the celebrated Guarnerius, which was Paganini's favourite instrument, which he bequeathed to the municipality of his native place (Genoa), and which has been untouched ever since, excepting once when his great pupil Sivori was suffered to play on it at a concert. People suggest that it should be played upon at concerts, that it should be sold to found a Paganini scholarship, and a hundred other uses are suggested to the Municipality, but really I cannot see that it is anybody's business to interfere, and I think it is most natural that the municipality of the Great Virtuoso's birthplace should like to keep his instrument sacred from all other touches.[2] Then again

<hr/>

[1] J. M. Fleming, " Old Violins and their Makers, including some reference to those of Modern Times " (London, 1883). Appeared originally as a series of articles in *The Bazaar, Exchange and Mart*, 1882, January 27th, *et seq.*

[2] This " Guarnerius del Jesù," dated 1743, was lent to Paganini in 1820 by a M. Livron, a merchant at Leghorn, to play upon at a concert in that place. After the concert, on Paganini's returning the violin to its owner, the latter said to him, " Je me garderai bien de profaner des cordes que vos doigts ont touchées ; c'est à vous maintenant que mon violon appartient," and from this moment it was Paganini's principal and favourite violin. Illustrations of this instrument may be found in G.Hart's " The Violin, its Famous Makers, and their Imitators " (London, 1875), *Frontispiece* ; and in the second edition of Mr. Wellington Guernsey's translation of F. J. Fétis's, " Notice Biographique sur Nicolo Paganini " (Paris, 1851 ; Translation, London. n. d.; 2nd Edit on, London, n. d. [1876]).

the second opinion is undoubtedly very well conceived, for had
it not been that these master-violins have been stored up,
untouched for years, from time to time, they would disappear
from the face of the earth very rapidly; but the third opinion
is the only really tangible one, and the only one that can be
discussed with anything like profit, for it is manifestly absurd
to dictate to men of means what they shall do with their pur-
chases. It would, of course, be of the most fascinating interest
if we could have periodical exhibitions like that of the year
1872 (vide note [1]), but, unfortunately, that requires an amount
of philanthropic self-devotion and trouble which we, in these
hard-living latter days of the nineteenth century, have neither
the time, patience, nor inclination to give.[1]

And this question of collecting brings us naturally to the
prices paid for violins. Although the wonderful prices we now
hear of as being paid for fiddles are things of comparatively
late years, still, every now and then, one hears some story of
fabulous prices paid for fiddles by "them of old time." The
Times of March 31st, 1876, contained a note to the effect that
at a then-recent sale by auction at Dresden, one of the objects
sold was the famous violin which the Count Trautmannsdorf,
Grand Equerry to the Emperor Charles VI., bought from the
celebrated maker Stainer on singular conditions. He paid in
cash sixty-six golden caroluses, undertaking to supply Stainer as
long as he lived with a good dinner every day, 100 florins in
specie every month, a new suit of clothes with gold frogs every
year, as well as two casks of beer, lodging, firing, and lighting;
and further if he should marry, as many hares as he should
want annually for himself, and as many more for his old nurse.
As Stainer lived sixteen years afterwards, the violin must have
cost the Count 20,000 florins in cash. The instrument, which
was last in the hands of an Austrian nobleman, was sold to a
Russian for 2,500 thalers (about 10,000 fcs.). The above story,
which purports to have been taken from the Globe, is rather
too "tall" (as an American would say) to believe, but that it
could have been thought possible shows in what estimation old
violins have always been held. Earlier than this the same
paper (November 4th, 1859) gives an account taken from The
Entr'acte to the effect that M. de Beriot had sold his famous

---

[1] Apropos of such exhibitions, a volume of the deepest interest to violinists
(apart from its great bibliographical rarity) is the magnificent Édition de luxe
of the " Catalogue of the Special Exhibition of Ancient Musical Instruments,
MDCCCLXXII " (London, 1873). Compiled by the late Carl Engel (vide note [1],
p. 6), and embellished with fourteen photographic plates, of which ten are photographs of celebrated Cremonese fiddles.

violin to M. Wieniawski for 20,000 francs.[1] The *Times* has often given notes of such prices, notably on June 24th, 1859, and June 28th, 1862, when it chronicles sales at Messrs. Puttick and Simpson's, among the items of which we find, Stradivarius violins sold for £249, £80, £56, £135, and £90 ; Stradivarius 'cellos at £129, and £210, and instruments by other celebrated makers at similarly varying prices.[2] W. Parke in his " Musical Memoirs " (vol i., p. 302) recounts a negotiation for a violin, which recalls the (to my mind) apocryphal one concerning the Stainer. Mr. Hay, a former excellent leader of the king's band, produced on his favourite violin, by Klotz, a German, a tone so sweet and powerful, that he was on one occasion offered by a noble lord £300 in cash and an annuity *durante vitâ* of £100. Mr. Hay, however, possessing a handsome independence, and not being desirous of parting with his instrument, rejected the offer,

[1] This announcement arose out of the following circumstance :—The two celebrated violinists happening to meet (in 1859) at Ems, Wieniawski, after playing on De Beriot's violin (a Maggini) in his apartments, asked him if he felt inclined to sell it. " Yes," answered De Beriot, " but not for less than 20,000 francs." Thereon M. Wieniawski expressed his desire to purchase it notwithstanding its high price. M. de Beriot having assured him that he would be most happy to see the instrument in his possession, the young artist asked permission to delay his final answer till the coming winter, after his return from St. Petersburg. The negotiation never came to a deal, but these are the facts concerning M. de Beriot's 20,000 franc violin.

[2] Those who are curious concerning the prices of violins will find carefully prepared tables of Celebrated Collections, Sales, and Prices of Violins in the appendix to Peter Davidson's " The Violin, a Concise Exposition of the General Principles of Construction theoretically and practically treated " (Glasgow, London, Edinburgh, and Aberdeen, 1871), and more fully still in the appendix to the 4th edition, 1881, p. 220. Mr. Davidson, besides being the author of the above little work, which is not without merit, is also the author of " Scintillations from the Orient," " Celestial and Terrestrial Fire," and " The Philosophy of Man," and also of the following advertisement which I saw in *The London and Provincial Music Trades Review*, June 15th, 1883, and which, like the advertisements I have reproduced on pages 14 and 15, I simply transcribe for the instruction and amusement of my readers :—

" Very important to all Musicians. A Ten Guinea Violin Given Away Gratis ! To every Subscriber to The Caledonian Collection of Strathspey's Reels, Gigs, Slow Airs, Songs, Hornpipes, Waltzes, Polkas, etc., composed and arranged for the Pianoforte, or Violin and Violoncello, by PETER DAVIDSON, Author of ' The Violin,' etc., and Honorary Member of the Bengal Academy of Music, Calcutta, Honorary Member of the Poonah ' Gayan Samaj Musical Society,' etc., etc. The Author will issue a beautiful Photograph of Burgie Castle, Morayshire—taken by him expressly for this purpose—upon which a Number will be imprinted, this serving as a Coupon, which will entitle each subscriber to a participation in the Drawing for the above Prize, viz. :— An Old Tyrolese (Oil Varnish) Violin, a copy of a Joseph Guarnerius, fecit Cremonæ, Anno 1720, I.H.S., being of magnificent Wood, Workmanship, Tone, and Brilliancy, and unanimously valued by Judges at Ten Guineas. The Violin will be delivered Gratis to the Holder of the Winning Number. The Drawing for such to take place within the year by a Committee selected by 'he Subscribers, etc "

and, dying some years after, this *rara avis* at the subsequent sale of his effects produced but £40. There are but few amateurs who would give £40 for a Klotz nowadays, and Mr. Hay must have been possessed of a very dull wit to reject so phenomenal an offer.

Stories such as these of the enormous prices which have been, and still are being, given for fiddles naturally suggest the recitals one constantly comes across of Stradivaris, Guarneris, Amatis, and so on, being "picked up for a mere song" in out-of-the-way emporia of second-hand goods. Now and then, indeed, such a thing happens,—indeed a "find" of this sort was chronicled in the *Orchestra and Choir* for October 1882. In this case a very fine violin by Antonius and Hieronymus Amati was bought by a gentleman in its *original* condition for five shillings at a broker's shop in Nottingham. But these things are of the days gone by ; the days of Luigi Tarisio and his extremely dishonest way of acquiring valuable fiddles on the "new-lamps-for-old" principle, are over. A fiddle will now always fetch its value, and second-hand furniture dealers who happen to get hold of the most inferior old fiddle will always nowadays affix thereto a price preposterously disproportionate to its value *for fear* of letting a treasure go for nothing. At the same time, an *excellent* fiddle can be bought nowadays for £25, which brings us back to my remarks on page 21 ; but if the amateur wishes to acquire a collection of undoubted masterpieces, let him first turn to the *Times* of May 26th, 1876, which chronicles the sale of a collection of fifteen Cremonas the day before at Messrs. Foster's in Pall Mall, for £1,682 ; two Stradivaris going for £240 each, and a Joseph Guarnerius del Jesù for £630 !

I meant this Introductory Essay to be but a short opening to the historical section of my work, but as I have worked, old memories have come upon me *currente calamo*, until my brief introduction has developed into a prolix treatise on matters connected with the Violin, which should find no place in a practical manual on Fiddle-making. The reader will, I hope, forgive me this extension of a labour of love, on my promise not to let my *calamus* carry me away again ; and if he (or She) has been interested in my long "gossip" concerning the instrument, I can only say that I lay down my pen preparatory to commencing the serious History of the Violin, with a joyful conviction that my labour has not been wasted.

PART I.

Historical.

DE FIDIBUS.

INTENSOS RESONA PRIMUM TESTUDINE NERVOS
  MERCURIOUS FERTUR SOLLICITASSE MANU,
CUM RAPTAS PECUDES QUÆRENTEM CARMINE PHOEBUM
  MOLLIVIT CREPITANS FILA CANORA LYRAE.
FLUMINA RIVORUM POTUIT CELERESQUE MORARI
  THREICIUS VENTOS VOCE POETA SUÂ ;
QUIN COMITES SILVAS DUXIT SCOPULOSQUE, FERASQUE
  DULCISONIS DOMUIT CANTIBUS ILLE LYRÆ.
TU GENUS HUMANUM, LACRYMAS, SPES, GAUDIA, LUCTUS,
  CALLIOPE CITHARÂ SUB DITIONE TENES ;
GAUDIA SI TREMULIS FIDIBUS MODULARIS OVAMUS,
  SIVE PLACET PLANCTUS CORDA DOLORE GEMENT ;
TU MISERORUM OCULIS DULCES REVOCARE SOPORES
  PECTORA TU FIDIBUS MŒSTA LEVARE QUEAS :
TU NISI SÆVORUM DOMUISTI CORDA VIRORUM
  IDALII PUERI VANA SAGITTA FUIT.

S. C. G.

CHAPTER I.

THE ANCESTRY OF THE VIOLIN.[1]

Difficulties in the Way of Research—Destruction—Errors of Description and Representation—Mention of Viols in the Bible—Bow Instruments among the Ancient Greeks and Romans—The Ravanastron—The Omerti—The Kemangeh a'gouz—The Rebab esh Sha'er—The Goudok—The Rebab—The Nofre—The Assyrian Trigonon—Pear-shaped Viols—The Rebec and the Viol—The Gigue and the Kit—The Viol-makers and their Instruments—French Claims to Invention—The Viol da Gamba—Playford—The Barytone—Prætorius—Chests of Viols.

> " 'Tis true, the finding of a dead horse head
> Was the first invention of string instruments,
> Whence rose the gitterne, viol, and the lute."[2]

In no subject of research, perhaps, has the Antiquary so many difficulties to contend with as in the consideration of the " Ancestry of the Violin," and the study of the precursors of instruments of music played with a bow.

The History of the Violin from the earliest times until comparatively recently has been one exclusively of pictures and sculptures. Metal and stone instruments may come down to us preserved in tombs, etc., in almost their original state, but the wooden instruments of music, especially those of such delicate build as those made to sustain the tension of musical strings, even had they been intentionally preserved by those whose ears they charmed, must long ere this have succumbed to the ravages of time and its attendant destroyers ; besides this, any instru-

---

[1] The following chapter (as also chapter ii. on the Welsh Crwth) is to a great extent the substance of a Lecture delivered by the Author on Friday, June 2nd, 1882, at the Freemason's Tavern, before "𝕿𝖍𝖊 𝕾𝖊𝖙𝖙𝖊 𝖔𝖋 𝕺𝖉𝖉 𝖁𝖔𝖑𝖚𝖒𝖊𝖘," which was subsequently printed in limited edition (210 copies for private circulation), and dedicated to "𝕿𝖍𝖊 𝕾𝖊𝖙𝖙𝖊 𝖔𝖋 𝕺𝖉𝖉 𝖁𝖔𝖑𝖚𝖒𝖊𝖘" under the title of " The Ancestry of the Violin, being a Discourse delivered at the Freemason's Tavern on Friday, June the second, 1882, to 𝕿𝖍𝖊 𝕾𝖊𝖙𝖙𝖊 𝖔𝖋 𝕺𝖉𝖉 𝖁𝖔𝖑𝖚𝖒𝖊𝖘 ; " Part I., *The Origin of the Violin;* Part II., *The Welsh Crwth* (London : printed for the Author by Mitchell and Hughes, 140, Wardour Street, 1882, forming No. 1 of a series of pamphlets on the Violin, entitled " De Fidiculis Opuscula").

[2] " *Lingua, or the Combat of the Tongue and the Five Senses for Superiority,*" an Allegorical Play written in 1607, and attributed to Anthony Brewer.

ment played with a bow or plectrum, has the additional disadvantage that this necessary appendage may easily become
separated from it and lost, whilst the instrument itself is
preserved. And, indeed, this is proved by the fact, that though
we know that many of the classic instruments were played with
plectra of various sizes, and of various materials, some of
them extremely hard and durable, in no instance has an
authenticated specimen of a plectrum been found, to give
us accurate information of what these prehistoric "bows"
actually were. This being so, we are thrown upon descriptions in prose and verse by contemporaneous writers, on
sculptures, frescoes, and carvings, and on pictures representing, or including in their subjects representations of, stringed
instruments. Undoubtedly of these four the first are the best,
but the inferiority of a written description to an actual repre-

Fig. 1.—Grotesque figures from panels in the roof of Peterborough Cathedral.
Date, 1194 (?).

sentation in carving or drawing needs no comment, and we
know from painful experience how intensely unsatisfactory and
doubtful any such representations must be when we reflect that
not only may the artist for his own artistic purposes have
"invented" an instrument, so to speak, to embellish his design,
regardless of the fact that he was recording, for the use of future
generations, a history of the dress, manners, and instruments of
his own time, but also the hand of the restorer may have been
at work ; and I doubt very much whether the good-natured
people who subscribe heavily in cash, and get up bazaars,
concerts, and what not, to raise funds for the "restoration"
(save the mark!) of the parish church, with its monuments,
frescoes, and ornaments, ever realize what irreparable mischief
such work is apt to do, unless carefully superintended, and
conscientiously and intelligently carried out by the artificers.

As an instance of the first of these contingencies, I would call your attention to the well-known Holy Family, painted by Carl Müller, who is, perhaps, one of the greatest living delineators of sacred subjects. The young Mother, the carpenter Joseph, the Infant Saviour, are all breathing images whose purity of expression and truth of colouring will render the picture immortal ; *but*, in an attitude of devotion, there kneels upon the ground an angel playing on a sort of three-stringed violoncello, more like the Kemangeh a'gouz of the modern Mohammedan (Fig. 7) than anything else. In a few centuries some sçavant will say—" In Germany, in the latter half of the nineteenth century, was played a modification of the Mohammedan Kemangeh : it would appear to have been used exclusively for devotional purposes." As an instance of the second of these casualties, in the lozenge-shaped panels in the roof of Peterborough Cathedral are grotesque figures playing violins (Fig. 1). Now, this roof is considered to be of the date 1194, but these violins—I use the word advisedly—are almost perfect ; the *f f* holes, scrolls, necks, finger-boards, strings and tail-pieces show a perfection not attained till the fifteenth century, and the bows are practically those of the eighteenth century. How account for this ? Simply thus—I quote the words of Messrs. Sandys and Forster [1]—" The ceiling was retouched a little previous to 1788, and repaired in 1835, but the greatest care was taken to retain every part, or restore it to its original con-

Fig. 2.—Viol attributed to Albinus (?). Fourteenth century.

dition, so that the figures, even where retouched, are in effect the same as when first painted." This is of course impossible . accurate tracings of the original designs would have been invaluable, imperfect though they might have been ; but as they are, though as ornaments they may be pretty, as antiquarian records they are comparatively useless.

A final instance that I will cite, as it concerns a frequently reproduced figure, is that of the so-called " Viol of Albinus." This (Fig. 2) is a figure found in a MS. of the fourteenth century in the library of the University of Ghent, entitled, " De diversis

[1] W. Sandys and S. A. Forster, " History of the Violin " (London, 1864).

monochordis, tetrachordis, pentachordis, extachordis, eptachordis, octochordis, etc., ex quibus diversa formantur instrumenta musicæ, cum figuris instrumentorum." The manuscript is not signed, but the viol purports to be the invention of one Albinus, and until we can find out who this Albinus was, and when he lived, the figure, which is a very interesting one, is not much use. Some have stated him to be identical with a certain Alcuin, who lived in the eighth century , but the viol is not only of a very fourteenth century shape, but its four strings are actually marked A, D, G, C, which renders it absurd to suppose it is a faithful representation of an eighth century viol. Others, more enthusiastic still (reminding us of Rousseau and Bartoloccius cited below), try to identify him with the Albinus mentioned by Cassiodorus (!), but the reader who peruses the next few pages will quickly dismiss any idea of this sort. No ; this remains one of those mysteries which we can only solve by analogy, and therefore, as we cannot identify Albinus, and the MS. is obviously fourteenth century, and appearances favour the assumption, we can almost safely say that we have here a fairly well-developed viol of the fourteenth century, represented with its mode of tuning and bow complete.

These three instances out of countless examples are enough to show the difficulties with which I enter upon a notice of the earliest forms of the fiddle. Plato,[1] indeed, tells us that among the ancient Romans "it was not allowed to painters or other imitative artists to innovate, or invent any form different from what were established, nor lawful, either in painting, statuary, or music, to make any alteration." This rule would, indeed, have been most useful if it had been adhered to throughout all ages, and would relieve the musical antiquary from the necessity of making my first complaint ; but the ravaging restorer would still rage around among the *monumenta temporis acti*, and nullify this far-seeing and provident law. It is to such meagre materials, therefore, that I turn for the information to be set forth at this present. Even later on in the Middle Ages, as will be seen, the sources of information are equally unsatisfactory; and in concluding these preliminary remarks, for the length of which I must crave your indulgence, I merely quote Bottée de Toulmont,[2] who says—" Si le moyen âge est l'époque où la nomenclature des instruments est la plus nombreuse, c'est aussi celle où les renseignements sur leur nature laissent le plus à désirer."

Before going further I will dispose, once and for all, of the

---

[1] " De Legibus," lib. ii. (B.C. 409).
[2] B. de Toulmont, " Dissertation sur les instruments de musique au moyen âge," dans " Mémoires des Antiquaires de France," tome 17.

From a Photograph by Wm. Field (Putney).

VIOLIN BY ANDREAS AMATI
One of 24 made by Andreas Amati for Charles IX, King of France,
(vide p. 73).

writers who have stated that the viol was known to the Israelites, citing in support of their theory many passages of the Old Testament where the word "viol" occurs. The word "viol" is of much more constant occurrence in old translations of the Bible than in the modern and accepted version. Thus the 2nd verse of Psalm lxxxi. used to read, "The pleasaunt harpe, with the viol;" the 12th verse of Isa. v. reads, "The harp and the viol, the tabret and pipe and wine are in their feasts." In an old Bible of the year 1551 the 5th verse of 2 Sam. vi. is rendered, "And David and al the house of Israel played before the Lord with al maner instrumentys of fyrre woode, wyth harpes, psalteries, timberelles, fyddelles and symbals." The 11th verse of Isa. xiv. reads, "Thy pomp is brought down to the grave and the noise of thy viols;"[1] and the 23rd verse of Amos ch. v. reads, "For I will not hear the melody of thy viols."[2] In all these cases the word translated is the Hebrew נֵבֶל, which is equivalent to the Greek ψαλτήριον and the Latin *psalterium*, and should be translated *harp*. In an old French Bible of the early part of the ninth century verse 3 of Psalm cxlix. is rendered, "Louent-il son noun en *crouth*; si chantent il à lui en tympan et psaltruy"—where the word *meaning* "dance" is rendered by the name of the instrument to which they used to dance (the crwth, *vide* p. 58), just as later on, the instrument known as the "gigue" (*vide post*, p. 49) gave its name to the dance it accompanied, which came to be called "jig."[3] In Gen. iv. 21 the word ψαλτήριον is translated *organ* in our version; but in the Lutheran version this passage reads, "Und sein Bruder hiesz Jubal, von dem sind hergekommen die Geiger und Pfeifer;"[4] and the same word (ψαλτήριον) is translated "viol" in the sixth chapter of Amos, ver. 5.[5] Again, the great divine, John Bale, talks of "the merye noyse of theym that play upon harpes, lutes, and fydeles."[6] These instances are enough, without unnecessary multiplication, to prove that as a matter of fact the equivalent of the word "viol" does *not* occur in the original text of the Bible, nor does any other word signifying *bow-instrument;*

[1] *Germ.*: "Dem Klange deiner *Harfen.*"
[2] *Germ.*: "Denn ich mag dein *Psalterspiel* nicht hören."
[3] This use of the word *crouth* reminds me of an absurd mistake made by Bishop Morgan in his translation of the Bible into Welsh, where he translated "*vials* of wrath" by the word "*crythan*"—*i.e.*, crowds or *viols!*
[4] "And his brother was named Jubal, from whom descended *fiddlers* and *pipers.*
[5] The German version gives the word "*Psalter*" in this place.
[6] "The Ymage of Both Churches after the moste wonderful and heavenly Reuelacion of Sainete John, &c. Compyled by John Bale" (London, 1550), Part III., ch. xviii., *not paginated*, leaf next before sig. Cc1, being the Commentary to the Revelation, ch. xviii., ver. 22.

and we can therefore be quite sure that the viol or violin was *not* in use among the Hebrews, for we may justly pause before believing the statements of Jean Rousseau, who declared that *Adam* used and understood the viol in the garden of Eden ! ! [1] and of Julius Bartoloccius,[2] who is cited by Gerbert,[3] and who mentions among the instruments of the Hebrews the "viola or chelys ; " but as he supports his statement by no evidence, and afterwards states that they had pianofortes (*spinnettæ* !), we are justified in doubting his accuracy. So much, therefore, for the claims of the Israelites to the possession of bowed instruments. If anyone would prosecute the enquiry, let him commence by reading Dr. Stainer's "Music of the Bible";[4] as for us—*moniti meliora sequamur.*

The history of the fiddle is as a matter of fact simply the history of the bow ; establish the existence of the bow, and you have the existence of the fiddle. It is a question yet unsolved whether the Latin word *plectrum* (which comes from *plango* = I strike), and the Greek word "$\pi\lambda\hat{\eta}\kappa\tau\rho\sigma\nu$" (which comes from "$\pi\lambda\acute{\eta}\sigma\sigma\epsilon\iota\nu$," to strike), can be translated "bow," *i.e.*, "instrument for *rubbing* the strings." The English word "bow" is often translated into Latin by the word *plectrum*, but it is a matter of considerable doubt whether this Latin word *plectrum* can be translated into English by the word "bow" ; and it remains to be found whether the bow was actually known to the ancients or not.[5] As a commencement to the question, I

---

[1] " Et comme la viole est le plus parfait de tous, parce qu'elle approche plus près du naturel qu'aucun autre, on peut juger que si ADAM avoit voulu faire un instrument, il auroit faict une viole, et s'il n'en a pas faict, il est facile d'en donner les raisons." (!) J. Rousseau, " Traité de la Viole," etc. (Paris, MDCLXXXVII.), p. 3.

[2] A monk of the order of St. Bernard, who lived in the seventeenth century (1613—1687), and who, being attached to the Library of the Vatican, left behind him two treatises of little value, entitled (i.) " De Psalmorum libro, Psalmis et musicis instrumentis " and (ii.) " De Hebræorum musicâ brevis dissertatio," which are to be found in the " Bibliotheca Rabbinica " (Rome, 1675).

[3] " De Cantu et Musicâ Sacrâ " (St. Blasius, 1774).

[4] John Stainer, " The Music of the Bible," etc. (London, n.d. [1880]).

[5] One of the most commonly quoted instances of the use of the word *plectrum* is the 647th line of the sixth book of Virgil's " Æneid " :—

> " Nec non Threicius longâ cum veste sacerdos
> Obloquitur numeris, septem discrimina vocum
> Jamque eadem digitis, jam *pectine* pulsat *eburno.* "

Mr. H. Nettleship in his " Abridgment from Connington's Virgil " (London, 1872— one of Whittaker's Grammar School Classics) gives the following note : " PECTINE —Though the Romans adopted into their own language the Greek word *plectrum*, they used the Latin *pecten* to denote the same thing, not because the instrument used in striking the lyre was at all like a comb in shape and appearance, but because it was held in the right hand, and inserted between the stamina of the lyre as the comb was, between the stamina of the loom."

will shortly enumerate what M. Vidal[1] says on the point. He cites the erroneous drawings and letterpress of one Valeriano,[2] who, in 1568, in his description and representation of a medal of the Æmilius and Scribonius families, B.C. 204 (Fig. 3), altered the two lyres hanging thereon to a violin (Fig. 4) ; a daring innovation truly, and one carrying out my first wail about pictorial history. He then refers to Blaise de Vigenère,[3] who, in 1605, reproduced Valeriano's errors, and gave a representation of Amphion raising the walls of Thebes by force of his viol playing. In conclusion, Vigenère cites Valeriano as his authority, just as, in 1735, l'Abbé de Chateauneuf[4] reproduces the theories of Valeriano and Vigenère. The work was never by him intended for publication, but was produced many years after his death full of uncorrected faults. Zaccharia Tevo, in 1706, asserts positively,[5] " Il violino fù inventato da Orfeo, figlio d'Apollo ; e Safo poetessa invente l'arco de crini di cavallo, e fù la prima che lo suonase come si costuma oggidi." This is probably in allusion to a

FIG. 3   Medal of the Æmilius and   Scribonius families. B.C. 204.   FIG. 4.—Same medal, erroneously figured by Valeriano. 1568.

well-known gem illustrated by Maffei,[6] representing Orpheus playing to wild beasts on a violin, reproduced as a frontispiece to his work[7] by M. Gallay, which was supposed to be antique, but subsequently proved to be comparatively modern. This is another illustration of misleading artistic imagination, than which no better specimen exists than the " Parnassus " of Rafaelle in the Vatican at Rome, where Apollo is represented as playing a viol.[8] My readers will, of course, all know the cele-

[1] A. Vidal. " Les Instruments à Archet " (Paris, 1876). 3 vols., 4to. *Édition de Luxe.*
[2] " Hieroglyphica Commentarii Joannis Pierii Valeriani per Thomam Guarinum" (1568).
[3] B. de Vigenère, " Les Tableaux de Philostrate, traduits en Français et commentés " (Paris, 1605).
[4] L'Abbé de Chateauneuf, " Dialogue sur la Musique des Anciens " (Paris, 1735).
[5] P. B. Zaccharia Tevo, " Musico Testore " (Venice, 1706).
[6] P. A. Maffei, " Gemme Antiche figurate " (Rome, 1708).
[7] J. Gallay, " Les Luthiers Italiens aux 17e et 18e siècles " (Paris, 1869)
[8] *Vide* the foot-note to p. 340 of " Raphael, His Life, Works, and Times," from the French of Eugène Muntz, edited by Walter Armstrong, B.A. (London, 1882), which runs : " It has often been asked why Raphael, instead of placing

brated picture by Paul Veronese in the Louvre, of the "Marriage
at Cana of Galilee," in the foreground of which is a figure (a portrait of Titian) playing on a perfectly-defined double-bass! It is
needless to multiply cases; all the supposed antiques that M. Vidal[1]
could get cognizance of were the works of comparatively modern
artists, and he consequently comes to the conclusion that to the
Greeks and Romans bow instruments were unknown. Sir John
Hawkins[2] cites a work on stringed instruments, written in
A.D. 60, by one Nichomachus Gerasenus, a Pythagorean, who
does not mention any mode of vibrating strings otherwise than
with the fingers or plectrum. Now, against all this Mr. J. M.
Fleming[3] makes some most interesting and valuable (if reliable)
statements, going to prove the existence of the bow in classic
times, quoting from an illustrated catalogue of the collection of
Greek and Etruscan vases, made by Lucien Napoleon, Prince
of Canino, published by subscription at Milan in 1836.[4] He
mentions " a tall-handled cup on which the figures are painted
red on a black ground. The subject is a man seated reading a
volume to two youths, who, leaning on knotted sticks, are
listening attentively. On a little table or box in front of the
principal figure is inscribed the name ' Chironeis.' On each
side of the reader is an object which authorities in these matters

the legendary lyre in the hands of Apollo, represented him playing the violin.
According to Passavant (' Raphael,' vol. i., p. 119) he was led to commit this
anachronism either by the pope or by some other great personage who was
anxious to have the portrait of some skilful player, possibly of Giacomo San-
secondo, whom Castiglione, in his ' Courtier,' eulogises as so accomplished a
musician. This is very far fetched, for Pinturicchio, in his frescoes in the
Borgia rooms, had already represented Music under the figure of a young woman
playing the violin (Pistolesi, ' Il Vaticano descritto,' vol. iii.). Lo Spagna, in
his Magliana frescoes, now in the museum of the Capitol, always substituted the
violin for the lyre. Raphael was also guided in his choice of this instrument
by special considerations, for the lyre had already been placed in the hands of
one of the Muses in this fresco, and he had also painted Apollo with it in ' The
School of Athens ' and in the ' Death of Marsyras.' He could not continually
be repeating the same motive,"
    [1] A. Vidal, "Les Instruments à Archet" (Paris, 1876).
    [2] J. Hawkins (Knt.), "General History of Music" (London, 1776), p. 73.
    [3] J. M. Fleming, "Old Violins and their Makers" (London, 1883). This
work first appeared serially, in the pages of the *Bazaar*, in 1882-3.
    [4] Micali, "Storia degli Antichi Popoli Italiani" (Milan, 1833), and Atlas
thereto Tav. ciii., "Tazza a un alto manico, figure rosse in fondo nero della
forma medesima num. 6 Tav. xcix., Pr. di Canino." The description runs thus :
" Molto singolare, quanto nuovo e gradito dovrà parere all' osservatore il tema
di questo dipinto. Vi si vede un uomo sedente παναίτιος ivvolte ligenocchia
nel suo manto che sta leggendo un volume o papiro. Duo giovanni uditori,
cinto del pallio, ed ambo appoggiati a un nodoso bastone attentamente lo ascoltano.
Dinanzi al leggitore è uno scrigno alto a contenere i volumi sul di cui coperchio
leggesi il titolo χιρονέις. Gli arredi appesi in alto possono essere *thecæ* deno-
tative la professione del maestro. A lato dei due Efebi e la solita epigrafe
καλόs nel mezzo dello scrigno καλέ." The drawing of which this is a description is reproduced at p. 250 of Mr. Fleming's work, cited in note [3].

term 'thecæ,' indicating the profession of this principal figure. One of these has a neck or handle, an oval disc, or sounding plane, and a tail-piece extending below this disc rather more than half the length of the neck. From the upper extremity of the neck to the lower extremity of the disc are stretched strings, and across these strings at the centre of the disc is placed a bow of as rational construction as anything that has come down to us prior to the days of Corelli. The instrument is indeed almost identical with the Ravanastron, the oriental precursor of the occidental fiddle. . . ." The bow above mentioned is placed so close to the instrument that it appears to have no hair, and it might on that account be claimed as a species of plectrum ; but when we remember that Paganini is reported to have played divinely upon his violin with a slender rush in a contest which he had with a vain young man in Italy, we need be at no loss to suppose that the ancients may have excited the vibrations of their strings by a similar contact before hair came to be used. This is a very important discovery, and its importance will be more fully appreciated when we remember the law I alluded to just now against artists altering existing forms in their works, and our not finding frequent representations of this instrument may very possibly be accounted for by the reason given by Mr. C. Engel,[1] viz., that the scenes transmitted to us are chiefly those of funereal, triumphal, or other rites in which instruments of such a primitive description as the fiddle must then have been (if it existed at all), would have taken no part.

Leaving, therefore, the consideration of the use of bowed instruments among the Greeks and Romans with these statistics, the earliest traditions and descriptions of a positive nature come from the East. M. Fétis has in more than one of his works remarked, " Rien dans l'Occident qui ne vienne de l'Orient ; " and certainly in the matter of the ancestry of the violin this is apparently the case ; nor is it at all unlikely, for, as we all know, the West (i.e., Europe) was civilized long after the Eastern continents. In his " Notice of A. Stradivari "[2] he says, very truly, " If we would trace a bow-instrument to its source we must assume the most simple form in which it could appear, and as such required no assistance from an art brought to perfection, and such a form we shall find in the Ravanastron (Fig. 5), made of a cylinder of sycamore wood hollowed out from one end to the other."

[1] C. Engel, " Catalogue of Musical Instruments in the South Kensington Museum " (London, 1874).

[2] F. J. Fétis, " Notice d'Antoine Stradivari " (Paris, 1856), translated into English by John Bishop (of Cheltenham), " Notice of Anthony Stradivari, the Celebrated Violin-Maker," etc.. (London. 1864).

The first tradition we have of this instrument is given by Sonnerat[1] who mentions the Ravanastron as having been invented, 5000 years ago, by one Ravana, then King of Ceylon. Mr Engel[2] says on this subject, " However this may be, there is a great probability that the fiddle originated in Hindustan, for Sanskrit scholars inform us[3] that there are names for the bow

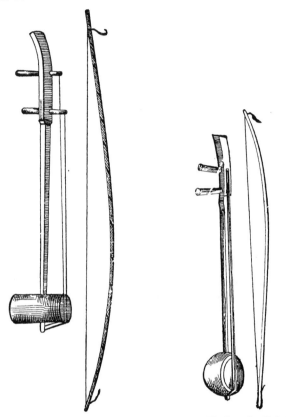

FIG 5.—The Ravanastron. (Ancient   FIG. 6.—The Omerti. (India.)
and Modern India.)

which cannot be less than 1500 to 2000 years old. These names are Kôna, Gârikâ, and Parivàdas. The kôna is described as the rudest kind of bow, consisting of a cane, perhaps without any hair ; it may have been made rough either by small incisions

[1] Sonnerat, " Voyages aux Indes et à la Chine " (Paris, 1782).
[2] C. Engel (vide note [1], p. 37).
[3] F. J. Fétis. " Histoire Générale de la Musique " (Paris, 1869).

THE ANCESTRY OF THE VIOLIN.

or by the application of some kind of resin. Howbeit, any one
may convince himself that a string, especially if it is of silk, as
the strings of Asiatic instruments generally are, may be made
to sound by the friction of a long rod drawn over it like a
bow." (This bears out the supposition of Mr. Fleming,[1] when
he alludes to the hairless bow, and throws a new light on the
plectrum, when we remember that we find representations of
plectra of considerable length among the works of the classic
authors and artists.) "The non-occurrence of any instrument
played with a bow on the monuments of the nations of antiquity
is by no means so sure a proof, as has been generally supposed,
that the bow was unknown. The fiddle in its primitive condition
must have been a poor contrivance, and probably was despised
by players who could produce better tones with greater facility
by twanging the strings with their fingers or a plectrum, and
thus it may have remained through many centuries without
experiencing any material improvement. . . . . In 2000 years
people will possibly maintain that some highly-perfected instrument popular with them was entirely unknown to us, because it
is at present in so primitive a condition that no one hardly
notices it." (Indeed, who shall say that in days to come the
Jew's harp may not become a leading instrument!) "Some
authors have supposed that the Ravanastron was introduced
into India by the Mohammedans; if this had been the case it would
most likely bear some resemblance to the Arabian and Persian
instruments, and it would be found rather in the hands of the
higher classes in the towns, whereas it is principally met with
among the lower orders of people in isolated and mountainous
districts. Moreover, it is remarkable that the most simple form
of Ravanastron (Fig. 5)—there are nowadays some varieties of
this instrument—is almost identical with the Chinese fiddle
called Ur-heen. This species has only two strings, and consists
of a small block of wood hollowed out and covered with the skin
of a serpent. The Ur-heen has not been mentioned among the
most ancient instruments of the Chinese, since there is no
evidence of its having been known in China before the introduction of the Buddhist religion into that country from India.
From indications, which to point out would lead too far here, it
would seem that several instruments found in China originated
in Hindustan." Another form of modern instrument almost
identical with the Ravanastron is the Indian Omerti (Fig. 6) and,
coming a step westwards, almost identical with the omerti is the
modern Turkish and Arabian Kemangeh a'gouz (Fig. 7). Now

[1] *Vide* note ², p. 36.

kemangeh is derived from the Persian word kemangeh, which
means " place of the bow," and " a'gouz " means "ancient," so
that the entire translation is in fact "ancient bow-instrument." [1]
Now the Arabs themselves say that they got the instrument from
Persia, and the word being Persian supports their own statement.
The Persian kemangeh is described by Sir William Ouseley [2] as
practically identical with the Turkish variety, and that it has not
had a changeful existence is proved by a treatise on Persian music,
written, in 1418, by one Abd-ul-cadir, which gives an identical
description of the instrument.[3]   Another modern Turkish and
Arabian instrument is the Rebab, of which there are many

FIG. 7.—Kemangeh a'gouz. (Modern Turkish.)

varieties, one of them (the Rebab esh Sha'er) differing from the
Kemangeh a'gouz only in that it consists simply of a four-sided
frame (Fig. 8), the top and bottom being composed of two pieces
of stretched skin. In one of his earlier works M. Fétis [4] derived the
origin of bow instruments from the Goudok (Fig. 9) of the Russian

[1] A. Christianowitch, " Esquisse Historique de la Musique Arabe " (Cologne,
1863).
[2] Sir W. Ouseley, Bart., " Travels in Various Countries of the East, especially
Persia " (London, 1819).
[3] Ben Gaibi Abd-ul-cadir was a Persian musician, whose work, quoted above,
(a manuscript entitled ملها في الألحامن مقاصد كتاب   تالـف ان ولاوز النقم [Treatise
on the reasons of modulation in chants and measures]) exists in the library
of the University of Leyden.
[4] F. J. Fétis, " Biographie Universelle des Musicians " 1835.

peasantry,[1] but in a later work[2] he corrects this, and ascribes the Goudok to its proper source, viz., the Rebab, and thence through the Kemangeh and Omerti to the Ravanastron of ancient and modern India. Al Farabi, a musical historian of the tenth century (whose work[3] was largely reproduced in 1841 by M. Kosegarten[4]), does not allude to the bow, but Ash-shakandi, in 1200, mentions the Rebab as having been in use in Spain for centuries without having been thought worthy of notice on account of its rudeness. It exists, indeed, still among the country people in Spain under the names " rabel " and" arrabel,"

FIG. 8.—Rebab esh Sha'er. (Modern Turkish and Arabian.)

almost identical with the Rebab of the north of Africa (Fig. 10). I have heard it played by the peasants of the Basque districts of the Pyrenees, but could never acquire a specimen by purchase or barter. A peasant whom I employed to compass

[1] The goudok has three strings, the first of which is touched with the finger while the other two are sounded with the bow, which is short, clumsy, and elementary.
[2] F. J. Fétis, " Notice d'Antoine Stradivari " (Paris, 1856).
[3] Abon-Nasr-Mohammed-Ibn-Obeydallah-Alkaysi Al-Farabi, " Istikasat-ilm-musike " [Elements of Music], a manuscript, written about A.D. 930, and now preserved in the library of the Escurial at Madrid.
[4] J. G. L. Kosegarten, " Alii Hispanensis liber cantilenarum magnus ex codicibus manuscriptis Arabice editus " (Greifswalde, 1841).

this for me, told me these " old violins " (*vieux-vielles*) are handed down from father to son, and are extremely scarce, and

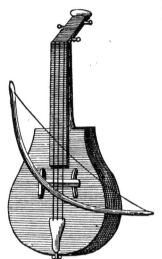

impossible to obtain from their owners. Now the Rebab was, without doubt, in use among the Moors in the seventh century, and, as they proceeded along the North of Africa and conquered Spain in the eighth century, that accounts for its presence along their track from that time to the present day. And as the Arabs themselves assert that they got the Rebab with the Kemangeh from Persia, we thus reach the intelligence again of another ancient Persian instrument, which makes another link

FIG. 9.—The Goudok. (Primitive Russian.)

FIG. 10.—Rebab. (North Africa).

in the chain which traces these instruments from India through Persia and Arabia into Turkey, on the north of the Mediter

ranean, and along the north of Africa into Spain on the south. There is no doubt that the Egyptians had an instrument called " Nofre," (or Nefer, or Nefru, or Nef) of the highest antiquity, with finger-board and bridge, and frets for producing different notes on one string (Fig. 11), and it seems astonishing that so highly civilized, inventive, and musical a people as the Egyptians should not have made the transition, which would be natural, were they in the habit of using a bridged and finger-boarded instrument with a plectrum, viz.,

FIG. 11.—Nofre, or Nefer. (Ancient Egyptian.)

that of rubbing the strings by the same means so as to produce continuous and slurred notes instead of the short sudden ones ; for, be it borne in mind, as I have suggested before, the use of hair is by no means essential to the existence of a bow. Of the high antiquity of the nofre (signifying, when used as a hieroglyphic, "good," [1]) there is no doubt, for we find it among the instruments used at concerts of the eighteenth dynasty (B.C. 1575—1289), and it occurs also in papyri of the date B.C. 2000, and even earlier. Mr. Chappell states that representations of it are found dating from the fourth dynasty. Some fragments of a nofre were found in a tomb at Thebes by Mr. Madox, on the neck of which some of these frets (which were formed of camel-gut tied round the finger-board) were still remaining. This most interesting relic is in the British Museum, and is figured by M. Fétis.[2] Mr. Chappell[3] gives many most interesting figures and descriptions of this instrument ; on page

FIG. 12 —Trigonon. (Assyrian.)

320 he reproduces one with three bridges, and a carved head, being played with a plectrum ; and on p. 62 he gives two figures of its use as a hieroglyphic, with two cross bars (or pegs) in the head, and one of them with a *perfect* bridge and tail-piece. His illustrations are from the " Denkmäler" of Lepsius, and are of the fourth dynasty, in the reign of Chephren (or Suphis II.), who erected the second great pyramid. This would give the instrument an antiquity of 3124 B.C. according to Lepsius, or of 2083 B.C. according to Sir Gardner Wilkinson.

[1] S. Birch, " An Introduction to the Study of the Egyptian Hieroglyphics " (London, 1857), p. 225.
[2] F. J. Fétis, " Histoire Générale de la Musique " Tome i., p. 271.
[3] W. Chappell, " The History of Music," vol. i. (all published) (London, n.d. [1874]).

Mr. Engel[1] gives a figure from an Assyrian slab in the British Museum, of about B.C. 880 (Fig. 12), playing an instrument of the trigonon species, holding a plectrum of considerable length in the right hand, whilst he stops the strings with the left, which, as Mr. Engel justly remarks, may very probably be a rude prototype of the modern violin bow, for these long plectra constantly occur; and, as they must have been very much more inconvenient to twang the strings with than a short one would have been, it is to my mind almost a certainty that the plectrum, when it got beyond a certain length, ceased to be an instrument of percussion, and became one of friction. From all these facts,

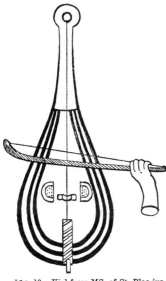

therefore, I deduce this one, that in ages of the highest antiquity bow-instruments, or at any rate stringed instruments from which the tone was produced by friction, existed among the primitive Asiatics. That with the Moors and Mohammedans these instruments journeyed westward into Spain and south-eastern Europe. From these two points they progressed to the north-west by the colonization of the British Isles and Brittany from Spain, and, without soaring into the Indo-European origin of the Celtic tribes, we may say that these great waves of population were progressing gradually into Northern Europe from the east and south-east, bringing with them their superior fiddles (keman-

FIG. 13.—Viol from MS. of St. Blas ius.
Ninth century. (Gerbert.)

gehs, rebabs, etc.) to supersede the more inferior bow instruments *already there* (to which I shall presently refer) There is no doubt that from Spain colonists were continually overrunning Europe, and this accounts for the presence in nearly all European languages of Moorish names for musical instruments, it being not at all improbable that names of crude and imperfect instruments have in all languages become transferred to newer and more perfect instruments as the former went out of, and the latter came into, use. From Spain colonists settled in Brittany, England, Normandy, and other

[1] C. Engel, "The Music of the Most Ancient Nations," etc. (London, 1864), p. 49.

parts of Europe, long before the Indo-European tribes had reached so far, and accordingly it is in these countries that we find records of the first pear-shaped viols, properly so called, bearing strong resemblance to a small variety of ancient and modern Moorish kemangeh. We do not find any actual and authentic representations of pear-shaped viols before the ninth century, which supplies us with a one-stringed viol (Fig. 13), from a MS. from the Monastery of St. Blasius in the Black Forest, which MS. was destroyed when the Monastery was burnt down, but of the illustrations of which the Abbot Gerbert had tracings, which he subsequently reproduced.[1] Representations of viols of supposed earlier dates have been now and then produced, but they have always been found to be ante-dated. In the earliest representations of bow instruments it is rather the exception to find a bridge, tail-piece, sound holes, etc.,

FIG. 14.—Viol from the Cotton MS. Tenth century. (Saxon.)   FIG. 15.—Viol from Eleventh Century Psalter. (British Museum.)

represented ; but as they occur frequently it seems certain that when they do not it is by the omission or ignorance of the artist or sculptor, or by subsequent " restoration " of his work.   A very favourite specimen is found in a MS. in the British Museum[2] (Fig. 14), of the tenth century, which bears a marked resemblance to a form of the ancient Moorish kemangeh and rebab, which is still found among the Breton and Basque peasantry under the name "rebec" (vide p. 41).   This is reproduced by Strutt, together with some others, from a like source.[3]   A Psalter of the eleventh century, in the British Museum, gives a fiddle[4] mounted with

[1] M. Gerbert, " De Cantu et Musicâ Sacrâ " (St. Blasius, 1774).
[2] Cotton MSS., Tiberius C. vi.
[3] J. Strutt, popba Ānʒel-cynnan ["Manners and Customs of the Inhabitants of England "] (London, 1775) ; and also " The Sports and Pastimes of the People of England, including the Rural and Domestic Recreations," etc. {London. 1855).
[4] The word " fiddle " is of immense antiquity, being derived in all languages

one string (Fig. 15), reminding us of the one from the St. Blasius MS. before referred to. A bas-relief of the same century from St. Georges de Boscherville (now in the Museum at Rouen), has two figures playing viols (Figs. 16 and 17), one of which (Fig. 16) is held like the modern violin, and the other (Fig. 17) like the modern violoncello, in which last we begin to see the inward curvatures, which, from this date, almost invariably distinguish the viol, properly so-called, from the more primitive gigue or rebec, about which I shall presently say a few words. The twelfth century supplies M. Potier (author of " Monuments Français ") with a viol of a similar but more ornate and cumbrous description from the porch of Notre Dame de Chartres (Fig. 18) ; and a number of similar ones, only of more definite

FIG. 16.—Gigue, or Rebec, from   FIG. 17.—Viol from the same
Bas-relief at St. Georges de   Bas-relief as FIG. 16.
Boscherville, Rouen. (Eleventh
century.)

and advanced form, are carved on the porch of a church at Santiago di Compostella, in Spain, built in the thirteenth century. At Exeter Cathedral, in the Minstrel's Gallery, a sculptured orchestra gives us perfect representations of the viol and rebec of the fourteenth century, after which we reach the fifteenth century, which saw the introduction of the perfect viols, the immediate predecessors of the modern violin, which were, indeed, for a long time its companions in harmony.

About the eleventh century the fiddle would seem to have

from the old Gothic. Thus we have in the old German " videl," a fiddle ; " videlære," a fiddler ; "videln," to fiddle ; in the modern "fidel." and " fiedel." In the Icelandic " fidla," in the Dutch " videl, viool, and veel.". As an Anglo-Saxon word " fythele " is of immense antiquity. In the legendary Life of St. Christopher, written A.D. 1200, we find, " Christofre hym serued longe ; Ye Kynge loued melodye of fythele and of songe " (G. Dubourg, " The Violin " : London, 1852).

divided into two classes—one the viol proper, having indentations at the sides, and probably two tables connected by sides ; and the other the rebec or gigue, which kept the most elementary or pear-shape, (which carries us back to the ancient Moorish "rebab" [Fig. 19], from which it was undoubtedly descended,) being first called the "rubebe," a most primitive instrument [1] probably only having two strings, thence to the "rebec" and "gigue," in which form it still exists among the Breton and Spanish peasantry and the inhabitants of the northern states of Africa. A friend, recently travelling in Poland, has sent me a most interesting photograph of a peasant rejoicing in the "un-in-one-breath-utterable" name of Stary Sabata Krzctowski r Sgstikanu Smyczhiem, who is playing just such an instrument as this, excepting that it has a head after the accepted form of violin-scroll, and a bridge and ff holes. It is played with a bow as long as the instrument itself, resembling both a double-bass bow, and what is known as a "Corelli" bow, and is altogether a most interesting relic of the Moorish rebab. The Germans called all their bow instruments "geige" (which is also the modern term), and divided them into "klein-geige," "gros-geige," which was of a very distinct form with long inward curvatures. sound-holes, and tail-piece, or rather string-holder like the guitar, and was mounted with from three to nine strings (Fig. 20). Most of the illustrations

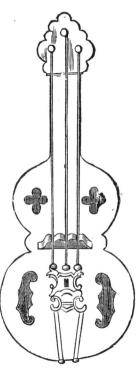

FIG. 18.—Viol from Sculpture at Notre Dame de Chartres.

of this instrument which have come down to us are bridgeless, but this is doubtless in every case an error of the artist, for they were very highly perfected instruments, and were used as late as the sixteenth century. There were four sizes (as with our bow instruments), the set of which are figured by Martin

[1] The rebab had various different names in the different countries of Europe in which it was found :—such as rebebe, rubebe, rebesbe, rebel, arrabel, rabel, rebelle, rebec, and so on (*vide* note [1]. p. 9).

Agricola in 1545,[1] and their names are discantus (Fig. 19), altus, tenor, and bassus. I came across a curious illustration which I take to be of this instrument, a short while since, in the British Museum, in a little black letter pamphlet, *beginning,* "𝕬𝖉 𝕵𝖑𝖑𝖚𝖘𝖙𝖗𝖎𝖘𝖘𝖎𝖒𝖚𝖒 𝕻𝖗𝖎𝖓𝖈𝖎𝖕𝖊𝖒 𝕻𝖆𝖓𝖉𝖚𝖑𝖘𝖚𝖒 𝕸𝖆𝖑𝖆𝖙𝖊𝖘𝖙𝖆𝖒 𝕬𝖗𝖎𝖒𝖎𝖓𝖎 𝖉𝖔𝖒𝖎𝖓𝖚𝖒 𝕵𝖔𝖆𝖓𝖓𝖎𝖘 𝕬𝖚𝖗𝖊𝖑𝖎𝖎 𝕬𝖚𝖌𝖚𝖗𝖊𝖑𝖑𝖎 𝕬𝖗𝖎𝖒𝖎- 𝖓𝖊𝖓𝖘𝖎𝖘 𝖈𝖆𝖗𝖒𝖎𝖓𝖚𝖒 𝖑𝖎𝖇𝖊𝖗 𝖕𝖗𝖎𝖒𝖚𝖘," and *ending,* "𝕵𝖒𝖕𝖗𝖊𝖘𝖘𝖚𝖒 𝖀𝖊𝖗𝖔𝖓𝖊 𝕬𝖓𝖓𝖔 𝖉𝖔𝖒𝖎𝖓𝖎 𝕸𝖈𝖈𝖈𝖑𝖝𝖝𝖝𝖎 (1491) 𝖉𝖎𝖊 𝖖𝖚𝖎𝖓𝖙𝖔 𝕵𝖚𝖑𝖎𝖎," to which it forms the frontispiece or title-page. It is a representa- tion of a viol and bow hanging on nails ; the viol hangs by a ribbon, and the bow by its own head, as bows are even now hung

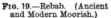

Fig. 19.—Rebab. (Ancient and Modern Moorish.)

Fig. 20.—" Gros-geig," from Illus- tration of M. Agricola. (1545.)

up in shops. The bow is of a very advanced type, having a nut button and head of almost the design of the modern double- bass bow. The viol is fanciful in shape, having a long body with a short neck and a perfect finger-board; the centre-bouts (*scilicet*) are set low in the body, the head is square, carved and provided with seven peg-holes in front, set, three on each side, and one in the middle, whilst at *the side* of the head there projects a peg with a perfect " thumb-piece," which supports two strings (just below the thumb-piece), whence they appear to go *into* the head at the top of the square box thereof. There are five strings on, and two off, the finger-board to the right. The bridge is identical with the modern violoncello bridge, and

[1] M. Agricola, " Musica Instrumentalis " (Wittenberg, 1545).

the tail-piece is like that of all the later viols, and has a tail
loop of twisted cord, which is not however tied on to the instrument ; the sound-holes are in the form of two C's facing one
another.   It is the most advanced representation of a bov.
instrument I have ever seen for the date.

The klein-geige, or gigue, which was identical in shape with the
old rebec (Fig. 10) and Moorish fiddle, was most probably never
more than the ancestor of the "kit," which was used up till late
years by our dancing-masters.   M. de Coussemaker describes one
from the Cathedral of Mans, of the fourteenth century, which has

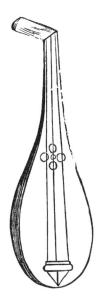

FIG. 21.—Gigue from the Cathedral   FIG. 22.—Discantus. Sixteenth
   at Mans. (Fourteenth century.)   century. (M. Agricola.)

the head thrown back [1] (Fig. 21), and Agricola, in the sixteenth
century (*vide* note [1], p. 48), gives a set of four of a similar but
very much improved shape and condition, which may be judged
from the discantus (Fig. 22).   They were used as late as the
seventeenth century, and they were illustrated by Mersennus [2]
in their last and most improved form.   The rebec is specially
mentioned among the rules of the "Roi des Violons," an

[1] C. E. H. de Coussemaker, "Histoire de l'Harmonie au moyen âge"
(Paris, 1852).
[2] M. Mersennus, "De instrumentis Harmonicis," Harmonicorum Liuri xii,
in quibus agitatur de sonorum naturâ, causis, et effectibus (Paris, 1648).

antique office of high emolument in France. We find [1] among
the rules of the corporation of musicians, confirmed by Louis
XIV. in 1658 (la Confrérie de St. Julien des Menestriers), the
following " . . . . il était défendu aux musiciens qui n'étaient pas
Maîtres, de jouer aux cabarets, etc., . . . à peine de prison," and
the author appends the following footnote, " Il y avait cependant
une exception en faveur de ceux qui
ne jouaient que du *rebec.* Le rebec
était un violon grossier qui avait
précédé l'usage de celui que nous
connaissons. Il avait la forme d'un
battoir échancré par les quatres angles,
au lieu d'être arrondi comme le violon,
et n'était monté que de trois cordes :
mi, la, ré. Il parait, par une sentence
du prévôt de Paris, du 2 mai 1664,
qu'il y avait des hautes-contres, des
tailles, et des basses de *rebec.* Cet
instrument s'est maintenu en France
jusqu'à la fin du dix-septième siècle
et y fut long-temps d'un usage général.
On connait ces vers de la 10e satire de
Régnier,—

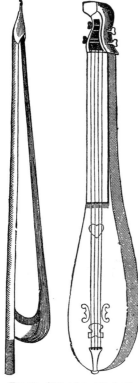

" ' O Muse ! je t'invoque, emmielle-moi le bec,
    Et bande de tes mains les nerfs de mon
       rebec.' "

The last relic that survived of this
form of fiddle was the Sordino
(French, *pochette ;* German, *Taschen-
geige*) of the dancing-masters of
the seventeenth and early eighteenth
century. Mersennus in his " De Instrumentis Harmonicis " [2] gives a
very good illustration of a " pera "

FIG. 23.—" Pera " or " Poche."
    1648. (M. Mersennus.)

or " poche " of the date 1648 (Fig. 23),
and this shape did not alter very much
till the eighteenth century, when it was practically abandoned.
There is in the South Kensington Museum a great beauty of this
date, made in ivory with a wooden belly, the head a carved,
female bust, the bow ivory, and the case leather stamped and
gilt. Both the instrument and the bow are fifteen inches long.

[1] F. J. Feüis, " Curiosités Historiques de la Musique " (Paris, 1830), p. 294.
[2] " Harmonicorum Libri xii, in quibus agitatur de sonorum naturâ, etc., . .
orbisque totius harmonicis instrumentis " (Lutetiæ Parisiorum, 1648).

From this time they would seem to have given way to the kit of the ordinary violin shape. It is from the word " gigue " that our word " jig " is derived, as being used by dancing-masters and so on. They are at all events most interesting, as being the last relics of, and descended directly from, the most ancient type of fiddle. Some twenty excellent specimens were exhibited in the Special Exhibition at South Kensington in 1872, and are described and illustrated by photographs in the catalogue.[1] This, therefore, brings us to the end of what is, to my mind, the right line of research into the ancestry of the violin, with this single conclusion : " Instruments with an elongated neck, finger-board, and bridge, played with the bow, are clearly derived from the Eastern nations of the highest antiquity."

It is now that we arrive at the time of the true viols, the immediate forerunners, and, indeed, early companions of the violin as it now exists. At the beginning of the fifteenth century, the sides of the viols began to be well incurved ; as makers we hear of Ott, and Frey, of Nuremberg ; and, about the middle, Joan Kerlino, of Brescia, the probable founder of the Brescia school. There was extant in 1450, according to Laborde, a viol of Kerlino, dated 1449, and we are told that one was exhibited by Koliker at Paris in 1804, which was converted into a viola by the substitution of a new head, which substitution, it has positively been stated, was Koliker's own work. It is said to have been soft and husky in tone. In the first half of the sixteenth century we come across Duiffoprugcar of Bologna, Linarolli of Venice, Dardelli of Mantua, and others, who have been cited by some as violin-makers ; but it is now certain that they only made the viol class of instruments, such as the viola d'amore, or treble viol, the viola bastarda, or alto viol, the viola da braccia, or tenor viol (hence the modern German word *Bratsche* for tenor), and the viola da gamba, or bass-viol. Of these Duiffoprugcar, though not an actual violin-maker, would seem to have been the most renowned. According to Mr. J. M. Fleming (whose serial papers on the old violin-makers in *The Bazaar*, before referred to [*vide* note [3], p. 36], rank among the best works written on the subject), he was a Tyrolese inlayer or mosaic worker, and this would seem to be borne out by the beautifully worked viola da gamba, a picture of which hangs upon the wall of the South Kensington Museum. His life seems to have been a most eventful one. We hear of him in Bologna, Paris, and Lyons, besides the Tyrol. He seems to have disappeared from Lyons,

[1] "Catalogue of the Special Exhibition of Ancient Musical Instruments, 1872 " (London, 1873), compiled and with an introduction by Carl Engel.

whence we find no trace of him, except a portrait of him, executed there by Pierre Wœiriot, which etching is reproduced by
M. Antoine Vidal in his wonderful work on the violin.[1] It is
supposed originally to have been copied from a portrait of himself on one of Duiffoprugcar's instruments, accompanied with
the verse quoted on the title of this work, the meaning of which,
it may or may not be necessary to state, is: "I lived in the
woods, until I was slain by the relentless axe. Whilst I was
alive I was silent, but in death my melody is exquisite." But
this portrait and motto has also been said to be that of one
Bandinelli, a sculptor in the service of Duke Cosmo of Venice,
in 1550. The great J. B. Vuillaume made a quantity of violins
at the beginning of this century, which were carved and inlayed
after the manner of Duiffoprugcar, and many an amateur has
fondly imagined himself the possessor of a genuine antique,
instead of a great maker's well-executed (not to put too fine
a point on it) "forgery."

The viols all had five or six strings at least, and frets to
stop the notes with. We sometimes come across tenors ascribed
to one or other of these old "Luthiers," but they can only
be thus described when they have new heads, necks, and finger-
boards. There were two such in the Exhibition of 1872, made
about 1520 by Ventura Linarolli, of Venice ; both of these had
the old six or seven-pegged heads replaced by the modern (or
rather sixteenth century) four-pegged scroll. As Mr. C. Reade
justly remarks, the immense breadth between the ff holes shows
that they were meant for five, six, or seven strings. They
were played *upon* the knee ; and as the same connoisseur points
out, old tenors and basses always appear much older than they
really are, from the fact that at that time (1550 *et seq.*) such
instruments were, as a rule, hung up against a wall when not
in use, not nursed in cases. According to Mr. Fleming, Giovanni
Cellini, father of the illustrious Benvenuto Cellini, was by his
son's statement an accomplished maker of viols of rare beauty,
about 1500 ; but beyond this noteworthy reference by his son,
Giovanni Cellini's work has not reached us. Prince Jousoupof,
the anonymous author of "Luthomonographie," [2] ascribes the
invention of the violin proper to one Testator of Milan, who
reduced the size of the viola to that of the violin contemporaneously with, or before, Gasparo da Salo. I cannot, however
find any notice of him elsewhere, except in the wok of,

[1] "Les Instruments à Archet" (Paris, 1877: J. Claye).
[2] "Luthomonographie historique et raisonnée, par un Amateur" Francfort
M/. 1856).

M. Antoine Vidal,[1] who quotes the same author, and utterly denies his statement, which I also class with the other mistaken which have crept into the work of this would-be anonymous Amateur. *Non nostrum tantas componere lites.* As to who really *did* first make the violin proper in its present form (*no one* can claim its actual *invention*) there seems to be very little doubt that it was the Italians. Mr. Hullah [2] pretty well sums up all that has been said on the subject when he says :— " The invention of the violin has been claimed for, or rather by, the French on, I believe, one single plea, that in some early Italian scores (*e.g.*, Monteverde's *Orfeo* [1608]) are found the words ' Piccoli Violini alla Francese.' There is good reason for believing that these 'piccoli violini' were instruments analogous to the kits used to this day by dancing-masters. But granting them to have been violins proper, their appearance in Monteverde's score (published as late as 1615) proves nothing. Vincenzo Galilei asserts in his " Dialogues " (printed at Venice in 1568) that the violino and the violoncello were both invented by the Neapolitans. Montaigne has recorded that he heard violins in the Great Church (St. Zeno ?) at Verona in 1578. Corelli possessed a violin which had been decorated by the Bolognese painter Annibale Caracci, who *died* in 1609, and to complete the case of the Italians, the first great *performer* on the violin of whom we have any account was an Italian named Baltzarini, who was brought, or sent for, into France, by Catherine de Medici, in 1577. No specimen of a French violin, no record of a French violinist, has come down to us of anything like these early dates. The invention of the violoncello again has been claimed on behalf of a certain Abbé Tardieu of Provence, who lived in the beginning of the last century. It is certain, however, that Baptistini, a Florentine, had brought the instrument into France at the end of the preceding century. Specimens of both the violoncello and of the contrabasso of Italian fabrication of the beginning of the seventeenth century are not rare."

Fig. 24.—Device of John Oporinus. (Basle, 1530.)

From about 1555 we find the instruments of Gasparo da Salo, the first maker of violas and violins, and as such he will be spoke of in his proper place in a future chapter; bu' he also was a maker of viols. In 1530, John Oporinus, a printer at Basle, had for his device a six-stringed instrument (Fig. 24),

---

[2] " Les Instruments à Archet " (Paris, 1877).

J. Hullah, " The History of Modern Music " (London, 186?), p. 190.

which comes very near the true tenor. The violin proper is first referred to by Zacconi in 1596, who describes it with a compass identical with the modern one, *without the shift*, which would imply that the shift was then unknown or little used, and it was certainly impossible, or at any rate ineffective, with the frets on the old viols, which were used fretted late on into the seventeenth century, with frets made, as a rule, of pieces of glued catgut tied round the neck at intervals, so as to form ridges on the finger-board.

One of the finest viole da gamba in existence is perhaps that

FIG. 25.—Viola da Gamba.
(C. Simpson.) 1667.

one which was formerly in the possession of Mr. S. A. Forster, who figures it in his "History of the Violin" (London, 1864), but now in the South Kensington Museum. My illustration of the instrument (Fig. 25) is from Christopher Simpson's "Division Viol."[1] At this period the viol had but six strings, but towards the *end* of the seventeenth century, a seventh was added.[2] The French gamba-player, Marais, added three bass strings of covered gut, but it was an innovation which did not in any way become general. Connected with the instrument, we find the names of two lady performers, Mrs. Sarah Ottey, in 1723, and Miss Ford, in 1760. These must have been ladies of great courage, when we consider the humour in which the world then regarded such performances (*vide* p. 5). The last celebrated performer on the viola da gamba was Carl Friedrich Abel, who died in 1784. A part was written for the instrument in Bach's *Passionsmusik des Mattheus*, and M. Caix d'Herveloix wrote some extremely pretty "Suites d'Orchestre" for the instrument in 1710. Its tone is nasal,[3] but extremely expressive; indeed, there are a few

[1] C. Simpson, "The Division Viol; or, The Art of Playing *extempore* upon a Ground" (London, 1667, fol.).

[2] Just as of late years a fourth string has been added to the double bass.

[3] Gostling was a great admirer of, and player upon, the viol da gamba, and he celebrated Purcell hated it, and could not stand Gostling's practising on the instrument. He therefore composed a "catch" for three voices in sarcastic eulogy of the viol, which he presented to his friend. The music is published

amateurs who play this instrument now, chief among whom I may mention Mr. Payne, over whose initials, E. J. P., most of the first-rate articles on subjects connected with the violin in Sir George Grove's " Dictionary of Music and Musicians " (London, 1879—1884) are to be found. It was tuned from the D below the stave in the bass clef thus,—D, G, C, E, A, D; but Playford[1] gives the following wonderful method of tuning it :—" When you begin to Tune, raise your *Treble* or smallest String as high as conveniently it will bear without breaking; then stop only your *Second* or *Small Mean* in *F*, and then Tune it till it agree in *Unison* with your *Treble* open ; that done, stop your *Third* in *F*, and make it agree with your *Second* open ; then stop your *Fourth* in *E*, and make it agree with your *Third* open ; then stop your *Fifth* in *F*, and make it agree with your *Fourth* open ; lastly, stop your *Sixth* in *F*, and make it agree to your *Fifth* open. This being exactly done, you will find your *Viol* in *Tune* according to the *Rule* of the *Gamut*." Imagine a modern violoncello-player tuning his instrument according to these principles !

A most interesting contemporary of the viola da gamba was the viola di bordone, or " barytone," which was mounted with six or seven gut strings (tuned from B below the bass clef, B, E, A, D, F, B, [E]), and twenty-two wire strings running from the head below the finger-board and bridge to an oblique row of pins under the tail-piece. The specimen exhibited by Mr. Lidel at the Society of Antiquaries in 1840, is now at South Kensington, and a full account and history of the instrument will be found in Mr. Engel's Catalogue, p. 264 (*vide* note [1], p. 37). Marpurg[2] states that it was originally called " viole de pardon," because it was invented in England by a prisoner about to be hanged, who was pardoned on account of the instrument ; but the origin of the name is undoubtedly " bourdon " (drone) from the noise made by the sympathetic strings.

It was usual to have a set of viols called " a chest of viols,"

---

in a collection called " The Catch Club; or, The Merry Companions."— W. H. Cummings " Purcell " (London, 1881), p. 31 : " The Great Musicians " series.

[1] J. Playford, " An Introduction to the Skill of Musick " (London, 14th Edition, 1700), p. 65. The first edition was published in 1654, but of this edition only *one* copy is known ; it was sold at the dispersion of the library of the late Dr. Rimbault in 1877 for ten guineas. This extreme rarity has brought about the consequence that the *2nd* edition of 1655 is generally cited as the first. Lowndes makes this mistake, which is probably copied from F. J. Fétis's " Biographie Universelle des Musiciens " (Paris, 1864), which gives 1655 as the date of the 1st edition.

[2] F. W. Marpurg, " Historisch Kritische Beyträge zur Aufnahme der Musik " (Berlin, 1756).

and players played on all indifferently (very indifferently I should think!). In the year 1620, Prætorius[1] gives a list of the viols then in use, mentioning the 1. "Gross contrabass-geig," like our modern contrebasse, with five strings, s s sound-holes, no frets, and modern scroll and bow; 2. "Violone," like our violoncello, modern scroll, six strings, six frets, two s s sound-holes; 3. "Viola da gamba," much the same as the violone, with two crescent-shaped sound-holes, carved head, seven frets, six strings; 4. "Viola bastarda," the same shape, six strings, modern scroll, two crescent and one round sound-hole, and seven frets; 5. "Klein posche" (or kit), a little oval instrument like a gigue, with one s hole in the centre under the strings; 6. "Rechte Discant-geig," almost identical with the modern violin; 7. "Tenor-geig," much like a modern short-necked viola; 8. "Bass-geig de bracio," like a clumsy short-necked 'cello. It is in allusion to the practice of having a set of instruments that Ben Jonson in *Bartholomew Fayre*, act iii., sc. 4,[2] makes his character *Cokes* say, "A set of these violines I would buy too, for a delicate young noise I haue in the Countrey, thatte are euery one a size lesse than another, iust like youre fiddles." The frets on the viols were never more than seven, for the shift was comparatively un-known; indeed, on the first introduction of the violin, the production of a note higher than the upper B was looked upon as something most rash, and only to be attempted by the best performers. To such a pitch was this carried, that Gallay tells us[3] that in violin solos, where it was known the high C occurred, the audience would murmur, as the crucial point was approached, " Gare l'ut!" (Mind the C!), and if the feat was achieved safely, a whirlwind of applause greeted the temerous player, whilst in case of failure a storm of hisses rewarded his rash efforts.

Having taken my readers well into the period when the violin proper was in full use, I must leave them, referring them to other and more historical works on the violin, if they would know more of the viols and their music, this being in the main a work on the actual construction of the instrument, to which these historical chapters are practically subordinate. Thus far, however, I have deemed it interesting and necessary to place before them the Ancestry of the Violin, so that they may have a clear perception of what its progenitors actually were. It will

---

[1] Prætorius, "Theatrum Instrumentorum" (Wolffenbüttel, 1620).
[2] "The Workes of Ben Jonson" (London, 1640), vol. ii., p. 39.
[3] J. Gallay. "Les Luthiers Italiens aux xvii⁰ et xviii⁰ siècles" (Paris, 1869).

be observed that I have made no mention at all of the Welsh crwth, and for this reason, that *it has nothing at all to do with the ancestry of the violin.* This is a statement so entirely at variance with all which has before been written on the subject, that I refer my readers to the next chapter for proof of my dictum.

" The woodman met the damsels and the swaines,
The neatherds, plowmen, and the pipers loud,
And each did dance, some to the kit or crowd,
Some to the bag-pipe, some to the tabret mov'd."

BEN JONSON : *The Sad Shepherd ; or a Tale of Robin Hood "* (*vide* note [2], p. 56)

CHAPTER II.

THE WELSH CRWTH.

Ancient Hebrew Lyre—Modern African Lyre—Greek and Roman Lyres—The Rotta—The Crwth Trithant—The Chrotta, or Crwth-proper—Gruffydd ap Howel—Daines Barrington—Wynne Finch—Genealogies of the Violin and Crwth.

LET us now turn to another branch of the study of bow instruments entirely apart from what we have already discussed, viz., the consideration of the instrument known as the Welsh Crwth. If we go back to B.C. 1700, among the records of the ancient Egyptians, we find on a tomb at Beni Hassan (that of Osirtasen I., who was the probable Pharaoh who protected Joseph) a group (Fig. 26), supposed to represent the arrival of

Fig. 26.—Ancient Hebrew Lyre. B.C. 1700.

the Israelites in Egypt, one of whom is playing a primitive lyre, the shape of which is very interesting to the musical antiquarian, as being very like the late Welsh crwth. This is reproduced by Sir Gardner Wilkinson,[1] who considers it to have been a Hebrew lyre. Almost identical with the true ancient Egyptian lyre is the modern Kissar of the African negroes of the north-east (Fig. 27), which, in its primitive rudeness, is acknowledged to rival the Ravanastron in its antiquity. I shall not go into the consideration of the progress of this instrument among the ancient Egyptians and Assyrians, but begin at once with the Greeks and Romans, to whom belongs the lyre *par excellence.* Their lyres were of various sorts and sizes, dating from B.C. 700, and many of them had bridges (Fig. 28), distinct curved bridges, as efficacious, and to my mind quite

[1] Sir G. Wilkinson, "Manners and Customs of the Ancient Egyptians" (London, 1878).

possibly for the same purpose as our modern ones, and as a rule these lyres were played by means of a plectrum. The Roman lyres were practically identical with the Greek in form and

FIG. 27.— Kissar. (Ancient and Modern African.)

mode of playing ; one kind of cithara, the barbitos (Fig. 29), is especially interesting to us, as having almost exactly the shape of the instrument which is now the subject of our inquiry.[1] The

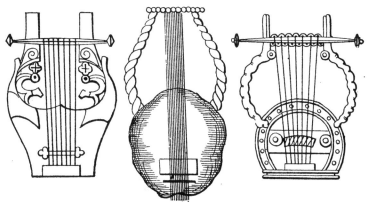

FIG. 28.—Ancient Greek Lyres, with Bridges

study of the lyre alone would fill a large volume, and I dare not enter upon it now for fear of being carried far from our

[1] This illustration (from Herculaneum) is taken from E. Pistolesi's work, 'Real Museo Borbonico descritto ed illustrato " (Rome, 1838-42), vol. iv., pl. 47.

subject; suffice it to say that the Romans had an instrument composed of a frame, one end of which was a hollow, rounded

FIG. 29.—Barbitos (from Herculaneum.)   FIG. 30.—Rotta of the Seventh Century.
                                               (MS, Psalter in British Museum.)

cavity, covered with a belly, on which was placed the bridge, and this instrument was played with the plectrum (*vide ante*, p. 34). The Romans subsequently colonizing France, Germany,

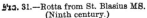

FIG. 31.—Rotta from St. Blasius MS.   FIG 32.—Crwth of the Ninth Century.
       (Ninth century.)   (Willemin.)

and Britain, introduced their instruments, which became modified according to the countries in which they were adopted; and in a MS. Psalter, in the British Museum, of the seventh

century,[1] we find the rotta, a primitive lyre-shaped instrument
(Fig. 30), strongly recalling the Hebrew specimen before alluded
to, and suggesting the later crwth, being merely a solid oblong
frame, one end being the sound board, and the other end being
open to admit the fingers (or plectrum) which twanged the
strings. In the ninth century we find this same rotta (in the
MS. of St. Blasius, reproduced by Gerbert, before referred to
(Fig. 31),[2] become more graceful in form, and having the sides
incurved as well as furnished with a well-formed bridge and
plectrum. Willemin[3] illustrates
a crwth from a Biblical MS. of
Charles the Bald of the ninth
century (Fig. 32), and the next
figure we have of it is in a MS.
from St. Martial de Limoges
(Fig. 33), in the Bibliothèque
Royale at Paris, of the eleventh
century, which gives us a figure
of a crwth, which, like Willemin's example, has only three
strings, and is played with the
rudest kind of bow. These last
two are probably the first instances we have of the crwth
trithant or three-stringed crwth.
This was not so much esteemed
as the proper six-stringed crwth,
of which it would appear to
have been only a primitive form.
Edward Jones, indeed, says, in
his work quoted below (p. 63),
" There was likewise the *Crwth
Trithant* or three-stringed crwth,
which was a sort of violin, or
more properly a rebeck; the

FIG. 33.—Crwth from MS. from St. Martial
de Limoges. (Eleventh century.)

performers or minstrels on this instrument were not held in
the same estimation and respect as the bards of the harp and
crwth; because the three-stringed crwth did not admit of
equal skill and harmony, and consequently its power was less
sensibly felt." The illustration, however, which he gives of the
crwth trithant, is precisely similar to the superior crwth,
excepting that it has but three strings.

[1] Cotton MSS., Vespasian A 1.
[2] M. Gerbert, " De Cantu et Musicâ Sacrâ." (St. Blasius, 1774.)
[3] N. X. Willemin. " Monuments Français inédits et pour servir à l'Histoire
des arts depuis le VIe Siècle jusqu'au commencement du VIIIe " (Paris, 1839).

Rühlmann[1] gives a most interesting specimen (Fig. 34) from a sculpture at Freiburg of the twelfth century, which is a most valuable link in the chain of evidence which connects the crwth with the rotta, for it is identically the latter instrument as illustrated from the St. Blasius MS. by Gerbert,[2] with the addition of a bow and a finger-board behind the strings. It has six strings, four on and two off the finger-board, as in the most perfect development of the instrument, differing only in that these two last,

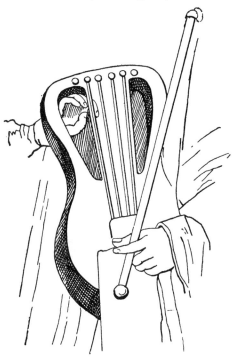

FIG. 34.—Crwth of the Twelfth Century. (Rühlmann.

instead of both being on one side of the finger-board, are placed one on each side thereof. Now the only difference between the earliest crwths (or chrottas) and the latest rotes (or rottas) seems to be (especially in the last instance referred to) the addition of the bow and finger-board, and so it would not be out of the way to assert that the instruments are identical, the former being the later and improved form of the latter, and certainly the similarity of

[1] J. Rühlmann, "Geschichte der Bogeninstrumente" (Brunswick, 1882).
[2] M. Gerbert, "De Cantu et Musicâ Sacrâ." 1774.

names is worthy of remark (though it must be borne in mind that, as I have said before, names have not unfrequently been transferred from one instrument to another ; similarity of names is of very little practical value to the antiquary). A crwth or crwd[1] of the thirteenth century from Worcester Cathedral (Fig. 35) given by Carter,[2] shows a very great improvement, being adorned with a tail-piece, sound-holes, and bow of very rational and practical construction, besides being held like a modern violin. And a somewhat similar but more cumbrous specimen from the Cathedral at Amiens (Fig. 36), dating from the same century, is given by M. de Coussemaker (*vide* note [1], p. 49). The principal authority on the crwth is Ed. Jones,[3] who gives the most accurate descriptions and illustrations of this

FIG. 35.—Crwth from Worcester Cathedral. (Thirteenth century.)

FIG. 36.—Thirteenth Century Crwth from Amiens Cathedral. (De Coussemaker.)

among his other national instruments. The supposition that it was the north-western portion of the continent which, by the application of the bow, first turned the rotta into the chrotta, receives confirmation from the words of one Venantius Fortu-

[1] There is no doubt that from the word crwth or crwd is derived the old English word " crowd " for fiddle, and " crowder " for fiddler.

" I'th head of all this warlike rabble
Crowdero marched expert and able."
BUTLER : *Hudibras.*

" Now the musicians
Hover with nimble sticks o'er squeaking crowds
Tickling the dried guts of a mewing cat."
MARSTON : *What You Will.*

[2] J. Carter, " Ancient Sculpture in England " (London, 1780).
[3] Ed. Jones, " Musical and Poetical Relics of the Welsh Bards " (London, 1825), p. 114.

natus, Bishop of Poitiers, in the seventh century, who says :—

> " Romanusque lyra, plaudat tibi Barbarus harpa
> Græcus Achilliaca, *Chrotta Britanna* canat."

The word crwth signifies in the ancient Saxon any bulging cavity, and the instrument is thus described in Welsh verse of the fifteenth century by one Gruffydd ap Davydd ap Howel : " A fair coffer with a bow, a girdle, a finger-board, and a bridge ; its value is a pound : it has a frontlet formed like a wheel with

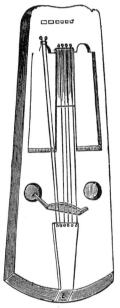

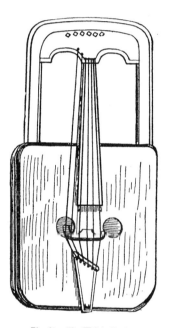

Fig. 37.—Figure of Crwth given by Daines Barrington, Fétis, Sandys and Forster, etc.

Fig. 38.—The Welsh Crwth. (South Kensington.)

the snort-nosed bow across. In its centre are the circled sound-holes, and the bulging of its back is somewhat like an old man, but on its breast harmony reigns, and from the sycamore melodious music is obtained. Six pegs, if we screw them, will tighten all its chords ; six advantageous strings are found, which in a skilful hand produce a hundred sounds ; a string for each finger is distinctly seen, and also two strings for the thumb. The inferior and primitive crwth trithant, to which I have already adverted, has been erroneously confounded by Ville-

marqué[1] and others with the ancient Moorish fiddle or rebek of
the Breton mendicant bards, which, as I have pointed out, has
an absolutely different form and origin. It has been urged in
favour of the theory that the crwth was the ancestor of the
violin, by MM. de Coussemaker and de Toulmont, that the
parallel sides of the crwth being inconvenient in bowing, they
gradually became hollowed out (as in Fig. 35), and thus the
crwth turned into the viol, but I think that, though this hollowing undoubtedly sometimes occurred, as in the Worcester
Cathedral instance, it was not carried out and adhered to, as is
proved by the ancient form having existed till the end of the
last century. M. de Coussemaker thinks that the word "rote,"
which was also undoubtedly the name of an instrument of the
viol kind, was a proof that the rotta or chrotta were part of the
progenitors of the violin, but this, I think, is quite accounted for
by the remark I made some way back, viz., that the name of one
instrument frequently got transferred to another, as the latter
superseded the former. The crwth properly so-called existed in
Wales to comparatively recent times, and we are told by Daines
Barrington, in 1770,[2] that it was then played only by one John
Morgan of Newburgh, in Anglesea ; but Bingley[3] mentions
having heard it played by an old bard in Carnarvon in 1801,
after which it seems to have disappeared, and with it ends this
branch of the study of the ancestry of the violin. The figure of
the crwth given by Daines Barrington (Fig. 37), and reproduced by M. Fétis, Messrs. Sandys and Forster, and others, is
misleading in its general appearance, and particularly as regards
the bridge, finger-board, and tail-piece ; the representation given,
however, by Mr. Engel,[4] of Mr. W. G. Wynne Finch's specimen
(the only genuine crwth in existence, and now in the South Kensington Museum[5]), is quite correct (Fig. 38), as I have found on

[1] H. de la Villemarqué, "Barzaz Breiz, chants populaires de la Bretagne"
(Paris, 1846).
[2] Daines Barrington was a judge of Carnarvon and Anglesea, who, on the
3rd May, 1770, read to the Society of Antiquaries some remarks on the crwth
and another Welsh instrument, which were published in "Archæologia, or
miscellaneous tracts relating to Antiquity; published by the Society of Antiquaries of London," vol. iii.. 1775, p. 32.
[3] W. Bingley, "North Wales, its Scenery, Customs, and Antiquities," etc.
(London 1804).
[4] C. Engel, "Catalogue of Musical Instruments in the South Kensington
Museum" (London, 1874).
[5] An *exact* counterpart of this instrument was made by M. Georges Chauot
when he had it for the purpose of repairing it. I have had this replica in my
hands, and it is certainly so marvellous a copy as to deceive any connoisseur.
The late Mr. Engel, to whom it belonged before his death, told me that he himself
could not possibly tell which was the original and which the copy when he saw
them side by side. Doubtless when this copy has changed hands a few times it
will be added to some national collection as a genuine antique Welsh crwth.

comparing it with the original. Messrs. Sandys and Forster, also figure it correctly, but without bridge, strings, or tail-piece. Mr. Wynne Finch's specimen is labelled 1742 in the inside, but as the condition of the wood betokens a much greater age, this was probably inserted by someone who repaired the instrument at that date. It is formed of one solid block of sycamore wood— except the belly, which is of pine and glued on. The bridge is very flat and curiously formed, one foot passing through the left sound-hole to the back, and thus serving as a sound-post; it is set obliquely on the belly. Its length is 22 inches, it is $9\frac{1}{2}$ wide, and 2 deep at its deepest part. It has a finger-board $10\frac{1}{4}$ long, and of its six strings four are set along the finger-board and vibrated with the bow, and two lie off it to be played pizzicato with the thumb.

Now this instrument is not a primitive essay which has become improved into the viol; it is a highly perfected instrument in its own unsatisfactory way, and I account for its being, as follows :—The Romans, colonizing the north-western part of Europe, introduced their lyres, where in course of time the use of the bow superseded that of the plectrum, the lyre becoming the rotta, and subsequently the crwth or chrotta. Meanwhile the Moors from Spain, and the Indo-European tribes gradually suffused the continent, bearing with them their more convenient bow instruments, and with them drove the crwth before them, till it had to take refuge among the aborigines or earlier inhabitants of the north-west, lingering on till it died a natural death in the wilds of Cambria (which, as we know, has remained more exclusively Celtic than any other part of the continent), until the last century. Indeed, the rude Norwegian "fidla" and the Icelandic "lang-spiel" are the only existing prototypes of the crwth. I consider, and I say it with all due deference in the face of all that has been written on the subject, but none the less positively, that the crwth had nothing to do with the Ancestry of the Violin; such a thing as the friction of a musical string was not a thing that could be discovered by any one nation alone. No; there were two distinct classes of musical instruments, of which, notwithstanding all that has been written and said to the contrary, I say the crwth was the younger, which, flourishing only so long as it had the monopoly of the bow in Europe, succumbed before the more successful and convenient rival, after trying in vain to hold its own among the Welsh, a primitive people whose conservatism in the matter of their nationalities is

---

¹ W. Sandys and S. A. Forster, "History of the Violin" London. (1864).

proverbial; and so to my mind it must for ever give up all thought of being considered part of the Ancestry of the Violin.

I have appended here the genealogies of the violin and of the crwth, according to the foregoing doctrines. These "pedigrees" will, I hope, elucidate any parts of these two chapters which have seemed obscure to the reader.[1]

---

[1] The above elucidation of the Ancestry of the Violin had never been suggested till the *Opusculum* mentioned in note [1], page 29, appeared in 1882. As the brochure was printed for private circulation only (as I intended prefixing it, as above, to this work) I did not place it in the hands of the public, and when, in the year 1883, after the death of Mr. Carl Engel (to whom I had presented a copy of my brochure), his work "Researches into the Early History of the Violin Family" (London, 1883) was published by Messrs. Novello and Ewer, Mr. A. J. Hipkins, the well-known musical historian (to whom was committed the task of preparing the MS. for publication) introduced the work with a short preface, in which he says : " I call attention especially to the interesting chain of reasoning which derives the mediæval rotte from the old Greek lyre." I wrote to Mr. Hipkins on the subject, and he, with a courtesy and generosity which I can never sufficiently esteem, made me the following prompt acknowledgment in *The Musical Review*, of April 21st, 1883. After calling attention to this obvious " Ancestry of the Violin," he says : " It shows how curiously ideas are 'in the air' when we find that Engel has not enjoyed this special one alone. A little pamphlet has been brought before our notice containing a lecture delivered last June to a society calling themselves " The Sette of Odd Volumes." This Opuscullum of twenty-eight pages has been privately circulated only, and is by Mr. E. Heron-Allen, who, by independent investigation has gone step by step with Carl Engel in the evolution of the bow from a longer plectrum." This is an instance of literary courtesy so marked that I feel a warm satisfaction in having this opportunity of publicly acknowledging my obligation, and of saluting the spirit in which this generous *amende* was made.

"Into the town will I, my frendes to vysit there,
  And hether straight again to see th' end of this yere,
  In the meantime, felowes, pype up your fiddles, I say, take them,
  And let your frendes here such mirth as ye can make them."

T. COLWELL : *Gammer Gurton* (London, 1575).

GENEALOGY OF THE VIOLIN,

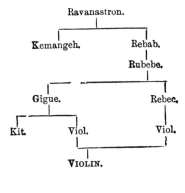

GENEALOGY OF THE CRWTH,

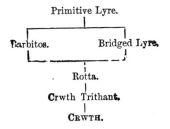

CHAPTER III.

THE differences in the models, styles, etc., of the greatest makers are so considerable, that my work would, to say the least of it be incomplete were I to enter upon the practical part of it without sketching, as briefly as possible, these "peculiarities of great men," for the guidance and instruction of the would-be fiddle-maker. To impart to the following notes any matter of a biographical description would be obviously outside the object of this work, so I shall confine myself absolutely and briefly to the mechanical characteristics of the " great few " whose names are household words alike to the amateur and the professional. I say the few, for though the name of the fiddle-makers is Legion, they mostly followed the principles of their chiefs, and it is only necessary to notice these great originals. For classification of names and biographical details I must refer our readers to Mr, Hart's work,[1] and for any one who requires a complete list of Violin-makers, I recommend the alphabetical list in the Appendix to Davidson's work, " The Violin,"[2] and the Tables of Diehl[3] and of Niederheitmann.[4] That the technical terms used in the fol-

---

[1] G. Hart, " The Violin, its famous Makers and their Imitators " (London, 1875 ; 2nd edition, 1884 : Dulau & Schott. *Popular edit.xn*, 8vo, 1880).
[2] P. Davidson, "The Violin, its Construction Theoretically and Practically Treated " (London, 4th Edition, 1881, p. 228).
[3] N. L. Diehl, "Die Geigenmacher der Alten Italienischen Schule," etc. (Hamburg, 1866).
[4] F. Niederheitmann, " Die Meister der Geigenbaukunst in Italien und Tyrol " [Vienna and Hamburg, n.d. [1876]).

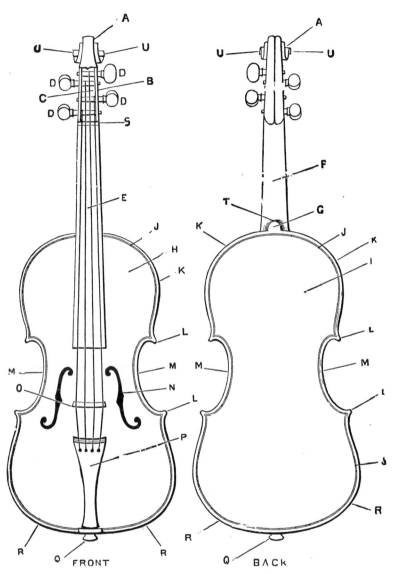

FIG. 39.—Diagram explaining technical terms used to denote the various parts of the violin. A, Scroll; B, cheeks of the scroll; C, peg box; D, pegs; E, finger-board; F, neck; G, button; H, belly; I, back; J, purfling; K, edges projecting over sides (or ribs), [upper bouts, centre (or middle) bouts, and lower bouts]; L, corners; M, centre (inner, or middle) bouts; N, *ff* holes; O, bridge; P, tail-piece; Q, tail-pin and rest; R, lower bouts; S, nut; T, shoulder; U, eyes of scroll.

lowing chapters may be fully understood, I have given in Fig. 39, on a tolerably large scale, diagrams of the front and back of the violin, showing its different parts, and the names that are applied to them. These diagrams will sufficiently explain their purpose without further description.

The Violin, as we have before seen, assumed its present form rather suddenly in the sixteenth century, and certain old " Luthiers " have been cited and their merits discussed in Chapter I. : these were Joan Kerlino (Brescia), 1449; Pietro Dardelli (Mantua), 1500; Gaspard Duiffoprugcar (Bologna, etc.), 1510 ; Ventura Linarolli (Venice), 1520; Peregrino Zanetto.(Brescia), 1540; Morglato Morella (Mantua), 1550—which last date brings us to the Brescian School, founded in 1555 or thereabouts. I shall notice the makers of this and the other schools in chronological order as nearly as possible.

Gaspard da Salo (Brescia), 1555—1610—so called from having been born at Salo in Lombardy—seems to have been originally a maker of viols, but set to making violins and tenors. It seems probable that the tenor was invented before the violin ; at any rate, Gaspard da Salo's tenors are much commoner than his violins.[1] His model is excellent in every respect, varying a

---

[1] As to the order in which the violin, viola, bass, and double-bass were invented, Mr. Reade, in a letter to the *Pall Mall Gazette*, August 19th, 1872 (*vide* note [2], p 19), has made the following notes : " Etymology decides with unerring voice that the violoncello was invented after the violono or double-bass, and connoisseurship proves by two distinct methods that it was invented after the violin. First, the critical method : it is called after the violon, yet is made on the plan of the violin, with arched back and long inner bout ; second, the historical method—a violoncello made by the *inventors* of the violin is incomparably rare, and this instrument is disproportionately rare even up to the year 1610. Violino being a derivative of viola, would seem to indicate that the violin followed the tenor; but this taken alone is dangerous, for viola is not only a specific term for the tenor, but a generic name that was in Italy a hundred years before a tenor with four strings was made. To go then to connoisseurship—I find that I have fallen in with as many tenors as violins by Gasparo da Salo, and not quite so many by Gio Paolo Maggini, who began a few years later. The violin being the king of all these instruments, I think there would not be as many tenors made as violins, when once the violin had been invented. Moreover, between the two dates came Corelli, a composer and violinist. He would naturally have created a crop of violins. Finding the tenors and violins of Gasparo da Salo about equal in number, I am driven to the conclusion that the tenor had an unfair start—in other words, was invented first. I add to this that true four-stringed tenors by Gasparo da Salo exist, though very rare, made with only two corners, which is a much more primitive form than any violin by the same maker appears in. For this and some other reasons, I have little doubt the viola preceded the violin by a very few years. What puzzles me most is to time the violon, or, as we childishly call it (after its known descendant), the *double* bass. If I was so presumptuous as to trust to my eye alone, I should say it was the first of them all. It is an instrument which does not seem to mix with these four-stringed upstarts, but to belong to a much older family— viz., the viole d'amore, da gamba, etc. In the first place, it has not four strings secondly, it has not an arched back. but a flat back with a peculiar shoulder.

little, but generally high; the centre bouts often short and primitive, and generally shallow; the *f f* holes (Fig. 40) running parallel, very long and pointed, but not out of proportion to the instrument; the scroll particularly marks the primitive state of the instrument.   He made many instruments of pear wood as well as of sycamore, especially basses.   His varnish is prin-

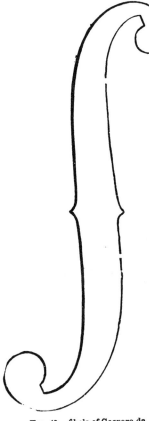

cipally a light brown amber, very rich and deep; the grain of his bellies generally very straight and even, but sometimes a trifle wide. The most perfect specimen I ever saw is a tenor in the possession of Mr. Edward Withers, a grand old primitive instrument, from which the *f* hole (Fig. 40) is traced. His tenors are unquestionably his best instruments; but the few known specimens of his violins, though uncomely, have great individual reputation from their very rarity. Mr. W. A. Tyssen Amherst, an English amateur of celebrity, has (or had) an exceedingly perfect specimen; but

copied from the viola da gamba; thirdly, the space between the upper aad lower corners is in the early specimens ludicrously short. And it is hard to believe that an eye which had observed the graceful proportions of the tenor and violin could be guilty of such a wretched little inner bout as you find in a double-bass of Brescia. *Per contra* it must be admitted that the *f f* holes of a Brescian double-bass seem copied from the four-stringed tribe, and not at all from the elder family; secondly, that the violin and tenor are instruments of melody and harmony, whilst the double-bass is one of harmony only. This is dead against its being invented until after the instru-

FIG. 40.—*f* hole of Gasparo da Salo. Tenor. (1555.)

ments to which it is subsidiary.   Man invents only to supply a want.   Thus, then, it is: first, the large tenor played between the knees; then the violin played under the chin; then (if not the first of them all) the small double-bass; then (years after the violin) the violoncello; then the full-sized double-bass; then, longo intervallo, the small tenor played under the chin." The author subsequently suggests very pertinently that the best way to solve these difficulties would be to find for what instruments the immediate predecessors of Corelli, and Corelli himself at the beginning, scored their music, details only to be obtained from the *original* MSS. or first editions.

perhaps da Salo's most celebrated fiddle was the highly ornamented one of the great Swedish artist Ole Bull, in the ornamentation of which he was aided (it is said) by the great Benvenuto Cellini himself, and which is referred to under that head (*vide* par. " Ornamentation," ch. ix., p. 167). It is said to have been almost as perfect as when it left the maker's hands ; and at the great virtuoso's death in the United States, was sold to some American amateur. His ticket is " Gasparo da Salò, In Brescia." His genuine tickets are never dated, which makes the period of his activity at least open to question and research, though one writer after another (*quorum pars fui!*) has accorded him chronologically the first place among the old fiddle-makers.

John Paul Maggini (Brescia), 1590—1640. Was probably a pupil of Gaspard da Salo ; his pattern is large, and broad in outline, the arching sloping away to the purfling and flattish, the sides rather shallow. The *ff* holes long and pointed, the scroll primitive, but not so much so as that of his master. He made the bellies of his instruments very strong, the back in proportion to the belly, rather thin, and generally ornamented by elegant curls of the purfling, which is generally inlaid in a double line (*vide* Fig. 91). Varnish, light yellowish, or deep brown, and very rich. The note of his instruments is grand and melancholy, the wood cut " on the layers." His instruments are often confused with those of Gaspard da Salo. The great violinist De Beriot used one of them (*vide* note [1], p. 25). Ticket, " Gio Paolo Maggini in Brescia ; " or, " Paolo maggini in Brescia."

Other makers of the Brescian school inferior to these were Mariani, Buddiani, and Bente, all from 1570—1620.

The Cremona school was founded by :—Andrew Amati (Cremona), born (about) 1520, died (about) 1580 ; the first of his illustrious family. Originally a maker of viols and rebecs, he only began in his later years to make violins. Possibly a pupil at Brescia before he started at Cremona. It is probable that he started the manufacture of violins contemporaneously with Gasparo da Salo, though the latter is generally named first. A rebec of his existed till very lately at Milan bearing date 1546. Most of his instruments are small or medium, model high towards the centre, bellies fairly strong. Backs often made of pear wood cut on the layers. Varnish, excellent light brown, or deep golden, work not unlike Gaspard da Salo, but that the *ff* holes (Fig. 41) are rather broad and inelegant. Ticket, " Andreas Amati Cremona, fecit 15—." Mr. Hart says, " Among the famous instruments of this maker were twenty-four violins (twelve large and twelve small pattern) six tenors and eight basses made in 1566 for Charles IX., which were kept in the Chapel Royal, Versailles, until 1790. These were probably the finest instruments of Andreas Amati, the workmanship being very perfect. On the backs were painted the arms of France and other devices, and the motto ' Pietate et Justitia ' " (*vide* p. 8). These instruments were taken out of the chapel and destroyed by the mob in the French revolution on the 6th and 7th October, 1790. Two of the violins were afterwards recovered by M. J. B. Cartier (*vide* Appendix D, No. 18). One

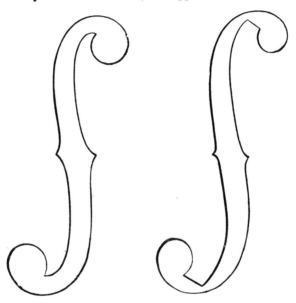

FIG. 41.—*f* hole of Andreas Amati. (1580.)   FIG. 42.—*f* hole of Antonius and Hieronymus Amati. (1570.)

of the small violins is now the property of George Somes, Esq., and through his courtesy I am enabled to give photographs of this unique fiddle as plates to this work. Its tone is mellow and beautiful in the extreme, but lacks brilliancy, and as a historical curiosity it is perhaps without its equal in the world of violins.

Anthony and Jerome Amati (Cremona), 1570—1635, sons of Andrew. They worked together for some time and then separated. Their wood was well chosen, and cut on the layers for the backs and sides, the bellies of fine even grain, their earlier instruments high built in the centre, but sloping gently to the edges, the *f* holes (Fig. 42) like Andrew's, but the wood scooped out a little round them. Their early varnish was deeper in tint than the later, and both were excellent ; their united label was " Antonius & Hieronym Fr. Amati Cremonen Andreæ fil. F. 1587." Their backs are cut variously in the whole or slab, or half form, their scrolls differ a good deal, and the purfling is perfect. In the instruments bearing this joint label the styles of the two brothers are quite distinct. Anthony made most of his instruments of Andrew's small pattern, flatter in the model though still high, and shallower in the sides than Andrew's. Their tone is sweet and pure, but not very intense ; his f holes are decidedly Brescian. Anthony died in 1635, or thereabouts, at about the age of eighty-five. Jerome, his brother, who died in 1630, is by some counted inferior to his brother ; he made some very large violins, suggestive of his son Nicholas Amati's *chef-d'œuvre*, the Grand Amati ; his model was original and graceful, the ff holes foreshadowing those of his son, who seems in some measure to have copied them. The edges of his instruments do not, as a rule, overlap the sides much, but are round and obtuse. His backs were generally whole, the purfling broad, and the varnish gold-yellow, or light brown. Tickets of this firm have been cited bearing date 1698, and thereabouts, by many learned authors, but as this would make the brothers average one hundred and forty-eight years of age, the statement has been made without due thought, being probably tickets used after their deaths by their pupils. (It will, therefore, be seen that the practice of labelling fiddles at random is by no means a new one ; in fact, for a long time Stradivari labelled his work " Nicholas Amati ! ")

Nicholas Amati (Cremona), born 1596, died 1684. Son of Jerome, and the best of this family of makers. At first he seems to have copied the small instruments of Anthony and Jerome ; working out the ideas of Jerome, his fiddles being more brilliant in tone than any other of the Amatis. His most celebrated fiddles are those known as Grand Amatis, which were large instruments with long corners ; he seems to have made but few of them, they are rather high in the centre, sloping rather sharply, so as to form a sinking-in round the edges. He improved Jerome's ff holes ; his later scrolls are better cut and bolder than his earlier ones, which were a trifle stiff. In all his design and detail he was perfect, his varnish superb, being deeper and richer than that of the other makers of the family ; his backs are beautifully figured, his bellies have a fine even grain, some of them being most beautifully mottled. Ticket, " Nicolaus Amatus Cremonen Hieronymi Fil. ac Antonij Nepos,

Fecit 16—." His son Jerome, the last of the Amati, was inferior to the rest of his family, and his works are very little known. The best known makers of the Amati school are Joseph Guarnerius, Francesco Ruggieri, Jean Baptiste Grancino, Francisco Grancino, Peter Guarnerius, and Sanctus Seraphino.

(Peter) Andrew Guarnerius (Cremona) 1630—1695 (little known as Pietro) the first of the Guarneri. Pupil with Stradivari of Nicholas Amati, whom he copied; his work was good but inferior to that of his great master. Later on he struck out somewhat of a new model, making his instruments flatter and altering the form of his scroll and ff holes. His varnish varied, but was generally a light orange. Ticket, " Andreas Guarnerius fecit Cremonæ sub titulo Sanctæ Teresiæ, 16—"

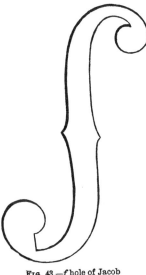

Jacob Stainer (or Steiner) (Absom), birth probably about 1620 and death uncertain. More properly a German maker, of whom he was the greatest. Was probably for some time a pupil of Nicholas Amati. His model was highly original; at his best his instruments were small in the pattern, the ff holes rather narrow and very round at the top and bottom (Fig. 43). His edges were very strong, the purfling set rather near them, the scroll shorter than Amati's but broader in front. The grain of his wood wide, and the varnish deep

FIG. 43.—f hole of Jacob Steiner. (1650.)

rose colour like Nicholas Amati's. His instruments are very high built, especially between the upper bouts, and often almost " tubby," the scroll often finished with a carved lion's or other animal's head; when of the ordinary shape, he made his scrolls broad and rather short. He has by some been preferred to the highest Cremonese masters (!). His most celebrated instruments were the " Elector Stainers," which were sixteen fiddles made by him, it is said, in a monastery at the end of his life, and sent by him, one to each of the Electors, and the remaining four to the Emperor of Germany. The wood is very handsome, and the varnish a lovely rose colour; they are decidedly Cremonese, or at least un-German in style. Of these, three are said still to exist, but according to Mr. Fleming these were not his work at all, he having died mad in his own house, —a story dismal indeed, and the merits of which it would be outside the province of this work to discuss, but the story of his madness, being well authenticated, must doubtless be accepted ; and as for these three fiddles, the difference they bear to his best known style is particularly in favour of the hypothesis that they were not his work at all. Ticket, "Jacobus Stainer in Absom, prope Œnipontum 16—" No maker has been more copiously, closely, or vilely copied ; his chief and best pupils and imitators being Matthias Albani (1654), the Klotz family (1670—1700), and in more modern times, Statelmann, Withalm, etc.

Francis Ruggieri (Cremona), 1668—1720, surnamed " Il per " from his ticket, which runs " Fran- cesco Rugger detto il Per Cremona 16—" A follower of the Amati school. His outline is original and graceful, his purfling broad, his arching perfect, his wood fine and left thick; his scroll is equal to the rest of the instrument ; the varnish, which is generally deep brown and very first-rate, is very well and evenly laid on. His *f* hole (Fig. 44) has been cited as a blending of that of Stradivari and Nicholas Amati.

Anthony Stradivari (Cremona), born 1644, died 1737, the greatest fiddle-maker that ever lived. He

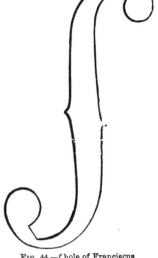

FIG. 44.—*f* hole of Franciscus Ruggieri. (1720.)

was a pupil of Nicholas Amati, with whom he worked till 1670 before which time he used not to sign his works. Between 1670 and 1690 he worked on Amati's "grand" model, but modified the extension of the corners ; these are known as " Amatese Stradi- variuses." The arching is not so high as Amati's, but his *ff* holes and scroll are something similar. The wood (often cut acros the grain), though acoustically good, is often not so handsome in his earlier instruments as it was later on. After 1690 his individuality began to assert itself, his model became more graceful and flatter, the *ff* holes elegant and reclining, the centre bouts gracefully drawn out, as also the corners ; the scroll is bold and striking, and the purfling rather narrow.

the varnish beautiful golden or light red. It was at the end of this period that he made the fiddles known as " Long Strads," so called from their narrowness between the *f* holes, giving them a lanky appearance, the actual size varying, the varnish amber or light red. The year 1700 brings us to his best period, the model flattish, the wood cut on the quarter, and thickest in the centre under the bridge, the curves gentle and harmonious, the wood of the blocks very light, often formed of willow, the scroll perfect in its symmetry. The graceful *f f* holes (Fig. 45), the transcendently glorious amber-coloured or rub varnish, are all character stics of this epoch of the greatest

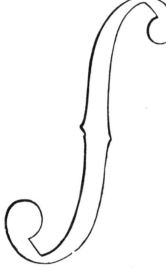

maker's greatest power. His best instruments have the purfling pointed across the corner instead of following it round, and it is not uncommon to find it running completely through the corner. His ticket runs, " Antonius Stra-diuarius Cremonensis faciebat Anno 17—" Between 1725 and 1730 the master began to show signs of approaching age (*Eheu! fugaces labuntur anni*), the arch-ing becoming more rounded. The fiddles made after 1730 show a decided falling off, many being made partly or wholly by his sons and pupils Omobono and Fran-cisco Stradivari and Charles Bergonzi, and signed "—sub disciplinâ Stradiuarii." In com-mon with all old Italian instru-ments, the sound bar is too weak

FIG. 45.—*f* hole of Antonius Stradiuarius. (1714.)

to support the modern high tension of the strings, and nearly all have to be rebarred. Stradivari made but few tenors, what he did make being grand and glorious instruments. He made many violoncello backs of poplar wood, some say because he had run out of maple, but the date of these instruments (all between 1698—1709) refutes such an argument. The elder Chanot possessed a violin by Stradivari which was guitar-shaped, in fact like the Chanot violin (*q.v.* p. 114), and it is said that from this instrument Savart and Chanot devolved their attempted improvements in shape.

Joseph Guarnerius (Cremona), 1690—1730, eldest son of Andrew, than whom he was a better workman. At first copied

Stradivarius and then his cousin Joseph del Jesù. The waists of his instruments are narrow, the lower and upper bouts wide in proportion, the curves so very graceful as to have served (as some suppose) as models to the great Joseph del Jesù himself. The *f f* holes a mixture of Andrew Guarnerius and the Amati and very like Gasparo da Salo's, whose idea he seems to have worked, and improved upon. They are rather lower in the belly and nearer the edge than is usual. Varnish very good, rather thickly laid on.

Peter Guarnerius, 1690—1725, known as " Peter of Cremona " in distinction to his nephew " Peter of Venice," second son of Andrew. Very broad model, arching rather too high, *f f* holes very round at the ends and vertical (like Stainer). Inner bouts rather weak, scroll very original, the eye prominent. Purfling very neat, the corners much drawn out, varnish perfect, golden or pale red and very transparent. The bellies are generally cut from an even wide-grained wood.

Laurence Guadagnini (Cremona), 1695—1735. This maker's model, which was flattish, was broad and very bold in its conception, his *f f* holes varied in form, being sometimes like those of Guarnerius del Jesù ; his scroll very good and original. His fiddles have a beautiful mellow tone. Ticket, " Lorenzo Guadagnini, Cremona, Alumnus Stradiuarius. Fecit Anno Domini 17—."

Jean Baptiste Guadagnini (Placentia), 1710—1750, probably was a brother of Lorenzo, and with him pupil of Stradivarius, whom he copied persistently, particularly in the form of his scroll. His backs are very handsome, and generally "joined," his bellies acoustically good, his varnish bright and highly transparent. Ticket, "Joannes Baptista Guadagnini, Placentinus, fecit Mediolani, 17—."

Dominic-Montagnana (Cremona and Venice), 1700—1740, pupil of Stradivari. A very excellent maker, indeed one of the best, but many of his fiddles are labelled " Joseph Guarnerius del Jesù " (whom he resembled in his *f f* holes), which has tended to eclipse his talent somewhat. His model is large, and all his curves are rather gentler than those of his master, the inner ones being particularly drawn out. The figure of his wood is usually large, and his scroll is larger and more powerful than that of Stradivari. His varnish is superb, and deservedly ranked among the best. Ticket, "Domenicus Montagnana, Sub Signum Cremonæ, Venetiis, 17—."

Santo Seraphino (Venice), 1710—1748, to my mind the neatest and most careful maker of the Italians. It is a pity he did not strike out and apply his care to a model of his own, instead of following a rather ugly German one, a cross between those of Stainer and Amati. (*Gratior et pulchro veniens in corpore virtus.*) His *ff* holes (Fig. 46) and scroll well cut, but of a poor model ; brilliant red varnish of a perfect quality, which, being sometimes too thick, gives his instruments an opaque appearance. His instruments are unmistakably like one another in style, though his model varied, the wood always showing the grain in clear even stripes. He branded his instruments with his initials S. S., in various places, particularly under the tail-piece. He used a very large, well-engraved, highly ornamented

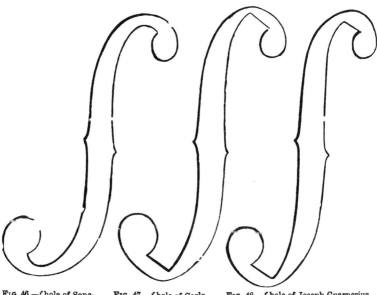

FIG. 46.—*f* hole of Sanc-tus Seraphino. (1740.)   FIG. 47.—*f* hole of Carlo Bergonzi. (1733.)   FIG. 48.—*f* hole of Joseph Guarnerius del Gesù. (1730.) *Sainton.*

label, worded, " Sanctus Seraphin, Utinensis, Fecit Venetijs, Anno. 17—."

Charles Bergonzi (Cremona), 1718—1755, the best pupil of Anthony Stradivari. At first copied his great master closely and well, and subsequently started a model of his own of fine size and good thickness of wood, flat and even, the wood hand-some, and the work excellent. The lower bouts being rather broad, the inner bouts set rather at an angle, the upper bouts larger than those of Stradivari, the scroll cut rather flat, but very bold, though not so well proportioned and finished as that of Stradivari; the eye of the scroll being rather prominent, the whole instrument possessing a considerable individuality. His ff holes (Fig. 47) are set lower in the belly than those of his master; in form they are between those of Stradivari and Guarnerius, and are set rather near the edge of the fiddle. His varnish varies from amber, through pale, to deep red, put on sometimes thickly, sometimes thinly. His fiddles are sometimes confused with those of Guarnerius, but are more Stradiuarian in character. His ticket runs, " Anno 17—. Carlo Bergonzi fece in Cremona." His son and pupil, Michael Angelo Bergonzi, 1750—1780, was inferior to his father as a workman.

Franciscus and Omobono Stradivari, 1720—1743, were pupils and sons of the great Stradivari, and worked together after the death of their father. As workmen inferior to their father, they worked up much of his refuse and unfinished material after his death. Francis was a better *luthier* than his brother, and his work, which shows his high tuition, is not without merit and originality, differing much from his father in outline of his f hole. The tone of his fiddles is very intense and good.

Joseph Anthony Guarnerius (Cremona), born 1683, worked 1725—1745. The best workman of the family of Guarneri ; surnamed " del Gesù," from the device ɪ H̵ s he was in the habit of placing on his labels. His work may be divided into four periods. In the *first*, his model varied, but he chiefly copied Joseph (son of Andrew) ; the scroll rather mean, the wood cut out at the shoulder, the ff holes long and marked. *Second period.*—Cut his backs chiefly " on the quarter ;" the pattern rather small, not too highly arched, gently sloping to the sides; the varnish very good ; the wood left rather thick, especially in his backs ; the pattern on the whole not unlike Stradivari in the rather drawn-out centre bouts and narrow waist. The ff holes were considerably curved, the scroll very bold and well cut, the purfling often running through both pegs, and the varnish of a rich golden brown. *Third period.*—The pattern rather large and very original ; the wood cut on the quarter ; the thicknesses perfectly proportioned, though sometimes a trifle excessive in the centre of the back. His varnish during this period was his best, and has been considered equal to Stradivari's. The fiddles of this period are broader in the waist, the inner bout long, but very elegant, the ff holes long and perpendicular (Fig. 48), the scroll perfect, and the varnish of a lovely orange shade. His f holes at this time may be described as the perfection of Gasparo da Salo's model In his *fourth peꞏiod*, Joseuh Guarnerius del Gesù seems to have cast away his high ideal and worked carelessly to satisfy present wants, so roughly and imperfectly finished are his later instruments. It is said that many (known as " Prison fiddles," " Drunken Josephs," etc.) were made in prison, with tools, wood, and varnish brought him by the gaoler's daughter. They are high built, the scroll stiff, the ff holes too long and clumsy, the wood and varnish alike inferior. In his better days it has been said that he made a great many of his bellies from one piece of wood, from a corresponding stain down each side of the finger-board in all of them. I have seen many " Josephs," but never such an one. He seems to have in a great measure varied his thicknesses according to the acoustic qualities of his wood. Paganini's celebrated violin (*vide* note [2], p. 23) was a Joseph Guarnerius (1743). The work of Joseph Guarnerius may be summed up in one old French couplet :—

" Quelques taches, quelques défauts
Ne déparent point une belle."

His ticket runs :—

" Joseph Guarnerius fecit,   +
Cremonæ, Anno 17—." I H S

Vincenzo Panormo (Palermo), born 1740, died 1813. Very perfect copyist of Stradivari, for whose fiddles his are often mistaken. His work is very neat and well-executed, the scroll and ff holes being particularly well cut.

Charles Ferdinand Landolfi (Milan), 1750. Model decidedly original, with a stiff inner bout not unlike Joseph del Gesù, his edges often deeply grooved, his ff holes not in keeping with the rest of his instrument ; his scroll rather mean, the varnish at times excellent He left a great many instruments unpurfled, and otherwise in an unfinished state. His wood was handsome, and his varnish very transparent ; he was the last maker who used the glorious old Cremona varnish. His ticket runs, " Carlo Ferdinando Landolphi nella contradadi santa Margarita al segno della Sirena. Milano 17—."

Lawrence Storioni (Cremona), 1780—1798. The last of the old Italian makers, a clever but inelegant workman, was as original and variable as Joseph del Gesù, whom he copied, the outline being often unsymmetrical, and the position of his ff holes constantly changing. The varnish a dark red Neapolitan, the purfling narrow and roughly inlaid, the scroll stiff and incomplete, the wood acoustically good, but not handsome.

This brings us to the end of our space for Italian makers; it remains, therefore, to glance at the best-known makers of

other countries, who, however, were, and are at best, but
mere copyists ; not indeed that I am, as too many connoisseurs
are, a bigoted *laudator temporis acti.* Far from it. It has been
said impartially (and also, I am sorry to say, for purposes of
advertisement), that fiddles are now being made in this country
and on the Continent, which in years to come will equal, if they
do not excel, the masterpieces of the old Italian fiddle-makers.
Though I do not go so far as the latter statement, I certainly
agree with the former, and consider that during the first half
of this century were made (and, were it not for the *auri sacra
fames* of the present day, still would be made) instruments
(mostly made by the following makers), which are, and will be,
well worthy to replace the works of the Italian masters when
they, in their turn, succumb like everything else to inevitable
age (*vide* p. 20).

Nicholas Lupot (Paris), 1784—1824. Is cited as the best of
the French makers. He copied Stradivari almost exclusively,
though his copies of the other great masters are also excellent.
Used a very good varnish, which varied from light to dark red.
He supplied M. l'Abbé Sibire with the information for " La
Chelonomie, ou le parfait Luthier " (Paris, 1806), in which his
praises are sung to an absurd degree, the author ending with
the following verse :—

> " Du plus grand des Luthiers imitateur fidèle,
> Lupot a recréé le vernis précieux ;
> C'est de son coloris le ton harmonieux,
> Et la copie est le modèle."

Jean Baptiste Vuillaume (Paris), born 1799, died 1875, is said
to have been one of the most perfect copyists and imitators that
ever lived. His original model founded on that of Stradivari
shows extraordinary merit.

Barak Norman (London), 1688—1740. Originally a viol-
maker ; copied Maggini very much, especially in his double
purfling. High build, *f f* holes decidedly German in style,
varnish very dark.

Benjamin Banks (Salisbury), born 1727, died 1795. Copied
Amati, and used a very excellent varnish. Left his wood
rather thick, so that his instruments have immensely improved
with age. His only weak point was his scroll, which seems
wanting in character. Many of his instruments are branded
with his initials, B. B., in several places. Ticket, " Benjamin
Banks, fecit Salisbury."

Thomas Dodd (London). Best known by his very perfect
varnish, the secret of whose composition he kept to himself.

He did not make fiddles himself, but employed Fendt and
Lott, whose instruments he received "in the white," and
varnished with his own hand. The instruments of Fendt and
Lott are among the best of English manufacture, Lott being
chiefly famed for his double-basses.

William Forster (London), born 1739, died 1808, one of the
best English makers, copied the Amati school. His varnish
was exceptionally fine.

Richard Duke (London), 1768. Copied Amati, his work
and varnish, which was yellowish, being excellent, the pattern
long. Has been most copiously and ruthlessly copied and
imitated. His tenors were small and very broad; some of his
instruments are poor, having merely been stained deep brown,
and then a coat of varnish laid on.

Peter Walmsley (London), about 1720—1760. One of the
best English makers, followed the Stainer model. He was in
the habit of artificially aging his instruments, consequently his
wood is often too thin to last well. His varnish was reddish, or
yellowish, brown; he often drew lines round his instruments,
instead of inlaying purfle.

John Lott (London), 1830—1870. One of our most talented
makers, and perhaps our best native copyist. Marvellous tales
are told of his cunning in the matter of repairs, which has been
compared with that of J. B. Vuillaume himself.

William Ebsworth Hill (London), 1830. Now living. The
last surviving representative of the old English school. Works
out an original model from the masterpieces of Stradivari and
Guarneri.

Georges Chanot (London), now living. Son of the celebrated Georges Chanot of Paris. Magnificent workman, and
marvellous copyist. Copies Stradivari, Guarneri, and Maggini.
Varnish light brown, and of magnificent consistency. Considered by many to be the finest fiddlemaker living, since his
father's death.

Edward Withers (London), 1860. Now living. Only pupil
of John Lott, whose style and varnish he has copied and
improved upon at times. Copies Stradivarius and Joseph del
Gesù. Varnish of a red gold colour.

Jacobs (Amsterdam), 1690—1740. So close and perfect a
copyist of Nicholas Amati that the two are often confounded.
Followed the "grand" pattern. His distinguishing marks are
his rather inferior scroll and whalebone purfling. Varnish, very
fine.

A word before we leave the consideration of the modern fiddle
trade, on the manufactories at Mirecourt; these turn out many

thousands of crude "noise boxes" annually, labelled, as a rule, Antonius Stradivarius, Joseph Guarnerius, or Jacob Steiner fecit. These are extraordinary for their quantity and cheapness. M. Gallay, in his report on the Vienna Exhibition, noticing the establishments of Thibouville-Lamy (who have a London house in Charterhouse Street) quotes as follows the actual cost of the manufacture of one of these fiddles. Wood for back 2d., wood for belly 2d., manufacture of same 1$\frac{1}{2}d$., wood for neck $\frac{1}{2}d$., making same 1$\frac{1}{2}d$., finger-board (stained) 2d., cutting 1$\frac{1}{2}d$., moulding back and belly 12$\frac{1}{2}d$., varnish 10d., fitting up, strings, tail-piece, bridge, etc., 7$\frac{1}{2}d$.—Total 4s. 2d. M. Gallay goes on to say that he heard such a fiddle as this, chosen from a number of similar ones and carefully mounted and strung and played, the tone and results obtained from which at a concert in Vienna were most satisfactory.

And here I must cease these memoranda, which for shortness I have confined exclusively to the fiddle proper (to the exclusion of the 'cello and double bass), apologising for their extreme brevity by the fact that we must hurry on to the practical part of our work. They are collected from the most reliable sources, and especially I desire here to record my best thanks to the collectors and dealers who have kindly placed both their trade-stocks and private collections of fiddles at my disposal for the purposes of these notes. To all such as are interested by them, and would care for more historical and biographical detail, I recommend Mr. Hart's book before referred to, as dealing most fully with all matters connected with the old and new "fiddle-makers."

"There sat dame Musyke, with al her mynstralsy ;
As taboures, trumpettes, wyth pypys melodyous,
rackbuttes, orgounes, and the recorder swetely,
Harpes, lutes, and croudes right delycyous."

S. HAWYS : *The Passe Tyme of Pleasure*
(London, 1509).

CHAPTER IV.

THE BOW.

Progressive History of the Bow.—The Corelli Bow.—The Crémaillère.—Tourte.—The Modern Bow.—Dimensions.—Hairing and Rehairing.—Rosin and its Action.—Folding Bow.—Vuillaume's Bow.—Withers.—Other Patents.—The Great Bow-makers.

It has been justly remarked that the History of the Violin is in point of fact the history of the bow, and this is indeed the case, for without the bow the fiddle (properly so called) cannot exist. Without it the fiddle would cease to express every human emotion, would cease to produce the continuous flow of melody that instruments of this class alone of all stringed instruments are capable of producing, and would, in fact, without this magic wand, at whose touch its marvellous powers are called into being, "become as the sounding guitar and tinkling banjo," and cease to merit the charming comparison drawn in Macheath's song in Gay's *Beggar's Opera* (*vide* note [4], p. 10). At the same time, if it is difficult to trace the progressive history of the Violin, it is infinitely more so to trace that of the Bow, and for very obvious reasons, for if in paintings and sculptures of the present day artists do not pay much attention to the execution of so (apparently) subordinate a part of the subject (as is evidenced by pictures and sculptures of our own day, in which though often the representation of the fiddle is accurate, yet " the fiddle-stick" is a very different concern from the bow of everyday use), how much less, therefore, are the representations of past centuries to be depended upon.

As to who invented the bow this is not the place to discuss ; the invention of the bow being, in fact, the origin of the violin, and as such already discussed in Chapter I. Of course we cannot take as absolute gospel the testimony of P. B. Zaccharia Tevo, who in his *Musico Testore*, published at Milan in 1706, asserts, " *Safo poetessa invento l'arco de crini di cavallo, e fù la prima che lo suonase come si costuma oggidi.*" It is most probable, however, that the Orientals were the first to use the bow, as seen in its primitive form (Figs. 49 and 50), which has continued among them even to the present day; as they were, in the opinion of M. Fétis set forth further on, the first to improve it by the addition of the nut.   As to when and where the actual word "bow," or its foreign equivalent "archet," was first used, opinions have differed, though it seems to me absolutely obvious that it is identical with the Latin arcus=bow, but some ingenious etymologists have tried to derive it from the Greek ἀρχή=dominion, from the dominion which it exercises over the violin, which seems to me to be, at any rate, very far-fetched.   As to its actual invention as the accessory, and in fact motive power of the violin, the value of pictorial representations may be proved by a glance at Figs. 51—60, which represent bows only taken from the most reliable sources, from pictures, sculptures, etc., of every century, from the eighth to the seventeenth.   The first thing that will strike you will be the great similarity which exists between all of them, from the first to the last, and also the close parallel which may be drawn between any one of them and the primitive modern bows represented in Figs. 49 and 50, which show two bows now in use among the Moors and the primitive Indians, which are indeed of the most simple and obvious form in which the bow could exist.   The conclusion we are brought to is consequently this : *either* all representations of bows which have come down to us are unreliable, *or*, the bow, instead of developing as the fiddle undoubtedly did, remained in a state of primitive simplicity, and bore till a comparatively recent date the same relation to its companion the fiddle, as do the early specimens of Delft ware and the exquisite Sèvres specimens, which recline side by side in the cabinets of the delightfully incongruous nineteenth century drawing-room.   If you ask me to which of these conclusions I incline, I think the two deductions are to one another as three times two are to twice three, and that a combination of the two would probably account for the present misty aspect of the past history of the bow.   Let us, however, dissect these figures and discuss in detail the extent (if any) to which they are reliable.

Fig. 51 is from Rühlmann's *Geschichte der Bogeninstrumente*,[1]

FIG. 49.—Bow of Indian Ravanastron.

FIG. 50.—Bow of Moorish Rebab.

[1] J. Rühlmann, " Geschichte der Bogeninstrumente, etc., mit einem Atlas von xiii. Tafeln " (Brunswick, 1882).

who quotes it from Herbé's *Costumes Français;* Fig. 52 is from the Abbot Gerbert's *De Cantu et Musicâ Sacrâ* (St. Blasius, 1774), and is taken from the MS. of St. Blasius, of the ninth century. It will be observed that this shows a very respectable form, as does

FIG. 51.—Bow of the Eighth Century, from Herbé's "Costumes Français."

also Fig. 53, which is reproduced from Strutt.[1] In Fig. 54, A, B, and D are crwth bows, the two former from a MS. at Neuberg, and the latter from the MS. from St. Martial de Limoges, and forms part of Fig. 33. c, Fig. 54, is from an enamelled plate, dug up at Soissons, on which we find two females playing bow instruments—one of them having a bow almost identical with the ravanastron bow, represented in Fig. 49, and the other having the bow here represented. A, Fig. 55, is from the crwth player, repre-

FIG. 52.—Bow of Ninth Century, from MS. of St. Blasius, from Gerbert, "De Cantu et Musicâ Sacrâ," 1774.

sented in Fig. 35; B, Fig. 55, from a window in the Cathedral of St. Denis, and c, Fig. 55, from Strutt in his work before referred to, are, again, a very considerable advance in point of

FIG. 53.—Bow of the Tenth Century, from Cotton MS. Tib. cvi., J. Strutt, "Sports and Pastimes of the People of England." (1855.)

shape. There is a figure of Neptune on a capital in a MS. at Douai of this century, holding a bow, which is absolutely and identically the same as that represented at c, Fig. 54; D, Fig. 55, is also from a sculpture at St. Denis, and its similarity to A in the same figure will be at once remarked.

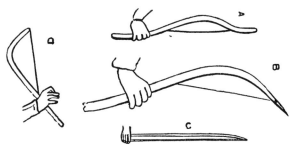

FIG. 54.—Bows of the Eleventh Century. A and B, from a Prayer-book in the Library of the Convent of Neuberg, near Vienna (Crwth bow). C, from enamelled plate dug up near Soissons (probably Thirteenth Century). D, from MS. in Library of St. Martial, Limoges (Crwth bow).

In the bows of the thirteenth century (Fig. 56) we find

[1] J. Strutt, "Glig-Gamena Angel-lcod ; or, Sports and Pastimes of England' (London, 1801).

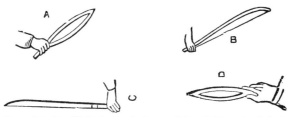

FIG. 55.—Bows of the Twelfth Century. A, from sculpture in Worcester Cathedral (Crwth bow). B, from Window at St. Denis. C, from MS. Bodleian Library. D, from sculpture at Portal of St. Denis.

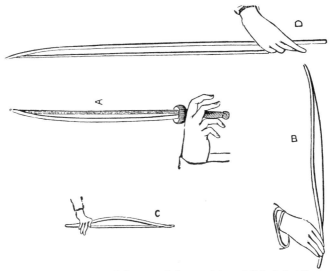

FIG. 56.—Bows of the Thirteenth Century. A, from sculpture at Cathedral of Rouen. B, from an Italian miniature (late) in the possession of J. B. Vuillaume. C, from A. Vidal, " Les Instruments à Archet," Paris, 1876. D, from picture by Cimabue in Pitti Palace, Florence.

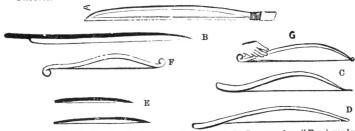

FIG. 57.—Bows of the Fourteenth Century. A, from MS. De Coussemaker, " Essai sur les Instruments de Musique." B, from painting by Barnabas de Modena, 1374. C, from " Liber Regalis of Richard II." (Strutt's " Manners and Customs," London, 1775). D, from Potier, " Monuments Français." E. from sculpture on Ely Cathedral. F. from MS. (De Diversis Monochodis, etc.,) in Library at Ghent. G, from sculpture at Cologne Cathedral.

another stride towards perfection, A, Fig. 56, from a sculpture in the Cathedral of Rouen, and D, Fig. 56, from a picture by Cimabue, in the gallery of the Pitti Palace at Florence, being almost perfect. B, Fig. 56, is again rather elementary by comparison, and C, Fig. 56, from a figure of a jongleur, given by M. Vidal, reminds us very much of Fig. 53, Strutt's Anglo-Saxon bow. In Fig. 57 we get more improvements and more retrogressions. A is from a MS. reproduced by M. de Coussemaker, D from a sculpture in Potier's "Monuments Français," B from a picture by *Barnabas de Modena*, E are from Ely Cathedral; and in them there is too much want of detail for them to be historically valuable to any great extent. We are indebted to Strutt again, in his "Liber Regalis," for C, Fig. 57, and to a Ghent MS. for F; these two are somewhat similar, and are again rather a reversion to simplicity than an improvement. In the fifteenth century the improvements in bow instruments drew with them like improvements in the bow, and though in Fig. 58 A, C, and D, which are from pictures, are elementary,

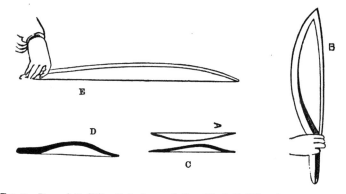

FIG. 58.—Bows of the Fifteenth Century. A, from Minstrel's Pillar, St. Mary's Church, Beverly. B, from Wood-carving in Choir, Church of St. Godehard, Hildesheim (Trumpet Marine). C and D, from painting by Hemling. E, from Raphael's "Crowning of the Virgin," in the Vatican.

yet E and B are most interesting, as showing respectively the violin and double-bass bow of the epoch. B, Fig. 58, the bow of a trumpet marine, is from a MS. in the Monastery of St. Godehard, of Hildesheim; and E we may consider trustworthy, being from a picture by Raphael, in the Vatican. In the sixteenth century, which saw the actual introduction of the violin, and when books began to be written on the instruments then in use, our evidence on the forms of the bow becomes

practically certain, though artistic representations of bows of
the most elementary description continued to be produced, just
as they are now. In Fig. 59, c and b (the latter especially)
may be considered trustworthy, being from illustrated works
on instrumental music. e, f, and g, the first and last particularly, may be taken as artistically fanciful. f is from
a musical work, but the designator has evidently paid little

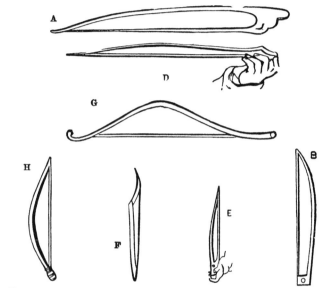

Fig. 59.—Bows of the Sixteenth Century. A, from St. Cecilia, by Raphael, at
Bologna. B and C, from M. Agricola, "Musica Instrumentalis" (Wittenberg),
1545. D, from "Marriage at Cana of Galilee," Paul Veronese (at Versailles). E,
from engraving by Altdorfer in German Museum, Nürnberg. F, from Gafurius,
"De Harmoniâ Musicorum Instrumentorum," 1518. G, from Potier. H, from
painting by Gerard Dow, Dresden Gallery.

attention to so minor a consideration as "the fiddlestick."
d is from Paul Veronese's well-known picture, the
"Marriage at Cana of Galilee," and as Paul was himself
a viol player, any representation of a musical instrument
by him we may accept as historic. The same remark
applies to h, which is from a picture by Gerard Dow in
the Dresden Gallery; for Gerard Dow's mother, we know,
played the viol da gamba, from her famous portrait by her son.
A, Fig. 59, we may also take as trustworthy, being from Raphael's
famous picture of "St. Cecilia" at Bologna.

After this, the bow as we now have it, was practically introduced, and our further representations thereof will be merely

progressive, and not including the results of artists' imaginings. With the figures we have before us, it remains, therefore, only to separate fancy from fact as near as we can ; and this division I think you may safely say will be as follows : Figs. 51, 52, and 53 we must take as they stand, but Fig. 52, it must be remembered, is the work of a priest, reproduced from the work of another priest, and we may, therefore, consider this figure as about right. In Fig. 54, c is about the best form, and most credible, a being a more elementary form, probably actually in use among the lower class of fiddlers ; c is from a well designed work of art, and is, therefore, most likely to be copied from existing specimens, but there exists some doubt whether it should not properly be dated thirteenth century. In the same way Fig. 53 gives probably a correct idea of the bow used by the peasants and lower classes. It is probable that up to comparatively recently the bows used with the rebecs, or lower bow instruments, continued to be hardly more than arcs, as depicted by Figs. 49 and 50, notwithstanding the great improvements in the bow with which the higher classes of viols were played.

In Fig. 55, a and d are probably artistic representations of a bow, nearly related to our double-bass bow; one side being probably represented flat; indeed, some authors have figured d, Fig. 55, almost identically our contrabass bow, but I cannot say for certain, as I have never noticed the original at St. Deni≈. b and c may be taken as approximately correct delineations of the viol bow, a and d being probably for the greater viols and trumpet marine In Fig. 56, c and b are artistically elementary, but a and d especially may be considered faithful representations. In Fig. 57, a, b, d, and e represent the actual, and c, f, g the fanciful element. d and g are, however, probably *near* the actual *gross-geig* bow. In Fig. 58, a, d and c representing fiction, b and e may be said to represent fact, in the form of the double-bass and viol bows of the period. In Fig. 59 we reach certain evidence, f and g being the last relics (as far as we are concerned) of that artistic imagination which always has, and always will stand in the way of the antiquary who searches after truth. And so by progressive stages we are brought to Figs. 60, 61, and 62, the last points in the history of the bow. These are all absolutely faithful diagrams of the existing bows taken from contemporary and reliable authors.

It is now that we see the nut minutely delineated for the first time, though it must not be supposed that it was a recent introduction. It is difficult to say where the nut was first introduced. M. Fétis is of opinion that it owes its origin to the east, and cites as evidence in his *Antoine Stradivari* (*vide* note [2], p. 37),

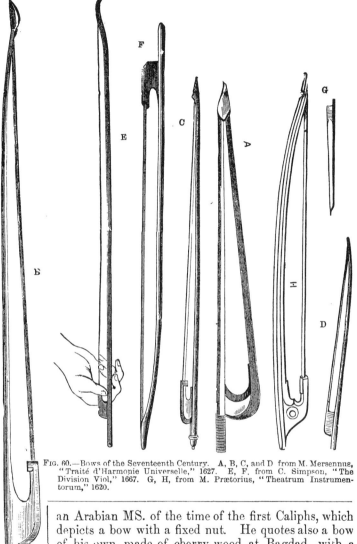

FIG. 60.—Bows of the Seventeenth Century. A, B, C, and D from M. Mersennus, "Traité d'Harmonie Universelle," 1627. E, F. from C. Simpson, "The Division Viol," 1667. G, H, from M. Prætorius, "Theatrum Instrumentorum," 1620.

an Arabian MS. of the time of the first Caliphs, which depicts a bow with a fixed nut. He quotes also a bow of his own, made of cherry-wood at Bagdad, with a properly constructed head and nut to receive the hair, the nut fitting into a notch in the stick.

The nut we see in Fig. 60 is in all cases fixed ; B represents perhaps the most ornate bow of the century, and E and F are most interesting as coming from an instruction book for the viol da gamba.[1] B, which shows the holding of the bow, is of the actual size of the picture from which it is reduced. G brings us apparently very near the modern bow, but is too small to be very useful as a representation. H introduces us again to the contrabass bow, and shows us we were right to accept as reliable Raphael's representation, A, Fig. 59.

It was in this century also that, it being found necessary to moderate the tightness of the hair, the *crémaillère* was added to the existing form of the bow. This is shown by Fig. 61, and

FIG. 61.—Bow of the Eighteenth Century, with Crémaillère to tighten the hair.

was a strip of notched metal as at A, fixed to the back of the stick. To the movable nut was added a band of metal which could be hitched over any of these notches, and the tension of the bow thereby regulated at will.

We now arrive at the eighteenth century, in which to the violins of Stradivari were added the bows of Tourte. It is to this latter, who lived at the commencement of the eighteenth century, when, for the first time, Corelli and Vivaldi were showing of what the violin was capable, that the invention of the nut worked by a propelling and withdrawing screw is generally attributed ; his bows were a great improvement on pre-existing forms, being better proportioned, and made of lighter wood, not to mention the elegant manner in which he was in the habit of fluting his bows, throughout half, or the whole, of their length. The head was generally long, pointed, and turned back, which gave the bow a very graceful appearance, as in Fig. 62.

FIG. 62.—Bow by Tourte aîné (with screw and movable nut).

The nut and head of the screw were generally of ivory. Mr. Arthur Hill has perhaps the best collection of old bows in England, for the bows of the old viols are much more scarce, unfortunately, than the viols themselves.

Tourte's eldest son was much inferior to his father as a workman ; it is his younger son, Francis Tourte, whose name connected with a bow is like the name of Stradivari connected with a violin. M. Fétis in his chapter on bows, at the end of his *Antoine Stradivari*, has given a most interesting and valuable

---

[1] Christopher Simpson, " The Division Viol " (London, 1667).

account of this king of bow-makers, which, as translated by Mr. John Bishop (of Cheltenham), is shortly as follows:—

"Francis Tourte, long known by the name of Tourte, junior, was born in Paris in 1747, in St. Margaret's Street, and died in April, 1835, aged eighty-eight years. Intended by his father for the business of a clockmaker, he entered, when very young, into a workshop, neglected every other study, and never knew how to read or write. Perhaps he was indebted to the trade which he at first followed for the skill and delicacy of hand which he afterwards displayed in the manufacture of bows. Disgusted with his condition after having passed eight years in the clockmaking workshops, because he did not there meet with sufficient remuneration for his needs, he took to the business of his father and brother. At this period the distinguished artists resident in Paris were making progress towards the art of singing on their instruments with the shades of expression of which the great Italian vocalists had given the example; and they all desired bows which should answer better to the effects which they wished to produce, and which should possess at the same time greater lightness, spring, and elasticity. Francis Tourte made his first essays with wood from the staves of sugar casks, with a view to determining the forms of the bow and to acquire skill in working without making use of expensive materials. He sold these early products of his manufacture for twenty or thirty sous each (ten or fifteen pence). Being an indefatigable investigator and fully sensible of the important action of the bow in the production of tone, he subsequently tried all kinds of wood which appeared to him proper to realize his views; but he was not long in discovering that Fernambuc wood alone would yield the results which he sought to attain, and that it alone combined stiffness with lightness. The period of the first and important discoveries of Tourte extends from 1775 to 1780. Unfortunately, the maritime wars of France and England then presented a serious obstacle to the importation of Fernambuc wood on the Continent, and the price of this valuable article used for dyeing rose to five shillings the pound. Fernambuc wood intended for dyeing purposes is exported in billets : that which is richest in colouring matter is likewise the best for the manufacture of bows ; but it is rare to find billets which are straight and only slightly defective, for the wood is nearly always knotty, cracked inside, and crooked in every direction. Sometimes eight or ten tons of Fernambuc wood scarcely present any pieces with a straight grain, and suitable for making good bow sticks. The rarity of this wood at the period here mentioned explains the enormous price which Tourte asked for his bows ; he sold a bow, the nut of which was made of tortoise-shell, the head inlaid with mother-of-pearl, and the mounting of the nut and button of gold, for nearly £12. His best bows mounted in silver with an ebony nut were sold at about £3 3s., and the ordinary unornamented bows fetched about thirty shillings."

Tourte finally fixed the length of the violin bow between 29·134 and 29·528 inches, and fixed also the requisite height from the stick of the head and nut, counteracting the weight of the head by the ornamentations in silver, gold, etc., with which the nut of a bow is loaded. Tourte bent his bows by means of heat to the required shape, and it is thus that all bows are shaped, not cut out of a plank the shape which we see them, as many violin players suppose, for the latter would cut the fibres of the wood across instead of preserving them intact throughout the length of the stick, as is essential to a good bow. It is most necessary that the stick should be heated right through the inner fibres before being bent, otherwise these inner fibres, being unheated, would in time cause the outer and heated fibres to resume their normal position. It is inattention to this point that causes the rapid deterioration and straightening out of apparently cheap bows.

Tourte paid as much attention to the hairing of his bows as to their sticks. On this point Fêtis says, " He preferred the hair of France because it is larger and stronger than that of other countries." The preparation to which he subjected it consisted in scouring it with soap ; he then put it into bran water, and lastly, after removing the heterogeneous particles which had adhered to it, he plunged it into pure water, lightly coloured with blue. His daughter was almost constantly employed in sorting the hairs, rejecting such of them as were not perfectly cylindrical and equal throughout their length. This is a most delicate and necessary operation, for not more than one-tenth of a given number of hairs are fit for use, the greater portion having one side flat, and presenting numerous inequalities. At the period when Viotti arrived in Paris, the hairs of the bow nearly always clustered together in a round mass, which impaired the quality of the tone. After making his observations on this point, Tourte conceived the possibility of compelling the hairs to preserve the appearance of a ribbon by pinching them at the nut with a ferrule (c, Fig. 63), which he made first of tin, and afterwards of silver. He subsequently invented " the slide," i.e., the little plate of mother-of-pearl which covers the hair on the face of the nut. He did not use quite as many hairs as are now generally put into a bow, the number now being, as a

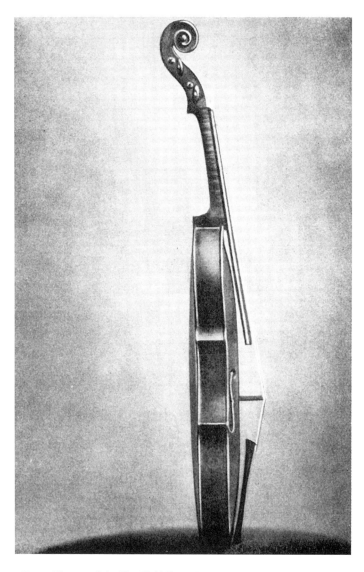

From a Photograph by Wm. Field (Putney).

VIOLIN BY ANDREAS AMATI
One of 24 made by Andreas Amati for Charles IX, King of France,
(vide p. 73).

rule, between 150 and 200. At the end of Fétis' *Antoine Stradivari* is given a most carefully and scientifically worked-out determination of the true working proportions of the Tourte bow, and how they may be obtained.

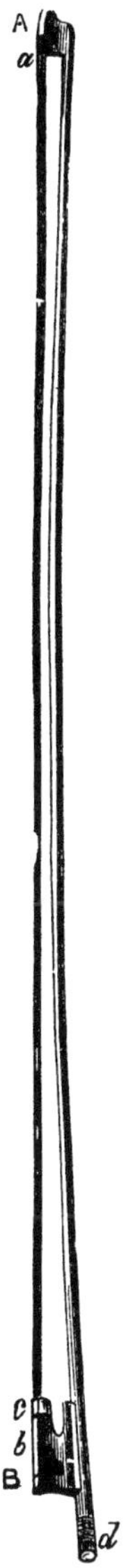

FIG. 63.—Modern Bow, after Tourte.

Fig. 63 represents the modern form of bow, as finally determined by Tourte, jun., in its entirety, Figs. 64 and 65 represent the head and nut, actual size, and Fig. 66 one of the wedge-boxes enlarged. Fig. 64 represents the nut and screw as set on the stick of the bow. In the nut is a small box (represented by Fig. 66), into which the knot M of the hair (Fig. 67) is fixed by means of the wedge N. The hair L being brought out and along the front of the nut E (Fig. 64), the ornamental plate H I J is slid over it along a mortised groove. The band K is then pressed into its place and fixed by the pressure of the thin wedge O, which being pressed in between the tongue of the nut E and the hair L, keeps the latter flat, firm, and fast. The entire nut E slides along the stick A by the action of the screw B C; the surface

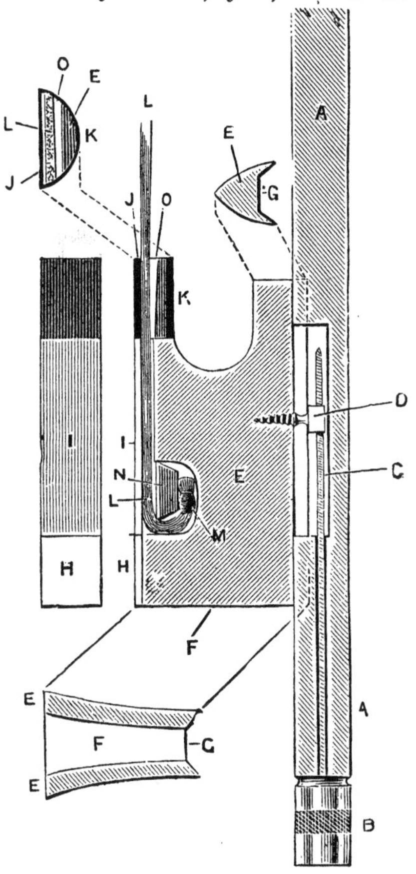

FIG. 64.—Nut and Screw of Modern Bow, showing method of fixing the hair.

which lies against the stick is cut angularly (as in G, Fig. 64), the cutting G being often lined with a thin bent plate of metal. The hair L leaving the nut E passes in a ribbon about half an inch broad to the head, where it is in a like manner fixed into a similar wedge-box (Fig. 66). The face of the head is generally protected by means of a metal or ivory plate (P, Fig. 65). The length of the bow is generally as near as possible 29½ inches (from the button to the tip of P, Fig. 65); the diameter of the stick is, at the screw (B, Fig. 64), ⅜-inch, and at the back of the head $\frac{3}{16}$. The diameter of the head across the plate (P, Fig. 65) is $\frac{7}{16}$, and the length of the head from top to bottom of P is one inch.[1] The hair with which the bows are fitted (which is horse, and not, as some people imagine, yak) is sold

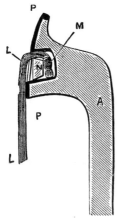

FIG. 65.—Head of Modern Bow, showing method of fixing the hair.

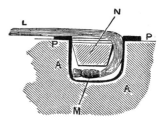

FIG. 66.—Wedge-box in head, and nut of modern bow (enlarged).

FIG. 67.—Knot at ends of hair.

by the pound, and, as I noticed before, in discussing Tourte's bow, it must be very carefully chosen and cleaned. It is also customary to lap or cover the sticks of bows for a space of a few inches above the nut with gold or silver thread or leather. This is doubtless a great convenience in holding the bow; it was for the same purpose that the elder Tourte, and some of the old bow makers, used to flute their stick over half or throughout their length, often in a most exquisite manner.

[1] Mr. W. S. B. Woolhouse gave some intensely scientific "Notes on the Suitable Proportions and Dimensions of a Violin Bow" to the *Monthly Musical Record* for July 1875, which are most interesting, but I fear hardly intelligible to the majority of bow-makers. He follows his remarks the next month (August 1875) with a "Supplementary Note" on the Bows of James Tubbs (*vide* p. 103).

To Hair, or Rehair a Bow.—If the latter, you must first unhair it ; commence by cutting the hair off short at the nut, then lifting the hair up pick the wedge N, Fig. 66, out of the head wedge-box, and pull out the knot M. Then take off the band K, Fig. 64, first pulling out the wedge O. Draw off the plate H I J, lift up the ends of the hair L, Fig. 67, pick the wedge N, Fig. 66, out of the nut wedge-box, and pull out the knot M. The stick is now clear of hair, wedges, and all, as if it had never been haired, and you can now proceed to hair it. The hair should either be kept in a large coil tied together loosely at one end, or straight out, wrapped round with paper in a drawer, the latter mode being the best. Lay out the bundle of hair on the bench and place a heavy weight upon it. Then take out enough for the bow, pulling it out from the bundle so as not to entangle the rest. You will be able to judge the quantity required by the eye after you have performed this operation once or twice. Take some waxed silk and tie round one end as at M, Fig. 67, and cut off the ends of the hair just beyond it ; hold these ends with a little stick of clear rosin in the flame of a spirit lamp for a few moments, so that the melted rosin permeates the ends and knot M, so as to harden and secure it. Take care not to burn too long and burn off the waxed silk doing this, or you will have all your trouble over again. Now cut a wedge (N in Figs. 64, 65, and 66), of such a size that it fixes the hair tight into the wedge-box in the head, the top of the wedge being just even with the plate P, so that the hair comes from it flat over the plate P. Put the knot M into the wedge-box, flatten out the hair so that it starts from the head in a broad ribbon, and lightly hammer in the wedge N so as to keep it thus, and as far as the head is concerned the hair is fixed. Now very carefully comb out the hair throughout its length with a fine comb, and then coiling it up near the head, steep it for a few moments in tepid water. Then hold it at the nut and re-comb it from top to bottom over and over again, till it is quite free, flat, and firm. The nut must be set, as in Fig. 64, with the eye D in the middle of the groove cut in the stick to receive it, or if anything rather towards the head. In this manner, holding the band of hair in your fingers, and allowing sufficient at the end for the knot to curl round the wedge in the box, make a tie and rosin the cut ends as at Fig. 67 in the same way as you did when preparing to set the other end in the head. Now take the band K off E and slip it (right way up !) over the hair, so that it can be brought back over the end of the nut when the hair is fixed, and taking E off the stick by completely unscrewing B, draw off the slide H I J, and fix the knot into the wedge-box as at Fig. 64, exactly as you fixed the other end into the head.

Now replace the nut E on the stick, by means of the screw B, and if you have nicely judged the length of the hair before making the tie M, the hair will be quite slack when D is as far rorward in the groove as possible, and per contra much too taut when it is drawn as near as possible to B, the proper tension of the hair being when D is in the centre of the groove as in Fig. 64. However, if the bow can be made slack, and tightened up by means of B, your work has been well done. Now finally comb the hair from head to nut, replace the slide H I J, and pull down the band K (which has been threaded loosely on the hair *before* placing it in the wedge-box in the nut), and slip it over J into its place. Now screwing the bow pretty tight, take the smooth *back* of the comb, and rub the surface of the ribbon of hair hard from the head to nut and back a few times. Then cut a little flat wedge O, or if necessary two, to slip in, and fill up the space between the ebony of the nut inside, K, and the under side of the hair, which will keep the ribbon of hair tight and flat against J, and the flat side of K, and the operation of hairing the bow is complete. When the hair is quite dry take some very finely powdered rosin, and sprinkling it on a sheet of paper, rub the hair on it so as to get well dusted and covered with rosin ; this, as it were, gives it a start, after which it is easy to keep the bow rosined.

As I have said in the chapter on fittings and appliances (*vide post*, p. 199), it is as well not to make changes in the kind of rosin one uses, except when the bow is rehaired, from which time one kind must be kept to, till the next re-hairing, and so on. It is a great mistake to use too much rosin, as young beginners are often apt to do ; it is only productive of a loud coarse tone ; and I prefer, personally, to err on the side of too little rosin, rather than to burden my bow and rasp my fiddle with too much. It is astonishing how few violinists know anything about the mechanical and scientific action of powdered rosin on tone production. Many people when they see you applying rosin, think you are " greasing your bow to make it go faster," and more still, including performers themselves, think that rosin renders the surface of the hair smoother, instead of, as it really does, making it rough. They know that if no rosin is used, the bow will make no sound, but *voilà tout*. The true function of rosin is as follows : It will have been noticed that whilst a string is vibrating, the least touch of the finger will make it instantly cease ; why, therefore, does not the continuous pressure of the bow militate against the production of sound ? Answer : because it is *not* continuous, owing to the presence of the rosin. If the bow were quite free from rosin, so long as it touched the string, or were drawn across it, the contact would be perfect and continuous, and as a natural result the existence of vibrations would be rendered impossible. When, however, the smooth surface of the horsehair is roughened by infinitesimal particles of rosin, the bow does not touch the string with a continuous pressure, but owing to the presence of the rosin, the string receives a constant, though infinitesimally intermittent succession of shocks, which renders the succession of vibrations so rapid as to appear con tinuous. It would take too long to discuss the scientific principles involved by this simple phenomenon, but the above exposition will show that the bow and hair are both secondary in importance, the true magical power of them both lying in the obscure and unnoticed rosin. Wherever bow instruments are used, rosin is an invariable adjunct. On primitive bow instruments, such as the urheen of the Chinese, and the ravanastron of the aboriginal Hindu, the rosin is always found in a little dirty lump, stuck on the top of the cylinder bearing the skin, which serves as the sound-board of those harmonious instruments. In the urheen especially, which has but two strings, and whose bow is worked *between* them, the convenience of this primitive arrangement is obvious, for with a couple of rubs the performer can rosin his bow during a half-bar's rest in his performance. Paganini is said to have played exquisitely on his violin with a rush, with a view to annihilating a self-confident Italian amateur, who matched himself against the " Immortal Trickster." If you gather a common rush, you will find that its surface is quite rough enough to have the mechanical effect of powdered rosin, which accounts for the possibility of the above performance.

Like the violin, the bow has been subjected to manifold improvements, and has survived them all in its absolute simplicity, as determined by Tourte. Amongst the most striking of these is the folding bow, made to go with the folding violin, mentioned in Chapter V. It comes in half with a joint and a ferrule, like a fishing-rod, and, curiously enough, does not seem to be as seriously affected by this eccentricity of construction, as it might be expected to be. The late J. B. Vuillaume introduced steel bows, but I have never come across any specimen of so ponderous an eccentricity, other than the one in the South Kensington Museum. One introduction, however, of his which has survived, is his self-hairing bow, which is still manufactured by Mr. George Withers, and is reproduced by his permission in Fig 68. The head, it will be seen, has no face-plate (P, Fig. 65), and though the nut and screw work in the usual manner, the nut is a plain piece of ebony (*i.e.*, it has no wedge-box, slide, etc.). The hair for these bows is sold in the right lengths, being terminated at each end by small cylindrical pieces, which slip into two holes cut in the head and nut, (as in the illustration), to receive them. It will be observed that though absolutely identical in outward aspect with the ordinary forms, not a particle of glue is employed at any point of the bow, and those who have ever taken a fiddle and bow through the Canal to India will fully appreciate the boon thus conferred upon them. In M. Vuillaume's original form the hair was fitted in a precisely similar manner, but the nut was glued fast and immovably to the stick ; the hair was fitted to a smaller brazen nut, which by means of the screw worked backwards and forwards *inside* the larger ebony one. The advantage claimed was that the distance between the nut and head (and consequently the length of the hair) never varied.

Mr. Bishop in his most valuable appendix to his translation of "Otto on the Violin" (*vide* note [1], p. 20) (which, with his notes on the text, constitute the great and sole value of the work) asserts that the variations of the movable nut are calculated to affect the tone of the performer. Mr. Bishop, of course, speaks *ex cathedrâ* ;

FIG. 68.—Self-hairing Bow.

but, personally, I do not consider the infinitesimal advance and retreat of the nut, to suit various styles of playing, to be in any way detrimental to execution or just intonation on the instrument.

Red horsehair has been recommended in preference to white, as "biting" better, consequently on the action of the dye ; but this is a fallacy, as its only effect is to produce a coarseness of tone. Dr. J. Nicholson, who invented a huge cumbrous form of fiddle, so heavy in wood and construction that it could be used for corking bottles much better than for "discoursing dulcet melodye," introduced for the purpose of evoking its "three-horse-power" tone, a huge bow, whose stick was half an inch thick at the nut, and *bombé* in the centre, which was fitted with red hair, and made of some light wood, which makes them wonderfully light in proportion to their size. These fiddles and bows (specimens of which may be seen in M. Georges Chanot's shop in Wardour Street) are curiosities in their way, but deadly in other respects.[1] The celebrated bow-makers are not many in

[1] A complete description of them, with *full size* diagrams, was printed for the inventor under the title of "Designs and Plans for the Construction and Arrangement of the New Model Violin" (London, 1880), large folio.

number ; after Tourte, jun., the first of any importance was Jacques Lafleur, of Paris (1760—1830). He was one of the best makers, his work being often as good as Tourte's, with which they are very frequently confused. After him came François Lupot, brother of Nicholas, the great Luthier of that name, who devoted himself solely to the manufacture of bows, in which he undoubtedly excelled.

In England our greatest maker was John Dodd, who has justly been called the English Tourte. He lived and was buried at Kew, living and working alone, for he never took an apprentice, who might learn the secret of his art, for the divulgence of which, it is said, he was once offered, and refused, £1,000. His violoncello bows are the best, but his violin bows, though sometimes a shade too short, are the best England has known of native manufacture, and as such command high prices. Nevertheless, Dodd died in Richmond workhouse. He was followed in the mastery of bow manufacture by Louis Panormo (the son of the violin-maker Vincent Panormo), whose bows are much esteemed by violinists. The only contemporary bow-maker with any claims to celebrity is James Tubbs, who, if so disposed, can be persuaded to make the most exquisite and scientific bows, on his own terms. The bows of James Tubbs are even now much sought after, and will, in time to come, be valuable from their scarcity and sterling qualities (*vide* note [1], p. 98).

---

[1] " Quelle est cet agent principal, qui tient en respect et soumet à ses ordres, l'air, le bois et les cordes. Quelle est cette baguette magique, enchantée, qui semble à chaque commotion recréer l'âme. Quel est, en un mot, ce Sceptre Dominateur, si non l'Archet lui-même, qui dit, et le son part. "

L'ABBÉ SIBIRE, "*La Chelonomie*" (Paris, 1806).

CHAPTER V.

THE VIOLIN, ITS VAGARIES AND ITS VARIEGATORS.

Perfection of the Existing Form.—Earthenware, Metal, Leather, Papier Mâché and Eccentric Violins.—Trumpet Violin.—Pear-shaped Violin.—Hulskamp's Violin. - Polychord Violins.—Isoard's.—Dubois.—Vuillaume.—Hœnsel.—Hawkins. — Sinclair. — Wylde's Nagelgeige, or Nail-Violin. — Boxwood Violin. — Howell. — Jacque's.—Bell. — Robertson. — Collins. — Howell.—Mollenhauer. —Guitar-shaped Fiddles. —Galbusera.—F. Chanot.—Savart's Trapezoid Violin.—Patent Repairs.

I HAVE often been asked by persons unacquainted with the construction or full powers of the violin, " How is it one never hears of improvements to the violin? Pianos, and indeed all other musical instruments, advance in perfection with the march of progress, but the fiddle seems to stand still." This is perfectly true; at least, it is necessary to search the most obscure sources for notices of " improvements to the violin,"—improvements only in name and on advertisements, which live their short existences, known only to the few who are brought into contact with the inventor, and go out without leaving a trace behind. The reason for this is not far to seek. The violin, called as it justly is " the king of instruments," is perhaps the only human contrivance, which, taken as a whole, may be pronounced to be—*perfect.* If you will turn to page 125 you will find the following paragraph: " Let us look at the *tout-ensemble* of a fiddle. What is it? It is a hollow box, from 13 to 14 inches in length ; at the widest part, $8\frac{1}{2}$ inches, and at the narrowest $4\frac{1}{2}$ inches, broad. It is about $2\frac{1}{4}$ inches deep at the deepest part, and weighs about $8\frac{1}{2}$ ounces. Beyond this we have a neck terminating in a scroll, which, with pegs, finger-board, and tail-piece of ebony, bring the weight up to about twenty ounces. The wondrous capabilities and wonderful equilibrium of all the parts may be summed up in one short sentence—it supports a tension on the strings of 68 lbs., and a vertical pressure on the bridge of 26 pounds."

This exquisite machine, standing apart in its mysterious simplicity from the vulgar herd of instruments of melody and harmony, is capable of expressing more by its unaided voice than all the rest put together ; and when this has been said,

are we not perfectly justified in ascribing to it the attribute of
perfection ? and is it extraordinary that any attempted improvement only proves to be a deterioration, and that to this day we
say to the fiddle in the words of Cardinal Wolsey :—

> " —— I charge thee, fling away ambition,
> By that sin fell the angels " ?

In the year 1804, Ernst, the celebrated violinist and Concert
director to the Prince of Saxe-Coburg-Gotha, who was also a
practical fiddle-maker[1] and experimentalist, wrote as follows[2] :
" After the numerous and repeated essays which I have made
in the construction of the violin for more than twenty years, 1
have come to the conclusion that its form and manufacture as
they have come down to us from the best Italian masters, are
not susceptible of any improvement, especially as regards the
body of the instrument." It has very justly been remarked,
Plura faciunt homines e consuetudine quam e ratione, and as
though to contradict this maxim, and from a feeling of independence, many daring innovations have been made (or rather
attempted), many of them the results of carefully-applied science,
and of the labours of intelligent and learned men ; as such, they
become most interesting to the violin-maker, and as such, it is
the intention of the present chapter to consider them. *Crimine
ab uno disce omnes.* First comes the list of instruments which
have been made of various and wildly unsuitable materials,
beginning with

Earthenware Violins.—There is a specimen of this vagary in
the Musée des Antiques, at Rouen, and another in Delft faïence
in the Musée of the Conservatoire at Paris, which has been
played on (with a result easily anticipated) by Mons. G. Choquet,
the compiler of the catalogue of the museum, who describes it
as " neither powerful nor pleasant." [3]

Metal Violins.—Copper, brass, and silver have all been used
for making fiddles, the tones of which may easily be imagined.
A notice of these may be found in the *Allgemeine Musikalische
Zeitung*, vol. vii., 1804, page 50. The silver violin which has
been on view in Mr. Davis's window in Green Street, Leicester
Square, longer than any living man can remember, is doubtless
a familiar object to many of my readers.

---

[1] He was the master in fiddle-making of J. A. Otto, to whose "Treatise on
the Construction of the Violin" reference has been made in these pages.

[2] *Allgemeine Musikalische Zeitung*, vol. vii., 1804, p. 49.

[3] Many of my readers probably know " Champfleury's " (pseudonym of
Jules Fleury the novelist) delightful story, " Le Violon de Faïence," exquisitely
" got up " in édition de luxe by M. Dentu (Paris. 1877), which relates the
adventures of one of these china fiddles.

Leather Violins.—There is one such to be seen in the museum of the Conservatoire de Musique, in Paris, of the date of 1776 ; and in the *Gentleman's Magazine,* vol. lxxxiii., for the year 1813, at page 312, we find mention of one Gavin Wilson, a bootmaker of Edinburgh, who, having invented a process for hardening leather for the construction of artificial limbs, etc., made therefrom a German flute and *a violin,* which are described as "not inferior to any constructed of wood."

Papier-mâché Violin.—M. Georges Chanot possesses one of these among the curiosities which characterize his shop. It is painted green and gold, and is as hideous and ghastly as anything can be which bears any resemblance to a fiddle.

Many of my readers will doubtless be familiar with the enterprising mendicant who perambulates the country playing on fiddles made of old meat tins and cigar boxes, which show a very considerable ingenuity in their manufacture, but which it would be obviously foreign to our purpose to describe in these pages. In the same category come the fiddles one sees made of broomsticks, and the various forms of sordini or mute violins, whose noise-producing capabilities are reduced to a minimum by various reductions and contortions of shape and size.

Next in order come the various eccentricities of shape, the application of various complications to the beautiful simplicity of the violin, and the various instruments which have from time to time been introduced, bearing eccentric arrangements and numbers of strings.

Trumpet Violin.—This was patented in 1854, in Germany, by Ferdinand Hell, and in England by W. E. Newton (1854, January 25th ; No. 186), and consisted in adapting a horn or a trumpet to a violin, the mouthpiece opening into the body of the instrument at the point where the neck joins it, the tube running down the neck under the finger-board, and the bell, or mouth, taking the place of the scroll. It is said not to have very much damaged the tone of the violin, but it was very hideous, as may be supposed.

The Pear-shaped Violin, of A. Engleder, was exhibited at Munich in the same year (1854) . The corners were abolished, the upper bouts contracted, and the lower bouts expanded, to produce the desired result. They were, it need hardly be said, a failure.

In 1862, at the London International Exhibition, one Hulskamp, a German resident in New York, exhibited a fiddle, the tables of which could, by a mechanism inside the instrument, worked by a key, be submitted to a regular tension to suit that of the strings. The back and belly were quite flat, which was considered an improvement on the score of expense in construction. Instead of *f f* holes, this fiddle had a round hole between the bridge and finger-board. One foot of the bridge rested on the belly, the other on a post set upon a rib glued to the back of the fiddle, through a hole cut in the belly, so that the lattei was not touched by bridge or post. This last arrangement seems to be based on the experiments of Savart, referred to on page 150, and reminds one of the arrangement of the Welsh crwth explained on p. 66 : the whole contrivance received good opinions from some high authorities (including Joachim, Laub, and Becker), but did not last longer than the generality of such vagaries.

Five-stringed Violins, or rather combinations of the violin and viola (*i.e.*, tenors with a high E string added, or violins with a low C string added), are frequently to be found among the curiosities on a fiddle-dealer's walls. M. F. Chanot made many of his guitar-shaped violins (those compendia of curious contrivances!) to mount with five strings, the size being between that of a tenor and a fiddle. About the year 1815, a German, named Hillmer, introduced such a combination, and called it the "Violalin ;" it was noticed in the *Allgemeine Musikalische Zeitung*," 1840, p. 245. He had the audacity to call it an invention, but of course, even if such a thing had not been made over and over again already, it was only reverting to the arrangement of the old violas, or viols, which were mounted with five or six strings.

One Prinz, in a work written in 1649, tells us that Lord Somerset invented a violin with eight strings, to which he attributed extraordinary advantages. A M. Urhan played on such a fiddle at a concert at the Paris Conservatoire in 1830.

A rather curious instrument must have been the " Violon-Général," invented by M. Vincenti, a Florentine lute-master, during the first half of this century. It had eighteen strings, and was played on with two bows, and derived its name from the fact that, according to M. Vincenti, it combined the effects of the violin, viola, violoncello, and violono.

A violin was presented to the Académie des Sciences (also in the first half of this century) by M. Isoard, the strings of which passed through two blades. Instead of being played on with a bow, the strings were vibrated at one end by means of a current of air, whilst they were stopped by the fingers at the other. Its tones were said to resemble the French horn and the bassoon !

Wettengel (in his " Lehrbuch der Geigen und Bogenmacherkunst," Weimar, 1869) mentions the *Violon-tenor*, invented by the elder Dubois (a Parisian amateur), the four strings of which were tuned an octave below those of a violin. The *raison d'être* of this instrument it is difficult to imagine, but as an idea it is about as original as the Violalin of Herr Hillmer. It was intended to supersede the viola, or act as an intermediary between it and the violoncello.

J. B. Vuillaume introduced, in 1855, a new model for the tenor, which was much broader and deeper, and consequently more difficult to play than that in ordinary use. These instruments were constructed on scientific principles, so that the mass of contained air should give a note of 341·33 vibrations to the second, giving the note F, which is the right scientific proportion according to the discoveries of Felix Savart. They were tried at the Brussels Conservatoire, and their tone was found to be more like that of a violin, and twice as powerful as that of an ordinary viola, but they did not come into universal use for the reasons given above.

Violins with the upper and lower bouts of the same size, have been constructed by more than one experimentalist. In 1808, we find a record of such an one, with the bridge set in the centre; and in 1811, one Jean Antoine Hœnsel, luthier and chamber musician to M. le Duc de Schœnburg, claimed attention for a similar one, which he asserted to have been invented by him in 1801.

In the year 1800 J. J. Hawkins took out a patent (No. 2446) for a violin, which had no sides or back, but only a strong rib running beneath the belly, on which was set the sound-post, which pressed up on the belly by means of a spring. We are told that the mere loudness of a fiddle was little impaired by this ruinous proceeding, though even this is a matter for considerable doubt; at any rate, it is acknowledged that the quality of tone was absolutely destroyed. It is said that he committed the vandalism of ruining a valuable Stradiuarius by the application of his ridiculous contrivance. *Fiat experimentum in corpore vili*, but spare the masterpieces of Cremona.

Mr. Davidson refers to the inventions of one Sinclair, a Scotch maker, who, at the commencement of the century, produced various triangular fiddles with arrangements of sympathetic strings for increasing the sonority of the bowed strings by consonant vibration, and also a structure with two sets of strings one above the other, and so far distant as to allow either set to be played upon by passing the bow between them. Of a similar nature are the productions of other makers, who, having time to experimentalize, have constructed violins with double strings (like a mandoline), tuned either in unison or octaves. A few years after the above, was born another Scottish vagary, which was a double violin, having one back, belly, and sides, but two necks, bridges, tail-pieces, and sets of strings ; it has been described as a loud, harsh-toned instrument, of little or no value, excepting as a curiosity.

In the year 1740 a German musician, named Johann Wilde, living in St. Petersburg, invented a curious instrument called a Nail-violin (in German, *Nagelgeige, Nagelharmonika, Eisen-violine*). Its invention seems to have been accidental, for it is thus described by Mr. Carl Engel : " One evening, after return-ing home from a concert, Wilde, in hanging his violin bow on a nail accidentally produced a tone by drawing the hair of the bow over the metal, whereupon he conceived the idea of constructing a musical instrument of nails. And that he has succeeded in producing a fine-toned, if not a practically recommendable instrument, will probably be granted by all who draw the large

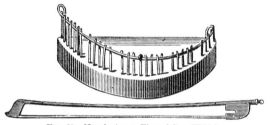

FIG. 69.—Nagelgeige or Eisenvioline (Wilde).

black-haired bow over the iron pins. The bow is best made with black hair, for white hair is softer, and does not 'bite' so well for such an iron fiddle. It must also be plentifully sup-plied with rosin to make it bite well." It was held in the left hand by a hole underneath. Mr. Engel gives a figure of it which I reproduce, Fig. 69. In 1780 it was improved by the addition of sympathetic strings, when Senal, an artist of Vienna, excelled upon it. The nails diminish in length as the notes get higher, and the chromatic nails are slightly bent. In 1791, one Trager produced an arrangement of it, worked by keys, called *Nagelclavier.* It is interesting as a curiosity in the way of bow instruments.

In the South Kensington Museum, and figured and fully described in the catalogue thereof, is a most curious violin, made of boxwood, dated 1578. It is of a queer and cumbrous shape, being in the form of a wedge, which narrows at the thick end to a sort of neck, which is formed by a round hole to admit

the hand, the shift being thus rendered impossible. It is **carved**
all over with various rural and allegorical scenes, and, as may
be supposed, the tone is very poor. It is described by Hawkins
and Burney in their Histories of Music ; the latter describes it
as having no more tone than a mute or violin with a sordine.
" It is said to have been given to the Earl of Leicester by
Queen Elizabeth, and has both their coats of arms in silver on
the finger-board. It is, perhaps, one of the most interesting
fiddles (if it can be so called) in exist-
ence " (*vide* p. 5).

In 1835 Thomas Howell took out a
patent (No. 6964) for a new form of
violin, which is represented at Fig. 70.
Its object was, by shortening the upper
bouts and lengthening the fingerboard,
to facilitate playing in the upper shifts,
and obviating "that inelegance of action
which is so much complained of, even
in the most expert performers." The
back and belly were flat, the tail-piece
glued to the instrument, to be " out
of the way of the chin," and the sound-
holes reverted to the form in vogue in
the fifteenth century.

In 1856 a clergyman (the Rev.
George Jacque) took out a patent (No.
1684) for adapting to the violin and
enclosing within it a series of sympathetic strings, set obliquely across the
interior of the instrument. They could
be taken out, tuned, and replaced by
an opening in the lower bouts. He
thought in this way to increase the
sonority of the instrument !

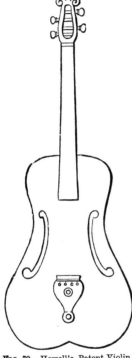

FIG. 70.—Howell's Patent Violin.
(1835, No. 6964.)

In 1858 one Henry Bell patented a
design (No. 2823) for applying a
flattened glass cylinder to the interior of a violin with the same
object.

In the same year (No. 2587) John Robertson patented a
device for increasing the tone of violins by grooving out the
soft part of the pine of the belly, so as to leave only the fibres
standing out. He thought that in this way the vibratory
surface would be increased, and the fiddle thereby improved.

In 1866 Henry Bell, the patentee of the last contrivance
but one, took out another patent (No. 2071) for increasing and

:mproving the tone of fiddles by placing in them a sheet of crystal or glass, with a hole through it to admit the sound-post. It was about as successful as his first " improvement."

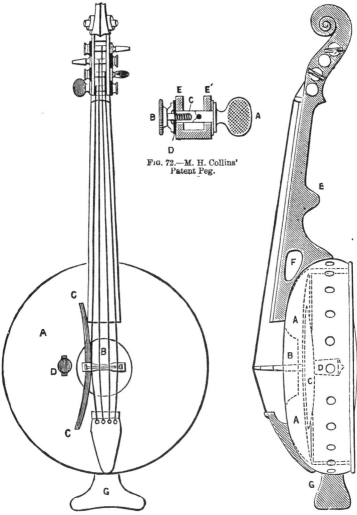

FIG. 72.—M. H. Collins' Patent Peg.

FIG. 71.—M. H. Collins' " Echolin " in plan and section.

In the year 1879 Michael Henry Collins, an American, took out an English patent (No. 2118) for a fiddle, which he termed an Echolin (Fig. 71). The body was quite circular, and inclosed inside a domed case A, which had a circular hole B in the middle to admit the bridge, which rested on the circular belly, and was formed like a violoncello bridge. Space forbids my going into the theory of this instrument here ; it is represented in plan and in section in Fig. 71. The bass bar was curved as at C, and the sound-post was replaced by a heavy mechanism which hung to the left side of the belly as at D. The neck had a protuberance E corresponding to the shoulder in the ordinary form, and another opening F for the high shifts. It was held by a chin rest G, and was fitted with patent pegs, which are represented in Fig. 72. The diagram explains itself. The string is tuned by turning A, an ordinary thumb-piece ; when the string is tuned, the screw C is turned by the milled head B, presses the plate D against the cheek of the scroll E, and prevents the peg from slipping.

Two years later (1879, No. 3022) one Howell patented a most curious instrument, the strings of which were set along the *side*, the neck being formed by a long hole in the side to admit the hand ; in its way it was interesting, and especially so to acousticians, who could thus test the results of the vibrations of the strings being transmitted longitudinally to the fibres of the wood, instead of vertically. He patented several modifications of the instrument on the same principle.

Still more lately (1881, No. 621) E. R. Mollenhauer, of New York, obtained protection for a design for dividing the inside of the fiddle into two chambers, by means of a fiddle-shaped plank resting on a supplementary side-lining, set round the centre of the ribs. He claimed by this means to increase the sonority of the instrument. Comment is needless.[1]

Another interesting vagary is the Folding or Traveller's Violin. The neck of this instrument, the body of which is long and narrow, comes off with the finger-board, as do also the bridge, tail-piece, and tail-pin, all of which, with a folding bow, fit into a small rectangular case. As a curiosity, it is good, and as a question of tone and convenience, it is not bad. At the same time, it will go into a portmanteau, and is amusing and handy on occasions when one does not want the fuss of carrying a full-grown fiddle.

I have received from Hanover a most interesting curiosity in the violin line. It is called the *Löffelgeige* (spoon-fiddle), and

---

[1] Count Luigi Francesco Valdrighi devoted one of his " Musurgiana " (No. 9) to the discussion of these fiddles, prompted thereto apparently by Mr. A. J. Hipkins' article in *Musical Opinion and Music Trades Review*. It is entitled, " Gli strumenti ad arco rinforzati del Sig. E. Mollenhaver. Cenni Monografici " (Modena, 1881), and gives descriptions in brief of many vagaries such as we are now discussing

is more a joke among musicians than anything else. It is formed of one solid piece of wood like a soup-ladle, and is represented in front and side view in Fig. 73. The bowl is scooped out, and decked, as it were, with a thin deal sound-board, pierced with two small oval sound-holes. The head is of a curious hook shape, and can boast of the same advantages that were claimed for the reversed scroll of M. Chanot, which is noticed below. An ordinary violin bridge is mounted on the belly, to raise the strings just clear of the long neck. It has no tail-piece, but the strings are attached to loops of D string, which come from pegs set underneath the fiddle, over a sort of rest made of tin, which protects the lower edge of the bowl. Its tone is curious, as might be expected.

The latest thing of the sort I have come across has been a fiddle of Russian manufacture (on Mirecourt principles of construction), which is now being sold at about a guinea in the music shops. This fiddle differs from the ordinary form in that it has no projecting edges, which is a great mistake, for it is practically impossible under these circumstances to take off the belly in case of need. However, like the "Seraphine," "Æoleon," "Zephyrophone," and other absurdly named eccentricities of bran-new violin manufacture, they are made I presume to find a market among amateurs who like to have something out of the common,

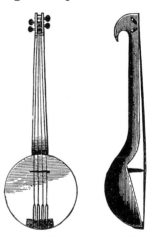

FIG. 73.—Löffelgeige or Spoon-fiddle.

at the expense of their own convenience and other people's ears.

Enough of these minor vagaries. If necessary, I could fill a thick quarto with them. Such as they are, they are interesting and beneficial as warnings ; it remains only to notice two intelligent and scientific experiments (I will not insult them by calling them vagaries). I allude to the guitar-shaped violins of M. François Chanot, and the trapezoid violin of M. le Docteur Félix Savart, to whom the world of violins owes so much for his valuable and devoted scientific researches into the forms and qualities of the Cremonese and other violins.

Guitar-shaped Fiddles have been made in all countries and all ages, since the invention of the fiddle proper in the sixteenth century. M. Gallay, in his "Luthiers Italiens," mentions the interesting fact that M. G. Chanot (brother of the naval officer mentioned below) had once in his hands a violin by Stradivarius, which was guitar-shaped, and had a flat belly. I have myself seen such—the work of Peter Walmsley, Benjamin Banks, and other of our native makers. It is a reversion to mediævalism, which is, to say the least of it, feeble and unimportant.

In the year 1832 Carlo Antonio Galbusera, an Italian officer, exhibited, in the Brera Palace at Milan, a violin of a guitar shape, which he claimed to have invented, but which was really a reproduction of M. Chanot's essay. He prepared his wood by chemical means, by which he claimed to get all the resinous particles out of it. They were criticised and argued against by M. Antolini in a pamphlet entitled, " Osservazzione su due Violini esposti nelle sale dell' I. R. Palazzo di Brera " (Milan, 1832).

The most celebrated instruments having this form were the violins of M. François Chanot, a French naval officer, and uncle of M. Georges Chanot, of Wardour Street, at whose shop several of these instruments of all types may be seen. M. Chanot would seem to have commenced with the same line of scientific consideration as did M. Félix Savart in the construction of his trapezoid violin, to which I shall presently allude.

These violins were very favourably pronounced upon by a council of the Academy, appointed to consider their merits, and, indeed, preferred to a masterpiece of Cremona with which they were compared—the instruments being alternately played in an adjoining room by M. Boucher, the eminent violinist. M. Fétis, on the other hand, stigmatizes them as not worth ten francs apiece, excepting as curiosities, and a musical critic in the *Allgemeine Musikalische Zeitung*, vol. xxxii., for February, 1820, finds considerable fault with their tone. However, for a few years they found a market, being sold at 300 francs each, and in late years M. Georges Chanot tells me they have realized £10 to collectors. I am fortunate enough to possess a copy of the " Rapport fait à l'Académie des Beaux Arts dans la Séance du 3 Avril 1819 au nom de la Section de Musique sur les nouveaux instruments de musique (violons, altos, violoncelles et contre-basses) suivant la facture brevetée de *M. Chanot*, Officier au corps du Génie Maritime, inséré au Moniteur du 22 Août 1817 " (Paris, 1819), four pages 4to. On the back of the report, which is headed " Institut de France, Académie Royale des Beaux Arts," is printed a statement that these instruments are sold at No. 216, Rue St. Honoré, Passage des Maures, at the following prices, viz.—Violins 300 fr., Violas 300 fr., Violon-cellos 500 fr., followed by the prices of bows and cases for these instruments. These violins may be seen, as I have said, in Wardour Street; they are covered with a light-coloured varnish, and specimens of both kinds, as represented in Figs. 74 and 75, may be seen.   Their tone is poor and unsatisfactory.

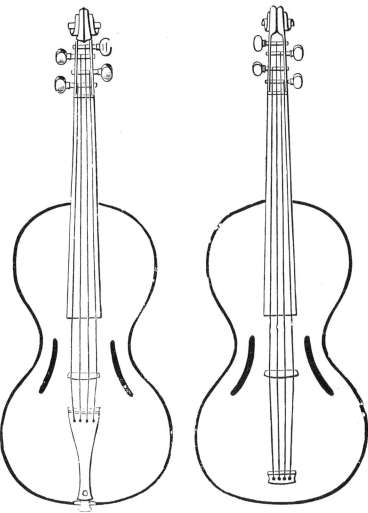

FIG. 74. The Chanot Violin.

75. The Chanot Violin, with reversed scroll and guitar string-attachment.

Fig. 79 represents the first form in which they were introduced in 1817 ; it will be observed that the corners are abandoned, which produces the guitar shape; the edges do not overlap

the sides, but end flush with them in a rim of ivory, or hard
wood, like a guitar.   The sound-holes are openings of the
same length as the ff holes of the ordinary form, but, following the curvature of the sides (to which they are set rather close),
they take the form of a segment of a circle.   The reason assigned
for this was that in cutting the ordinary f form, a large number
of fibres had to be cut through, and were therefore no longer
affected by the vibrations of the bridge.   The new form claimed
the merit of reducing these cut fibres to a minimum, and of thus
producing a maximum of long fibres.   It had been determined
by experiment that the low notes of a fiddle were principally
produced by the long fibres, and the high notes by the short
fibres (and it is on this principle that the sound-post, by pressing
upon the belly against the bridge, divides the violin into two sets
of short fibres on the side on which the high notes are produced,
whilst on the other side, on which the low notes are produced,
the fibres are intact throughout the length of the instrument).
For when the fibres under the low strings were similarly divided
(by shifting the sound-post to the left foot of the bridge), the
low notes lost all their power.   M. Chanot claimed for his violin
the merit, therefore, of having more long fibres to produce the
low notes, and more short ones to produce the high ones.   The
bass bar is set as in Savart's fiddle, down the exact centre on the
join of the belly.   Close to the tail-pin will be seen a screw,
which, passing through the tail-piece and pressing on the belly,
enabled the tail-piece to be raised, so as to lessen the angle
formed by the strings passing over the bridge, and reduce the
pressure on the belly at this point.   A similar contrivance to
this was patented in England by one Claggett, in 1788.   Passing
through the back of his fiddle was a screw, which, acting on the
sound-post, enabled the pressure of this latter, against the belly,
to be regulated at will.   M. Chanot at first proposed to place
frets upon the finger-board, but abandoned this design on the
suggestion of the Council.

Two years later (in 1819), M. Chanot discarded (as in Fig. 75)
the tail-piece and tail-pin, and the strings were fastened by pins
to two plates of wood, one glued outside and the other inside
the belly, like the string attachment of a guitar.   The bar was
removed from the centre join, and shaped like an arc, the centre of
which was under the left foot of the bridge, and whose *ends only*
approached the centre join.   The sound-post was set in front
of instead of behind the bridge.   The volute of the scroll was
turned *back* instead of forward, as is usual, to give greater
facility in manipulating the ends of the strings, especially that
of the A string, inside the peg-box.   His memorial on the

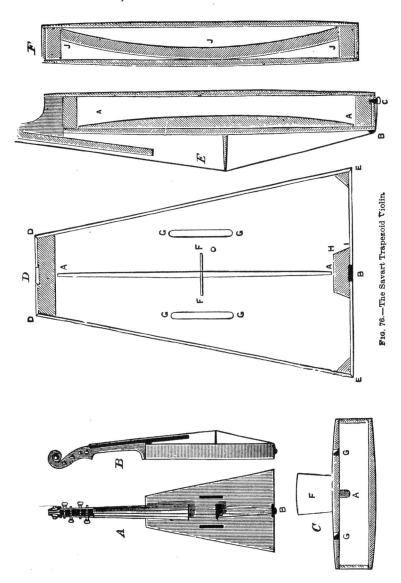

Fig. 76.—The Savart Trapezoid Violin.

subject was read to the Académie des Sciences, on the 24th of May, 1817.

A full description of it may be found in the "Description des Machines et Procédés Spécifiés dans les Brevets d'Invention,"

tome xv., p. 161 (Paris, 1828). And a report of its trial before
the Council of the Academy may be found in the " Moniteur
Universel," 22 Août, 1817.

Savart's Trapezoid Violin or *Box-fiddle* was one of the most
celebrated and satisfactory experiments ever tried on the construction of the instrument. He was led to its production by
a series of carefully conducted experiments, which went to
prove—(1) that a plane surface vibrates much more readily than
an arched or curved one ; (2) that consequently there are points
on the surface of a violin of the ordinary form where the vibrations are reduced to a minimum, or cease altogether ; (3) that
the bouts, corner blocks, and *f f* holes are the principal causes
and localities of this reduced vibration. He therefore constructed
a violin, the general aspect of which is shown in Fig. 76 A and B,
the tables of which were practically plane, as shown in B,
C, and E—*i.e.*, they were plane on the inner surfaces, but very
slightly raised on the outer, to support the increased pressure of
the strings, caused by the extra height which it was found
necessary to give to the bridge to allow the play of the bow.
The cause of this trapezoid shape was not founded particularly
on any scientific reason, but that it being necessary to have a
certain contained mass of air, this shape was best adapted to
give the instrument a narrowness at the bridge, which would
allow the play of the bow, and yet have the same interior capacity
as if the sides were parallel but broader at this point. Arguing
that the sound-holes of an ordinary violin are cut *f*-shaped only,
so as to counteract the resistance the curved surface offers to the
vibrations, this necessity being absent in the Savart fiddle, he
cut his sound-holes straight, as shown in A and D, Fig. 76, on
the same principle as those of the Chanot fiddle—viz., that it is
expedient to cut as few fibres of the wood as possible ; and their
exact position in the belly and distance from each other, as
shown in D, Fig. 76, he determined by a series of practical
experiences. The bar he placed down the central joint of the
fiddle by an erroneous course of reasoning, thinking by this
means to equalize its influence over the entire surface, which
was, of course, a mistake. He also constructed, in some cases,
a bar, as shown in F, Fig. 76, only touching the belly at a point
below the bridge, which he found had the same effect as the
other form (shown in C, D, and E, Fig. 76), and was more durable
but more difficult to construct and fix to suit the instrument. He
gave to his sides (which were made of the same wood as the
back) a thickness of $\frac{1}{12}$ in., and, considering that the absence
of the curves would support this substance, and again, with this
thickness, he used no side-linings. His sound-post, it will be

observed, was set behind the bridge, as in an ordinary violin, but
more to the right of the instrument. The tail-piece was suppressed
on the same principle as in the Chanot fiddle of 1819 (Fig. 75),
but, as he justly remarks, the full tug of the four strings on a
tender part of the belly being very detrimental to the instrument,
he carried them over a nut set at the bottom of the instrument
(B in A, D, and E, Fig. 76) to the tail-pin, which was set rather
below the centre of the lower side, as shown at C, in E, Fig. 76.

The merits of the new fiddle were duly considered by a
council of the Académie des Sciences, composed of MM. Biot,
Charles, Haüy, and De Prony, to whom were added MM. Berton,
Catel, Le Sueur, and Cherubini, members of the Académie des
Arts. The new fiddle was tested with another, a Cremona
master-piece, both being played alternately in an adjoining
room by M. Lefebvre, the eminent violinist, in exactly the
same way as the Chanot violin had been compared, and with
the same result—viz., that the new instrument was pronounced
equal, if not superior, to the work of the Italian master. It is
interesting to note how these councils of enthusiastic Frenchmen
were ready, apparently on all occasions, to rush into the arms
of any innovator and reward him in terms of the most fulsome
eulogy, but that the musical public on each occasion refused to
indorse their opinion and adopt the innovations. At the same
time the construction of Savart's "Box Fiddle," as it has con-
temptuously been called, was based on sound sense and scientific
principle; and there is no doubt that a violin properly constructed
on the Savart model, though falling far short of a first-rate
fiddle of the ordinary kind, would be very much superior to the
common Mirecourt wholesale production, besides being very much
easier for an amateur to construct. This will be acknowledged
readily enough by any one who will take the trouble to compare
the diagrams that are supplied in Fig. 76 of Savart's Trapezoid
Violin with those of the ordinary form of the violin which are
given in subsequent chapters. It is well known that in carpentry
it is far more easy to execute rectangular work than it is to manage
rounded or curved work, and this pertains in an equal degree in
fiddle-making, as far as amateurs are concerned. The appearance
of the trapezoid fiddle, our readers will observe, is by no means
so attractive as that of the violin proper.

For the benefit of any persons sufficiently interested to construct one of these trapezoid violins, I give the exact measurements [1] of its various parts, which are as follows [2] :—

[1] The measurements in French inches are the more exact; the sizes in English
represent their nearest English equivalents without considering high fractional
divisions.

[2] For full description of this instrument and report thereon, see F. Savart's

	French inches and lignes.		English inches.
Length of the body (D, E, and F, Fig. 76) . .	13· 0	=	$13\frac{13}{20}$
Breadth of upper end (D D in D, Fig. 76) . .	3· $1\frac{1}{2}$	=	$3\frac{4}{16}$
Breadth of lower end (E E in D, Fig. 76) . .	8· 4	=	$8\frac{3}{4}$
Height of bridge (F in C, Fig. 76) . . .	1· 6	=	$1\frac{5}{8}$
Breadth of bridge (F in C, Fig. 76) . . .	1· 6	=	$1\frac{5}{8}$
Length of sound holes (G G in D, Fig. 76) . .	2· 7	=	$2\frac{3}{4}$
Breadth of sound holes	0· 3	=	$\frac{1}{4}$
Diameter of back and belly at edges . .	0· 1	=	$\frac{1}{12}$
Diameter of back in centre	0· $2\frac{1}{4}$	=	$\frac{1}{5}$
Diameter of belly in centre	0· $2\frac{3}{4}$	=	$\frac{1}{4}$
Height of blocks and sides	0·$15\frac{1}{4}$	=	$1\frac{7}{20}$
Diameter of sides	0· 1	=	$\frac{1}{12}$
Diameter of blocks	0· 8	=	$\frac{17}{24}$
Length of bass bar (A A in D and E, Fig. 76) .	11· 2	=	$11\frac{7}{10}$
Breadth of bass bar at ends	0· 2	=	$\frac{3}{16}$
Breadth of bass bar in centre (A in C, D, and E, Fig. 76)	0· 3	=	$\frac{11}{40}$
Breadth of lower block, narrow side (H in D, Fig. 76)	1· 6	=	$1\frac{5}{8}$
Breadth of lower block, broad side (I in D, Fig. 76)	2· 0	=	$2\frac{1}{8}$
From nut to top of bridge	12· 2	=	$12\frac{31}{40}$
Depth of bass bar at ends (A A in D and E, Fig. 76)	0· 1	=	$\frac{1}{12}$
Depth of bass bar in centre (A in C, Fig. 76) .	0· 6	=	$\frac{17}{32}$
Depth of bent bar throughout (J J J in F, Fig. 76).	0· 6	=	$\frac{17}{32}$

These, therefore, are the principal alterations which have been attempted, a careful study of which only determines the would-be fiddle maker, *stare super vias antiquas.*

Patent Repairs have been the ruin of many splendid fiddles in former years, though nowadays people are more careful of trusting valuable instruments to the first quack who invents some patent operation which will increase the value of any fiddle, according to his own account, tenfold. One Maupertuis, in an article, "Sur la Forme des Instruments de Musique," in the *Mémoires de l'Académie Royale des Sciences*, 1724, p. 215, declared that the tone of a fiddle is to be improved by breaking it to pieces and having it pieced together again by a good workman. He argues thus :—that the violin ought to be made up of fibres of different lengths, so as to have some of a size to suit every note on the compass of a fiddle. An idea complimentary to the musical powers of glue, but deadly in practice.

Other fiddle-dealers and owners are always tinkering up their instruments by gluing in slabs of wood here, gouging out layers there, shortening or lengthening the bass bar, and shifting the bridge and sound-post about, till the violin, as it were, in very indignation at such treatment, relapses into a sullen or confused silence, until properly regulated by an artist of the trade. It

"Mémoire sur la Construction des Instruments à cordes et à archet" (Paris. 1819), and an excellent *resumé* of this "Mémoire" appears at p. 246 of No. 400 of the *Penny Magazine* for June 30th, 1838, entitled, "How to make a Cheap Violin."

is, as has been already pointed out, almost fatal to destroy, by thinning the wood in old violins, the provision the conscientious old makers laid up for time to expend its strength upon. It is almost equally so to patch up a fiddle, which has been subjected to this destruction, with new wood ; it stands to reason that the vibrations must be very seriously impaired by a stratum of glue and a slab of new wood, whose fibres do not coincide with the rest of the instrument. The acme of short-sighted and destructive repair is reached in a case which occurred, according to Mr. Davidson, at the beginning of this century. He mentions the case of a Scotch amateur, who being possessed of a splendid Stradivari violin of the large pattern, had it *cut down* smaller, *mirabile dictu*, at the suggestion of the celebrated J. P. Salomon. The fiddle subsequently sold for £56. Letters patent were granted to J. P. Grosjean, in 1837 (No. 7450), for coating the surfaces of violins with glue and powdered glass, to improve their tone, a practice about as intelligent as that of one Weickert, of Halle, who, at the beginning of the century, imagining that the loss of the resinous particles from the wood of violins by reason of their age, (which is the great advantage of age !) was detrimental to their quality, made a practice of *soaking* violins in a mixture of rosin dissolved in pine oil, to close the pores, an operation which, of course, caused complete and irremediable damage. Similar experiments have been tried to close the pores of the wood, (which it is most important to have open,) with white of egg and other such matters, all of which operations may be classed with the rest of the " patent repairs " I have here enumerated, and on all of which comment is needless. But they serve as warnings to the owners of valuable instruments, not to entrust their fiddles to the hands of musical quacks. If you think your violin wants anything doing to it, go to one of the heads of the profession for advice ; a respectable dealer or repairer will never do anything superfluous to your fiddle for the sake of the job ; and the love of his art will be subservient to his interest in his profession. I cannot do better than conclude this chapter with the highly epigrammatic remark made by Mr. J. Pearce in his " Violins and Violin Makers," " Beware of ignorance which assumes the mask of knowledge, and of designing roguery which apes the appearance of innocence."

"IL VIOLINO."

Canto popolare Toscano.

Musica di L. GORDIGIANI.

Oh ! quante volte l'ho desiderato,
 Un damo aver che fosse sonatore,
Un angelo del ciel me l'ha mandato,
 Io lo ringrazio del gentil favore.

Quando il mulino di grano manchera,
Con il Violino se ne trovera,
Oh ! quante volte l'ho desiderato
 Un damo aver che fosse sonator
 Un angelo del ciel me l'ha mandato,
Lo ringrazio del gentil favor
 Bravo ! Caro !
 Oh ! che bravo sonator !

PART II.

Theoretical.

FO'C'S'LE YARNS.

"And Tommy had a fiddle too,
And I don't know what there was he couldn't do
With yonder fiddle, the way it'd mock
Everything—it'd crow like a cock,
It'd hoot like a donkey, it'd moo like a cow;
It'd cry like a baby, it'd grunt like a sow,
Or a thrush, or a pigeon, or a lark, or a linnet,
You'd really a-thought they were living in it.
But the *tunes* he was playin'—*that* was the thing,
—Like squeezin' honey from the string;
Like milkin' a fiddle—no jerks, no squeaks—
—And the tears upon the misthress' cheeks
She'd often stop him and ask would he change
To a nice slow tune, and Tommy would range
Up and down the strings, and slither
Into the key ; then he'd feather
The bow very fine, and a sort o' hum
Like a bee round a flower, and out it'd come."

L. L. C. Koelle, "Music in Song" (London), 1888.

CHAPTER VI.

THE WOOD—THE MODEL.

The Violin—The Woods used—Chemically prepared Woods—The Qualities of the Woods—" Whole," " Half," and " Slab " Backs—The Model—Method of Copying an Old Model—Method of Drawing a Mathematical Outline.

It is a matter of considerable astonishment to many persons that the fiddle took its present familiar shape, apparently quite suddenly in the sixteenth century, and, in spite of all attempts to change it, and in spite of all experiments made with a view of introducing other forms, has kept it ever since. It is the object of the present and following chapters to explain, (1) Why this form is the best ; and (2) How it is obtained. Many experimentalists, many of them men of undoubted ability (among whom are most noteworthy Chanot and Savart), have applied their skill, science, and labour to the discovery of a model to supersede that which has prevailed from Gasparo da Salo (1555) to the present time ; and, as many of these innovations have been most interesting to all, and especially instructive to the fiddle-maker, I have made these scientific vagaries the subject of a recent chapter (Chapter V., p. 104). At present, I shall confine myself to pointing out the arrangement of the seventy parts of a violin[1] in the manner best calculated to charm by its results the musical ear. And I shall point out the advantages of this generally accepted arrangement, more from a theoretico-scientific point of view than from a purely mechanical one, leaving this latter to its proper place, i.e., to be set down in Part III., when we have acquired sufficient of the theory and science of fiddle-making to be able to put our knowledge into practice.

Let us look first at the *tout ensemble* of a fiddle. What is it?

[1] The seventy parts are made up as follows : Back, 2 ; Belly, 2 ; Blocks, 6 ; Sides, 6 ; Linings, 12 ; Bass Bar, 1 ; Purfling, 24 ; Tail-piece rest, 1 ; Tail-piece, 1 ; Tail-piece fastening, 1 ; Tail-pin, 1 ; Pegs, 4 ; Finger-board, 1 ; Bridge, 1 ; Nut, 1 ; Strings, 4 ; Sound Post, 1 ; Neck and Scroll, 1. The Back and Belly are often formed of one piece only, and the purflings are often let in, in 36 instead of 24 pieces. The Neck also is frequently separate from the Scroll, as will be hereafter seen.

It is a hollow box, from 13 to 14 inches in length, at the widest part $8\frac{1}{2}$ inches, and at the narrowest $4\frac{1}{2}$ inches broad. It is about $2\frac{1}{2}$ inches deep at the deepest part, and weighs about $8\frac{1}{2}$ ounces (avoirdupois).[1] Beyond this we have a neck, terminating in a scroll, which, with pegs, finger-board, and tail-piece of ebony, bring the weight up to about a pound. The wondrous capabilities and wonderful equilibrium of all the parts may be summed up in one short sentence—it supports a tension on the strings of 68 lbs.,[2] and a vertical pressure on the bridge of 26 lbs.[3]

Let me answer my own question, "Why is this form the best?" The only attempt I have ever seen made to answer this question

[1] I here append the exact measurements of noted Stradiuarius instruments as given by M. Vidal. I give them more as mere statistics than as guides for the practical luthier in building a fiddle :—

	1.—VIOLIN.*		2.—VIOLA.†		3.—VIOLONCELLO.‡		
	Millimetres.	in.	Millimetres.	in.	Millimetres.	ft.	in.
Length of body from base of button to tail-pin	355=	14	410=	$16\frac{3}{16}$	750 =	2	$5\frac{17}{32}$
Breadth across upper bouts ...	165=	$6\frac{9}{16}$	185=	$7\frac{5}{16}$	340 =	1	$1\frac{5}{16}$
,, lower ,, ...	206=	$8\frac{3}{16}$	240=	$9\frac{15}{32}$	440 =	1	$5\frac{11}{32}$
,, inner ,, ...	109=	$4\frac{5}{16}$	130=	$5\frac{5}{32}$	240 =	...	$9\frac{15}{32}$
Length of inner bouts, from corner to corner perpendicular)	076=	3	095=	$3\frac{3}{4}$	170 =	...	$6\frac{11}{16}$
Length from base of button to notch of *f f* holes	193=	$7\frac{5}{8}$	220=	$8\frac{11}{16}$	400 =	1	$3\frac{3}{4}$
Height of sides, upper bouts ...	030=	$1\frac{3}{16}$	038=	$1\frac{17}{32}$	118 =	...	$4\frac{21}{32}$
,, inner ,, ...	030=	$1\frac{3}{16}$	038=	$1\frac{17}{32}$	118 =	...	$4\frac{21}{32}$
,, lower ,, ...	031=	$1\frac{1}{4}$	039=	$1\frac{9}{16}$	119 =	...	$4\frac{11}{16}$
Neck, from chin of scroll to base of button	130=	$5\frac{5}{32}$	...	...	...		...
Length of finger-board.........	260=	$10\frac{1}{4}$	...	...	...		...

* Measurements taken from "The Vuillaume," or "La Messie," Stradiuar.

† Measurements taken from Stradiuarius Viola, date 1723, in the possession of M. le Vicomte de Janzé.

‡ Measurements taken from Stradiuarius 'Cello, belonging to M. Franchomme, the celebrated violoncellist.

[2] First string, 23 lbs.; second string, $18\frac{1}{2}$ lbs.; third string, 14 lbs.; fourth string, $12\frac{1}{2}$ lbs. In 1734 Tartini discovered the tension of the strings to be 63 lbs. It must be remembered that in his day strings were thinner and bridges were lower than they are now. L'Abbé Sibire, in 1806, estimated the tension at 64 lbs. In 1835 M. Fétis stated the tension to be 80 lbs., but this is excessive, and is an error.

[3] This weight has, of course, increased to this amount only with the rise of pitch of the present century. L'Abbé Sibire in "La Chelonomie" (*vide* note [2], p. viii. Preface) estimates it (in the year 1806) at only 24 lbs. This indeed was an increase on the pressure of the time of Stradiuarius, and in the time of the Abbé Sibire (1806) certain daring "restorers" (save the mark!) used to place *transverse* bars across the belly to support this increase. This, of course, is never heard of now, being one of those vagaries invented for the enrichment of what M. L'Abbé rather quaintly calls "le luthier instrumenticide."

explicitly, is that of Mr. T. Porter, whose little pamphlet[1] "How to choose a Violin" is, I think, one of the most valuable additions which have of late years been made to the literature of the violin. First of all, the length of the violin, about 13 to 14 inches, is the best possible for the free play of the muscles of the arm, and if it were longer, the tension required to stretch the strings up to pitch would probably break them. The "upper and lower bouts" are rounded so as to resist the strain on the body of the instrument, to allow the hand to come up the finger-board with ease in the high positions, and to take the chin of the performer comfortably; for this latter object the edges are grooved round. The "centre bouts" curve inwards to allow the passage of the bow from string to string, and to enable the bow to put the first and fourth strings into vibration, without having to make the bridge disastrously high (vide p. 161). The "button" holds the "shoulder" of the "neck," so as to help it to resist the strain which would pull it forward.[2] The "bulge" or "arching" of the back and belly resists the strain of the strings and assists the escape of the tone through the "ff holes," which are of the f shape, as conducing to a maximum vibration of the convexity of the belly. These are the reasons why this form is the best. And what are the results of this arrangement? The results are notably three :—Power, Delicacy, and Penetration. Power : for volume and sweetness are imparted to the inaudible vibrations of the string. Delicacy : for the slightest touch of the bow draws forth a tone sweet and true and pure. Penetration : for the tones of the instrument, even when played pianissimo, carry further than ten times the volume of mere noise. The object of the present and following chapters is therefore to give the scientific rules which must regulate the construction and arrangement of the various parts of the instrument with a view to the production of this desired result.

First of all, then, let us consider the materials :—

The Wood.—This is, of course, the first consideration when setting about to make a fiddle. *Ex quovis ligno non fit Mercurius!* And when I speak of the wood, I mean, of course, that used for the back, belly, linings, blocks, neck, scroll, bar, sound-post, and sides of the instrument, without regard to the ebony or rosewood used for the pegs, nut, finger-board, tail-piece, rest, and tail-pin.[2] The wood most generally employed for backs of fiddles is maple, though pear and sycamore are also

[1] T. Porter, "How to choose a Violin, with Directions for Keeping the Instrument in Order," etc. (London, n. d. [1879] : Pitman).
[2] For explanations of these terms *vide* Fig. 39.

sometimes used, and the wood is cut either *sur maille* (on the quarter) or *sur couche* (on the layers). As to these modes of cutting, we shall speak farther on (*vide* p. 133) ; it is the nature and quality of the wood, on which so much depends, that we must now consider. The wood most sought after for bellies is Swiss or Tyrolese white pine, of a fine (not too close), even grain.[1] Both the maple and the pine (says M. Fétis, *vide* note [2], p. 37) should be not only that of the trees growing on the south side of the forest, exposed to the sun, but also only the wood of the south side of the tree should be used. L'Abbé Sibire[2] goes so far as to say that the wood must be taken at a certain distance between the bark and heart of the tree, and between the boughs and root, and should be cut in the months of December or January. According to M. Fétis, in his notice of Anthony Stradivari, the maple used by the old Italian makers came from Croatia, Dalmatia, and even Turkey ; he goes on to say that it was sent to Venice prepared for galley oars, and that the Turks, always at war with the Venetians, took care to select wood with the greatest number of waves in it, *i.e.*, having the curliest grain, in order that it might break the sooner ; that it was from these parts of the wood, intended for the rowers, that the Italian makers chose what suited them for the manufacture of violins. The maple and pine from the Cantons of Schwytz and Lucerne are the best. M. le Docteur Félix Savart,[3] indeed, considered this preference for Swiss and Tyrolese wood to be unfounded, adding that he had made bellies of pino from the Vosges, which was superior to the other sorts of pine when very dry, and when it had *not* been rafted.[4] Simoutre (*vide* note [1], p. 20) gives the following as the order of superiority among pine-woods : first, that which comes from Silesia ; secondly, that which comes from La Valteline, Les Grisons, Le Simmenthal (in the Bernese Oberland), the Valley of the Lac de Joux, and Les Brassus (Canton of Vaud) in Switzerland ; and thirdly, that which comes from the southern slopes of the Jura-Bernois. The best maple to be had for our purpose, is that which grows on the southern slopes of the Carpathians,

---

[1] L'Abbé Sibire, Prince Youssoupof, and Savart mention cedar as material for the belly, but this is an error, or, at any rate, only an experiment.

[2] L'Abbé Sibire, "La Chelonomie, ou le parfait Luthier" (Paris, 1806). 2nd Edition (Brussels, 1823, *vide* note [2], p. viii. Preface).

[3] F. Savart, "Mémoire sur la construction des Instruments à cordes et à archet" (Paris, 1819).

[4] The pine, when cut in the great forests of the Continent, is generally floated down the rivers to its destination in large rafts, which process of transport would naturally affect it and retard its desiccation for purposes of violin-making

and in some parts of the Eastern Alps. It is of the greatest importance that the wood used in fiddle-making should be thoroughly dry and well-seasoned, and for this purpose should be laid fully exposed to the sun and air (but not to rain) for some five or six years, *at least*, before it is used. If the wood is not thoroughly dry before it is used, the chances are that it will shrink or otherwise alter after the fiddle has been made some time, and thus thicknesses properly apportioned (as will be seen further on), at the time the violin leaves the workshop, will, by the final drying of the wood, become out of proportion to the instrument, and the original maker will receive unmerited blame. Stradivari, like many of the other great Cremona makers, had a kind of open shed or awning on the roof of his house in Cremona, where his wood was stored on rafters all ready for use, and this shed is still to be seen by those visitors to Cremona who venture to explore the house of the great luthier.[1] It is well nigh established that no advantage is derived from artificial preparation of the wood, though many recipes for such an operation have been suggested, and, indeed, recommended. There is no doubt that the earlier instruments of Vuillaume were made of wood, baked and otherwise tampered with, operations which certainly improved their immediate appearance, but they could not last, and are now his worst instruments. He himself very soon discarded all artificial preparation. Mr. Bishop, in his translation of Otto's "Treatise on the Violin" (a useful little work, whose value is quadrupled by the translator's valuable and intelligent notes, *vide* note [1], p. 20), mentions a process discovered in 1839 by one Schlick, "for depriving wood of water, acid, resin, etc., by which means he was enabled to make violins with a tone scarcely distinguishable from that of the best old Italian instruments." A bold assertion, truly! (*Credat Judæus Apella, non ego.*)

Amongst others he mentions a process (noticed in the *Bulletin*: Paris, 1822) in operation at Vienna for preparing wood intended to make musical instruments of, by steaming it in a room or chest 10 ft. by 5 ft., made of strong boards well joined. He says, " This steam by penetrating the pores of the wood softens the vegetable parts, and renders them susceptible of being dissolved. The steam condensed in the chest forms, in the lower part, a liquor, at first but slightly coloured, which gets deeper as the operation proceeds; at length it is quite clear, and

[1] The Rev. H. R. Haweis in his most recent work, "My Musical Life" (London, 1884), gives (on p. 314) a most delightful account of a visit to the house of Stradivari in the Piazza San Domenico at Cremona.

The internet (amazon.com) shows
Treatis on structure and Preservation of Violin
by Jacob Augustus Otto, Translated by Bishop

acquires a very decided acid taste. This is let off by a proper pipe. The operation commonly lasts sixty hours. The wood is afterwards taken out and dried in a stove, heated to 42° or 48° Réaumur (=126½° or 140° Fahrenheit). The desiccation lasts two or three days when the boards are half an inch thick ; but if thicker several weeks, or even months, are necessary. This wood acquires such a degree of dryness as to resist all the variations of the atmosphere ; its colour increases in intensity, particularly the wood of the walnut, cherry, or maple. It becomes firmer and more sonorous, which is a great advantage for musical instruments. Violins acquire the quality of the esteemed old instruments, of which the true merit is due perhaps to the slow desiccation which the wood composing them has undergone." Mackintosh, in a pamphlet on the "Construction and Materials employed in the Manufacture of Violins " (Dublin, 1837) remarks :—" I am borne out by traditionary accounts in believing that the Cremona makers actually put their wood through some process for the purpose, not only of preserving, but of cleansing it, and making it, consequently, a better conductor of sound." The same author, according to Mr. Bishop, states that " the wood must be not only of firm and regular texture, but have pores of a certain size and formation ; and, above all, it is essential that it shall have attained not only full maturity of growth, but shall have remained for some years after being felled, in order to make it fit to go through a process, by which the pores (for that is the great object to be arrived at) may be rendered so perfectly dried and cleared as not afterwards to be liable to close or alter their natural position, or become crooked or irregular, as would be the inevitable consequence if cut up immediately into thin pieces, as it is then liable to shrink, which is also objectionable, as being injurious to the pores. . . . When experimenting I have had recourse to steaming, steeping, stoving, boiling, and baking the timber : I have also used all kinds of spirits, caustics, and acids ; but all these disorganized the pores and impaired the fibres of the timber, which ought to be in a sound and perfect state." Mr. Fleming (*vide* note [1], p. 23) claims an advantage from steeping wood in the mother-liquor of salt works, as greatly increasing the elasticity of pine, and he points out the fact that beneath the pine forests of the Tyrol, whence the Italian masters got their wood, there extend considerable salt mines, which, as he justly remarks, had doubtless then, as they have doubtless now, considerable beneficial effects upon the quality of the wood, which they thus *naturally* impregnate, but it is also hopeless to try to produce this natural effect by artificial means.

Abele, in his book " Die Violine,"[1] assures us that there is no proof in existence that the old Italians used any artificial means for drying or preparing their wood. Notwithstanding all that has been written on this point (which would fill a large book), it seems that the wood, if carefully selected, is better if left to nature, to mature and fit for our purposes. Apart from its maturity the maple must be thoroughly sound, without knots or cracks, the grain must run evenly and not in curves or waves. (The reader will distinguish the difference between " grain," and " figure " or " curl," of the wood.) It must be neither too hard nor too soft : if the former, the vibrations will be sluggish and the tone harsh ; if the latter, the tone will be dull and wofully lack brilliancy. Above all things, never dream of using a piece of maple which the worms have touched ever so slightly ; for sooner or later such ravages will either be continued or become the seat of a thousand ills. M. Maugin, in his ' Manuel du Luthier,"[2] mentions a wood, called "azarole," as being used by the Cremonese masters, but states that the wood is unknown to him. So it was to me, until I read the following explanation of the term in M. Simoutre's little brochure.[3] He says :—" Among pine-woods, the species named Epicea, or red pine, *known by the Italians under the name of Azarole*, is the best." The same author gives some interesting notes on the use of plane-wood as a material for backs, stating that a plane-wood back causes a soft and muffled tone in a violin, in distinction to the pure, clear tone of the maple back. I have not verified this by trial, but it is quite probable, owing to the greater density and toughness of the plane-wood.

Lastly, never let the maple be spotted in any way ; for the sake of both appearance and sound the wood should be of a uniform silvery cream colour under the planing-iron. The pine should be quite white and brilliant like silk when split open, avoiding anything like a reddish tinge, which indicates a most unhealthy growth. The grain must not be too close or too wide, and must be disposed evenly and straight from top to bottom of the belly. The grain of the back should also run from top to bottom of the instrument. One is often asked, why the belly should not have the grain setting crossways, and it is often argued that the best makers have sometimes cut their backs so that the grain ran across them. In the

---

[1] H. Abele, " Die Violine, ihre Geschichte und ihr Bau " (Neuberg, A.D. 1864 ; 2nd Edition, 1874).

[2] Maugin et Maigne, " Nouveau Manuel Complet du Luthier " (Paris, 1869), p. 9. 1st Edition by J. C. Maugin alone, " Manuel du Luthier " (Paris, 1834)

[3] N. E. Simoutre, " Aux Amateurs du Violon. Historique, Construction, Réparation et Conservation de cet instrument " (Bâle, 1883). *Vide* note [1], p. 20.

first case experiment has proved to us that the vibrations are transmitted along the fibres of wood quickest in this position and under these circumstances, and in the second it will be remarked that the tone of the Cremonese masterpieces is always most brilliant when this perpendicular setting of the grain has been adhered to. Care must be taken to select the pine neither too hard nor too soft in texture, and without any defect, knot, stain, or other fault.

Deal owes its great recommendation for bellies to its slight density, elasticity, and vibratory powers. If a rod of steel, another of glass, and another of deal be taken of identical dimensions, they will, when similarly struck, produce the same note ; therefore, of these three bodies deal is equal in elasticity and immeasurably superior in lightness. Maple is much more slow to vibrate than deal, and consequently a fourth rod made of maple would give a lower note than that made of deal ; and consequently the back of a violin (maple) when struck, or vibrated alone with a bow, would yield a lower note than the belly (deal), if the plates were of the same thickness, but being made of *different* thicknesses, the back, when finished, is about a tone HIGHER than the belly when finished by the cutting of the *ff* holes and the affixing of the bass bar.[1] And M. Fétis, in his " Notice of Anthony Stradivari "[2] (a book much more instructive to the practical luthier than its title would denote), fixes this difference of sonority at exactly one tone, and M. Savart coincides in (though he has sometimes been made to contradict) this statement, and his numerous experiments went to prove that if by a reduction of the thickness of the back it were made to coincide in intonation with the belly, a feeble and unsatisfactory tone would characterize the fiddle so formed. If the difference were less than a tone, the tone of the instrument would be throbbing, and if more than a tone an even more unsatisfactory result would be

---

[1] Nearly every author who has written on this subject has declared that *the back should be a tone lower* than the belly. It is useless (as many of them probably never actually *made* a fiddle) to persuade them that exactly the reverse is the case. Mr. Davidson is the only author who ever reproduced M. Savart's *right* words on this point. All the others have made him say that the back should be a tone lower : the verbatim report of his own words is in *L'Institut* (" Sciences mathématiques, physiques, et naturelles," Nos. 319, 321, 323, 327), where he rightly states that the back should give a tone *higher* than the belly. It is extraordinary that such an error should have so long been an authority. Mr. Bishop, indeed, seriously criticises and reproves the correction of his own error, or rather the *correct* rendering of his own authority. Let any one make a fiddle, and this will be proved to him more satisfactorily than by a volume of " premeditated pleonasm " on the point.

[2] F. J. Fétis, " Notice of A. Stradivari," translated by J. Bishop (London, 1864). *Vide* note [2], p. 37.

obtained. To ascertain the normal tone of a plate of wood, it must be clamped firmly at a point where two nodal lines cross one another,[1] and vibrated with a bow drawn along the edge. The note it then renders is the lowest of which it is capable, and is called "its normal tone." Some interesting experiments of this kind have been made with some fragments of Stradivarius violins of various dates. Thus :—rods were made $7\frac{3}{4}$ inches long, $\frac{3}{4}$ inch broad, and $\frac{1}{8}$ inch thick of maple and deal from one of these fiddles which had been destroyed. Two rods of maple, one plain, the other figured, dated respectively 1708 and 1717, gave, when struck, identically the same note. Three rods of deal, dated 1690, 1724, and 1730, gave identically another higher note,[2] and the coincidence of tone with the disparity of dates and appearance must surely indicate that Stradivari had a standard of acoustic intonation, and relation between back and belly, to which he paid more attention than the mere appearance of his fiddles. (*Vide* Fétis' "Notice of A. Stradivari " [note [2], p. 37], p. 78.)

Let it be noted that blocks or planks for fiddle-making should not be cut with a saw, but split with the axe, as the marks of the saw will hide any defects in the wood, which would at once be revealed on the shining silky surface of a plank or block split open by the axe, and besides this splitting with the axe ensures the fibres being left whole and straight, and not cut into as they are by the teeth of the saw. In Chapter III. I made frequent use of the terms " whole," " half," or " slab " backs, referring to the way in which the wood forming that part of the instrument was cut, and I here give a woodcut of a section of a tree trunk (Fig. 77) with cuttings to explain these terms. As bellies are almost invariably joined, and very 'requently (nay, almost always) backs are cut in this manner, I will shortly explain this figure before proceeding. It represents a trunk cut at D " on the layers " (*sur couche*) for the whole back, and at A " on the quarter" (*sur maille*) for the half or joined back. The wedge A is squared at the thick end

---

[1] I have tried to exclude such terms as these from this work, as being difficult to understand, and confusing. This one, however, I cannot avoid. If a plate be strewed with sand and then vibrated with a bow, the sand arranges itself in certain lines, called " nodal lines." It is at a point where two of these cross one another that the plate must be clamped. As good a way as any is to place a piece of cork near the edge of the bench, balance the plate on it, and hold it firmly with the finger, pressing it on to the cork. The edge overhanging the edge of the bench may then be vibrated with a well rosined bow.

[2] The belly (deal) here also sounded higher than the back (maple). *Parfaitement !* because the rods were identical in point of size and volume In the mass (*i.e.*, the whole plates) the intonation of the back and belly is found to vary correctly, the former being a tone higher than the latter.

and redivided down the middle, as shown at B ; the two halves are then joined at the broad ends in the manner shown at C. It is often asked why backs and bellies are so often joined when it would be simpler to construct them all in one piece. The reason (setting aside the fact that this form of cutting is nearly always far prettier than the " whole " or " slab " form) is, that it is very seldom that you find a wedge of deal or maple good for fiddle-making of sufficient breadth to make a fiddle back or belly out of it without joining (*i.e.*, in the " whole " form), and it is better to have both halves of your tables acoustically good, than to let the unsuitability of the wood of one side of the back or belly counteract the good qualities of the other. " Slab " backs,

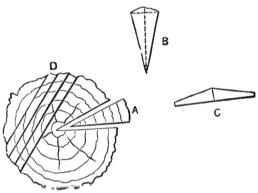

Fig. 77.—Diagram explaining methods of cutting wood for Violin-making. A, wedge cut *sur maille*. B, the wedge marked for cutting. C, the wedge cut and joined. D, planks cut *sur couche*.

i.e., cut as at D Fig. 77, are of course always all in one piece. The model, or outline, is then traced on the flat surface, cut out with a fret-saw and file, and the work proceeds. At D is shown the cutting for slab form ; the planks thus cut are worked without any further preparation. A " whole " back is so called when it is made out of the breadth of the wedge in the manner laid down in another place. (*Vide* Part III., p. 285, Fig. 177.) As much depends upon the model you cannot be too careful to draw an outline correct in every particular, and for this purpose either copy some old master, or trace an outline for yourself mathematically in the manner to be hereinafter laid down. A word about storing wood to mature. It is best to keep the maple stored in wedges, blocks and strips for the back, neck, scroll, and sides ; the pine also in wedges, for the belly ; in these forms they occupy but little space, and are ready to hand when wanted. The maple for the backs is cut into wedges 15 inches long, by 5 inches broad, being 1⅝ inch thick at the thick side, and ¾ inch at the thin side (B Fig. 77). The maple for the neck should be in blocks (also slightly wedge-shaped) 10½ inches long, 2¾ inches broad, the thick edge 2 inches deep, the thin 1½ inches, and that destined to make the sides should be cut into strips 15½ inches long, by 1⅜ inches broad by 1/16 inch thick. The pine for the belly should be in wedges 15 inches long by 5 inches broad, 1⅝ inches thick at the thick side, and ¾ inch thick on the thin side. The object and convenience of keeping the woods in these dimensions will become apparent when we reach the practical part of our work.

The Model.—To copy an old master's model. Having decided what fiddle you will copy, very carefully remove the belly of the instrument to be reproduced. This is done by applying a rather blunt knife to the edges where the belly is glued to the sides in the manner described farther on (*vide* p. 306). This done, the belly or back is held down on to the planks of deal and sycamore prepared for the belly and back of your fiddle, and the outline sharply and cleanly traced round it with a sharp pencil or point. This is a very certain, and the most convenient way, if you happen

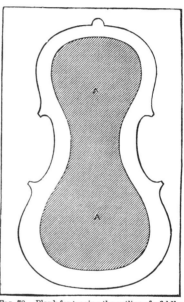

FIG. 78.—Plank for tracing the outline of a fiddle.

to have access to a good instrument in course of repair, but if not, the following method is a very good one. Take a piece of thin, stiff wood, rather longer than, and about one and a-half times as broad as the violin you wish to copy, and cut a piece out of the centre about two inches smaller than the approximate outline of the said violin as at A in Fig. 78, which shows a guitar-shaped cutting. If this be laid upon the fiddle it will lie flat round the outline, the guitar-shaped opening receiving the bulge or arching of the back, which would otherwise interfere with the tracing. The outline may then be traced round (as in the figure), and you will have an exact tracing of an entire outline. To copy the rise or arching of the back or belly, proceed as follows: Take a piece of wood, **2 inches** across, ½ an inch thick, and a little longer than the body of the instrument you wish to copy.   Place this edgeways on, and at right angles to, the back or belly, holding it firmly, or wedging it at the ends, so that it cannot see-saw on the rise in the middle. Take a pair of compasses with a fine point or lead, and opening them about an inch, place one point sideways on the back or belly, so that the other point touches the piece of wood held at right angles to it ; then draw the point touching the surface to be copied, down the centre of that surface, so that the arm touching the piece of wood will, by following the motion of the lower arm, exactly reproduce on the lath thus held for the purpose, the contour of the back and belly to be copied.   Be very careful that the wood is held, and the lower arm is drawn down the exact centre of the surface being reproduced.   Similar models should be taken of the rise across (i) the broadest part of the upper bouts, (ii) the narrowest part of the inner bouts, and (iii) the broadest part of the lower bouts.

To trace an independent outline mathematically on a given, graduated, perpendicular straight line, you must proceed as follows.   And I beg, before commencing the explanation of this operation, which is illustrated by Fig. 79, to record my indebtedness to Mr. John Bishop, by whose courtesy I am enabled to reproduce this diagram and descriptive letterpress from his translation of Otto's work on the construction of the violin (*vide* note [1], p. 20) :—

Draw a perpendicular line down the middle of a sheet of paper or of the flat side of the piece of wood intended for the back, of the *exact* length required for the body of the instrument (without the button *b*, Fig. 79), and divide it into 72 equal parts, as shown in the figure.   This must be done with the greatest accuracy, for on it depends the correctness of the whole.

Then intersect this perpendicular, by 20 horizontal lines at the points named below.

Line (1) A at the point	8		Line (11) L at the point	33
„ (2) B „	14		„ (12) M „	34
„ (3) C „	16		„ (13) N „	37
„ (4) D „	20		„ (14) O „	39
„ (5) E „	21½		„ (15) P „	40
„ (6) F „	22		„ (16) Q „	44½
„ (7) G „	23		„ (17) R „	48
„ (8) H „	27		„ (18) S „	55
„ (9) I „	28		„ (19) T „	56
„ (10) K „	31		„ (20) V „	65

This being done, open the compasses to an extent of **9 parts** of the perpendicular, and describe the two arcs *a a* from the point b. Then place the compasses on the point 24, and opening them to b, draw the curve $a\,b\,a$.

Next set off 2 parts c, on each side of the perpendicular, on the horizontal line c. Place the compasses on the point c, and opening them to a, draw the curves $d\,d$, from a to the horizontal line A.

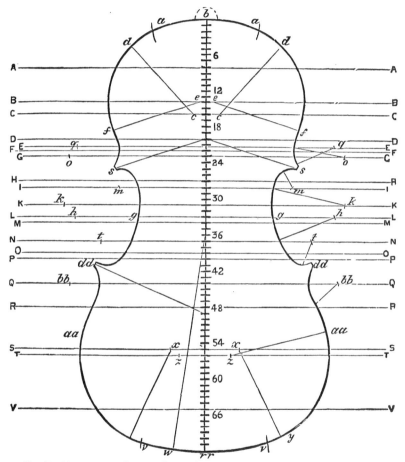

Fig. 79.—Method of drawing an outline mathematically on a given graduated straight line.

Now set off one part e, on each side of the perpendicular on the line B. Place the compasses on these points, and opening them to the line A, where the curve d ends, draw the curves f from the line A to that of D. This completes the draught of the upper portion of the instrument without the corners.

For the middle or narrow portion proceed thus:—On the horizontal line L set off 11⅓ parts from the perpendicular to the point *g ;* and then 11 other parts, from *g* to *h*, from which latter point draw the curve from the line L to that of P.

Next set off 23¾ parts on the line K, from the perpendicular to *k ;* open the compasses to the point where the curve *i* intersects the line M, and draw the curve from the line M to that of H. The little angle formed by the curves b tween the lines L and M, must be worked off so as to bring the sides into proper shape.

The lower portion is obtained as follows :—Open the compasses 11 parts, and describe the two arcs *v v* from the point *r r*. Then place the compasses on the point 35, and opening them to *r r*, draw the curve *v w v*.

Next set off 6 parts *x* on each side of the perpendicular on the line S. Place the compasses on the point *x*, and opening them to *v*, draw the curves *y y* from *v* to the line V.

Now set off 4 parts *z* on each side of the perpendicular on the line T. Place the compasses on these points, and opening them to the line V, where the curve *y* ends, draw the curves *a a* from the line V to that of R.

For the upper corners, set off 24½ parts on the line G, from the perpendicular to *o*, and placing the compasses on this point, open them to the line D, where the curve *f* ends, and draw the curve from the line D to that of F.

Then on the line I set off 14⅔ parts from the perpendicular to *m*. Place the compasses on this point, and opening them to line H where the curve ends, draw the curve from the line H to *s*.

Now on the line E set off 22 parts from the perpendicular to *q*. Place the compasses on this point, and opening them to where the curve meets the line F, draw the curve from the line F to *s*. Again place the compasses on the point 20, and opening them 16⅓ parts mark off the length of the corners *s s*.

For the lower corners set off 24 parts on the line Q from the perpendicular to *b b*, and, placing the compasses on this point, open them to the line R, where the curve *a a* ends, and draw the curve from the line R to *d d*.

Then on the line N set off 16½ parts from the perpendicular to *t*. Place the compasses on this point, and, opening them to where the curve meets the line P, draw the curve from the last-named line to *d d*.

FIG. 79A.—Method of tracing rise of arching along centre join of Fig. 79.

Lastly, place the compasses on the point 49, and, opening them 19¾ parts, mark off the length of the corners *d d, d d.*

This completes the entire model, and the belly can now be marked from the back thus traced.

To obtain the proper rise or height for the back or belly, take a thin piece of hard wood, about 2 inches broad, and a little longer than the violin you propose to make (Fig. 79A), and mark it in the middle at the point A, which must be three " parts " (of the foregoing scale) distant from the edge, shown here by the dotted line. Then, placing a large pair of compasses on the point A, open them 216 parts, or three times the length of the body of the instrument, and with this radius describe the arc shown in the figure, which, by being sawed out, will serve as a guide for the height or rise required.

The small semicircular piece seen at the top of Fig. 79 is the " button," which is part of the back, and made in one piece with it, to which is glued the shoulder when the neck is fixed to the body.

This method of tracing an outline (which has been given by more than one author) is, though terribly complicated, the most ingenious piece of mechanical drawing I have ever come across. Nowadays any one can get access to a good outline, which may be copied as before set down, but I have given the above method as it is extremely interesting, and clever in construction.

Vivebam in sylvis, et tunc sine voce cupressus
Mortua facta chelys, nunc ego vocem habeo.

CHAPTER VII.

THE BACK, BELLY, AND SIDES.

The Thicknesses of the Back and Belly—Copyists—The Sides—Mass of Air contained in a Fiddle—Height of the Sides.

I HAVE described the models and the modes of tracing them ; it remains, therefore, to notice the relative thicknesses of the different parts of the back and belly of a properly proportoned fiddle. Important as is the selection of wood acoustically good, it must be appreciated at once, that the tone of the instrument depends quite as much on the wood being properly cut and apportioned, as on the wood itself, for it stands to reason, that however good the material may be, its intrinsic merit must be absolutely nullified if it fall into the hands of an unskilful workman. Of course, to lay down hard and fast rules to fix the proper amount of wood to be left in an instrument, either in the back or in the belly, would be quite impossible, for it must necessarily vary with the quality of the wood : thus the closer the grain and the harder the material, the thinner must it be left ; and the proportions which would be perfect with one piece of wood, might produce a very unsatisfactory result with another.

It is always, however, better to err on the side of excess than of meanness, for the best authorities allow that an instrument with plenty of wood left in it has a much finer tone than one which has been chiselled down to a minimum of thickness ; and again, instruments which have been spared the chisel in their infancy (*Haud inscius ac non incautus futuri!*) have a much better chance of maturing to perfection than weaker ones. The great thing is to avoid extremes. If too thin, the tone of the fiddle will be weak and feeble ; if too thick, the result will be a sluggish, dull tone ; in fact, the elasticity of the deal, and the rapidity with which it transmits sound, will be neutralized by the quantity of it which has to be put into vibration. It is in the adjustment and regulation of these thicknesses that the true talent of the fiddle-maker asserts itself, or is conspicuous by its absence. In high breasted models (like the German, for instance) the consequently necessary thinning out of the wood under the finger-board causes such a weakness at this point, that the neck is very apt to be dragged forward by the strings, the wood of the belly not being strong enough to resist the pressure at this point, and good tone is rendered an impossibility.

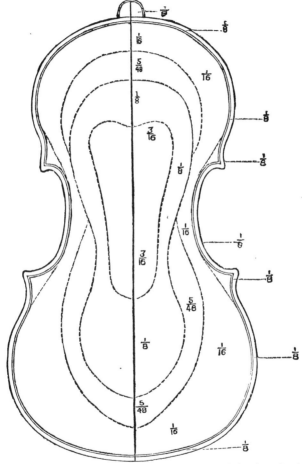

Fig. 80.—Diagram of a well-seasoned back, with thicknesses in fractions of an inch.

To obviate the difficulty of these variations in the quality of the wood, and the obscurity which would be involved in a long verbal description, and to serve as a guide for the amateur fiddle-maker, I have obtained a back and belly from well-made violins, which I have very carefully gauged all over, and made maps of (reproduced in Figs. 80 and 81), with imaginary lines on them, to denote where the thicknesses merge into one another, as far as it is possible to determine those boundaries; and I

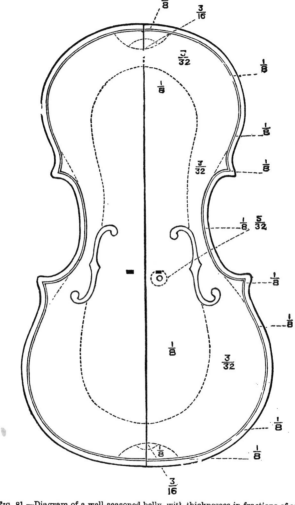

Fig. 81.—Diagram of a well-seasoned belly, with thicknesses in fractions of an inch.

present these two diagrams to my readers with every confidence in their practical value. The thicknesses, as they merge into one another, are indicated in fractions of an inch, and may be taken as those of the average number of violins; **the denser the wood**, of course, the thinner it will be, but the proportions remain the same. The margins beyond the purfling (which is the extreme edge which overlaps the sides), and in Fig. 80 the button at the top, have no influence on the vibration of the plates, and are left to the discretion, art, or instinct of the fiddle-maker; naturally, a good strong obtuse edge has a tendency to strengthen the entire instrument. In Fig. 81 it will be seen that the thicknesses are very uniform, in the semi-circular pieces at the top and bottom, having the thickness of $\frac{1}{8}$, the wood is merely left flat to fasten on to the blocks, and the little pieces left thicker $(\frac{3}{16})$ in each of these semicircles are caused by the rise of the belly. The little triangular pieces in the corners (in both figures) are left thick $(\frac{1}{8})$ for the same purpose. In reality the thickest part of the belly (Fig. 81) is, it will be seen, just over the sound-post, but it is only *just* thicker $(\frac{1}{32})$ (as will be seen in the figure) than the surrounding wood, and this slight increase covers a space of about a shilling.[1]

Before dismissing this question of thicknesses, a word about copies. Of these, there are two sorts: Firstly, the genuine copy made by the skilful workman, who recognizes a high original, and tries, not unsuccessfully, to obtain the same results, by making his bran new fiddle exactly what the master-pieces of the Amati, the Guarneri, and Stradivari were, when they were bran new, and leaving time to work its magical improvements. Such were the instruments of Panormo, Lupot, Vuillaume, and others. And, secondly, the vile imitation which leaves the workshop dirty, damaged, and otherwise disfigured by artificial age, produced in a few hours by the artful fiddle-forger. These sham antiques can generally be told by the abominable smell which characterizes their insides, and which is the result of the acids, etc., used to prematurely age the modern work. The first are left properly proportioned, and with their proper age and parents recorded inside them; the second, being antedated some centuries, are thinned down to aid the deception, and the time which should perfect, only destroys them. This was the great fault of Peter Walmsley, and applies to the forgeries, more or less artistic, which are turned out every year by the wholesale fiddle trade. "The *wholesale* fiddle trade." *Ô tempora! O mores!*

The Sides.—People are apt to imagine that the six strips of maple wood which compose the sides of the violin have no

---

[1] These are, of course, the thicknesses of an old and seasoned back and belly. The thicknesses set down further on in the practical directions for *new* instruments, it will be seen, vary slightly from these.

influence on the tone, and consequently serve no other purpose than to keep the whole structure together. It is true they do not vibrate themselves, but they help in a great measure to transmit the vibrations of the belly to the back; and on their proper measurement and height depends the volume of air contained in the interior of the instrument; and the importance of this point cannot be better expressed than in the words of M. Fétis, who says:[1] "The intensity of the sounds rendered by the violin depends upon the mass of air contained within it, which ought to be in a certain relation with the other elements, a relation which it is here the question to determine. By a series of ingenious experiments, made with an apparatus which permitted the mass of air in a violin to be augmented or diminished at pleasure,[2] we are assured that if the strings are put into vibration while the mass of air is at a medium, we obtain sounds at once mellow and powerful; if the volume of air be too great, the low notes are weak and dull, and the high ones sharp and thin; if it be too little, the low notes are coarse, and those of the first string lose their brilliancy. If we examine the sound produced by the air in the body of the instrument, when the tone rendered by the strings is most beautiful and intense, we find that it keeps within certain limits, which depend on the form and the other elements of the instrument. In trying the mass of air contained in several instruments of Stradivarius by means of a wind conductor formed of a simple brass tube slightly conical, and flat at its larger end, so as to leave only a little slit for the escape of the air, it was found by placing the flat end of this apparatus over one of the f holes, and blowing through the other end, that the air always produced a sound corresponding to 512 vibrations in a second, which was that of the Middle C in the time of Stradivarius, but which in 1838 (when Savart made his experiments) answered to B natural (a semi-tone below). Through the excessive rise in the pitch for about the last eighteen years the sound produced by 512 vibrations is now nearly in unison with B flat. All the excellent violins of Stradivarius and Guarnerius have yielded the same result. This then is another fact acquired for science: the air contained in a violin should produce a sound equal to 512 vibrations in a second, when set in motion by the apparatus of which we have spoken. If the intonation of the air be higher, the low notes of

[1] "Notice of Anthony Stradivari," p. 84 (*vide* note [2], p. 37).
[2] This was a flat, square violin, with a chamber attached to it at right angles, in which worked a piston, which permitted the mass of air contained in the instrument to be increased or diminished at pleasure. The strings were vibrated whilst the piston was worked, and when they sounded best the mass of air was found to produce a note corresponding to 512 vibrations in a second.

the instrument are dry ; if lower, the notes of the first string are sluggish and dull, and those of the fourth resemble the notes of a tenor." M. Fétis goes on to say that though it is not probable that Stradivari made such experiments as this, yet his skilful hand, guided by his knowledge of his own work, always enabled him, by the model or arching of his violin, the outline, and the height of the sides, to produce an identical interior capacity.

In the same way the body of air inside a violoncello must be equally scientifically proportioned to the depth of the tone it is destined to produce, and as the correct capacity would too greatly enlarge the outline if made in the proportion of a violin, the difficulty is obviated by giving to the instrument an increased depth. Therefore it is a great pity that many writers have loosely stated (doubtless with the best intentions) that " the proportions of the fiddle, the tenor, the bass, and the double-bass should be all identical with one another." The late J. B. Vuillaume constructed some tenors the dimensions of which were arranged so as to produce the *quality* of tone of the violin, but they were found to be too cumbrous to be of much practical value (*vide* p. 108). The measurements of the sides of a violin, as nearly as it is possible to set them down, are as follows : they should have a uniform thickness of $\frac{1}{24}$ of an inch at the most. M. Savart has remarked that the lower the sides are, the thinner they must be, and he has observed that when they are fairly strong they lend a certain softness to the tone of the fiddle. In the lower bouts they should be $1\frac{1}{4}$ inches deep, diminishing gradually $\frac{1}{16}$ to the upper bouts, where they should be $1\frac{5}{32}$ broad. With an ordinary elevation of the model and outline, the above dimensions will produce the desired capacity of air inside the instrument, especially with the flatter models like those of Stradivarius and Joseph del Jesù. When the outline is large, and the arching high, the sides should be rather shallower, as in the instruments of Paul Maggini. L'Abbé Sibire, in " La Chelonomie," says that if a violin be too small in model-dimensions the first string will be brilliant, the second fair, the third tolerable, out the fourth dull and harsh ; but that if, on the contrary, the model be too voluminous, the first string will be weak, the second nasal. the third very full but uncertain, the fourth soft and hollow, like a viola. These faults are more likely to be produced by the rise or arching of the back and belly than the actual size of the outline ; the most typical specimens of these two errors are the almost flat instruments of Cuni, a little-known maker of the eighteenth century, and the great tubby instruments of some of

the Klotz family, and of the German school generally. Some
of the old fiddle-makers lined the sides of their fiddles with
paper or cloth. Stradivari himself is said to have done this
sometimes, but the practice is entirely abandoned, as it does
not improve the stability of the sides, and certainly injures
the tone.

"Vissi nel bosco un di: poi caddi steso
Per dura scure: ma, se tacqui tanto
La divina dell' uomo arte m'ha reso
La vita! . . . e or canto!!"

CHAPTER VIII.

THE INTERIOR OF THE VIOLIN.

The Blocks—The Side Linings—The Sound Post—Its Measurement—Position in the Fiddle—Functions of the Sound Post—Petizeau's Sound Post—Hänsel's —Davidson's—The Bass Bar—Its Measurements—Position in the Fiddle—The Old Bars—Vagaries attempted with the Bass Bar.

The Blocks.—These are the six pieces of wood which being fixed at the top, bottom, and corners (F, Fig. 82) of a violin, serve to strengthen the whole structure, and thereby give a firm base for the vibrations of the back and belly,[1] and there is no doubt that they perform a considerable duty in transmitting the vibrations of the belly to the back in the same way as the sound-post and the sides. In some of the commonest and most inferior fiddles which come into the market, the corner blocks and side linings are altogether omitted. It is hardly necessary to comment on the utter worthlessness of such instruments, which, however, are now happily only to be found in toy shops, or at the most inferior musical warehouses. The blocks are made of pine, of an even and not too wide grain (which is set perpendicularly to the back and belly), excepting in the instruments of Stradivarius, who nearly always used willow for his blocks, doubtless with the object of giving a greater specific lightness to his instruments. The top and bottom blocks should have a length of 2 inches, a breadth of $\frac{9}{16}$ inch, and a height of course identical with that of the sides. The corner blocks should just fill up the corners (as in the figure), so as to produce the guitar-shape that the interior of a violin would present if the corners were removed. The greatest care must be exercised, in fitting the blocks to a fiddle, to use the smallest quantity of glue so as to fix them most closely, accurately, and immovably to the sides, to avoid the catastrophe of their coming loose. The tail-pin (G, Fig. 82) is fastened into a hole bored through the middle *of the breadth*, rather *below* the *middle of the height* of the bottom block. The neck fits into a chamber cut *through* the upper bouts into the top block, as is hereafter

[1] Fig. 82 represents the interior *only* of a violin, *i.e.*, the *sides* are not represented.

laid down. In olden days the neck was often fixed to the back with a nail or screw, an expedient extremely deleterious to the fiddle, and I have seen instruments in which the top block was dispensed with altogether, the shoulder being extended into the

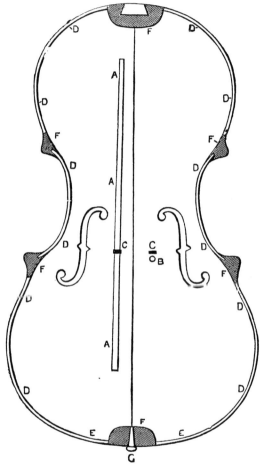

FIG. 82.—The Interior of the Violin.

body of the instrument sufficiently far to act as the top block of the violin.

The Side Linings.—These are the twelve strips of wood which run round the top and bottom of the sides (D D, Figs. 82 and 83), and connect the blocks with one another. They are made of the

same wood as the blocks,[1] which they touch, but do not run
into them (except in the cases of Stradivari and Guarneri, who
used to prolong the linings of the *centre* bouts into the corner
blocks, as shown in Fig. 82, and hereinafter laid down, *vide*
Fig. 142). It is needless to say they run in the direction of the
grain of the wood of which they are made. As shown in the
section (Fig. 83), they are wedge-shaped, being $\frac{1}{16}$ inch in
diameter, where they join the back or belly, and slant down
(or up) to a fine point. They are $\frac{5}{16}$ of an inch deep, and serve
the purpose of strengthening the sides when the back and belly
are glued on to them, for otherwise the extreme thinness of the
sides ($\frac{1}{24}$) would not be enough to ensure the stability of the
juncture. The same remark applies as to fitting them very
closely and evenly to the sides, as to the fitting of the blocks.

The Sound Post, with the *Bass Bar*, constitutes the entire
nervous system of the fiddle, and on their proper construction and
position depends the tone of the in-
strument. By a wrong arrangement of the sound post or bass bar,
what are termed " wolf-notes " are
produced, and when present, they
may generally be cured by the proper adjustment of the bar or post.

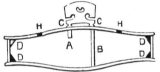

FIG. 83.—Section of the Violin across
the *f f* holes.

The sound post is a little round stick of fine, even-grained pine,
varying, of course, in length with the distance from each other
of the back and belly of the fiddle, both of which it must
just firmly touch. It must not be long enough to force the
back and belly apart ever so slightly, and must not be so
short as to fall down when the instrument receives a jerk,
or when the strings are let down. The violin, as I have said
before, must be so constructed as to be able to sustain the
pressure of the strings without giving way. If the sound post,
in addition to its most important duties (set out below), has to
bear a part in sustaining the belly, or if originally it is cut too
long, the result will be a feeble tone ; for the sound post will in
this case check the vibrations of the belly, instead of communicating them to the back. It has a diameter of $\frac{1}{4}$ inch, and its
fibres must form a right angle with, that is, must be set *across*,
the fibres of the belly. Its diameter must be, to a certain extent,
adapted to the fiddle in which it is set, for if it is too slight the
tone will be thin, and if it is too thick the tone will be rendered
dull. Its exact position depends entirely upon the quality and

[1] J. A. Otto says that the side linings are made of maple, but this is an error
They are always pine, unless the blocks are made of willow, in which case the
linings are made of the same wood.

peculiarities of the fiddle, and must be carefully regulated by an experienced workman, but it is almost invariably within ½ inch behind the right foot of the bridge, as indicated at B, in Figs. 82 and 83. A high-built instrument will require the sound post nearer the bridge than a flatter model. It is the more important to trust this work only to a skilled hand, for the only access to it being through the right-hand f hole, an inexperienced operator is very apt to destroy the appearance of this f hole, not to mention injuries to the internal surfaces of the fiddle. A poor violin is often improved by placing the post nearer the bridge, but a violin thus arranged requires very careful playing to render the tone even. When, though even, the tone is rough and harsh, the post must be moved back a little ; if the high strings are weak and the lower ones harsh, the post must be moved a little outwards towards the f hole ; if the low notes are weak and the high ones shrill, it must be moved very slightly towards the centre. Experiments have been tried, placing it behind the left foot, but the pressure of the two left-hand strings being lighter than that of the two high ones, it would not be so much acted upon in this position, and again, following an argument set out a little further on, it would cause the production of short fibre vibrations where long ones are required, and *vice versâ*. So important, indeed, is the action of this little post on the tone of the instrument, that the French term for it is " *l'âme* " (the soul) ; without it the tone of a fiddle is harsh and feeble, but with it the effect again becomes good. M. Savart has made many most interesting experiments on the functions and action of the sound post, amongst which were the following.

He removed the sound post from a violin, and applied it *outside*, and on the top of the belly by means of two uprights on the corner blocks, and a crossbar, between which and the belly the sound post was set up. Again, fixing this arch to the back of the instrument ; by cutting a hole in the back, he set the post up against the belly, *without touching* the back at all. Again, removing the sound post altogether, he applied a weight to the belly, and in all these three experiments the same results were produced, as if the sound post were there in its normal position. In fact, the same effect is produced whether the post presses against the belly outside by means of the arch, or the belly is pressed against it by means of a clamp. It was based upon this peculiarity that Hawkins in 1800 patented his violin, in which the back and sides were replaced by a bar, and a spring in place of the sound post, which produced the same effect (as far as mere *noise* was concerned) as if the post had been still there. This and similar vagaries have been mentioned in a previous chapter. The object of the sound post is not so much to communicate the vibrations of the belly to the back, as to render the vibrations of the two plates similar (or normal), *whilst* it communicates them. If, instead of being continuous, the vibration of the string were instantaneous, like that of a guitar, the sound post would only deaden the sound. It is for this cause that the pizzicato note on a violin has no resonance, unless the sound post be absent, when it is as full as a guitar note.

The sound post has, therefore, the same effect upon the belly and back as the bow has on the strings ; it continues the vibrations and keeps them regular with one another. The succession of shocks given to the strings by the bow, are communicated to the back by the sound post, and, being placed just behind the right foot of the bridge, it holds it firmly there, whilst it allows the vibrations of the left foot to be transmitted to the bass bar beneath it, which directs the vibrations of the belly. To prove this, if a hole be cut in the belly, so that the right foot of the bridge rests on the top of the sound post without touching the belly at all, the effect of the post is not neutralized or destroyed, and the left foot acts upon the bar as usual. Again, if in another violin the wood is cut out from under the left foot, so that the left foot cannot communicate with the belly, but is independently supported, and to allow this the bar is shifted to the middle of the belly, the sound post being in its normal position with regard to the right foot of the bridge, the effect of the sound post is produced, though the effect of the bar is neutralized.

These, then, are the functions of the sound post, and to make it perform those functions properly, the greatest care should be exercised in determining its position, and pressure on the back and belly. It must, however, be borne in mind, that every time the post is moved the equilibrium of the instrument is deranged, and it will take some time to get accustomed to the change, and as these changes are naturally deleterious to the fiddle, they must be made as seldom as possible. As I have said before, the mass of air contained in a fiddle ought to yield a certain note (*vide* p. 144) ; if the post is too short, a lower note will be produced, and the upper notes of the violin will suffer ; if it is too long, the contrary will happen. In fact, if your sound post is too short, it will have the same effect as if the back and belly had been worked too thin, and *vice versâ*. It sometimes, however, occurs, that when a sound post has been made of unseasoned wood, it contracts after being set in a fiddle ; this, if suspected, should be ascertained by relaxing all the strings, when, if the sound post has shrunk, it will fall, and a new

one must be put in, fulfilling the proper conditions. **A few**
years ago, M. Petizeau announced to the Academy of Sciences
in Paris that considerable advantages were to be derived from
the use of *a hollow glass* sound post, and in the *Allgemeine
Musikalische Zeitung*, for 1881 (p. 75), one John Anthony
Hänsel, a luthier and musician, pronounces in favour of a
broad, flat, and thin sound post, though difficult to adjust, and
requiring great accuracy to ensure success. Mr. P. Davidson
claims especial merit for a sound post, which he calls "an
ancient form lately re-adopted," which is made as follows :
"Drill a longitudinal hole through a square, clean piece of
cedar wood, about $\frac{1}{8}$ of an inch in diameter ; now drill a
number of holes crossways through two opposite sides, so as
to have a space of about $\frac{1}{2}$ an inch between each ; then in the
other two sides of the square drill a number of holes of the
same size as the preceding, so as to pass through the middle
of the former spaces, in a direction thus crossways to the
others ; now reduce and cut the post to its proper rounded
dimensions, and fit it to the violin in the usual manner." This
operation is, of course, superfluous and ridiculous, but is
interesting as showing how complicated may become even so
simple a piece of mechanism as the sound post of a fiddle.

The *Bass* Bar or *Sound* Bar, which is the other great nervous
regulator of a fiddle, is the bar of fine soft even-grained pine,
about $10\frac{1}{2}$ inches long, which extends along the belly of the fiddle
in a slightly oblique direction, underneath the left foot of the
bridge (A, Figs. 82 and 83). This obliquity of position is often
much exaggerated, on paper, in diagrams, and in the fiddle itself
The right deviation, measured from the centre join of the belly, is
as follows : at the top it is $\frac{15}{20}$ or $\frac{3}{4}$ inch from the centre join ; in
the centre, under the bridge it increases to $\frac{16}{20}$ or $\frac{4}{5}$ inch; at the
bottom end it has increased the distance to $\frac{17}{20}$ or $\frac{5}{6}$; a total
deviation of $\frac{2}{20}$ ($= \frac{1}{10}$) of an inch throughout its entire length.
These distances include the $\frac{3}{16}$, which is the diameter of the bar,
i.e., they are taken from the outer side of the bar to the centre,
and they are subject to slight alterations according to the model
of the violin. Thus on a narrow fiddle they would be slightly
less, and on a broad one a trifle more. Its width at the edge
glued to the belly is $\frac{3}{16}$ inch broad, the other edge is slightly
rounded. This last rounded edge is slightly undulated, and
the edge glued to the belly throughout its entire length takes a
concavity regulated by the longitudinal arching of the belly.
Its depth is also, of course, similarly regulated, but is generally
in the best fiddles $\frac{2}{7}$ inch in the centre or deepest part. It is set
quite at a right angle with the belly (*vide* Fig. 83). The would-

be anonymous author of "Luthomonographie" (*vide* note *⁸*, p. viii. Preface), citing Félix Savart and his trapezoid violin, says that the bass bar should be placed down the centre join of the belly, a statement based purely upon an *argumentum ad ignorantiam*, which gives a fair notion of the practical value of Prince Yousoupof's otherwise well-meaning " Essay." The purely mechanical influence of the bass bar is interestingly illustrated by the following experiment taken from Mr. Davidson's work on the violin.   Having procured a piece of well-seasoned and sonorous pine, a belly was formed out of it in the usual manner, adopting the plan of thickness according to the method used by Stradivarius.   This plate, when thus finished (the *f* holes not as yet cut), gave the note C.   Subsequently the *f* holes were cut of the usual size and pattern, when the sound was found to be lowered half a tone, now being B.   A bass bar having afterwards been glued on, of a somewhat larger size than commonly employed, the plate gave the note D, but the bar having been reduced to its proper dimensions the sound was again lowered, and now the belly gave the same tone as originally, C.   We can now easily perceive that the bar perfectly compensates for the difference of tone, arising from the cutting of the *f* holes, but at the same time we can raise or lower the tone very considerably by altering the dimensions of the bar ; for the stronger the bar the higher the tone, the sound lowering as the bar is decreased in dimensions.

And this brings us to the fact that the original bass bars put in by the Italian masters have all become too weak for the modern high pitch, and consequently a bar of the dimensions given above (about $10\frac{1}{2}$ inches) must now be substituted for the original one ; but this operation, if your fiddle is worth anything at all, must only be performed by a first-class workman. The functions of the bass bar are to transmit to the entire belly the vibrations communicated to it by the left foot of the bridge, and to prevent it from entering into a series of segmental vibrations, and not, as has so often been laid down, to strengthen the belly.   As Otto justly remarks, " A properly constructed fiddle ought to be able to stand screwing up to pitch without giving way, in the absence of either bass bar or sound post."   Care must be taken not to make the bass bar too long in proportion to the instrument, or, instead of promoting, it will check the vibration, and render the tone of the fiddle dull.   The same care ought to be taken in the selection of the wood of which the bar is made as with the material for the belly, and for the same reason it should be made of the pine, which yields the highest note when struck or vibrated with a bow, or by rubbing with the fingers.

Perhaps no part of the violin has been more assailed by the inventors of vagaries applied to the violin than the bass bar. Everything that could be done to alter it has been done, and called " an improvement," beginning with one Baud, a maker at Versailles, in 1810, who introduced a violin without a bass bar at all, because he considered that it "interfered" with the vibrations.[1] He therefore left the belly much thicker than usual to compensate for the absence of the bar, but (as might be expected) the tone was seriously impaired. In 1852, an American (William B. Tilton) patented a design by which a second bar was fixed to the inside of a fiddle, extending between the top and bottom blocks, which were cut sloping, so as not to check the vibrations at these points. In 1867, Miremont reproduced the same vagary, but without obtaining for it any successful recognition. M. Fétis[2] mentions the arrangement of a violin in 1855, with two bars, by M. Rambaux, of Paris : one in the usual place, the other glued to the back, *on which* was set the sound post. In his notice of it, M. Fétis says that, though superfluous in the case of a first-rate fiddle, inferior instruments were decidedly improved, especially on the fourth string, by this arrangement. Dr. Stone and Mr. Meeson's elliptical tension bars, which were exhibited to the Musical Association in 1874, are described as " four strips of white deal, curved to an elliptical figure, passing parallel from end to end on the inside of the belly. Thus they intercept the *ff* holes, and remove a well-known cause of weakness, and a break in the vibrating body." The highest eulogia were heaped on this contrivance by the inventors, but it is certain that, whilst spoiling a good fiddle, they would not improve a bad one. A Mr. Walker introduced, a few years back, a new form of bass bar, which was " cut on the slab, and had the grain consequently running on the edge." It measured 10 inches long, ⅝ broad, and ⅛ thick. It was bent to the arching and glued on the *flat* side in the usual place. This would probably augment the *quantity* of sound produced, but the *quality* would be seriously deteriorated. Some have suggested that no bass bar ought to be necessary, but that the belly ought to be made thicker, so as to support the strings and vibrate as well. This was the principle of Dr. Nicholson's violin (*vide* p. 102) and of M. Baud's violin, mentioned above, both of which demonstrated the fallacy of the suggestion, for the increase of the thickness effectually checked all possibility of vibration.

[1] A full description of this invention, or rather vagary, will be found in "Bibliographie Musicale de France et de l'Etranger," etc. (Paris, 1822 : Niogret), p. 348.
[2] " Rapport sur les Instruments de Musique dans l'Exposition Universelle de Paris en 1855."

CHAPTER IX.

THE EXTERIOR OF THE VIOLIN.

WE have now discussed the interior construction and parts of the violin; it now remains, therefore, to consider those parts of the instrument which meet the eye, and which, whilst serving each its allotted purpose in the building-up of the perfect whole, and in producing the perfect result, tend to give the fiddle that graceful appearance and elegance of detail which at once strikes the eye of the most casual observer.

The ff Holes or Sound Holes.—For the model or outlines of these there exists no rule. As will be seen from the Figs. 40 to 48, from the earliest days of fiddle-making each maker of any originality has designed, and to a great extent invariably kept to, his own particular form of *f* hole, so that the amateur or beginner has only to devolve his own idea, or follow the pattern of one of his great ancestors in fiddle-making. In striking out a new outline certain rules below set forth must be followed, for the reasons there given, but before considering the *f* hole from its scientific aspect, I will shortly enumerate a couple of perfect methods for copying the *ff* holes of any given fiddle. (1) Having got the instrument of which you desire to copy the *f* hole, place over either of the *ff* holes a piece of soft white paper. Then, holding the paper firmly with one hand to prevent it slipping, with an old dirty glove, or with the slightly dirtied finger of the other hand, rub the paper just over the *f* hole strongly, and the outline will appear on the paper, in the same manner as patterns for fretwork, etc., are obtained with a heel-ball. I find that my gloves, or my fingers when at work, are always dirty enough for this purpose. (2) To obtain the exact outline and position in the belly of any particular pair of ff holes, as in Fig. 84 (or Plate VI.), the following excellent method is given by MM. Maugin et Maigne. Having detached the belly of the instrument whose ff holes you wish to reproduce in facsimile, take a piece of strong parchment large enough to cover the portion of the belly indicated in Fig. 84. Take any large piece of cloth, and folding it several times place it on the table. Stretch the parchment over this cushion, and press the belly upside down into the cushion covered with parchment, and with a finely-pointed pencil draw the interior outlines of the ff holes and the exterior outline of the belly, as shown in the figure, and there you have Fig. 84 complete. This parchment outline may either be kept in a portfolio for future use, or transferred to a thin leaf of wood ($\frac{1}{18}$ or $\frac{1}{20}$ of an inch thick), which is more durable and more convenient to work with. The interior of the ff holes and the exterior of the outline are to be very carefully cut out, and the centre line of the belly should be drawn down the model

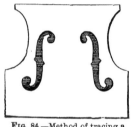

FIG. 84.—Method of tracing a pair of ff holes.

exactly as in the original. A pair of ff holes taken like this may be seen in their actual size in Plate VI.

Now as regards the ff holes with respect to their influence on the entire fiddle and its tone. Of course, nothing need be said about the exact position of the ff holes in contra-facsimile to one another; if they were not set in the belly so as to exactly balance one another, the setting of the bridge and sound post would be reduced almost to an impossibility, let alone the ghastly effect on the appearance of the fiddle! As M. Fétis justly remarks, it would be a great mistake to suppose that the position and form of the ff holes are arbitrary. The f shape of the sound hole is rendered necessary by the arching of the belly. If this latter were plane the sound holes need only be straight and parallel (as in the Savart trapezoid violin, vide Fig. 76). They influence the entire system of vibrations of the belly, and thus govern the vibrations of the whole instrument. This has been proved by experiment; i.e., if the ff holes were cut in the back of the fiddle it would be immediately muted, for the belly would not have sufficient elasticity without them to vibrate and communicate its vibrations to the rest of the instrument. The position of these ff holes, their form, and the minutest details of their cutting, are such essential points that no alteration whatever can be made in them without injuring the quality of the tone, and for this reason, that the ff holes influence to a powerful degree the sound of the mass of air contained within the body of the instrument. If they are too small, or if one be covered up, the sound of the contained air becomes lower, if they are cut too large it rises. The *ff* holes must, therefore, be regulated by the size of the fiddle, and the proportion of the *ff* holes must be so adjusted that the contained mass of air renders the requisite 512 vibrations. If they be too large, or set too near to one another, the tone of the violin becomes harsh and shrill, and when too small, or set too far apart, they make it more woolly or viola-like. Savart has observed that the *ff* holes in some of the larger violins of Maggini are too large, consequently that the note given by the mass of air in the interior is heightened, and the tone is thereby impaired; but time has in a great measure repaired this defect, at any rate it is one that I have never noticed. After all, what can be more consummately graceful than the *ff* holes of Stradivari or Santo Seraphin, and why should we try to improve upon them?

The Neck (or Handle), and the Scroll (or Head).—On the proper proportion of this part of the instrument depends its entire " personal appearance," quite as much as on an elegant outline; however graceful may be your fiddle, a weak or uncouth scroll will utterly mar its symmetry, and besides this, it has considerable influence on the tone of a fiddle, according to the nature and quality of the wood, which must be neither too hard nor too soft, because it is one of the channels by which the vibrations of the strings are conveyed to the body of the instrument (the bridge being the other). This is proved by the following experiment. If the *body* only of a violin, without the neck, be held in a vice, and the strings, instead of being connected with it by the neck and scroll, are stretched up to pitch by pegs having no connection therewith, the tone will not be so powerful as if they were screwed up in a peg box communicating with the body. The difference is only slight, but enough to prove that the neck does some of this part of the work. And again, it has to bear the entire strain of the four strings united, and if not of good seasoned wood, and properly proportioned, this comparatively gigantic pull would twist it out of shape. Great care must, therefore, be taken to make it in proper proportions, angles, and curves, and above all to set it upon the violin properly; that is, that it be in a line with the centre join of the instrument, that it be so fixed that the finger-board shall have the proper rise proportioned to the instrument, and that when you look at the fiddle edgeways, holding it perfectly upright, the eye of the scroll is in a line with the *edge of the back.* If it is set too far back, the bridge has to be made high to accommodate it, and as a natural consequence the tone of the fiddle is weak and poor ; on the other hand, if it is set too far forward, the bridge has to be proportionately low, and the tone becomes acute and metallic. Care must also be taken not to make it too strong and massive at the place where it joins the body of the instrument, or, acting as a clamp, it will deaden the tone. The proper proportions, as shown in Fig. 85, are given below, as taken from a very perfect neck and scroll kindly placed at my service by Mr. W. E. Hill. It must be prefaced this is an

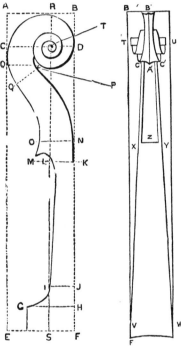

excellent *average* head, but, of course, the measurements will vary slightly in different styles, and secondly, the neck as now made is quite $\frac{1}{4}$ inch longer than the old makers used to make it, and it is for this reason that so many (in fact, nearly all) old violins have been re-necked. The neck and scroll are cut from a block of maple $9\frac{3}{4}$ to 10 in. long by 2 in. deep by $1\frac{5}{8}$ in. wide (all the following measurements are in inches and *fractions of an inch*), and when finished ought so to touch all these dimensions at its most prominent parts (front and back of scroll, front and back of shoulder) as to lie perfectly flat on a smooth surface, if placed on its face, back, or sides. The following are the measure-

FIG. 85.—The Neck and Scroll. Front and side views.

ments : A B, C D, E F, 2 in. ; R S, $9\frac{5}{8}$ in.; G H, $1\frac{1}{2}$ in. ; L K, $\frac{9}{16}$ in. ; I J, $\frac{5}{8}$ in. ; R L, $4\frac{1}{4}$ in. ; L S, $5\frac{3}{8}$ in.; R T, $\frac{11}{16}$ in.; O N, $\frac{7}{8}$ in. ; Q P, $\frac{11}{16}$ in. The peg-box is $1\frac{3}{8}$ in. deep on the line O N; $\frac{11}{16}$ in. deep on the line Q P; and 3 in. long on the line P N. Looking at the neck and scroll as in the front view, the measurements are : V W, $1\frac{3}{8}$ in. ; X Y, $\frac{5}{8}$ in. ; T U, $1\frac{1}{2}$ in. The peg-box is $\frac{3}{4}$ in. broad at A'. The cheeks of the peg-box are $\frac{3}{16}$ in. thick. The summit of the scroll B' is $\frac{7}{16}$ in. broad. The base of the volute C C', $\frac{7}{8}$ in. broad. The eyes of the scroll, T, are $\frac{1}{4}$ in. in diameter. From these exact measurements, and the figure, if carefully followed, a most exquisite scroll may be traced (far better than the figure, which merely illustrates the method).

To copy in facsimile the scroll of any given fiddle, the following is the best plan. Take, as directed for copying ff holes, a cushion and piece of strong parchment, and arrange them as there set down. Take the scroll you wish to copy, and from which the pegs have been removed, and pressing it into the cushion, draw a line round it with a pencil from L to K as nearly exactly as possible, and removing the scroll, correct it as far as possible by the eye. Or, having cut a hole in a leaf of wood just large enough to lay the volute into (so that the cheek of the scroll, with the pegs removed, lies flat upon the plank), lay the scroll upon the plank, and with a marking-point draw the outline in the ordinary manner. Then draw upon it the lines R L and C D, crossing each other exactly at a right angle at T. From the point T where they meet, measure exactly, with a pair of dividers, the breadth of the scroll on either side of it (the point T will be indicated on the outline by the dent which the eye makes in the paper or parchment). Then, in the same manner, measure off the distances from T of the respective volutes at the four points where they touch the lines R L, C D; and thus, with the dividers constantly comparing your drawing with the original, you will get an exact copy of the profile of the scroll you wish to reproduce. The elevation is traced and compared at the points B′, C′ C′, T U, A′ and Z, in exactly the same manner. The elder Chanot (*vide* p. 116) introduced an alteration at this part of the fiddle by reversing the scroll; *i.e.*, making the volute curl over backwards instead of over towards the front of the violin (as in Fig. 75). His reason for this was the difficulty there is in getting at the peg of the *A* string inside the peg-box under the scroll, but as no fiddle-case ought to be without a pair of fine tweezers to get at this end with, and the innovation is intensely ugly, it never superseded the well-known graceful form. The necks of old violins, as originally affixed by the old Cremonese masters, were too short for the present alteration in pitch ; a new neck must, therefore, be adjusted when a fiddle turns up untouched since it left its maker's hands. This must be done by a really first-rate work-man, splicing the old head on to a new neck just below the chin of the scroll; this may be done in a manner to defy detection by an unpractised eye. It should be added that this alteration in no way decreases the quality or value of an old and valuable fiddle.

The Bridge.—As we saw in Chapter I. the bridge, as we *now* see it, was an improvement introduced comparatively late in the history of bowed instruments, though, as I have said before, the records from which we have to collect the history of the violin —namely, pictures and sculptures—leaves much to be desired in the matter of completeness of detail. The early bridges would, however, appear to have been very rude, as will be seen by turning to Figs. 18 and 22, and in the time of the viols not much progress had been made. M. Fétis gives three figures of bridges : Figs. 86, 87, and 88. Fig. 86 is a viol bridge to support seven strings, and, as will be seen, is very elementary. Figs.

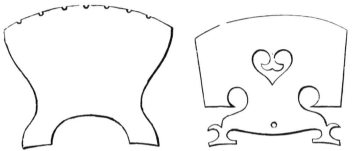

Fɪɢ. 86.—Bridge of 7-Stringed Viol (F. J. Fétis).   Fɪɢ. 87.—Antique Violin Bridge   Antonius Amati (F. J. Fétis).

Fɪɢ 88.—Antique Violin Bridge. Nicolaus Amati (F. J. Fétis).   Fɪɢ. 89.—Bridge of 5-Stringed Viol (W. E. Hill).

87 and 88 are two old violin bridges of the time of the Amatis, distinctly approximating the modern form, which design was settled upon by Stradivarius, and has never since been altered. Fig. 89 is from a curious old five-string treble viol, in the possession of Mr. W. E. Hill.

It must not be imagined that the design (Fig. 90) thus fixed upon by the greatest fiddle-maker the world has seen was merely his idea of what was most pretty, though to this day there are a great many violinists who are firmly under the impression that the ornamental cutting of the bridge is merely a matter of taste. Very far from it; for countless experiments have been made with a view to altering the accepted design, any deviation from which has proved injuriously to affect the tone of any instrument to which it is applied. It is difficult to imagine the reason of this; how it is that a little piece of maple, which merely serves to keep the strings off the finger-board, should have such a powerful effect on the tone of the instrument to which it is not fastened in any way, being merely kept in its place by the pressure of the four strings. The first explanation of this influence must be sought for in the fact that it is the principal channel by which the vibrations of the strings pass, to the belly by way of the bass bar, and to the back by way (in a lesser degree) of the sound post. In consequence of these its important functions, its proportions, and position on the belly must be very nicely adjusted to the quality of the violin to which it is affixed. For instance, if it be too thick, the vibrations of the strings will not pass with sufficient rapidity to the belly. Its height must also be most carefully adjusted to the quality of the instrument, for if it is too high, the tone will be dull and sluggish, and if it is too low, a harsh, piercing tone will be the result. As it is of the greatest importance (as will be discussed further on) that the strings be supported at a proper height from the end of the finger-board *and as it is of equal importance* that the bridge be not raised or lowered to maintain this distance, the height of the finger-board must be suited to that of the bridge, *not* the height of the bridge to that of the finger-board. Again; it was noticed by M. Sibire in 1806 that at that time the augmentation of the height of the bridge $\frac{1}{12}$ of an inch raised the pressure on the strings by seven pounds, and this proportion has, of course, increased with the since-raised pitch.

FIG. 90.—The Modern Violin Bridge.

According to Otto, a good violin, whose wood has not been worked too thin, will require a higher bridge, as the vibrations are easier to produce, though the higher the bridge the more perceptible become the faults of the fiddle; and, on the other hand, certain faults may, in some measure, be glossed over by a low bridge, at the expense, however, of the power of the instrument. In an earlier edition of the same work, the author contends that the suitability of a bridge depends more upon its weight than its height; and mentions a somewhat ingenious mode of discovering the precise weight of bridge which any

Too high makes dull tone, Low makes harsh

Higher bridge for power

Weight more important

See p129 of this volume for Otto's book "Treatis on the Violin" translated by Bishop

5
Wood
clips

instrument requires. He made six little wooden clips, like one-pronged mutes, weighing respectively 2, 4, 6, 8, 10, and 12 grains. Having found that any bridge was unsuitable to the instrument to which it was applied, he tried on it successively these little wooden weights, clipping them between the D and A strings. Having found thus with which clip the result was best, he weighed the clip and the bridge together and proceeded to make a new bridge, the weight of the old one *plus* the satisfactory clip. Of course the clips must only act as weights, and *not* hold the bridge so as to act as mutes ; and I do not see how the latter contingency can possibly be obviated.

Spotted
maple
Thickness
feet arch

The bridge must be made of spotted maple, neither too hard nor too soft, the grain horizontal, and its proportions should be, just half as thick at the top as at the feet. Care must be taken to select a bridge made of wood which accords with that of the fiddle in its consistency, grain, etc. The greatest care must be taken that the feet of the bridge fit the arching of the belly, where they rest, so as to leave no interval beneath them, as such will render the tone hollow and dull. The top of the bridge must only so far be rounded as to prevent the bow touching two strings at once, unless required to do so by the performer ; and, lastly, the four little grooves made to receive the strings must be as shallow as possible consistent with effectiveness. It has probably befallen all my readers, at one time or another, to be worried by their strings " sticking "—*i.e.*, when the peg is turned, the string, instead of rising in tone at once, "hangs fire," so to speak, and then tightens (or loosens) with a jerk and a creak. This is in consequence of the nicks on the bridge being too *deep*, and when it occurs they must be made shallower by filing the sides of the nick. The first string is particularly liable to be thus affected, by reason of the extra work it has to do, and of its greater tension and consequent pressure on the nick. It is good to have a little shallow " extra " nick at the side of the principal one, in which a new string is placed to be screwed up to pitch before transferring it to the principal nick. This keeps the principal nick shallow, and the noisy squeaking of the string, as it is screwed up to pitch, is obviated.

left foot
over bass
bar

As regards its position on the belly of the fiddle, its exact position is just between the two nicks in the *f f* holes (unless the position of such nicks, or the *f f* holes themselves be eccentric), at an exactly equal distance from each, and the left foot must stand exactly over the centre of the bass bar. The most extensive and instructive experiments on the bridge are those of M. Savart. As determining the necessity of the Stradivarian cutting, he commenced by making a bridge quite plain, and without cuttings in it at all, and the tone of the instrument was almost entirely destroyed. On cutting feet in his bridge an improvement was perceptible, which greatly increased as he made lateral incisions in it ; and the tone gradually improved till it reached perfection, as the bridge attained its present system of ornamentation (Fig. 90). The feet of the bridge are particularly necessary in determining its shape. The centre join of the belly is, in all cases, what Savart calls " un nœud de vibrations ; " *i.e.*, along the centre join the vibrations are at a minimum, and it is consequently from thence that they start (*vide* note [1], p. 133), and it is of the utmost importance that this centre of vibration be not interrupted or checked. Any change in the wood of the bridge has similarly proved prejudicial to the tone of the instrument. As we have seen before, the right foot of the bridge is comparatively rigid, whilst the left foot vibrates the bar and belly ; therefore, if the right foot of the bridge be held (as by a mute), the effect will not be nearly so perceptible as if the action of the left foot were similarly impeded. The bridge has, like the rest of the violin, been subjected, from time to time, to the eccentricities of would-be improvers, such as fitting the top of it with little wheels for the strings to run over, and so on *ad infinitum*. In a later chapter I shall notice Zebrowski's patent bridge, or rather combination of bridge and mute.

The Purfling.—This is the last trace which is left us of the extraordinary amount of ornamentation with which violins used to be loaded, and which I shall shortly notice in its proper place. It is composed, as a rule, of a strip of plane-tree, glued between two strips of the same wood stained black, which sandwich is exceedingly brittle, and difficult to bend into shape and inlay, when bought (as it may be) ready made and glued together. This difficulty is, to a great measure, obviated if the three strips are inlaid separately as set down in Part III. It is inlaid in four or six pieces : either, from corner to corner, or, from the centre join, three on each side of the back, and the same number on each side of the belly. It is the mark of a good workman to make these joins at the corners and ends as imperceptible as possible ; Stradivari, as will be seen on looking at any one of his fiddles, excelled in this respect. Some makers have used whalebone for this purpose to get over these difficulties (Jacobs of Amsterdam) ; and others have merely painted   line round their instruments (Peter Walmsley), and this latter method is often still pursued with the commonest class of instruments. Maggini and his copyists have made use of double rows, and curls and designs executed in purfling (as in Fig. 91), but this has been said to injure the tone of a fiddle, and certainly, to my mind, whilst it can do no good, it does not improve the appearance of an instrument. The usual diameter for the purfling is about $\frac{1}{16}$ inch, and it is set at a distance of $\frac{3}{16}$ of an inch from the edge of the fiddle. Its only real *use* (which has preserved it after the relinquishment of profuse ornamentation) is, that it serves to preserve the edges of the instrument from splintering, by, as it were, binding the fibres together as with a border.

The Pegs, or Points.—These are the little round dots of wood that are not unusually seen at the top and at the bottom of the backs and bellies of old and new violins. As many violinists are

wholly at a loss to account for the *raison d'être* of their presence there at all, it may be well here to go into the origin and motive of their existence. In the first place, they are not absolutely necessary at all (as is proved by the large mass of violins bearing no trace of this superfluity), but many of the Cremonese masters used them, and, when present, they are accounted for as follows :—When the back (or belly) is ready to fix on to the sides or ribs, it was not unusual to commence by setting it on them and making it fast by thrusting a bradawl through the back (or belly) at top or bottom (or in both places), into the end blocks, so as to keep it fast at these

FIG. 91.—Ornamentally inlaid Purfling.   points whilst you proceed to fit the sides to the table all round and set on the screws. When this is done, and the bradawl is removed, it leaves a hole, which is then filled up with a peg, made and fixed in manner set down in Part III. The pegs of Stradivari, as we shall see in a future chapter, were always placed as shown at A in Fig. 92, and as in making copies of great masters it is necessary to attend to this, particular instructions for their application will be given in due course ; though, as will be seen, the more scientific use of cramps to secure the tables at these points is the invariable practice of the best modern makers.

Ornamentation.—The ornamentation of fiddles is practically obsolete, as I have just remarked, but in former times the very best makers ornamented their fiddles occasionally. Before the days of the violin, of course nearly all viols were ornamented in some way, and after their extinction violins could not quite get rid of this superfluous charm, which has come down to us in the shape of eccentric purflings. Maggini was especially fond of a fantastic arrangement and reduplication of the purfling, of which Fig. 91 is a specimen, and nearer home it was a favourite peculia-

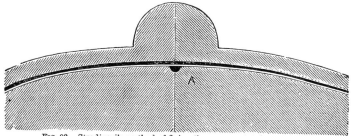

FIG. 92.—Stradivari's method of fixing the *pegs* or *points* (actual size).

rity of Barak Norman, our last native viol-maker. The practice of using a simple ornamental purfling (or rather two rows with a design worked between them) has been followed by the highest members of the fraternity of fiddle-makers. Fig. 93 is an ornamental purfling copied from a violin of Stradivarius, the one that is figured by Mr. Hart from the Plowden collection.[1] Another mode of ornamentation once very much in vogue, but now entirely obsolete, is the practice of inlaying. The instruments were inlaid with views, medallions, crests, or fancy designs. Fig. 94 is a fiddle of the Maggini model, very finely inlaid, which also presents another form of ornamentation, namely, the sculptured scroll or head. This was another relique of the viols, which nearly always had sculptured heads. Jacob Steiner

FIG. 93.—Ornamental Purfling of Stradivarius.

was the most frequent adopter of this form of ornament; and his followers of the German school have very freely reproduced this peculiarity of their great master, his favourite form being the lion's head, but he not unfrequently seems to have executed human and other heads, probably reproductions of the crests of the patrons for whom the instruments were made. There exist also instruments with carved heads by Stradivari; they are

[1] G. Hart, "The Violin, its Famous Makers and their Imitators" (London, 1875). 4to and 8vo. Plate 18, p. 230. (Popular Edition, 1880, 8vo, and 2nd (Enlarged) Edition of the original, 1884.)

beautifully executed, but are inestimably rare. *Apparent rari nantes in gurgite vasto!* I have before noticed the principal makers of violins abroad and at home, and have alluded to the peculiarities of form, etc., by which the instruments of these

makers are distinguished, but I have said but little about their ornamentation with painting, branding, etc. With regard to the former mode of ornamentation, I have already noticed the twenty-four violins of Andreas Amati, one of which has furnished us with the plates II. and III., and which are described on page 73. Another specimen, made in 1620 by Nicholas Amati, was shown in the special Exhibition of Ancient Musical Instruments, held at South Kensington in the year 1872. It was a viola (No. 136), lent by Mr. W. L. Adye, very beautifully illuminated on the back, and reproduced in the illustrated catalogue of that exhibition. (*Vide* note, p. 24.) It is not uncommon to find very old violins painted with medallions and other similar ornamentation. Some makers, notably Benjamin Banks, of Salisbury, and Santo Seraphin, have embellished their instruments by branding them with their initials or other devices. The favourite spots for this kind of initialling seem to have been under the tail-piece, on the rib close to the tail-pin, and under the fingerboard. Lastly, the most (and only) modern form of embellishment is the practice of fitting up

Fig.94.—Violin with Inlaid Back and Carved Head.

instruments with inlaid accessories, such as tail-piece, pegs, and finger-board—the first most usually, the second sometimes, the third seldom. The first are so familiar in the show-cases of any violin-dealer that they need no description ; the second are not so much used : but undoubtedly a small gold stud or small plate let into the peg is not at all amiss with very old or first-class new instruments ; the finger-board is seldom ornamented in any way, but at one time it was not at all uncommon to inlay it with fancy designs of various sorts, and particularly with little pearl spots, where the notes are formed, sometimes with a complete scale up to the highest E. The same remarks apply to all these (excepting as aforesaid)—namely, that they are a mistake : apart from the fact that they do not improve the look of a clumsy fiddle, and certainly mar a good one ; these inlaid slabs of pearl, silver, and ivory are very apt to come loose and jar unpleasantly, and are generally more bother than they are worth. Mr. Hart has a tail-piece and set of pegs made of boxwood, very beautifully carved by the late J. B. Vuillaume. The former bears in relief a carving of the Orpheus of Maffei, reproduced by Gallay, and referred to in Chapter I. (page 35). And lastly, one remark applies to all the forms of ornamentation above mentioned— namely, that except as curiosities they are not a success. De gustibus non est disputandum, but what can be wanted more than the plain line of purfling, which merely emphasizes the graceful outline of a well-made fiddle ? What carved head was ever more graceful or pleasing than a perfectly cut scroll ? What art can inlay a design so perfect and æsthetic as the natural waves of a handsome slab of figured maple ? and is it not a sin to cover up these beauties with a coat of paint ? Branding does not do much harm, but is unnecessary, for the original work of a first-rate maker requires not his name burnt into it to identify it, and is a practice which only serves as something else for the unscrupulous to copy, and for the charlatan to insist upon. Perhaps the most celebrated ornamented violin whose fame has reached us of the latter days, is Ole Bull's celebrated Gasparo da Salo. Its head, finger-board, bridge, and tail-piece, we are told, were magnificently carved by the illustrious Benvenuto Cellini. An accurate description of Ole Bull and his Gasparo, with excellent representations of both, were given in No. 368 of Harper's Magazine: January, 1881 (No. 2, vol. i. English Edition : Sampson Low & Co.), by an intimate friend of the great master.

" La Lutherie n'est pas seulement un métier, c'est un art.'
L'Abbé Sibire, " La Chelonomie " (Paris, 1806).

CHAPTER X.

THE VARNISH.

Charles Reade on the Old Varnishes—Old Recipes—Alexis the Piedmontese, 1550—Fioravanti of Bologna, 1564—Anda, 1663—Zahn, 1685—C. Morley, 1692—Bonanni of Rome, 1713—Qualities required by Violin Varnish—Amber Varnishes—Spirit Varnishes—Application—Sizing—Tests for Purity of Ingredients—Coloration of Varnish—Composition—Time for making Varnishes—Recipes.

WE have now reached the point at which our fiddle is completed "in the white" : there only remains, therefore, before proceeding to fit it up and string it, to discuss the question of Varnish. So much has been written on the subject of the " Lost Cremona Varnish," with such infinitesimal result, that it would be worse than useless to start a new theory to solve an apparently insoluble difficulty. Mr. C. Reade, in a letter in the *Pall Mall Gazette*, of August 31st, 1872,[1] has shortly epitomised all that is known of this lost but glorious compound, and his remarks on the subject are, in the abstract, as follows :—

"It comes to this, then," says he, "that the varnish of Cremona, as acted on by time and usage, has an inimitable beauty ; and we pay a high price for it in second-class makers, and an enormous price for it in a fine Stradiuarius or Joseph Guarnerius. No wonder, then, that many violin-makers have tried hard to discover the secret of this varnish, many chemists have given days and nights of anxious study to it. More than once, even in my time, hopes have run high, but only to fall again. Some have even cried, ' Eureka ! ' to the public ; but the moment others looked at their discovery, and compared it with the real thing, ' inextinguishable laughter shook the skies.' At last, despair has succeeded to all that energetic study, and

[1] These most interesting and valuable letters were (owing to the medium of their publication) not nearly so widely spread amongst the musical world as they ought to have been. In the year 1873, Mr. G. H. M. Muntz, of Birchfield, reprinted them in the form of an ornate little pamphlet, entitled, " A Lost Art Revived ; Cremona Violins and Varnish, by Charles Reade ; " it was printed by J. Bellows. at the Steam Press, Eastgate, Gloucester ; but only a small number were printed, and the circulation was necessarily limited

the varnish of Cremona is sullenly given up as a lost art. I have heard and read a great deal about it, and I think I can state the principal theories briefly but intelligibly.

"1. It used to be stoutly maintained that the basis was amber; that these old Italians had the art of fusing amber without impairing its transparency: once fused by dry heat, it could be boiled into a varnish with oil and spirit of turpentine, and combined with transparent yet lasting colours. To convince me, they used to rub the worn part of a Cremona with their sleeves, and then put the fiddle to their noses, and smell amber. Then I, burning with the love of knowledge, used to rub the fiddle very hard, and whip it to my nose, and *not* smell amber. But that might arise, in some measure, from there not being any amber there to smell.[1] (N.B. These amber-seeking worthies never rubbed the *coloured* varnish on an old violin. Yet their theory had placed amber there.)

"2. That time does it all; that the violins of Stradivari were raw, crude things at starting, and the varnish rather opaque.

"3. Two or three had the courage to say it was spirit-varnish, and alleged in proof that if you drop a drop of alcohol on a Stradivari, it tears the varnish off as it runs.

"4. The far more prevalent notion was, that it is an oil varnish, in ~apport of which they pointed to the rich appearance of what they call the bare wood, and contrasted the miserable, hungry appearance of the wood in all old violins known to be spirit varnished (for instance, Nicholas Gagliano of Naples, and Jean Baptiste Guadagnini of Piacenza, Italian makers contemporary with Joseph del Gesù).

"5. That the secret has been lost by adulteration. The old Cremonese and Venetians got pure and sovereign gums that have retired from commerce.

"Now as to theory No. 1. Surely amber is too dear a gum and too impracticable for two hundred fiddle-makers to have used it in Italy.[2] Till fused by dry heat, it is no more soluble in varnish than quartz is; and who can fuse it? Copal is inclined to melt, but amber to burn, catch fire, do anything but melt. Put the two gums to a lighted candle, you will then appreciate the difference. I have tried more than one chemist in the fusing of amber; it came out of their hands a dark brown, opaque

---

[1] This "rubbing" test has been in great favour with many experimentalists. A fiddle by the "brothers Amati" is said to have given off a smell of mastic and linseed oil; and instruments by Joseph Guarnerius (filius Andreæ), and by Joseph "del Gesù," submitted to the same test, suggested to the seekers after the mystery the presence of benzoin, as well as of mastic and linseed oil!

[2] It must be borne in mind that amber is much cheaper and commoner in Italy and the Tyrol than in the northern countries of Europe.

substance, rather burnt than fused. When really fused, *it is a dark olive-green, as clear as crystal.* Yet I never knew but one man who could bring it to this, and he had special machinery invented by himself for it ; in spite of which he nearly burnt down his house at it one day.[1] I believe the whole amber theory comes out of a verbal equivoque. The varnish of the Amati was called amber to mark its rich colour, and your *à priori* reasoners went off on that, forgetting that amber must be an inch thick to exhibit the *colour* amber. By such reasoning as this, Mr. Davidson, in a book of great general merit, is misled so far as to put down powdered glass for an ingredient in Cremona varnish. Mark the logic. Glass in a sheet is transparent ; so if you reduce it to powder, it will add transparency to varnish. Imposed on by this chimera, he actually puts powdered glass, an opaque and insoluble sediment, into four recipes for Cremona varnish.[2] But the theories, 2, 3, 4, 5, have all a good deal of truth in them ; their fault is that they are too narrow, and too blind to the truth of each other. In this, as in every scientific inquiry, the true solution is that which reconciles all the truths that seem at variance.

"The way to discover a lost art, once practised with variations by a hundred people, is to examine very closely the most brilliant specimen, the most characteristic specimen, and, indeed, the most extravagant specimen—if you can find one. I took that way, and I found in the chippiest varnish of Stradiuarius, viz., his dark red varnish, the key to all the varnish of Cremona, red or yellow. (N.B.—The yellow varnish always beat me dead, till I got to it by this *détour*.) Look at this dark red varnish, and use your eyes. What do you see ? A red varnish, which chips very readily off what people call *the bare wood.* But never mind what these echoes of echoes call it. What *is* it ? It is *not* bare wood. Bare wood turns a dirty brown with age ; this is a rich and lovely yellow. By its colour, and by its glassy gloss, and by disbelieving what echoes say, and trusting only to

[1] This was the late John Lott (*vide* Chapter III., p. 84).
[2] The use of powdered glass has by many authors been held up to derision, and rightly too, if it is to be understood as an *ingredient* of the varnish ; but though some short-sighted plagiarists may have copied into their works recipes including powdered glass *as a part of the varnish*, if you could find the originals from which they derived their information, you would probably find that they included powdered glass with good intent, expecting from it merely a *mechanical* action in the preparation of the varnish, not a *chemical* influence on the nature of the completed article. Thus M. Eugène Mailand (*vide* note p. 186) recommends the use of a stratum of coarsely powdered glass at the bottom of the phial in which the resins, etc., are mixed, *to prevent the resins from adhering to the bottom of the vessel,* never dreaming that any one would take him to be recommending the glass as " adding transparency to the varnish."

our own eyes, we may see at a glance that it is not bare wood, but highly-varnished wood. This varnish is evidently oil, and contains a gum. Allowing for the tendency of oil to run into the wood, I should say *four coats of oil varnish;* and this they call the bare wood. We have now discovered the first process —a clear oil varnish, laid on the white wood with some transparent gum, not high-coloured. Now proceed a step further. The red and chippy varnish, what is that? ' Oh! that is a varnish of the same quality, but another colour,' say the theorists No. 4. ' How do you know?' say I. ' It is self-evident ; would a man begin with oil varnish, and then go into spirit varnish?' is their reply. Now observe, this is not humble observation, only rational preconception. But if discovery has an enemy in the human mind, that enemy is preconception. Let us, then, trust only to humble observation. Here is clear varnish, without the ghost of a chip in its nature ; and upon it is another, a red varnish, which is all chip. Does that look as if the two varnishes were homogeneous? Is chip precisely the same thing as no chip? If homogeneous, there would be chemical affinity between the two. But this extreme readiness of the red varnish to chip away from the clear marks a defect of chemical affinity between the two. Why, if you were to put your thumb-nail against that red varnish, a small piece would come away directly. This is not so in any known case of oil upon oil. Take old Forster, for instance : he begins with clear oil varnish ; then on that he puts a distinct oil varnish, with the colour and transparency of pea-soup. You will not get his pea-soup to chip off his clear varnish in a hurry, except where the top varnish *must* go in a played bass. Everywhere else his pea-soup sticks tight to his clear varnish, being oil upon oil.

" Now take a perfectly distinct line of observation. In varnishes, oil is a diluent of colour. It is not in the power of man to charge an oil varnish with colour so highly as this top red varnish is charged. And it must be remembered that the clear varnish below has filled all the pores of the wood ; therefore the diluent cannot escape into the wood, and so leave the colour undiluted. If that red varnish was ever oil varnish, every particle of the oil must still be there. But this is impossible, when you consider the extreme thinness of the film which constitutes the upper or red layer. This, then, is how Anthony Stradivari varnished the instruments such as the one we are considering. He began with three or four coats of oil varnish, containing some common gum. He then laid on several coats of red varnish, made by simply dissolving some fine red unadulterated gum in spirit ; the spirit evaporated, and left pure gum lying on a rich oil varnish, from which it chips by its dry nature and its utter want of chemical affinity to the substratum. This solution of the process will apply to almost every Cremona varnish. The beauty, therefore, of varnish lies in the fact that it is a pure glossy oil varnish, which serves as a foil to a divine unadulterated gum, which is left as a pure film on it by the evaporation of the spirit in which it was dissolved. The first is a colourless oil varnish, which sinks into and shows up the figure of the wood; the second is a heterogeneous spirit varnish, which serves to give the glory of colour, with its light and shade, which is the great and transcendent beauty of a Cremona violin. Gum-lac, which for forty years has been the mainstay of violin-makers, must never be used, not one atom of it. That vile flinty gum killed varnish at Naples and Piacenza a hundred and forty years ago, as it kills varnish now. Old Cremona shunned it, and whoever employs a grain of it commits wilful suicide as a Cremonese varnisher   It will not wear ; it will not chip ; it is in every respect the opposite of the Cremona gums. Avoid it utterly, or fail hopelessly, as all varnishers have failed since that fatal gum came in. The deep red varnish of Cremona is pure dragon's blood ; not the cake, the stick, the filthy trash, which, in this sinful and adulterating generation, is retailed under that name, but the tear of dragon's blood, little lumps, deeper in colour than a carbuncle, clear as crystal, and fiery as a ruby. The yellow varnish is the unadulterated tear of another gum [Gambogo], retailed in a cake like dragon's blood, and as great a fraud, as presented to you in commerce ; for the yellow and for the red gum, grope the city far eastwards. The orange varnish of Peter Guarnerius and Stradivarius is only a mixture of these two genuine gums."

For this long extract from Mr. C. Reade's letter, copied practically verbatim, I must crave the reader's pardon ; but as it is perhaps (to my mind certainly) the most intelligent, practical, and scientific solution of the fiddle-builder's greatest difficulty, presented to a limited number of people by a great connoisseur, and by one eminently qualified to give an opinion, it is far more honest and satisfactory to give the writer's own words, than to adapt it (as so many " bookmakers " unblushingly do) to my own phraseology, and call it original observation. (*"Palmæm qui meruit, ferat."*)

So much, therefore, for the *modus operandi* of the old Cremona varnishers as far as we can say. What were the component parts of their varnish, it were very difficult, nay, impossible, to. determine, for it must be borne in mind that a period of close upon two hundred years has elapsed since it was last applied as we see it—a time quite long enough to oxidize the gums, resins, and their diluents beyond the reach of the most careful quantitative or qualitative analysis, besides which, the costliness of the operation of depriving a Cremona masterpiece of its greatest beauty, would place it far beyond the reach of the most enthusiastic experimentalist. This varnish had an existence extending only from about 1550 to about 1750, at the end of which time it would seem to have vanished as completely and mysteriously as it appeared, superseded by the new spirit and lac varnishes which possibly seemed better then, but as they have turned out, were very much worse, for the purposes of the violin-varnisher. All the data we have to go upon are the printed works of some few individuals, who have written pamphlets on the various varnishes in common use for various purposes, and it is not unreasonable to suppose that the varnish used by the luthiers or fiddle-makers, was, to a certain extent, familiar to them ; again, the reading and proper construction of these formulæ is rendered more difficult by the fact that many of the gums, resins, and solvents mentioned, no longer exist under the names by which they were then known,[1] and some would seem almost entirely to have disappeared. I will now recapitulate a few of the most likely formulæ enumerated in these ancient brochures.[2] The first I have been able to obtain is a treatise called " Secrets of the Arts," first published in 1550, by one Alexis, a Piedmontese.[3] He gives the following recipes :—

1. Place some powdered benzoin (a) in a phial and cover it with two or three fingers' depth of pure spirits of wine, and leave it thus for two or three days. Into this $\frac{1}{2}$ phial of spirits, put five or six threads of saffron (b) whole, or roughly broken up. With this you may varnish anything a golden colour, which will glitter and last for years.

2. Take white resin (vide note [1]) 1 lb., plum tree gum 2 ozs., Venetian turpentine (c) 1 oz., linseed oil 2 ozs. ; break up the resin and melt it. Dissolve the gum in common oil and pour it into the resin, then add the turpentine and oil, and placing it on a light fire, let it thoroughly mix ; remove and keep for use ; apply slightly warmed. This is a good picture varnish.

· Under this head would come a kind of copal, known variously as " Indian copal," " dammar," and " gum animi," which flows from a Sumatran tree called *Vateria Indica*, which was, in former times, known as " white amber," or " white resin," or " white incense," which names were also given to a mixture of oil and Grecian wax, sometimes used as a varnish.

[2] As the names of many of these gums, etc., may be unfamiliar to my readers, I have placed an Appendix, descriptive of them. at the end of the book (Appendix A.), and the reference letters in the text refer thereto.

[3] D. Alexii Pedemontani de Secretis Libri Septem. (Basle, 1603.)

3. A quickly drying varnish. Take frankincense (*d*) and juniper gum, powder them and mix them finely. Take some Venetian turpentine, melt it in a little vessel, and add gradually, mixing thoroughly, the aforesaid powders. Filter through cloth and preserve ; apply warm, and it will dry very rapidly.

4. Take gum-mastic (*e*) 2 ozs., Venetian turpentine 1 oz., melt the mastic on a light fire, adding the turpentine, let it boil for some time, mixing them continuously, but not long enough for the varnish to become too thick. Put it away out of the dust. To use it, warm it in the sun and lay it on with the hand.

5. Boil 3 lbs. of linseed oil till it scorches a feather put into it, then add 8 ozs. juniper gum and 4 ozs. aloes hepatica (*f*), and thoroughly mix them ; filter through cloth, and before using, warm in the sun.

6. Gum-mastic 2 ozs., gum-juniper 2 ozs., linseed oil 3 ozs., spirits of wine 3 ozs., boil in a closed vessel for an hour.

The author cites as colouring matters, sandal wood (*g*), dragon's blood (*h*), madder (*i*) steeped in tartaric acid, log-wood (*j*), Brazil wood (*k*), all dissolved in potassa lye, and alum, and boiled. Also saffron (*b*), cinnabar (*l*), and orpiment (*m*). He says, " Linseed oil will dissolve mineral and vegetable colours, but kills others."

Fioravanti in a brochure called " The Universal Mirror of Arts and Sciences," published at Bologna in 1564, gives the four following formulæ :—

1. Linseed oil 4 parts, spirits of turpentine 2 pts., aloes 1 pt., juniper gum 1 pt.

2. Powder, benzoin, juniper gum, and gum-mastic, and dissolve in spirits of wine. This varnish dries at once.

3. Linseed oil 1 pt., white resin (*vide* note [1], p. 173) 3 pts., boil together, and colour as you will.

4. Linseed oil 1 pt., resin 2 pts., pine resin ½ pt., boil till it thickens. Juniper gum must never be added to the linseed oil till it boils, or else it will be burnt. The oil should be boiled till it scorches a feather dipped into it.

He gives the same directions as Alexis, as to colours, and the solvent powers of linseed oil.

Beyond these two authors, formulæ become rather scarce, being chiefly brought from China. All these last, and the coming. formulæ are not to be taken as invented at the dates given, for they are from works in the nature of Encyclopædias, and consequently post-dated.

A priest of the name of Anda, in a pamphlet entitled " Recueil abrégé des Secrets Merveilleux," published in 1663, gives the following recipe :—Oil of turpentine 2 ozs., turpentine 1 oz., juniper gum ½ dram ; to be mixed over a slow fire.

One, Zahn, in 1685, in " Oculus Artificialis," vol. iii., p. 166, gives two recipes :—

1. Elemi (*n*), anime (*o*), white incense, and tender copal (*p*), 2 drams each ; powder and dissolve in acetic acid in a glass vessel, adding 2 drams of gum tragacanth (*q*) and 4 drams crystallized sugar ; dry off this mixture and powder finely. Take 1 lb. of oil of lavender (*r*) or turpentine and 6 ozs. Cyprian turpentine (*s*), and boil them on a water bath. When the turpentine is well dissolved add the powder and mix thoroughly ; boil for three hours.

2. Oil of lavender 2 ozs., gum-mastic 1 oz., gum-juniper 1 oz., turpentine ½ oz. ; powder the mastic and juniper, and boil the oil, then add the turpentine, and when dissolved add the powders and mix thoroughly.

The Rev. Christopher Morley in 1692, in " Collectanæa Chinicæa Lydensia," gives under the name of " Italian varnish," the following recipe :—

Take 8 ozs. turpentine and boil on a fire till it evaporates down to 1 oz. ; powder when cold, and dissolve in warm oil of turpentine. Filter through a cloth before use.

And, lastly, a Jesuit, named Bonanni, in his " Traité des Vernis," published at Rome in 1713, gives a list of substances used, in which he includes—1, Gum-lac in sticks, tears, or tablets (*t*) ; 2, Sandarac (*u*) or juniper gum;[1] 3, Spanish or American copal, hard and soft ; 4, Amber (*v*) ; 5, Asphalte (*w*); 6, Calabrian resin or pitch ; 7, A little-known gum which flows from the wild olive-tree, resembling red scammonium.

Besides these he mentions as gums not used for varnishes, elemi, anime, arabic (*x*), pear-tree, cherry-tree, azarole-tree (*vide* p. 131), and other tree gums. He also alludes to gamboge (*y*), incense, myrrh (*z*), oppoponax (*a a*), ammonia, oils, such as turpentine, copaïba (*b b*), etc. It will be observed that he omits benzoin, and mistakes when he classes amongst useless gums elemi and anime, which (especially the former) are much used for violin varnishes on account of their tender qualities, otherwise his list is practically one of the modern ingredients of varnishes for all

---

[1] Sandarach, or rather what is sold as such, is a mixture of the resin described in note *u*, Appendix A, with dammar and hard Indian copal, the place of the African sandarach being sometimes taken by true gum juniper. These gums are insoluble (or nearly so) in alcohol, and consequently the sandarach (or pounce of the shops) is useless to the violin-maker. True sandarach is the pure gum of the common juniper, and appears in the form of long yellowish dusty tears, and such you must see that you get. And for this reason I have always in this chapter made use of the term gum juniper in preference to the better known term sandarach

purposes.   He gives many formulæ, the bases of which are principally mastic, juniper gum, copal, linseed oil, and oil of lavender.
It would be easy to multiply these old formulæ, but space
forbids it; the foregoing are doubtless the most important
and useful of them, as giving us a good idea of what materials
the old Cremona varnishers had at hand; their varnishes, of
course, had to be most carefully suited to their peculiar requirements, and properly to ascertain this it is necessary to finc.
(a) what part it plays in the construction of a fiddle, and (b)
what qualities it must consequently necessarily possess.   L'Abbé
Sibire in "La Chelonomie" thus sums up its *raison d'être* :—
" Il faut que ces pâtes, parfaitement délayées, plus légères que
massives, nourrissent les matériaux sans masquer leur vertu, et
adoucissent les sons sans les obstruer.   Ce ne serait pas la peine
d'avoir pris tant de précautions avec le compas [*du violon*], pour
les annuler avec les drogues.   Émaillez tant qu'il vous plaira,
mais n'assourdissez pas.   Quand je vous commande un violon,
je souhaite qu'il soit joli, mais j'entends qu'il soit bon ; et mon
oreille, indignée et jalouse, ne vous pardonnerait pas d'avoir, à
ses dépens, travaillé pour mes yeux."
Before beginning to consider the matter we must get rid
of all notion of colouring the wood *before* varnishing, or staining
it with acids and other corrosives to give the appearance of
age and all such inventions of the Evil one, which acids sink
right into the unprotected wood as into blotting-paper, and
invading the innermost heart of the fiddle, where they have no
business to be, destroy its most sovereign qualities without
performing any of the proper functions of varnish.   Its first
and great function is, of course, the preservation of the wood ;
without it no fiddle could attain an age of more than a very few
years, and the tone would lose sweetness and power after a very
short existence of harmony.   On its nature also a great deal
depends : it must be tender, in a manner soft ; that is, it
must yield to the movements of the wood, and not encase the
fiddle like a film of rigid glass.   It is well known that in hot
weather the wood expands, and in cold weather contracts on a
violin, imperceptibly perhaps, but none the less actually, and
the nature and quality of the varnish must be such as to allow
of its following these movements of the wood to which it is
applied, without checking them in any way, as it certainly would
if it were too hard.   It is this that gives the oil varnishes such a
vast superiority over spirit varnishes, though the former are more
difficult to compound and apply, and take weeks, months (nay,
years), to dry properly.   Gum-lac has this same hardening effect
upon varnishes, though it has been most freely and disastrously

used. In the recipes given below I have specially excluded all such, and all spirit varnishes. To obtain this suppleness, the gums must be dissolved in some liquid not highly volatile like spirit, but one which mixes with them in substance permanently, to counteract their own extreme friability. Such are the essences of lavender, rosemary, and turpentine, combined with linseed oil.

If these conditions are borne in mind, a glance at the above formulæ will show that they are all adapted for application to musical instruments in a greater or lesser degree, though most of them would require, at any rate, diluting. For instance, among those of Alexis, the Piedmontese, No. 1 is hardly more than a stain, and would require the addition of gum mastic and juniper to give it consistency. No. 2 would be tender, but too heavy ; the same remark applies to Nos. 3 and 4 ; they all require diluting with essence of turpentine, and so on throughout. A moment's consideration of each will suggest the dilution or alteration required to make it useful for the purposes of the fiddle-maker. Again, by a looseness of diction the old masters have been cited as covering their fiddles with an " oil-varnish," without stating whether the oil employed were an *oil* properly so called (as linseed oil and the like) or an essential oil (such as oil of turpentine). It has appeared in the foregoing remarks that the old varnishers used to begin by boiling their oils to an extent sufficient to render them siccative, and then after cooling they mixed in the necessary powders, having re-heated the oil to a lesser degree, otherwise the high temperature necessary to boil the oil would burn the delicate resins and gums which they employed. And in this they differed from the manner in which the hard glassy spirit varnishes of to-day are made.

M. Savart has made the extraordinary mistake of preferring a hard spirit varnish of gum-lac, but it is difficult to imagine by what circuitous route he can have arrived at such an erroneous conclusion. It has been said that Stradivarius and his predecessors varnished with amber, but strong evidence against this is brought by the fact, that the secret of dissolving amber and hard copal was not known until 1744, when letters patent for the discovery were granted to one Martin. His operation was to fuse amber and hard copal by dry heat, and dissolve it in boiling oil, which was diluted with an essence raised to the same heat before it was added. This operation was, indeed, invented in 1737, but as this was the year in which Stradivarius died, he could never have used it, much less his predecessors, as stated by Otto, and besides, a varnish so compounded would be much too hard to use on violins for the reasons before stated.

It was towards the decline of the Cremona violin manufacture that gum-lac was introduced, and with it J. B. Guadagnini spoilt the tone of many of his instruments. It is impossible to impress the fact too strongly, that the vehicle in which the resins are dissolved must be, and remain soft, so as to keep soft the resins, which by themselves are naturally hard ; and consequently any varnish from which the diluent has completely dried out must of necessity become hard and glassy, and chip off. On the other hand, if the varnish be too soft, and. in fact, remain tacky, it will in time cake, and destroy the tone of the fiddle. The hard spirit varnishes might be improved by oil of turpentine, castor-seed, lavender, etc. ; but surely it is better to use these at once than use them merely to counteract faults in an inferior composition. It is impossible to say how the old luthiers dissolved the highly-coloured resins which tint their deeper coloured varnishes ; but the means of dissolving the most delicate gums has already been discussed, and certain it is that nowadays varnishes of the highest colour can be prepared without a vestige of cloud or sediment ; and such recipes are given below.

The author of " How to Choose a Violin " (*vide* note [1], p. 127) makes the following most pertinent remark :—" It is certain that the varnish used by the old Cremona makers was superior to any now existing : it was more pliant, or it would have impaired the tone : it was adhesive, or long use would have parted it from the wood. *Yet writers err who assign to the varnish the cause of the wonderful tone of Cremona violins.* Their beauty and value are in their construction. No varnish could make an inferior instrument sound well, while a superior one would still be good, even if ill varnished." This is one of the wisest remarks of this marvellously wise little book, and I quote it that my readers may bear it in mind whilst they read this chapter.

It has been a much-debated question whether wood ought to be sized, and to my mind there can be no question about it. It seems to me certain that the old Italian makers sized their wood in some way before applying the varnish, and this accounts for the yellow substratum noticed where the varnish has worn off, alluded to by Mr. C. Reade, in the extract quoted at the beginning of this chapter, where he distinctly describes this operation of sizing with one kind of varnish, and then varnishing, in the ordinary acceptation of the term, with another, rather different in its nature—in fact, as he says, heterogeneous. The use, or rather necessity, of this operation is at once apparent when we consider the following facts. The nature of the wood

being porous or spongy, it would absorb the first two or three
coats of varnish, and, in fact, be sized by the varnish itself, and
the vehicle being absorbed, and leaving behind its resinous and
colouring particles on the surface, these last would dry rapidly,
and lose the elasticity which they should acquire by the presence
of their softening diluent. Also the instrument would want a
larger number of coats of varnish, the lower ones of which, when
the upper had worn away, would be hard and friable, and the
very quantity of varnish necessary to be applied would infallibly
destroy the power and brilliancy of the tone for a great number
of years ; in fact, the filling up of the pores with varnish
would entirely counteract the advantages derived from a complete desiccation of the wood, the result of years of preservation.
Fiddles must not be sized with common " size," like furniture,
but with quickly-evaporating washes, composed of some such
gums as gamboge or aloes, dissolved in spirits of wine to produce
the familiar yellow ground (*vide* p. 294). Such a size only pene-
trates very slightly into the wood, and leaves the resinous
ingredients on the surface in a state of infinitesimal subdivision,
which forms no check on the movements and vibrations of the
wood. It is thus, doubtless, that the old Cremonese workmen
prepared their fiddles before varnishing them, when this yellow
tint is observable ; and when not, the wash used was probably
juniper gum dissolved in alcohol. However, the yellow size
seems to be the best, and is to be made as follows :—1, Gamboge, finely powdered, 20 grammes ; spirits of wine, 100 cubic
centimetres ; or 2, gamboge, 10 grs. ; aloes, 8 grs. ; spirits
of wine, 100 cubic centimetres. Place the spirits in a vessel
with half the powdered resins, and let them dissolve for eight or
ten days, periodically stirring them, then filter out the insoluble
gummy particles through a cloth, and into the filtered portion
put the rest of the resins, and repeat the process. It is better
to do this in two operations, as the liquid is thereby more
saturated and better coloured ; and it is also better and safer to
do it thus than by means of heat. The second recipe is the best
as being more tender. One coat is sufficient, if well and evenly
laid on. It is better to use alcohol than water for this solution,
as it is a more complete solvent of the resins, and evaporates
with greater rapidity. You must be careful to have your alcohol
absolutely pure, or your troubles will be greatly increased. You
can test alcohol by letting a few drops evaporate in your hand,
when, if it has been mixed with any essential oil, the latter may
be detected by the smell left behind. If it has been adulterated
with wood spirit it is impossible to detect it, but this admixture
does not spoil the alcohol for our purposes. It is not much use

to test alcohol with areometers or hydrometers, for by a careful addition of sugar the feloniously disposed can always increase its specific gravity at will. However, when pure it ought to register 76 on the government scale, at a temperature of 60° Fahr. (or 16° Cent.) The essential oils must also be quite free from adulteration ; if they are mixed with turpentine, this latter may be discovered by rubbing the oil smartly in the palm of the hand, which will expose the turpentine by its smell. If the essential oil has been adulterated by any fixed oil it may be discovered by letting fall a drop on a piece of paper and warming it, when, instead of entirely evaporating, it will leave a transparent spot on the paper. If it is adulterated with alcohol, place a little in a graduated tube with a little water. The two will keep separate and the bulk of the oil may still be registered, but on shaking it up, the water dissolves the alcohol out of the essential oil, and the latter becomes smaller in bulk than before. If on shaking up the oil smartly in a bottle it becomes milky or opalescent, it indicates the presence of water as an adulterant. If the essence be distilled in a small retort, any resin or fixed oil which may have been mixed with it will be separated. By all these methods, therefore, you may test the purity of your materials before commencing operations. And this brings us to the colouring of varnishes, which is a much more difficult matter than one would suppose, for many essences, such as essence of turpentine, lavender, rosemary, etc., will not (or only very slightly) act as solvents of coloured resins, or will only hold them in suspension, which would be fatal to the transparency of the varnish. Such resins (which include gamboge, dragon's blood, etc.) are, however, soluble in spirits of wine ; and in the following manner they may be used to colour the essences before-mentioned :—

Let the colour-resin be dissolved in alcohol, and the solution may be poured into the essence without losing its clearness. Now, the boiling or evaporating point of alcohol being much power than that of the essence, the mixture may be kept above the boiling point of the alcohol and below that of the essence, and thus the alcohol will evaporate, and leave behind it the colouring matter stationary in the essence, which is thus, as it were, deceived into holding the colour in clear solution. Any colour resin may thus be incorporated with any essence (except that of turpentine), which may then be used in the composition of a varnish ; but it must be borne in mind that *all* the materials employed must be *absolutely* pure ; and their purity must be ascertained by the means given above. As the best essence wherewith to incorporate the colour is that of turpentine, and essence of turpentine in its clear, pure, recently-distilled state will not mix with alcohol, a slightly different mode of procedure must be followed—namely, the essence must be exposed to the air in an uncorked phial, and periodically stirred before adding the alcoholic solution, so as to mix it with the oxygen of the air. It must remain exposed until a few drops taken from the exposed essence mix readily with a similar quantity of alcohol; the exposure required to oxidize the essence will seldom exceed two months. The resins employed for giving a red tint to varnishes are those of the *Pterocarpus indicus* which imparts an orange colour; the *Pterocarpus santalinus*, which gives a darker red; and dragon's blood, which gives the deepest scarlet. The woods or the resins must be powdered fine, and steeped in alcohol for some eight or ten days, and then filtered off for use. The best essence is that of turpentine, combining, as it does, properties at once tender and siccative. After it come in order, rosemary and lavender, of which the former is the better.

All operations requiring heat should be performed on a water bath, the nature of which is too well known to require explanation here, and the compositor of varnishes should always have close at hand a wet cloth and a pail of water, in case the compound should catch fire; but this contingency seldom happens if the inner vessel be not filled to more than half its capacity. The alcoholic solution of the colouring resin should first be evaporated to half its bulk, to obviate the essence being too freely diluted by its addition. When cold, this saturated solution may be added to the essence of turpentine, which has been oxidized as before described, and the two boiled together, *being most careful to keep it below the boiling point of the essence;* in this way the alcohol will be entirely dissipated. It may be occasionally stirred with a *wooden* stick to hasten it, and instead of letting the alcoholic solution cool, it will have the same effect if the essence be heated to a like temperature before the alcoholic solution is added. When all the alcohol has passed off, which will be seen when bubbles cease to be evolved, let the mixture remain on the water bath for a few minutes, to drive off any water which may be left there by the alcohol, but it must not be left long enough for the essence to commence to evaporate, or the colouring matter will be precipitated in proportion as the liquid diminishes. Of course, the above directions are given for the preparation of small quantities of varnish; if large quantities were constantly being made, it would be worth while to regain the alcohol hereby dissipated by means of special apparatus, which it is needless here to describe. It is always better to perform these operations in the summer, for in winter oils and essences have a tendency to alter in their nature and consistency from either cold or absorption.

From the beginning of July to the end of September is the best time to prepare varnishes. The three red resins mentioned above, pass through many shades of colour, and may be lightened with gamboge, and darkened with asphalte or dragon's blood; but these tone-modifiers must not be used in sufficient quantity to alter the nature of the varnish. For instance, gamboge dissolves more readily in essential oil (especially that of turpentine) than the sandal woods which have to be added by means of the alcoholic solution ; so to lighten an essence coloured with sandal wood the gamboge must not be added *direct* to the solution, or, by reason of its greater affinity, the essence might precipitate the sandal wood in favour of the gamboge. This latter, therefore, must be added by means of an alcoholic solution, and the alcohol evaporated off as described above. Dragon's blood, however, is not so readily precipitated from the essence ; therefore this may more safely be added directly to the essence without the intervention of the alcoholic solution. It is best to finish the colouring of the essence before commencing to compound the rest f the varnish. Finally, it is necessary to state that the essence of turpentine has been dealt with hitherto as being the best, for reasons given above ; essence of rosemary may also be used, and is easier to deal with, but not so good in the final result. The alcoholic solution of sandal wood is apt to oxidize and deepen in tint on exposure to the air, though an essential solution does not present this peculiarity to so marked a degree, all its solutions, however, are powerfully acted upon by alkalies of all kinds.

In conclusion of this somewhat lengthy subject, there remains only to formulate the final operations necessary for the completion of the varnish. The resins appropriate to our use divide into two classes, the hard and the soft. The hard comprise copal, amber, and gum-lac, and the soft are subdivided into two other classes, viz., dry, such as juniper gum, gum-mastic, and dammar ; and elastic, such as benzoin, elemi, anime, and turpentine The first, or hard kinds, would be unsuitable used alone, for they would check the vibrations of the instrument and chip off on the slightest provocation; the second, or dry kind, counteract this chipping tendency of the hard kinds, but used alone would powder off; the third, or elastic kinds, are not solid enough to use alone, besides, by their heavy glutinous character,

rendering the tone of the fiddle woolly and viola-like, but they
impart elasticity to the hard kinds, and consistency to the dry
kinds, when mixed with them. The art, therefore, of making
varnish lies in so combining these three classes that each
conveys its good qualities and counteracts the bad ones of the
other two. In spirit varnishes the dry and elastic kinds must
be mixed, to ensure tenderness and solidity, for the alcohol
evaporating leaves the resins as they are, on the wood, and if the
soft resins unduly preponderate they will remain tacky for a
long time. The most wearable resin is mastic, but as it is not
wholly soluble in pure alcohol, it must be added last of all the
ingredients, when the insoluble parts mingling with the other
constituents obviate this difficulty. It is easy, therefore, to see
that formulæ for varnishes can be varied *ad infinitum* according to
requirements. Thus taking as a basis 100 cc. (cubic centimetres)
of alcohol, to produce a terrifically hard varnish, we would use
gum-lac 20 grammes, juniper gum 8 gr., elemi 4 gr. For a good
wearing, and at the same time, tender varnish, juniper gum
20 gr., mastic 10 gr., elemi 4 gr., or juniper gum 25 gr., mastic
6 gr., Venetian turpentine 10 gr. (turpentine must always be
added to a spirit varnish *last*). It must be remembered (and it is
shown in these three formulæ) that alcohol will only dissolve
one-third of its weight of resins. A good formula for spirit
varnish is that of Watin, who prescribes juniper gum 125 gr.,
gum-lac (in tears) 62 gr. 50 centi-grammes, mastic 62 gr. 50 c.,
elemi 31 gr. 25 c., Venetian turpentine 62 gr. 50 c., alcohol
1 litre (= 1000 cc.). This would yet be too hard a varnish,
but Watin was (erroneously to my mind) in favour of this
quality, and it must be remembered that he was hardly a fiddle-
maker. The best spirit varnish for our purpose is composed as
follows :—Juniper gum 80 gr., mastic 100 gr., elemi 30 gr.,
concentrated essence of turpentine,[1] 60 cc., castor oil 50 cc.,
alcohol 1 litre. Before the addition of the resins the spirit must
be coloured, as described above. If a thick varnish (of which
one coat will be sufficient) is required, the resins may be proportionately increased, but not the turpentine or castor oil, for
they would make the varnish sticky if overdone.

However good this may be as a spirit varnish, and however
convenient to work with, it is, and must be inferior to an oil
varnish, for the latter is at the same time more tender, and more
solid, for it continues its softening and binding presence, whereas
the alcohol becomes promptly dissipated. It is always better to
compound varnishes without heat than with it ; for the former

[1] By concentrated, I mean evaporated to one-tenth part of its bulk. Turpentine is here indicated, but as elsewhere stated rosemary might also be used

is only a matter of time, and the latter is liable to carbonize or otherwise alter the constituents; and, secondly, there is no denying that all the substances used are highly inflammable, and without exceedingly careful handling, considerable danger to life and property ensues if heat is used in a laboratory not specially constructed for the purpose. It will be seen that the materials ready to our hand now, are the same (with the exception of some useless ones, such as frankincense, etc.) as were enumerated in the old recipes. In our favour we can cite, that, *when* unadulterated, resins are to be had purer than they were then,[1] and the operations of concentrating essences, and fusing the hard gums, then unknown, are now fully understood. It has been explained that we must relinquish the use of the four hard resins, and also benzoin, because by swelling it renders the varnish gummy; and juniper-gum, because it requires so much heat, and tender copal (or dammar) is just as good, and much easier to work with.

We are reduced, therefore, to 1, mastic (in tears), which is the most tender and wearable of all resins; 2, tender copal (= brittle dammar), which by its dryness counteracts the more elastic resins, and renders the varnish more siccative; 3, Venetian turpentine, which we avoid, as rendering the varnish tacky; 4, elemi, and 5, anime, both very soft and elastic gums. Camphor is sometimes mentioned as having been used, but it has a tendency to kill colour. The formula left us as the best, becomes therefore, mastic 10 gr., tender copal 5 gr., essence (coloured at will as described) 100 cc. To this is added finally 5 cc. of linseed oil, not boiled, but the older the better. More than this quantity might be used, but with the effect of lessening the siccative properties of the varnish. The above formula may be prepared as follows :—Place the 100 cc. of coloured essence in a glass vessel, and into it put the mastic, which will take from twenty-four to thirty-six hours to dissolve. When quite dissolved add the copal, which will take a like time. Periodically shake the bottle. Then finally mix in the oil. Put this fluid away in a dark, cool place, in a stoppered bottle, for ten days or a fortnight, to let it settle ; then filter (through filter paper for choice), and keep the varnish six or eight months before using it In this varnish elemi, anime, and turpentine are left out, the linseed oil taking their place in contributing the tenderness to the varnish. The resins appear to bear a small proportion to the essence, but it must be remembered that

[1] It has been suggested that in these very adulterations, the natures of which we cannot now ascertain, lay the " secret of the Cremona varnish," a hypothesis which, to say the least of it, is exceedingly improbable.

the colouring matter will have already, to a certain extent, charged it, and it is better to have the varnish thin, and varnish often, than to have it thick and lay it on blotchy. When the essence is tinted with dragon's blood, it is better even to reduce the weight of resins proportionately to 12 gr. instead of 15, as above. Such a consistency will not require warming before use, as is necessary if the varnish be too thick.

When varnishing, you will discover the absolute necessity of having your wood thoroughly dry and well seasoned. If it is not, the varnish, instead of preserving the wood, will hasten its decay by preventing it from drying properly. It must be borne in mind, that to lay on varnish evenly is very difficult, for every stroke of the brush tells on the porous surface of the wood. Of a really well compounded, thin, and transparent varnish, the requisite depth of colour and thickness of varnish is not generally reached till the twelfth to the fifteenth coat, and each coat must be thoroughly dry before another is applied, or else the varnish will chip and powder off; it saves a good deal of trouble to wait a week or more between each coat, on the principle of "more haste worse speed." If after a few coats you find the colour is deep enough, instead of continuing you may finish with one coat of the following transparent varnish—mastic 20 gr., copal (= brittle dammar) 10 gr., essence (new and pure) 100 cc., linseed oil 12 cc. The essence must be the same as that used in the first or coloured varnish. It is possible to varnish with one or two thick coats, but it is neither so satisfactory nor so good. Varnishing should always be done on a dry, warm day, in some place out of a draught, or the operation will become much more difficult : the full particulars of the operation being elsewhere laid down (*vide* p. 294).

To recapitulate the foregoing rather protracted details, the operations to be performed are, in brief, as follows:—(1) Steep 100 gr. of sandal-wood (or 80 of dragon's blood) powdered, in 1 litre of alcohol, set it in the sun or some warm place for ten days, shaking it periodically. Then filter through a cloth, and repeat the process with another 100 (or 80) gr., in the same litre of alcohol. To lighten the colour, use an alcoholic solution of gamboge; to darken it, use similarly asphalte or dragon's blood Always use deep, large vessels, and never fill them more than half full at a time. (2) Now take 300 cc. of this coloured alcohol in a graduated vessel, and reduce it, by evaporation on a water-bath, to half its bulk. Then pour into it 200 cc. of essence and volatilize the alcohol as before described, after which you will find you have 200 cc. of coloured essence.

(3) When this is cold add your resins, shaking periodically as before described. Leave the liquid to settle for a fortnight, then filter through paper and preserve.

Thus far it has seemed necessary to enter into the minutiæ of the rather distinct art of varnishing, and I hope that these notes, gathered from the most reliable sources and from personal experiences, may, at any rate, serve as guides for the experiments and practice of the would-be Cremona varnisher. To any one more particularly interested in the subject, I beg to recommend the work of M. Eugène Mailand, to whose " Découverte des Anciens Vernis Italiens " I am indebted for much valuable information contained in the foregoing pages.[1]

The violin is now theoretically finished, *i.e.*, we have scientifically discussed all its parts, and have only to add the fittings and strings (which will be the subject of the next two chapters), before playing on our fiddle. The reader will by this time have fully appreciated the host of trifles to which deference must be paid, for if not, *hæ nugæ in seria ducent mala*. Their importance must not be judged by their number (which alone is calculated to impress the unlearned), but by the immense influence every trivial part has on the combined whole ; *non numero hæc judicantur, sed pondere*.

[1] E. Mailand, " Découverte des Anciens Vernis Italiens, Employés pour les Instruments à Cordes et à Archet " (Paris, 1859), Second Edition, 1874.

Nelle selve io vivea cipresso muto
Oi, morto, ho voce, poi che me fer liuto.

CHAPTER XL

FITTINGS AND APPLIANCES.

The Fittings.—Having completed our Violin by varnishing it, the next step to be considered is the fittings. These, taken as a class, may be said to consist of the pegs, the nut, the finger-board, the tail-piece, the rest and the tail-pin, as necessary to the existence of, and fastened on to, the violin when in use, in manner hereinafter appearing. Beyond this, other miscellanea, which might more properly be called "appurtenances," exist, and consist of chin-rests, mutes, and other accessories, which have a local habitation in the pockets of a well-organised fiddle-case. It has been the tendency very frequently to consider these fittings either too important or too unimportant, the results being, in the former case, to produce complications which end in agony and vexation of spirit and a reversion to simplicity, and, in the latter, to produce endless worry and difficulty. The true secret of a well-fitted violin is to have all these things, good in themselves, simple in construction and application, and properly and scientifically applied to the instrument, and how to produce this result is the object of the present chapter. Besides noticing them and their arrangement, I shall also advert to some of the patent fittings, which have begun and ended their useless existence unknown, and, in fact, though years old, my readers may probably hear of them for the first time through the medium of these pages.

To take all things in their order, we begin with the pegs (D, Fig. 39). These are made of boxwood, ebony, or rose-wood ; in their simplest form they are represented in Fig. 95 (A and B). All forms are, however, liable to ornamentations, which have been noticed in Chapter IX., and are represented in their most ordinary design at c in the same figure. Of the three components named boxwood is the most inferior, being hard and unyielding, which causes the pegs to stick ; the most convenient are made of rosewood, which, being springy and soft, are easily fitted, and turn in the holes for tuning purposes with an ease and firmness which commends itself at once to amateurs, and especially to ladies, who should always use them, as they reduce the operation of tuning from a tiresome and lengthy to an easy and instantaneous one. Their only disadvantage is that they wear out sooner than ebony pegs, which, if really thoroughly well fitted, eclipse all others both for ease in tuning, wear, and appearance. But the fitting must be done by some one thoroughly experienced in violin fitting, for a badly-fitted peg is an abomination. It is also most important and essential to the convenience of the player that the pegs should be so set in the head, that each string can pass from the peg to the nut, quite clear of the other three pegs. Otherwise one string will rub over the peg of another, and each time one is

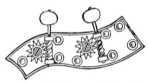

FIG. 95.—Violin Pegs.   FIG. 96.—Machine-Head for Violin.

tuned the other will be thrown out, which immensely increases the difficulty of tuning the instrument. Such a defect in an instrument can, however, be remedied by having the old holes filled up and new ones bored by an intelligent workman, but this operation certainly does not improve the appearance of the head. Full instructions will be given for fitting pegs in a future chapter. The best size is $1\frac{1}{5}$ inch long, the stem tapering from $\frac{3}{8}$ of an inch to $\frac{11}{40}$ of an inch. Pegs have been made also of rhinoceros horn, ivory, and other fancy substances, but after a short trial they have been pronounced utterly unsatisfactory, and rejected. Fig. 96 represents a machine head ; these certainly carry the palm, so far as ease in tuning is concerned, but they soon wear out, and if they become loose anywhere a jar is produced, calculated to qualify the possessor for election to the first vacant post of county lunatic. Patent pegs are all much of a muchness. Fig. 97 represents one of these, the invention of Mr. Joseph Wallis, and has, at any rate, the merit of complicated ingenuity to recommend it. A is a metal stem ; B a metal screw, passing through an ordinary peg-head c, and fitting on to the end of A ; D D are two metal discs lying against the cheek of the scroll. When the peg has been adjusted in the ordinary manner, it may be rendered immovable, by turning the serew B by means of the key E. It is not, however, by any means a new idea, the same principle having been in-vented and patented before, both for guitars and violins. The principle is in itself wrong, the action of the screw being to compress the cheeks of the scroll, which is highly un-desirable ; for in the first place old and dry wood will not stand it, and in the second place it is necessary, in apply-ing them, to fill up the old holes and bore new ones, a process absolutely scouted by owners of valuable fiddles with their heads in the original condition. Owners of such will often rather put up with the inconvenience of one string rubbing over the other pegs inside the box, rather than have the head altered.

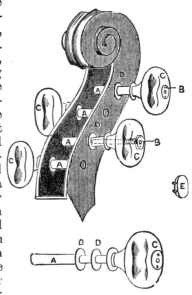

FIG. 97.—Wallis's Patent Peg.

In 1876 a patent was taken out (No. 4525) by Wm. H. Cooke, for applying the ratchet system to ordinary pegs in a manner which, in fact, was merely a complicated machine head, the machine screw pegs turning ordinary ones. Another very fairly good peg patented in 1876 by M. H. Collins (No 2118) was introduced by him in connection with his patent and eccentric violin. It will be found figured (Fig. 72) and described under the head of vagaries in Chapter V., page 111. The best patent peg yet introduced is (to make use of an "Irishism") not a patent at all ;

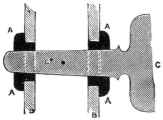

FIG. 98.—Patent Peg to ensure Firmness.

it simply consists in having the peg holes made a little larger, as in Fig. 98, and having them fitted with an ebony collar A, which so much increases the surface of resistance offered to the shaft of the peg (by projecting beyond the cheeks of the scroll) that slipping becomes practically unknown. Mr. Stuttaford has introduced a peg for the A string to obviate the difficulty always experienced in getting at this string consequent on its being covered by the volute of the scroll (*vide* M. Chanot's violin, p. 115). A screw runs down the stem of the peg from the end of the thumb piece, which presses upon the string as soon as it is put through the hole in the peg, and holds it tight, so that the peg can be turned at once without the trouble of pulling out the end with tweezers, and doubling it under the string to fix it. A good idea, but likely to weaken the peg, and get out of order.

The Nut (s, Fig. 39) is the small piece of ebony $\frac{1}{4}$ inch high, $\frac{9}{40}$ in diameter, $\frac{5}{8}$ long, which intervenes between the peg-box and the finger-board, and over the hard cross-grain of which the strings pass (on small grooves cut in it), to the bridge clear of the finger-board, its elevation above which is only $\frac{1}{18}$ under the first, and $\frac{1}{32}$ under the fourth string.

The Finger-board (E, Fig. 39) is the most important of the fittings of the violin; its most ordinary and correct measurement being $10\frac{3}{8}$ inches long, the breadth tapering from $1\frac{5}{8}$ inch at the bridge, to $\frac{5}{8}$ inch at the nut. Its thickness so long as it is glued to the neck, is $\frac{3}{16}$ inch, from which point it tapers to $\frac{2}{16}$ inch. At its broad end it is $2\frac{15}{32}$ inches (just under $2\frac{1}{2}$ inches) from the bridge. Its distance below the strings at its broad end must be very nicely adjusted, the correct distances being about :— below the E, $\frac{5}{32}$ inch ; below the A, $\frac{11}{64}$ inch ; below the D, $\frac{3}{16}$ inch ; below the G, $\frac{5}{32}$ inch. The *cutting* of the bridge must follow the contour of the finger-board, but *not* its height, for the finger-board must be raised or lowered by cutting away the wood of the neck at either end, rather than that the bridge be made to suit the finger-board. (See on this point Chapter IX., par. " The Bridge," p. 161.)

Of course the finger-board must be rounded to coincide with the ordinary cutting of a bridge. If the finger-board be not rounded enough, the E and G strings will be too close to it, and the A and D too far away, if the bridge be properly cut ; if it be too round, the opposite will be the result, and in high shifts the bow will be apt to strike three strings at once. At the same time at the broad end of the finger-board the G string is furthest from it, and the E is the closest (*i.e.*, about $\frac{1}{8}$ inch), for the vibrations of the G string being the largest they must have most room, on which principle the distance between the strings and the finger-board decreases, as the open note is pitched higher, till the minimum is reached under the E string. The bridge and finger-board must each oblige one another, and not each try to compel the shape of the other. The boundary for the length or the finger-board has been set down as far as the upper corners of the fiddle, and no farther. From the end of the neck to the end of the finger-board, its under side will be hollowed out following the decrease in thickness. So far as it is glued to the neck, the thickness must be perfectly uniform, to preserve a level surface. M. l'Abbé Sibire, in " La Chelonomie," inveighs in unmeasured terms against a practice which certainly I have never come across—namely, that of hollowing out a semicircular space between the neck and the finger-board. The practice seems to have arisen with a view to lightening the finger-board. The finger-board must, of course, be glued closely and firmly to the neck all over the surface of the latter.

The wood of which it is made should not be too close and dense, or it will influence the elasticity of the neck, and consequently the tone. The height of the broad end above the belly will vary with the model of the fiddle, but it may generally be taken as $\frac{7}{10}$; the finger-board should be made of ebony, which must be thoroughly dry and well seasoned, and its cutting and fitting will be set down further on. Finger-boards have been, and are still on cheap fiddles, made of stained or veneered wood; these are an endless trouble, as they are constantly wearing out. Curiously enough, M. Savart recommended such finger-boards for the sake of obtaining an increase of elasticity and vibration, but this is proved to be a mistake. Formerly, finger-boards used to be made curiously ornamented, and of fancy materials. Mr. Arthur Hill has a wonderful collection of such curiosities, which have been discussed under the head of ornamentations in Chapter IX. (page 166).

Spohr is said to have recommended the hollowing out of the finger-board under the G string to allow for its greater vibrations, but my experience of this vagary is that it is a worrying and useless eccentricity, whose superfluity is only equalled by its unsightliness. I am told by Mr. John Bishop (of Cheltenham) that Spohr got this idea from Romberg the Violoncellist. One can understand that it might be advantageous for the C string of a Violoncello, but not for the G of the Violin. In a word, the finger-board should be perfectly plain, polished, and true, as in Fig. 99.

As for patent finger-boards their name has been legion, and countless contrivances, " born to blush unseen," have increased the revenue, as is testified by the records of the patent office.

In 1845, Robert Brooks took out a patent (No. 10,719) for various improvements in finger-boards, the principle of all of

which was similar—viz., a double finger-board, between the two
surfaces of which the strings ran, and were acted upon by
means of studs passing through the upper one, and kept above
the strings by a spring, which could be pressed down at the
right spot like the keys of a pianoforte. In 1852, R. A.
Brooman patented (No. 567) a similar, but not so complicated
a contrivance. In 1876, Daniel Semple took out a patent
(No. 3723) for a finger-board, which had between the strings
rows of raised points on flexible wires to guide the fingers.
(Pleasant to slide up and down !)

The *Tail-piece* (P, Fig. 39) is made, as a rule, of ebony,
though useless, fancy things are sometimes to be found beneath
the glass cases in a fiddle dealer's shop, made of ivory, glass, and
other such utterly unsuitable materials. Enough has been said

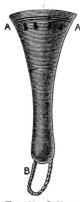

FIG 100.—Ordinary
Form of Tail-piece.

in another place of ornamental tail-pieces; they
are generally a delusion and a snare, as regards
their superiority over the simpler forms (as in
Fig. 100). The tail-piece is attached to the
tail-pin of the fiddle by a loop made of a D
tenor string (as at B in Fig. 100), sufficiently
long for the ebony to be supported by the
tension of the strings, just clear of the edge of
the fiddle (protected by the " rest "). The
orthodox dimensions are $4\frac{3}{8}$ inches long, $\frac{1}{8}$ inch
thick, $1\frac{3}{4}$ inch in diameter at the broadest, and
$\frac{5}{8}$ inch at the narrowest part. The holes to
receive the strings should be at equal distances
from one another (as in the figure), the slits
into which they run diverging towards the edge,
in such a manner that the strings run to the
bridge parallel with one another, and not fanwise, as in this
latter case the bridge gets dragged forward by the operation of
tuning. The strings pass from the tail-piece to the bridge
over a kind of nut (A A, Fig. 100) formed of ebony or ivory,
and let into the tail-piece at $\frac{3}{16}$ inch from its broad edge.
The distance from the bridge to the edge of the tail-piece should
be $1\frac{3}{4}$ inches.

In Mr. Bishop's translation of Otto's work, a most lucid
description is given by the translator of a tail-piece invented
by L. Spohr, by means of which the portions of the strings lying
between it and the bridge could be so regulated as to produce
certain intervals, which might tend, perhaps, to modify little
inequalities of tone in some instruments, or prove advantageous
in other respects. Fig. 101 represents this contrivance ; A, B,
and C being drawn half their actual size, and D, E, F full or

actual size. A consists of a fore part *e*, and a hind part *f*, and is formed out of one piece of wood (or metal). The fore part is perfectly flat on the top, but is worked out underneath, to the extent and in the manner shown in the section of the tail-piece c, and in the view of the front end of it B. This fore part has four long openings *a a a a*, placed at a suitable distance from each other, and made to receive the like number of little pegs

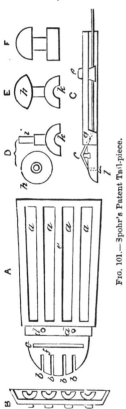

FIG. 101.—Spohr's Patent Tail-piece.

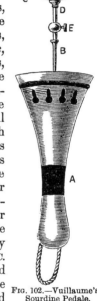

FIG. 102.—Vuillaume's Sourdine Pedale.

formed as at E. The hind part *f* of A, which is semicircular, stands a little lower than the fore part *e*, and has its upper edge rounded off, as shown at c It is chiefly remarkable for four little slits, *b b b b*, made to receive the knots of the strings, and for a little nut *c c*, formed of bone or brass, which is let into the middle of the semi-circular part *f* There are also two small holes, *d d*, through which the gut-loop is passed which connects the tail-piece with the tail-pin. Four other small holes pass obliquely from the upper to the under side of the tail-piece, as shown by the dotted lines *g* in c. E and F are front and side views of the little pegs which are placed in the openings *a a a a* of A, and press on the strings beneath the fore part of the tail-piece, as shown at c. By moving them to and fro in their respective openings, those portions of the strings between them and the bridge are lengthened or shortened, and thus the different intervals are obtained. These pegs consist of two parts, as at D, where *h* represents the knob or cap, and *i* the pin, which is firmly glued into a hole in the middle of it, after having first been passed through one of the openings *a* from the under side; the little furrow *k* at the bottom of the peg is intended to receive the string. From the section c the mode of attaching the string may be seen. After tying a knot in the string *l*, it is drawn into one of the slits *b*, then carried over the nut *c*, and passed through one of the holes *g*. It then passes into the furrow *k* of the peg E, and over the bridge in the usual way. This contrivance is very scientific and ingenious, but has been but very little used.

Vuillaume's Sourdine pedale (Fig. 102) is an ingenious combination of mute and tail-piece, which enables an instrument to be immediately muted or unmuted by a player during a performance ; it is very useful for effects, such as sudden echoes or short muted passages, but it is too great a strain for the chin to keep it in action long. Its principle is as follows : the plate A stands up in the centre of the tail-piece, as shown in the figure ; this acts upon a bent spring below the tail-piece, to the end of which is attached the arm B, bearing the mute C on a sliding fitting D. By the pressure of the chin upon A this spring is straightened, and therefore lengthened, which pushes the mute C by means of the rod B against the bridge. Its distance from

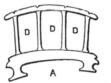

FIG. 103.—Zebrowski's Bridge and Mute.

the bridge is regulated by the telescope fitting D, which carries the mute C, and fixes it on the rod by the screw E. Its great disadvantage is that it deadens the tone of the fiddle, and is very apt to come loose and jar.

A somewhat similar contrivance, or, rather, combination of bridge, mute, and tail-piece, was patented in 1881 (No. 3915) by Felix von Zebrowski. This bridge, which is figured at A, Fig. 103, was, as will be seen, composed merely of four uprights, with a base of the ordinary sort and a top connecting piece. This tail-piece was in appearance much like Vuillaume's, but Zebrowski's stud A (Fig. 102) was fitted into a slot, into which (A being a screw) it could be fixed. The arm B, instead of carrying a metal mute C, carried a plate shown at B, Fig. 103, bearing three cushions of leather C C C, which fitted into the three openings D D D of the bridge A. To apply the mute, the stud A had to be unscrewed, pushed forward in the slot till the plate B embraced the bridge, and there refastened. It was very ingenious, but not nearly so simple in application as the ordinary mute, which it did not exceed in efficacy, whilst the tone of the fiddle was seriously

impaired by so unorthodoxly-shaped a bridge. Mr. Stuttaford
has recently patented a tail-piece whereon the strings pass
through slots at the broad end from small buttons placed behind
them, over which the strings are looped. The idea is an excellent one, for the strain on the knot consequent on the present
form is thereby reduced to a minimum, but, unfortunately,
fiddlers are so loth to make use of any innovation, which is a

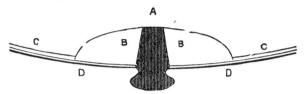

FIG. 104.—Section of Tail-pin with sides, side linings, and block (Guarnerius block).

departure from the old-established forms, that it is doubtful
whether it will ever come into use among violinists.

The *Tail-pin* (Q, Fig. 39) is the peg of ebony or box-wood, which
is firmly fixed into the bottom block, as in Fig. 104, through the
centre of the join of the lower bouts, as in Fig. 105, to which is
fastened the loop, or gut-attachment of the tail-piece (B, Fig. 100).
It requires to be very carefully fitted, as it has to withstand the
entire tension of the strings. Directions as to its fitting, etc.,
will be given in a future chapter. Its length is regulated by
the depth of the block ; the diameter of the knob is $\frac{5}{8}$ inch.

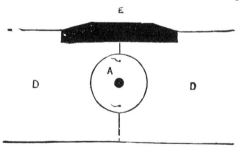

FIG. 105.—View of Tail-pin with Rest at base of Fiddle.

The *Rest* is that small piece of ebony, or other hard material
(E, Fig. 105), over which the gut passes from the button A to the
tail-piece. It measures, in length, $1\frac{2}{3}$ inch ; breadth, $\frac{11}{48}$ inch.
Its depth and shape are regulated by the edge of the fiddle
whose shape it follows, its only office being to protect the edge
of the fiddle from the gut-loop (B, Fig. 100), which would otherwise cut into it with the tension of the strings.

These fittings, therefore, having been duly apportioned to the

instrument, there remains only to string the fiddle to have it
ready to play upon. In the next chapter I shall shortly describe
the operations through which the guts in the natural state pass
before they reach us as strings ; but in the meantime we must
consider, before leaving our fiddle, the various appliances which
are to be found in every fiddle-case, and which include chin-
rests, mutes, gauges, string-box, rosin,
tuning-forks, etc. The first and most important of these is—

The *Chin-rest*, which in its most primitive form (represented in Fig. 106) is said
to have been invented by L. Spohr, and
is, without doubt, a great convenience to
violinists, as the hold which it gives the
chin, which could not otherwise be obtained
but by great pressure, imparts a freedom

FIG. 106.—Chin-rest
(L. Spohr).

and ease to the left hand in shifting, which comes of its being
rendered absolutely irresponsible as far as the retaining of the
fiddle in its proper position is concerned, beyond merely sup-
porting it at its proper angle. Some people prefer to place a
pad to fill the hollow beneath the collar bone, but it is not
so certain ; others again aver that it checks the vibrations of

the belly, but the field
of contact at an almost
quiescent point being
so small, and in the
newer forms being re-
duced absolutely to a
minimum, I think we
may dismiss this com-
plaint as practically
without foundation. It
was founded on this
supposed disadvantage
that Ole Bull took
out an English patent
in 1879 (No. 1604),

FIG. 107.—New form of Chin-rest.

for several wonderful
and cumbrous arrangements of rest, or holder, embracing
almost the entire base of the fiddle, and attached to the tail-pin or
bottom block of the fiddle. Following the same line of thought,
Zebrowski, at the same time that he patented his tail-piece and
bridge-mute (Fig. 103), projected a holder of the ordinary shape,
which instead of clipping the fiddle, was attached to a strap
extending by a hook from the lower left-hand corner of the

fiddle to the tail-pin, to which it was firmly attached. His principle seems to have been, with a view to prevent the imaginary checking of the vibration by a tiny clamp, to clasp the entire left hand lower bout with a thick strap ! Comment is needless. The name of the fiddle-holders is legion in their improved form. A good typical specimen, and one which is beyond the reach of the " vibrationists," is the latest introduction (from America) of Mr. W. E. Hill (Fig. 107), which is formed of vulcanite and nickel. Its composition gives it ascendency over its rivals, than which in other respects it is neither better nor worse. A chin-rest forming one piece with the tail-piece, and with it affixed to the tail-pin, is represented

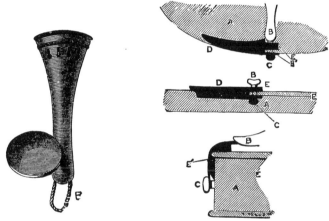

FIG. 108.—Tail-piece and Chin-rest combined.

FIG. 109.—Newest Improvement of Chin-rest.

by Fig. 108. It has this disadvantage, that the chin pressing upon it, twists the tail-piece, and throws the strings out of tune.

Mr. G. A. Chanot, of Manchester, has made me a most excellent chin-rest, to my mind the best I have seen. It is composed simply of one piece of ebony, and is shown at Fig. 109 in plan, elevation, and section. A represents the sides and tables of the fiddle. The chin-rest D is furnished with two ends or tongues E E' at right angles to one another, so that they can be slipped under the loop (B, Fig. 100), which connects the tail-piece B with the tail-pin C. In this way the point of contact is reduced to a minimum, the rest being held on to the fiddle by means of the loop-attachment of the tail-piece. Its great charm is its simplicity; its only fault, if any, is that a good hard pull, such as is sometimes in difficult passages made on the chin-rest, is liable to give the tail-piece a twist, small in itself but quite enough to throw the strings out of tune. It is a simplified form of a chin-rest, which I saw once on a fiddle years ago. In this instance, the ebony chin-rest proper was mounted on a plate of brass which extended some inches on each side of the tail-piece, in consequence of which not only was the chin-rest extremely heavy, but the fiddle had to be entirely unmounted to put it on. There has lately been introduced in Italy a rest, the principle of which is that it is attached *round the neck* by a band fixed to the tail-pin, which is peculiarly constructed to admit of its application. In theory it is doubtless good, for it leaves the neck and head free, no pressure of the chin being necessary, but in practice a trifle outrageous, for it takes a considerable time under these circumstances to disembarrass oneself of one's fiddle, which would be a trifle awkward, not to say ludicrous, after a solo in a concert room.

The *Mute* is that appliance formed of metal or other material which, being clipped on to the bridge, checks its vibrations, and thus deadens the tone of the entire instrument. The common

and most familiar form is executed in metal, and a very efficacious one is that one known as the Mysterious Mute, which is composed of horn and brass. After trying all sorts I have discarded all others in favour of the one represented full size in Fig. 110, introduced a short time since by Mr. W. E. Hill, which is formed of vulcanite, moulded all in one piece, which precludes the possibility of jar, and, being formed of an elastic, though resisting material, clips tightly, without injuring the bridge. On the action of the mute enough has been said when discussing bridges (page 163). The Vuillaume and Zebrowski mutes have been already described under the heading of tail-pieces. As effective a mute as any may be extemporized by placing a penny or half-crown behind and against the bridge, setting it under the A string with its edges resting on the E and D.

FIG. 110.—Hill's Vulcanite Mute.

A word about rosin, which, without doubt, is the most essential necessity of the fiddler, for as Wilkins said in 1607,[1] " My fiddlestick cannot play without rosin," and, in truth, however good the player, the fiddle or the bow, all is dumb and useless without the humble, necessary " colophane." There are an immense number of different kinds of rosin, or rather different arrangements of rosin. Many soloists of celebrity use a common lump of kitchen rosin, in spite of what all the books ever written in

[1] Wilkins, *The Miseries of Enforced Marriage* (1607), Act V. *Vide* "The Ancient British Drama" (London, 1810), vol. ii., p. 180.

the subject say. The more ordinary forms are all equally good
in spite of the eulogies inscribed on the labels ; the only thing
to be noticed is, that as there are trifling differences in their
composition and substance, you should never change your rosin :
that is, that if you want to try a new sort of rosin, do not do so
till you have your bow re-haired, and the older your rosin is
the better. I have some put up by M. J. B. Vuillaume which
is perfect on account of its age. To my mind the most convenient form is the book-form, introduced by M. Georges
Chanot, which is enclosed in a leather case, which keeps the
rosin dust from filling one's fiddle-case, and besides is convenient
to hold, presents a long surface to the friction of the bow in
applying it, and does not wear into a groove, which always cuts
one's bow-hair to pieces. Stuttaford's " Spherical Rosin and
Case " is a ball of rosin in a round case, with a slit in it to
receive the bow-hair. I have not found any advantages accru-
ing from its use, for it cuts the bow-hair and *covers* one's fingers
with rosin-dust. The operations by which the clarified rosin or
colophony of the fiddle-dealers' shops is prepared are as follows,
as stated by Otto. Put a quantity of Venice turpentine in a
pipkin, add a little water to it, and boil for two or three hours
over a slow fire. As it rises pour in small quantities of cold
water to keep it from overflowing, and allow a drop now and
again to cool on a plate, when, if it rubs clear between the
fingers without sticking, it is sufficiently boiled. When thus
boiled, pour it into cold water ; work it well with the hands to
press out the water, and break it into pieces when cold, expose
to the sun and air until all the moisture is evaporated and the
rosin quite transparent. Many violinists adopt a method of
purifying and rendering the rosin more transparent by boiling
it in vinegar, and whilst it is warm pouring it into paper-moulds,
after which it is exposed for some time to the sun and air. The
purest and finest rosin for the violin is that made from pure
Venice turpentine. These particulars are given as likely to be
of interest to the violinist, but surely no amateur will go so far
as to *prepare* his own rosin. The violinists of Vienna, and
several of the other continental capitals, are now, I am told,
using liquid colophane instead of solid rosin. The mixture is
applied with a camel's hair brush, and is said neither to injure
the bow nor the strings of the instrument, and to last out one
hundred hours' playing. It is also stated that the strings give
out a clearer tone than when solid rosin is used. The *action* of
rosin has been already discussed on page 100.

Gauges are all more or less of the same pattern, and are
almost all equally deceptive and unsatisfactory. The right plan

is to get a gauge of the ordinary form and efface the markings; then, when by chance you happen to have on your fiddle a set of strings true to one another, and well suited to your instrument, pass the gauge on to them (below the bridge; not above, where they are thickened with rosin), and mark your gauge for yourself, in which way you get a guide more reliable than the common brass fork which is usually supplied for the purpose. Mr. G. A. Chanot has introduced a rather complete gauge called the "Quartett Gauge," which has round its sides incisions of the varying diameters of all the strings of all three instruments, violin, viola, and violoncello. It will be principally useful to tradesmen laying in a stock of all kinds of strings at the same time, and for leaders of quartette parties, for few players require to be constantly buying strings for all three instruments at once. Mr. Hart has shown me a very sensible and ingenious, if rather cumbrous, appliance, termed a chordometer, with which, by means of a lever arm and micrometer scale, the exact diameter of any string from a double bass C, even to one no larger than the finest hair, can be accurately ascertained and recorded.

Tuning-forks are toys always convenient, and sometimes useful in settling disputes as to pitch or for pieces in which the violin has to be tuned to uncommon intervals, and notes to which the ear is unaccustomed. I have found most useful a tuning-fork which, by means of sliding weights embracing the prongs, can be altered at will to give any required note. Otherwise an A tuning-fork is always handy.

String-boxes are another requirement of the fiddler. I have seen it recommended to wrap up spare strings in a piece of oiled bladder, but a more messy, horrid performance it is to my mind difficult to imagine. It is also suggested that a piece of oiled flannel be kept in the string-box, but the effect is equally nasty. Unless you live far away, it is never necessary or convenient to keep more than one or two spare sets of strings by you, and if you are a long way off, a note to a London dealer will always bring them down by post. The best receptacle to contain the strings is an ordinary japanned box with two openings on opposite sides, in one of which the gut strings, and in the other the covered strings, are kept. Mr. Hill has introduced a very neat and sensible string-box, which is a japanned tin box with a hinged lid, which just fits into the semi-circular division at the head of a fiddle-case, and is divided into four compartments, to keep the different strings separate. But a better one still has followed it, consisting of a round box with three movable trays, which lift out and keep the strings separate.

Every case should contain a small strong pair of scissors, and

a pair of long-pointed tweezers for manipulating the strings
inside the peg box. An ingenious appliance, long in use in the
fiddle-dealer's workshop, but only just lately offered to the
public by Mr. George Withers, is the peg-turner, that is, a large
peg-head, which is attached to a sort of oval box or bell, which,
clasping the peg, turns it with irresistible force. It is recom-

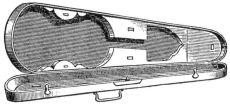

Fig. 111.—Single Violin Case.

mended for the use of ladies and persons with weak fingers, but
is comparatively useless to the amateur, who can always have
his pegs refitted to make them turn quite easily. However, it
is very useful for dealers, makers, and repairers, who constantly
have many and very hard-set pegs to turn. They are sold
neatly made in ebony and silver, but the practical amateur can
easily make one for himself out of any piece of hard wood.

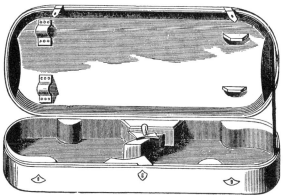

Fig. 112.—Double Violin Case.

The fiddle, on being put away in its case, should be wrapped in
an old silk handkerchief, and many people use a fiddle-blanket,
that is, a thin pad of flannel or quilted satin, shaped to the inside
of the case and covering up the fiddle. A common accessory of
the amateur is a pad or cushion used for holding the fiddle.
This is not, to my mind, so efficacious or convenient as a chin-
rest, but this has been discussed before in the paragraph on

chin-rests. And, lastly, a word on the case in which the fiddle is kept ; these are either single, as at Fig. 111, or double, as at Fig. 112. These last are very handsome, but wofully massive and heavy. If you carry your fiddle about much, nothing can beat the American cloth oblong cases, which hold music, and are very light, but are bad as permanencies, as people have a knack of sitting upon them, very considerably *ad damnum* of the contained fiddle (and its owner). The papier-maché or American cloth cases which follow the shape of the fiddle (commonly known as "baby alligators") are very convenient, but they do not hold music, and, if the fiddle is high built, it runs a chance of being cracked by the bows in the lid. Some amateurs have such an objection to being seen carrying a fiddle about, that they have cases made only *just* the length of the *fiddle*, rounded similarly at both ends. These are, to my mind, as wicked as they are cowardly, for they necessitate the bow being *cut in two*

Fig. 112A.—Patent Violin Bag (G. A. Chanot).

above the lapping, and jointed with a plug and ferrule. Ye gods ! what a sacrifice to appearances ! After trying all sorts, I have come to the conclusion that nothing is better than Fig. 111 of French, or light English make.

Fig. 112A represents the latest improvement in fiddle cases, recently patented by Mr. G. A. Chanot, of Manchester. It consists of a strong frame, which holds the body of the fiddle, the head being covered by a lined waterproof bag. The large opening (whereby the fiddle is put in) is similarly closed with waterproof ; and the bow goes into a box similarly covered and closed, which can be detached from the case itself. This is very light and strong, and will, I think, come into very universal use.

The next chapter (on strings) will bring us to the end of the theoretical discussion of the violin ; after which I shall proceed to the detailed exposition of the practical manual processes required to solve the problem, " Given, a log of wood : make a fiddle."

CHAPTER XII.

THE STRINGS.

Choice of Strings—Theory of Vibration—Relations to One Another—" True " and " False " Strings—True and Harmonic Octave and Fifth, Tests—Appearance of a Good String—Preservation of Strings—Different Sorts of Strings—Their Composition—Method of Preparation and Manufacture—Covered Strings—Silk and Acribelle.

HAVING finally adjusted all the fittings of the violin, and having got together all the miscellanea of the fiddler's art, there remains but one particular to be attended to before proceeding to the consideration of the actual manual operations necessary for the carrying out of the scientific principles which have been the subject of the preceding chapters. This matter, which, though left till the last, is almost as important as the construction of the fiddle itself, is the consideration, selection, and manufacture of the strings. It is not an uncommon thing to see an amateur enter a violin-dealer's shop and say, " Give me two firsts, and a second, please," and walk off with the first three given him by the individual in charge, without even looking at them. The chances are a hundred to one that the result of that amateur's expenditure of capital will be a source of considerable misery to himself, and to his sorrowing family or neighbours. It cannot be too strongly borne in mind, that not only must the size, quality, and substance of the strings be perfect, but that the individual strings chosen must suit the instrument to which they are to be applied, for a string that would produce a mellow and full tone on one fiddle might very probably be harsh and " criard" on another. Again, you must choose your strings to suit your style of playing ; some virtuosi use very thin strings by choice, whilst others use them exceptionally thick. Parke in his " Musical Memoirs " (*vide* note [1], p. 5), says, " At this meeting (Worcester musical festival, September 1776), I first heard the popular violin-player Giardini execute a concerto, in which he displayed a fund of grace and expression, with a tone so sweet, and at the same time so powerful, that he appeared to be performing on strings so large, that I really thought his fingers must have been blistered by the necessary pressure he gave them." There is a great deal in what the biographer here says, which strengthens the stress which I lay upon choice of strings. When, however, you have found a diameter of strings, which suits your fiddle, keep to that and do not experimentalize with new thicknesses, for it is as deleterious to change one's style of strings as to be constantly shifting about the sound-post. The strings must be in proper relative proportion to one another ; I mean you must not use a thick E, a thin A, and a medium D they must all be relatively thick, thin, or medium. This care in choosing particularly applies to the first string, or chanterelle, and proportionately to the others.

The appliance known as a string-gauge is well known, and has before been referred to (p. 199) ; but each violinist ought to have one to his own fiddle—*i.e.*, he should get one quite plain, and as he gets good, sweet, and true strings on to his fiddle, which suit the instrument, he should mark it for himself by them, and as nearly as possible always choose strings the same size by its aid. Properly to understand the relative duties of, and the correspondence between, the strings and the body of the violin, let us turn for a moment to the scientific principles which regulate and determine these relations. A string, as is of course well known, only becomes capable of emitting a musical note under the influence of tension. Again, if we be gifted with the strength of Hercules and stretch a gut or other string between our fingers, in the open air, the sound produced by that string under the influence of the bow, or upon twanging it, is practically imperceptible, but if at one or both ends we attach a slab of thin wood, the sound increases in intensity as the molecules of the wood vibrate in sympathy with the string. In the construction of a violin and the choice of its strings we have to aim at as near as possible a perfection in these relations, with this difference, that not only is it the molecules of the wood forming the instrument that vibrate sympathetically with the strings, but the mass of air contained inside the fiddle as well. The tone, therefore, depends on the thickness of the strings, the force with which they are vibrated, and the quality of the magnifying body (*i.e.*, the fiddle). The actual note produced depends, of course, merely on the diameter of the strings, their substance, their length, and the amount of tension applied to them. The more the vibrations entered into by a string, the higher will be the note produced, and *the number of vibrations produced by a string are in the inverse ratio of its length*—*i.e.*, the shorter the string the greater the number of its vibrations, and consequently the higher the note. Thus, in Fig. 113, if the whole string A B produce one hundred vibrations, and consequently gives (say) the note D : when stopped at C, the parts a' or b' vibrated alone would produce two hundred vibrations, and consequently the note D an octave higher. Dr. Arbuthnot remarked this more than a century and a half ago,[1] saying :—" I have found that the single fibres, both of animal and vegetable substances, are lengthened by water or by moist air ; a fiddle-string moistened with water will sink a note in a little time, and consequently it must be (*i.e.*, it *is*) relaxed or *lengthened one-sixteenth.* The steam of hot water will sink it a note in five or six minutes." It is in consequence of this natural phenomenon that when one is playing, one's breath will often make the strings "go flat," and that in a concert room, if the heat of the room is a moist heat, one's fiddle gets flat, whereas, if the heat is dry and burning, the strings lose their natural moisture and get sharp, a circumstance often very disastrous to singers accompanied by an orchestra towards the end of a concert, unless carefully guarded against.

Again, the thicker the string the fewer its vibrations, and consequently the lower its note ; therefore, *the number of vibrations produced by a string are in the inverse ratio of its diameter.* Thus : one string, having a diameter represented by 2, gives a note (say) D ; another of the same length, and subjected to the same tension, having a diameter represented by 1 (just half), the note produced would be D an octave higher. Again, the denser and heavier the substance which composes the string, the lower will be the note produced. It is from this that, to obviate the use of an immensely thick string for the fourth string of the fiddle, we *increase the weight* of a string thinner than the third, by covering it with wire. Again, the heavier the tension applied to a string, the higher the note produced ; therefore : *the number of vibrations produced by a string are in the direct ratio of the tension applied to it.* Thus : if a string drawn by a weight of fifty pounds gave a note, (say) D, increase the weight to one hundred pounds, and the note produced would be D an octave higher. The action of these weights is, in the violin, replaced by the pegs. This, therefore, is the theory of vibrations of a musical string as far as they are likely to interest us. For any further particulars on this

FIG. 113.—Diagram illustrating the influence of *length* on the note produced by a string.

• Dr. J. Arbuthnot, "An Essay concerning the Effects of Air on Human Bodies " (London, 1732), p. 61, ch. iii., par. 20.

most interesting subject, the reader is referred to any of the standard works on sound (such as Professor Tyndall's[1]). The above notes may, however, as far as they go, be of considerable use and interest to the violinist. The scientific and mechanical action of that very necessary accessory, the rosin, in vibrating a string continuously by means of a bow, has been set forth in a previous chapter (p. 100).

As to the strings themselves, besides being suited to the fiddle to which they are fixed, they must also possess certain qualities which are absolutely indispensable to tone, and which are technically summed up in four words : *They must be true.* True, not only individually, but true to one another ; and this truth is only to be obtained, in the first case, by being properly constructed and chosen, and in the second case, by being accurately proportioned or gauged to each other. It is absolutely necessary that a string be of even thickness throughout,—*i.e.*, one end must not be thinner than another, or else the production of perfect fifths and harmonic octaves will be rendered impossible. As the sounding of these two harmonies is the best, and most absolutely certain test for falseness in a string, it may be advisable here to consider the conditions necessary for their perfect production. When a string is divided into two equal halves by a light pressure of the little finger (c, Fig. 114), in the fourth position (or by extension in the third), the well-known sound of the harmonic octave is produced by the two halves of the string vibrating simultaneously and consonantly, as in Fig. 114. If redivided at a quarter of its length from the nut by the first finger (D, Fig. 115), in the third position, a second octave (higher) is produced by the four quarters c, d, e, f, of the string vibrating simultaneously and consonantly, as in Fig. 115, and it is immaterial whether the little finger c be removed or not (though in many instances it is advisable that it be kept in position as in the figure) ; now if the thickness of the string be not uniform, and the string be divided by a firm pressure, as in Fig. 113, and the two halves thus isolated be separately struck

FIG. 114.—The Harmonic Octave.

[1] *Vide* A. Guillemin, " The Applications of Physical Forces," translated and edited by Mr. and Mrs. Norman Lockyer (London, 1877), pp. 138—152 ; and [2] Rambosson. " Les Harmonies du Son, et l'Histoire des Instruments de Musique " (Paris, 1878), p. 374, and other similar works.

with the bow, the thinner end of the string will give a higher note than the thicker, and consequently, if to such a string a light pressure be applied, as in Fig. 114, the two halves vibrating simultaneously *but not consonantly*, a false, squeaky note will be produced in place of the clear flute tone of the true harmonic octave. The higher harmonic octave (as in Fig. 115), constitutes in similar manner a yet finer test for the truth of an individual string.

The next test for the truth of a string, both individually and to its neighbour, is the production of perfect fifths. By this is meant that if two strings are stopped by the finger *both together* at any given point, the interval known as "a fifth" will be produced, the same as it was when the two open strings gave a perfect fifth sounded together. If the harmonic octaves of both open strings are sounded together by one light pressure, as in Fig 114, they will (if the two strings are true) produce a perfect *harmonic* fifth, an octave above the perfect fifth produced by the open strings. The reason for this is obvious, for if one string is finer at one end than at the other, the two equal halves will have a different intonation, and the fifth produced by vibrating such a string simultaneously with another true one will not be perfect, but harsh and dissonant. Therefore, if a string will render two perfect harmonic octaves, and if another vibrated simultaneously with it gives perfect fifths when stopped at an identical point, those two strings are true in themselves, and true to one another. It has been suggested that when strings are thus falsified by want of similarity throughout their breadth, the defect may be to a certain extent remedied by passing a moist finger along the finer portion of the string (*vide* Dr. Arbuthnot's experiment, *supra*, p. 205), and thus swelling it. An approach to equality of thickness produces somewhat the desired result, but it will always be found best to take another string at once, rather than try to remedy a false one.

It will be said that this is a lengthy mode of judging of a false string, and that a string once mounted and removed, is useless alike to the buyer and seller ; the only chance, therefore, is to be guided by the eye in choosing strings in the shop, and a very short acquaintance with the exterior signs of a good string will effectually guard the fiddler from ever investing in a false one. A string, as seen in the coil or bundle at a shop, ought to be

FIG. 116.—The Harmonic Double-Octave.

transparent, and without spots or blotches throughout its entire
length. It should be pliant and elastic, returning to its former
shape (like a watch spring), without breaking when pressed or
pulled out; it should not be too white, for this betokens improper
materials or excessive bleaching, both of which render a string
brittle and false. A good string must not lose its transparency,
and become cloudy and yellow when bent. Seconds and thirds
may be without harm much whiter than firsts, but otherwise the
same rules apply. It is often laid down that the truth of
a string may be determined by vibrating it between the fingers,
and that if it present only two even lines it is true, and if more,
false. It is certain that if it produce an irregular or multiplied
figure it is false, but it does not follow that if the lines be clear
and distinct it is true ; and again, a string which may seem true
at a slight tension, may quite possibly be false at the higher
tension to which it is subjected when applied to a fiddle, though
as a rule a string will be false at a low tension whilst it is true
at a higher. The reader will appreciate this if he has ever been
forced as a *pis aller* to mount an E string as an A, or *vice versâ.*
It remains, therefore, that the only way to ensure choosing good
strings is to go as far as possible by the appearances before
mentioned, and, above all, to deal only with the best goods of
the best dealers. It is a mistake, to my mind, for amateurs to
think they can save money by buying a bundle of fifteen or
thirty strings at once ; some of them are almost sure to go wrong
before they are all used, unless the greatest care is taken of
them. Some people wrap their spare strings in bladder or
flannel moistened with oil, a process which, even if the oil does
not go rancid (as it generally does), can only be characterized as
"horrid." The mess involved in putting on a new greasy string
is enough, if you are not of a seraphic disposition (I am not), to
make you touchy for the rest of the performance. I never buy
more than two strings at a time, and always keep just one
double set handy. It has been recommended by various authors,
following J. A. Otto (*vide* note, p. 20), to keep in one's case a
piece of silk moistened with almond oil, which must be passed
down the strings, from nut to bridge, every time the fiddle is
put away, and that before playing the strings should be rubbed
free from the effects of this unction with a linen rag. I do
not know whether this has ever been done ; it would certainly
be quite impossible to play on strings so treated.

The different strings now in the market are described by
Mr. Hart in his work, " The Violin : its Makers and Imitators,"
as follows " Musical strings are manufactured in Italy,
Germany, France, and England. The Italians rank first in

this manufacture, their proficiency being evident in the three chief requisites for strings—viz., high finish, great durability, and purity of sound. There are manufactories at Rome, Naples, Padua, and Verona, the separate characteristics of which are definitely marked in their produce. Those strings which are manufactured at Rome are exceedingly hard and brilliant, and exhibit a slight roughness of finish. The Neapolitan samples are smooth, and softer than the Roman, and also whiter in appearance. Those of Padua are highly polished and durable, but frequently false. The German strings now rank next to the Italian, Saxony being the seat of manufacture. They may be described as very white and smooth, the better kinds being very durable. Their chief fault arises from their being over bleached, and hence faulty in sound. The French take the third place in the manufacture. Their strings are carefully made, and those of the larger sizes answer well, but the smaller strings are wanting in durability. The English manufacture all qualities, but chiefly the cheaper kinds ; they are durable, but unevenly made, and have a dark appearance."

The cause of variation in quality of the several kinds arises simply from the difference of climate. In Italy an important part of the process of manufacture is carried on in the open air, and the beautiful climate is made to effect that which has to be done artificially in other countries. Hence the Italian supe-riority. Southern Germany adopts, to some extent, similar means in making strings ; France to a less degree ; while England is obliged to rely solely on artificial processes. It therefore amounts to this result, the further from Italy the more inferior the string. The best strings in the market to-day are imported from Signor Andrea Ruffini, of Naples, which are sold by all the leading violin-dealers in London.

It is a matter of every day occurrence to hear people talk of fiddle strings as " catgut " ; indeed, one great writer has alluded to a violinist as a man who " stretches the bowels of a cat over a wooden box and rubs them with the tail of a horse." However this may be, it is one of those carefully-persisted-in errors made on the *lucus a non lucendo* principle. One, Baptista Porta, seems to have made some most intelligent experiments in the sixteenth century on the materials of which strings were made, the astounding results of which were, that strings made of combined wolf and sheep gut produced no music, but only jar and discord. The painful effect of playing on strings made from the intestines of serpents was to make women miscarry, especially when vipers supplied the material. Porta, probably, got his informa-tion from Pythagoras, who tells a similar " story " ; at any rate, Kircher, the well-meaning, but often sadly misguided author of "Musurgia Universalis,"[1] strung two instruments, one with wolf gut strings, and the other with sheep gut strings, and sitting in a fold, played to the assembled sheep, who, however, failed to express any objection or alarm at either form of tone production!

Setting aside for future consideration the silk, metal, and acribelle strings, we will turn our attention to the manufacture of the ordinary strings, which are all similarly composed, the only difference being that the fourth (or G) string is covered with a layer of fine wire, whose composition and object will be hereafter noticed. Strings for the violin, and nearly all other string instruments, are composed of the small intestines of sheep, and have been so composed, as Mersennus very justly remarks,[2] ever since the time of the ancient Egyptians. Mr. Chappell[3] gives an interesting note on the ancient Egyptian strings, in his "History of Music" (vol i., p. 26), quoting the remark of the simple-minded M. Fétis,[4] who "wondered at the Egyptians making this use of the intestines of cats, seeing that with them the cat was a sacred animal." (!) The best intestines are those of lambs which have lived on dry mountainous pastures; and it is said that the best lambs are those from the province of Berry, and from some parts of Germany, and that they are at their best for the purpose of string-making in the month of September, which is, consequently, the string-making month in each year.

The intestine used is that one which is composed of the duodenum, the jejunum, and the ilion; it is composed of three membranes, the external (or peritoneal), and the mucous membranes, both of which are removed as useless, but which enclose between them a third, the muscular or fibrous membrane, which is used in the manufacture of fiddle strings. The intestine are fetched direct from the butcher's, whilst the carcasses are still warm, and they are detached by workmen, who are specially employed for the purpose, by whom they are at once stretched upon an inclined plane and scraped with a knife blade, to clean and empty them of all foreign substances, grease, etc. This must be done quickly, and whilst the intestines are yet warm, or the cooling matters would hopelessly colour the intestines;

[1] A. Kircher, "Musurgia Universalis, sive ars magna consoni et dissoni" (Rome, 1650). Condensed and translated into German by Andreas Hirsch (Hall [Swabia], 1662).
[2] M. Mersennus, "Traité de l'Harmonie Universelle," 1627.
[3] W. Chappell, "The History of Music (*Art and Science*). From the Earliest Records to the Fall of the Roman Empire." Vol. i. (All ever published.) (London, n.d. [1874]).
[4] F. J. Fétis, "Histoire générale de la Musique" (Paris, 1869—1876), 5 vols.

after this operation the intestines are tied up in bundles and placed in vessels to carry them to the manufactory, where they are tied in bundles of ten, and placed in cold water from twelve to fifteen hours ; this may be done in a running stream, or in a vat of spring water, slightly corrected with carbonate of soda. After this they are immersed four or five hours in tepid running water. These soakings produce a slight fermentation, which aids the separation of the fibrous from the mucous and peritoneal membranes, which is done by women scraping the intestines with a split cane on a slightly inclined slab, down which a current of water constantly runs ; the internal membranes run off into a trough and are used as manure, the external are used for racquets, whips, and other rougher articles composed of gut. The fibrous membranes, separated in bundles of about ten, are now placed in stone jars to soak for three or four hours in potassa lye (or ammoniacal solution, which is preferable), whose strength must be most carefully apportioned to the work to be done. At the end of this time they are carefully rubbed through the first finger (protected by a gutta-percha glove), and the thumb (armed with a copper thimble), of the left hand ; by this means are removed any of the fragments of the two superfluous membranes which may have escaped the first scraping. This operation is generally repeated at two hours' interval three times during the day, after each of which repetitions they are put into a similar stone jar of solution of permanganate of potassa. The fourth time this is repeated they are not replaced into the same solution, but are dipped into a weak solution of sulphuric acid. These operations are repeated for two or three days, morning and evening, always similarly increasing the strength of the solution used.

The guts are now sufficiently cleaned to be sorted, and, if necessary, split. They are sorted by experienced workmen into qualities, lengths, thicknesses, and strengths, so that each may be devoted to its proper uses and tones. As the guts, in their natural state, are not sufficiently uniform in diameter to obtain that cylindricity and parallelness that is the great aim of the string-maker, they often require to be split into long threads by means of a knife specially prepared for the purpose, which threads are then placed in a jar with their thick and thin ends set alternately The next operation is the spinning, which is performed on a frame about three times as long as a fiddle. It is done as follows : two, three, or more fibres (according to the string required to be made) are taken and set alternately ; that is, the thick end of one opposite the thin end of another. The usual number apportioned to the four strings of a violin are as follows : for the first, or E string, 3-4 fine threads ; for the second, or A, 3-4 strong ones ; for the third, or D, 6-7 strong ones. Beyond this, double bass strings reach as many as 85 fibres, but this is a branch of the manufacture which does not concern us.

At one end of the frame is a little wheel, the centre or axle of which bears two hooks : at the other end of the frame are little fixed pegs. The guts selected are fixed to a peg which is set in one hook of the wheel, and carried to the other end of the frame, twisted round a fixed peg, brought back to the other end and fixed to the other hook of the wheel by another peg ; this wheel is rapidly revolved by a multiplying fly-wheel, and the guts are twisted up into a fiddlestring, the fingers being passed along it meanwhile to prevent the formation of inequalities in its length. The pegs are then removed from the hooks and set into holes opposite the fixed pegs at the other end of the frame (in the same way as the pegs are set into the head of a fiddle), and the work proceeds in the same way with a new bundle of guts from another fixed peg to the hooked wheel, until the frame is full. The strings are then sulphured to whiten them in a sulphuring chamber, into which the frames are placed, and flowers of sulphur ignited in the centre. The chamber is then hermetically sealed and left for the night, during which time the strings become bleached by the action of the sulphurous acid gas evolved by the combustion of the sulphur. They are next morning exposed to air (but not rain) till nearly dry, when they are again moistened, twisted on the frame, and replaced in the sulphur bath. This operation lasts from two to eight days according to the size of the string being made. The strings are then thoroughly polished and rubbed to get rid of all inequalities, grease, or other foreign particles. This is done whilst they are still on the frame by means of a set of hair cushions, which, enveloping the strings, by a lateral movement submit them to a rapid and forcible friction, they being from time to time during the operation moistened with a sponge soaked in an alkaline solution of potassa. The strings are then wiped to get rid of all impurities, moistened with pure water, and replaced for the night in the sulphur bath, after which they are again twisted and dried. When dry they are polished, an operation which first or E strings are frequently allowed to go without, but which for the others takes place as follows :—The frames are laid flat upon trestles or other supports, and the strings are polished by hand or machinery by means of little gutta-percha cushions, olive oil and pounce, or whitening, being used for the purpose. These polishers are run from end to end of the strings till the requisite polish has been obtained. The strings are then carefully wiped and lightly moistened with olive oil, after which they are thoroughly dried, which is accomplished when, on loosening the pegs, they do not contract. The strings are now cut from the frames close to the pegs, and rolled into coils as we see them in commerce, after which they are made up into bundles of fifteen or thirty. With all these operations it is not to be wondered at that it is exceedingly difficult to obtain *absolute* cylindricality throughout the entire length of a string, and as a matter of fact the extreme ends of a string generally taper slightly, and are therefore useless, producing false, and "wolf" notes. To get over the effects of this circumstance it is best when putting on a new string to uncoil its *entire* length, put the two ends together, and cut it in two exactly in the middle, tie the knots in the two strings thus made *at the cut ends* (*i.e.*, in the *middle* of the string) ; you thus have two strings (it is false economy to try and make a string run to three lengths), which are pretty sure to be true from the tailpiece to the nut, whilst the defective four or five inches at the ends serve to coil round the pegs, and the superabundance is cut off. It is following this line of action that it is the custom when a string is false to "turn it round" on the fiddle, which often remedies the defect.

It remains to us now (before noticing patent strings) to turn to the consideration of covered strings. On the violin only one such is used, the fourth, or G string ; but going a step farther to the tenor (or viola), we get another covered string, the C, which balances the absence of the violin E. It is doubtful who first invented covered strings, but J. Rousseau[1] attributes the invention to Sainte-Colombe, the celebrated violinist of his epoch (1687). For violins it is generally gut which is covered with copper (plated or pure), or with silver. Silk is also used, but it is difficult to tune accurately, and will not remain in tune when once screwed up ; undoubtedly the best are the copper-plated gut ones. I always obtain my covered strings for violin or viola from Mr. G. Hart, who covers them with alternate spirals of gun-metal and plated copper. The best (recommended by Herr Strauss) are wrapped over close to the knot with red silk. The gut of which covered strings are formed is not sulphured, nor is it oiled. The string is fixed at one end to a hook set on a wheel, and at the other to a turning swivel, which holds the string stretched by means of a weight. The turning of the wheel turns the strings and the swivel, and the workman carefully wraps the wire on to the string as it revolves, taking the

* "Traité de la Viole" (Paris, 1687), *vide* note [1], p. 34.

greatest care to preserve its regularity and close winding, and checking the vibrations of the rotating string with a cork. The gut used must be perfectly uniform in diameter throughout its length, and incapable of further stretching. Consequently it is strongly stretched before the wire is wound on, or else by subsequent stretching the core would recede from the helix, and the effect can only be described by those who have suffered from it.

All violin players are familiar with the now-common acribelle, or silk, strings, which are composed of an infinity of filaments of silk so twisted together and polished as to exceed in uniformity and transparency the finest gut strings. For players troubled with perspiring hands, and for hot or damp climates, they are, without doubt, invaluable, for they are but little affected by damp, and they make up in convenience in these respects what they certainly lack in tone. They are apt also to fray and get ragged, and though it has been recommended when this is the case to draw the string quickly through the flame of a spirit lamp, to remove the frayed fibres, an acribelle string once gone wrong, is ghastly with a ghastliness more easily imagined than described. The same remark applies to the twisted or plaited strings, sometimes known as Chinese water-cord. These are quite the best for players with hot hands, and are almost exclusively used by violinists in India and other hot countries, where the ordinary strings not only break very easily, but are very difficult to keep. But, of course, their tone is inferior to gut.

In conclusion, by-the-bye, a word on knots. It seems a simple thing to tie a knot in the end of a string so that it shall not slip through the slit of the tailpiece, but the common " booby " knot is very apt to break off, and in so doing the knot flies against the belly and produces those four little chipped holes so often seen beneath the tailpiece of a fiddle. If in tying the knot you do not pull the short end right through, but make a slip-knot of it, you will find that the long end coming out of the slit is much securer and less likely to " fly " than if the dear old " booby "-knot of our childhood is made. It should be remarked that in the knot of the *first* string the long end should be twisted round the slip-knot once again to make it larger, and, therefore, more secure So shall your strings hold well, and not " fly " out of " pure cussedness." In putting on a string *never* (as so many amateurs do) put the end through the peg, and then draw it down to the tail-piece and fix it there with a knot. This is certain to bruise the string all along, and utterly spoil it. Make your knot as above directed, and fix it to the tail-piece ; then carry the string up to the head, cut off what you do not want, and fix the end thus made to the peg. Never have a coil of loose string hanging about the scroll of the fiddle, or twisted round the pegs; it is unsightly, and often produces a buzzing noise. When you require to put an entire new set of strings on (fiddlers with cool hands seldom break strings, but have to replace the whole set when it is worn out), *do not, on any account,* take all the old strings off and then put the others on; the sudden relaxation of the pressure, and consequent " working " of the fibres of the fiddle, may throw the instrument " out of temper " for days. Take off one at a time, and put on the new one, and screw it up to pitch before changing the next one.

" Est contra figulum figulus fabrum faber odit,
Contra cantorem cantor premet Irus ad Irum :
Dic mihi cur donata viris sit Musica doctis:
Ut Re-levet *Mi*-serum *Fa*-tum *Sol*-itosque *La*-bores."

Volker von Alzei.

„Und Gunther sprach: „Freund Hagen, Töne klingen
   Herübe. ..t dem Spielmann durch den Saal,
Die durch der Hunnen Mark und Beine dringen;
   Sein Fiedelbogen ist von rothem Stahl."
„Daß ich bisher ihm vor," versetzte Hagen,
„So war's nicht recht; das muß ich selbst nun sagen." . . .

„O König, was spielt er für schöne Weisen!
   Wohl sind sie Deines Gold's und Silber's werth!
Sein Fiedelbogen bringt durch Stahl und Eisen
   Wenn er auf Helm und Schilde niederfährt.
Noch keinen Spielmann hab' ich je gesehen
So durch sein Spiel begeistert vor mir stehen."

(„Das Niebelungenlied." 1210.)

PART III.

Practical

FIDDLE AND I.

By **Frederic E. Weatherly**.

By road and river,
  Country-side and town,
I roam for ever
  With my fiddle brown.
Creeping under barns so gladly
  When outside the winter howls,
Playing sadly, playing madly,
  Waking up the rats and owls.
      Ah! it was gay, night and day
      Fair and cloudy weather,
      Fiddle and I wandering by,
      Over the world together!

Down by the willow
  Summer nights I lie,
Flowers for my pillow,
  And for roof the sky.
Playing all my heart remembers,
  Old, old songs from far away,
Golden Junes and bleak Decembers
  Rise around me as I play.

On, on, for ever!
  Till the journey ends,
Who shall dissever
  Us two trusty friends?
Who can bring the past before me,
  Make the future gaily glow,
Lift the clouds that darken o'er me,
  But my trusty fiddle bow?
      Ah! it was gay, night and day
      Fair and cloudy weather,
      Fiddle and I wandering by,
      Over the world together'

MUSIC BY MRS. A. GOODEVE. *By permission of the publishers, Messrs. Enoch.*

CHAPTER XIII.

THE TOOLS.

Ordinary Tools—Special Tools—Toothed Planes—Scrapers—Knives—Marking Point—Bending Irons—Oval Planes—Spring Compasses—*f f* Hole Piercers —Gauging Callipers —Screws — Clips — Cramps — Compasses — Purfling Tools.

I HAVE now enumerated at length the Scientific Principles on which every good fiddle must be constructed. I am now going in detail into the practice of actual fiddle-making, and hope to be understood by my readers in proportion to the amount of pains which I have taken to make myself so. I shall proceed as if I were actually working with the reader, and he were using my moulds, models, and tools, with a view to facilitate which I have given outlines of all the former in their actual size (Plate IV.), so that they need only be traced or cut out, and pasted on slips of wood for immediate use. By way of introduction I give in this chapter drawings and descriptions of all such tools as are peculiar to the fiddle-maker's *atelier*, which must be high and light. The mould I have chosen, which is represented in Plate IV., is of the best shape of Stradivarius, and all the outlines (neck, scroll, *f f* holes, etc.), which are also reproduced actual size, are those which go with this mould, and have been most carefully and accurately taken from the same fiddle. It must be observed that there are two ways of performing many of the operations by which a fiddle grows under our hands. I have embodied these in Chapter XXI., giving another plate (Plate V.), this time *an in-side mould* of *Guarnerius*, with its models and outlines in facsimile.

The first great consideration in the practical science of fiddle-making is that of the tools. Many of these are what are to be found in any cabinet-maker's shop, such as saws, planes, chisels, gouges, etc., of the ordinary patterns ; but there are certain original tools and modifications of the common ones which must form part of the *lares* and *penates* of the fiddle-maker, and it will be to the consideration of these that we are now about to turn our attention. Firstly, then, for the common tools, a large saw. a tenon saw, and a bow saw of the ordinary forms are

required ; a long, or " trying " plane, a small, or " smoothing "
plane, and a set of carving gouges and chisels.   The workshop
must be fitted with an ordinary bench, with a vice affixed to it,
shelves for reception of wood and other massive miscellanea, and
racks for tools and small objects, bottles, and other paraphernalia,
which in well arranged confusion furnish the fiddle-maker's
workshop.   Rules and T-squares of ordinary dimensions are
also required, and I always carry in a leather case in my pocket
a small three-inch rule, divided to $\frac{1}{96}$, $\frac{1}{80}$, and $\frac{1}{64}$, of an inch, with
a pair of small spring bows for fine measurements and calcula-
tions.   This was beautifully made for me by Messrs. Aston and
Mander, of Soho.   One rule should have a perfectly true edge
of steel or some other hard substance, for the purpose of trying
edges and surfaces.

You will want a pair or so of common iron cramps (Fig. 116),
for fixing wood, etc., to the bench when in use.   A small bench-
vice, such as can be quickly screwed on and off the bench, is
frequently needed, as also is a medium-sized hand-vice.   The
ordinary whetstones and sharpening media must be provided.

FIG. 116.—Common Iron Cramp.   FIG. 117.—Sections of   FIG. 118.—Scrapers.
Files required.

A glue pot of the common sort will do, but I like one made of
copper enamel, as being cleaner.   Many violin-makers use the
best Salisbury glue, but to my mind none is better for our
purpose than that which comes over in thin light brown leaves
from Cologne.   An ordinary cutting and marking gauge will be
required, and also a set of files of the sections shown at Fig. 117.
The only hammer you will want is one of the light small
hammers used in joining fretwork or carvings, such as is used
by watchmakers for rough work.

We now arrive at the consideration of the tools peculiar to
our art which it is necessary to have ready to one's hand before
commencing to work, and these I shall enumerate and describe
in the order in which they are mentioned and required in the
following chapters on the actual manual labour required in
fiddle-making.

1. *The Toothed Plane.*—This is a small iron plane, like what
are known as the ordinary American planes, whose edge, instead
of being smooth like an ordinary plane, is toothed or serrated.

2. *Scrapers.*—These are small pieces of steel plate shown in

Fig. 118, three inches broad, whose upper side is rounded at the corners, and whose lower side is kept quite straight and flat. Several should be prepared, and they must be kept very sharp, being held in a hand-vice whilst being ground. They are sharpened by bevelling one edge, as at A, along the flat side, and round the curved side as at B B, for getting at places inaccessible to the flat side. If preferred, and to obviate the danger of cutting the fingers with the side not in use, instead of sharpening the flat and curved side of each scraper, some may be sharpened on one side and some on the other if you have plenty. During

FIG. 119.—Sharpening Steel (for Scrapers).   FIG. 120.—Violin-maker's Knife.

use they are kept keen by means of a sharpening steel (Fig. 119), which is a round plain bar of steel, $\frac{1}{2}$ inch in diameter, set into an ordinary handle. To re-set the edges it is drawn strongly down the flat side and then down the bevel, repeating the process once, when, unless the steel wants re-grinding, it will be found to have remedied any slight bluntness of the scraper.

3. *Knives.*—Two or three of these must be at hand, fixed in good strong handles. Their blades should be fine and well tempered, and they must be kept thoroughly keen (Fig. 120).

These knives are made by setting a strong steel blade down through an ebony (or other hard wood) handle (like the lead in a cedar pencil); then, as the knife wears out or gets ground down at the point and so shortened, more of the wood is cut away and a further piece of the blade sharpened. Photographers use knives with sliding blades, fixed in a grooved handle by means of a screw, which do very well for our purpose. I

FIG. 122.—Another (and better) form of Bending Iron.

FIG. 121.—Bending Iron.

have bought them at Messrs. Shew's in Wardour Street, but I suppose they are to be had from any purveyor of photographic apparatus and accessories.

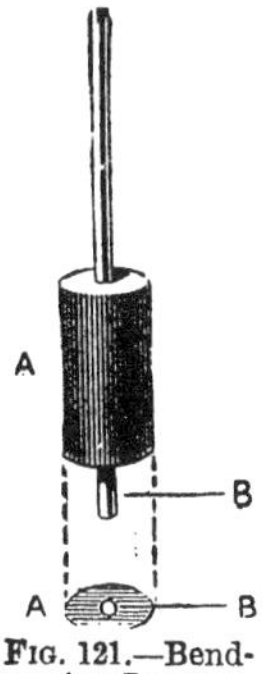

4. *Marking Point.*—This is merely an old bradawl sharpened to a fine point for marking exact outlines with, which would be difficult with a soft pencil.

5. *The Bending Iron.*—This is used for bending the sides, and though called a "bending *iron*," like a "soldering *iron*," it is best made of copper. It is formed (Fig. 121) of a bar, bearing at one end the oval mass A, at the end of which is the narrower round piece B. The object of this shape will appear later on.

Another, and perhaps better, form is represented at Fig. 122, and is crutch-shaped. It is fixed in a hole in the bench or in the vice when in use.

6. "*Lining*" *Chisel.*—This is used in letting the linings into the blocks, and is an ordinary chisel, only ¹ of an inch broad, as in Fig. 123, sharpened to a long edge, as at A.

7. "*Oval Planes.*"—A set of these will be required for finishing the model or arching, and the scooping out of the back and

FIG. 123.—
Lining
Chisel.

FIG. 124.—Oval Plane, upper and lower sides (actual size).

belly. They must be in three sizes, the largest and smallest of which are represented actual size by Figs. 124 and 125, there being also an intermediate size. The under surfaces are curved, as they are used for planing down the arching, and for planing smooth the gouging out of the tables. The edges of the irons, as will be seen in the figure, must be toothed, the brittle nature of the maple and the tenderness of the pine rendering this necessary.

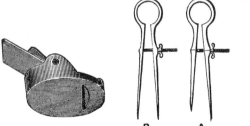
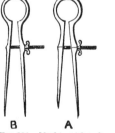
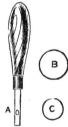

FIG. 125.—Oval Plane (smaller size).   FIG. 126.—Marking (A) and   FIG. 127.—*f* hole
Measuring (B) Compasses.   Piercer.

8. *Spring Compasses.*—You will want two pairs of these, as at Fig. 126, one pair having one leg *just* longer than the other, as at A, for use as a marking gauge. The other ordinary, as at B, for measuring and dividing.

9. *f Hole Piercing Tools or Punches.*—These are two punches, represented at Fig. 127, used for piercing the round holes at either end of the *ff* holes, and are, therefore, of two diameters,

indicated at B and C in the figure, the smaller one being for the upper, and the larger for the lower hole of the *f*. They are hollow cylinders of steel, having the open end ground to a fine circular edge, and having (about an inch up the bore) a round hole in the side A, whence to pick out any chips of wood, which would otherwise, by filling them up, choke the punches. They are also made with the "bore" extending right through the handle, so that a thin rod may be pushed down the cylindrical chamber thus formed for the purpose of pushing out the plug of wood cut out by, and therefore sticking in, the punch. This is the better form, for the "picker" is apt to injure the cutting edge of the punch when removing the cut-out plug of wood.

10. *Gauging Callipers*—Fig. 128—are what are used for determining the thicknesses of the back and belly. They consist of a frame A, somewhat like that of a fret-saw, and a movable arm B, which is attached to A by a hinge C. This arm carries a metal or ivory plate D marked with sixteenths of an inch down the

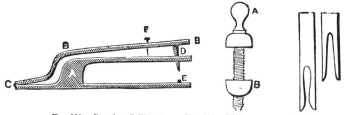

FIG. 128.—Gauging Callipers.   FIG. 129.—Violin-screw.   FIG. 130.—Sound bar Clips.

straight side, which passes through, and works in, a slot cut in the upper arm of the frame A, and which is of such a length that when the arm B is shut close down on to A, the tip of the plate D just touches the ivory stud E, set on the lower arm of A. The tip of D can be set and maintained at any required distance from E (as marked by its own scale), by screwing the screw F, which permits any distance to be adjusted very exactly and accurately. There are many forms of these, but this one is, I think, the best, as being the most steady and certain to work with.

11. *Violin Screws.*—Fig. 129. These are used for fixing the back to the sides and the belly similarly. They are made of wood, and about three dozen, varying a little in size, will be required.

12. *Sound Bar Clips.*—Fig. 130. These wooden contrivances, strongly resembling clothes-pegs, are used to keep the bar in position in the belly when being fitted. A pair must be provided.

13. *Sound Bar Cramps* are wooden screw cramps, Fig. 131, which are used to fix the sound bar in position when glued into the belly. Three or five are used in cramping a bar into its place.

14. *Bow Compasses.*—Fig. 132—are required for copying and registering diameters when working from a model. They are principally used when chiselling the head.

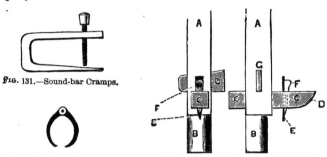

FIG. 131.—Sound-bar Cramps.

FIG. 132.—Bow Compass.

FIG. 133.—Purfling Gauge or Marker (front and side views).

15. *Purfling Gauge.*—This (Fig. 133) is an ebony gauge composed of an ordinary stem A, rounded at one side as at B, which bears a sliding beam C, one end of which, bearing the cutter E, and its wedge F, is rounded as at D. The cutter E is made fast at any distance from the stem A by knocking the

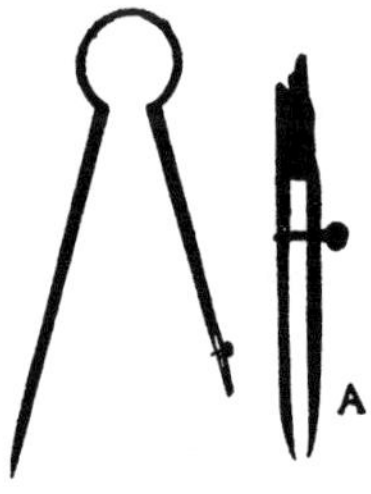

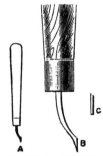

FIG. 134.—Purfling Compasses.

FIG. 135.— Purfling Chisel.

wedge G into the opening cut to receive it. It is used for tracing the lines of the purfling round the edge.

Another form of purfling tool shown me, and recommended by Mr. Hill, is represented at Fig. 134, and its object and construction will be readily understood by looking at the figure. Doubtless it is very certain, but it lacks the " sympathy " (if I may be allowed the expression) of the ebony one, Fig. 133, as it goes round the edges of the fiddle.

16. *Purfling Chisel or " Picker."*—Fig. 135.—The shape of this is shown at A, and enlarged to actual size at B ; C shows the *actual* breadth of the blade. It is used for picking out the wood between the cuts or tracing made to receive the purfling.

17. *Oblong Plane.*—This, which is represented almost actual size by Fig. 136, is made entirely in steel, and is used more

FIG. 136.—Oblong Steel Plane.   FIG. 137.—Lining-clip.

properly for bow-making, but you will often find it very useful during the course of your fiddle-making.

18. *Lining Clips.*—(Fig. 137). These are used for fixing the glued linings to the ribs when working with an " inside mould." About half a dozen should be kept handy.

These are the special tools required for the actual building of the fiddle;[1] others which are used only for the fitting up and repairs will be described and figured in the chapters devoted to these subjects.

---

[1] When the substance of this work was appearing serially in *Amateur Work Illustrated*, an arrangement was made with Mr. W. E. Hill, of No. 72, Wardour Street, London, W., to supply readers of that magazine with woods for violin-making, and the tools mentioned in this chapter, at moderate prices. This is, of course, no part of Mr. Hill's profession as a violin-maker and dealer. but I have no doubt that he will still oblige my readers by obtaining their requirements for them.

CHAPTER XIV.

Copying the Outline—Making the Mould—Its Diameters—The Outline Models—
The Arching-Guides—The Cramping-Blocks.

THE first thing to be done is to decide upon the model of your
instrument, and make your Mould. Moulds are of two sorts—
"the inside mould," which is solid, and *round* which the fiddle is
made ; and "the outside mould," which is cut out like a frame,
and *inside* which the fiddle is made. Of the former I shall
speak later on (Chapter XXI.) ; at present we are going to make
this fiddle on the latter or "outside" mould. The first step is to
decide upon your model and outline ; if you wish to copy any
given master, or if you wish to produce your own original
model, you will find directions for this on page 135. (I may say
that unless you wish particularly to copy any particular fiddle,
you cannot do better than adopt the model, outline, mould, etc.,
given in Plate IV., which is that of a Stradivarius of the most
finished elegance.) The first thing is to take an outline, as exact
as possible, of the fiddle to be copied, then transfer this to
a sheet of wood $\frac{1}{20}$ inch thick, rather larger than the outline.
Then with the *finest* fret or bow-saw cut this out *as evenly as
you possibly can*, sparing no pains to keep your cutting free from
all irregularities. Mark, on the fiddle-shaped piece thus cut out,
and on the frame from which you have cut it, the exact centre
of the outline, drawing a line down the centre, as at A B in the
plate. Having ascertained that your outline is correct, take
a slab of hard wood, the size and shape of the mould figured in
the plate, $1\frac{3}{4}$ inches thick, and mark the exact centre of it by
drawing from top to bottom the line A B. Take your plank
outline (down the centre of which a line is drawn), and place it
on this slab which is to form the mould, so that the line down
the centre of your outline coincides exactly with the line A B
down the centre of the mould. Holding the outline very firmly
in this position, so that the centre cannot move at either end
from the line A B (if necessary, fixing it thus with cramps), draw

with a fine point the *exact* outline of your plank on the board, and make it indelible by scratching it into the surface of the wood. You will then have the outline O, O, O (Plate IV.) drawn on your mould.

To measure the breadth from the extreme edge to the sides, allowing for wear, and being guided by the eye, draw a line right round inside the line C, about $\frac{3}{16}$ inch from it, preserving the same distance between them all round ; you will then have traced on the plank the line D, D, D. Then cut out very gradually, and with the same amount of care as you devoted to cutting your outline, all the wood inside the line D (left white in the plate). Your mould is now cut out, having a thickness all over of $1\frac{3}{4}$ inches. But we have seen (p. 145) that the sides of a fiddle are shallower in the upper than in the lower bouts, and in the case of the fiddle from which we are now working, the deviation is from $1\frac{1}{4}$ in the lower bouts to $1\frac{5}{32}$ in the upper ; your mould must therefore have the same deviation, which is arrived at by turning it over (so as not to plane away the lines C and A B), and planing round it very carefully, con-stantly measuring the depths till the gradual decrease in diameter is obtained.

You have now got (i) a hollow mould of the proper thick-ness, on the top of which are drawn with perfect symmetry the lines A, B, and C, and (ii) a thin plank outline exactly corre-sponding with the line C, down the exact centre of which runs a line corresponding with the line A B on the mould. Mark the word " front " on the front of this latter thin plank outline, so that you may always know which surface to have uppermost (for the two sides of this outline are *not* in exact *contra-facsimile* —Stradivari's outlines seldom, or never, were perfectly true).

Before we go further, it may be well to explain fully the nature of this plate. For purposes of working it may be as well to take two tracings of it, so as to separate the various things it illustrates. All the shaded part represents a violin mould, round the cutting of which is traced C, C, C, the actual ouline of the fiddle from which it has been made. Make tracing number one, of all the shaded parts (including the line C, O, C), and showing at top and bottom the ends of the centre line A B. Then make tracing No. 2 of the outline C, C, C as exactly as possible, bearing the line A B down its centre (and the sound-post E, and the f hole F, so that you may know which is the front of the model). Glue this tracing to a leaf of wood, sufficiently large, and cut it out most carefully, as it is your plank outline to which I have referred before. It will be noticed that at the bottom of the mould (or shaded part) the words " back " and "belly" are printed ; this means that to save room, and as the outline on both sides of a back and belly are nearly (if not quite) identical, I have made the right-hand half represent the belly, and the left-hand half the back. The *f* hole and sound-post in the right-hand (or "belly") half are merely put there to distinguish it still further from the left-hand (or "back") half.

Draw right across the traced outline of the back, the lines 1, 2, 3, 4, 5, 8 (which traverse the left-hand or "back"-half of the outline c, c, c). Draw across the traced outline of the "belly" the lines 7, 9, 10, 11, 12 (which traverse the right-hand or "belly"-half of the outline c, c, c). You have, therefore, now a tracing from which to make your mould, and a tracing of the outline c, c, c with *f* hole, and sound-post from which to make your plank outline. Next, make of thin hard wood the eleven "guides" (figured actual size). These are respectively (1, 2, 3, 4, and 5 in the plate), the model or elevation of the arching of the back, taken from the edge to the join (A B on the plate), along the lines 1, 2, 3, 4, and 5 respectively ; 8 shows the arching of the back between the centre bouts (or C's), along the line 8 ; and 9, 10, 11, and 12 show the arching of the belly, taken along the lines 9, 10, 11, and 12 ; 7 shows the entire arching of the belly between the centre bouts (or C's) along the line 7, in the same way that 8 gives the entire arching across the back. A similar guide to the entire arching along the line A B, is made by cutting a similar piece of wood i to the curve of the line G, G, G on the plate. It will be observed that the guide No. 8 is merely a doubled form of No. 3, and shows the arching of the centre of the back.

The last accessories of the mould are the cramping-blocks, which are represented in their actual size at H, I, J, K, L, M. These are pieces of wood cut the same depth as the mould, to fit its curves at the points H, I, J, K, L, and M respectively marked on the shaded part representing the mould. The outer edges (those which touch the sides), are lined with a thin sheet of cork (represented in the figures of the cramping blocks by the shading). These pieces are used to cramp the sides into their final shape in the mould, in manner hereinafter appearing.

So much for the construction and accessories of what is called "the outside mould." The other form, or "inside mould," will be described in another place, among the instructions for making a fiddle of the Guarnerius pattern, on an inside mould, and otherwise differing in many particulars from the fiddle we are now going to construct. Outlines and models for the neck and scroll of our present fiddle, and taken from the same instrument that has served us as a pattern for this mould, are also given in the plate. Having, therefore, prepared our mould and arching models, let us set to work to build our fiddle, and remember— *Priusquam incipias consulto, et ubi consuleris, mature facto opvs est.*

Multos multa juvant,   Me vero musica primuM
Voce suâ moesto   Vindicat à gemitV.
Salve supremi   Soboloe domumquo tonantiS,
Ipse favet Phœbus,   Iuppiter ipse tibI.
Constabit tua laus.   Clarissima sidera doneC
Alta poli decorant   Atria luce suAl

CHAPTER XV.

THE SIDES, OR RIBS, BLOCKS AND SIDE-LININGS.

Selection of Wood—The Sides—Bending the Sides—Fitting the Sides—The Top
and Bottom Blocks—The Corner Blocks—The Side-linings—Bending the
Side-linings—Fitting—Fixing the Linings—Levelling—Finishing the Sides,
Linings, and Blocks, Inside and Outside.

THE first step to be taken towards the making of a fiddle is the
selection of the wood. I have already pointed out the advisabi-
lity of keeping woods stored in certain dimensions (p. 134) ; it
will therefore be simply a matter of search and taste to select a
" set " of wood (*i.e.*, a wedge for the back, a block for the neck,
six strips for the sides, and a wedge for the belly), handsomely
figured and acoustically good as regards the maple, and finely and
evenly grained as regards the pine. Having decided this, we
proceed to " prepare " the wood for the various operations to
which it is to be submitted :—beginning with the Sides. If the
wood has been stored in strips $15\frac{1}{2}$ inches long, by $1\frac{3}{8}$ broad,
three such strips will be required ; but I recommend the selec-
tion of six, to provide for accidents of all sorts, which *will* come
about when an amateur is working with a brittle strip of
wood $\frac{1}{16}$th of an inch thick. Before proceeding further, let me
give a word of warning about the selection
of these strips. It is this : beware of
extra-handsome wood ; that with the finest
and boldest curls is excessively difficult to
work with, chipping away under the knife, plane, and scraper
to an alarming degree ; and, worse than all this, when the work
is finished, and your sides are set, and your fiddle varnished,
handsome wood will often take the wavy surface shown in the
section, Fig. 138, a phenomenon often observable on fiddles
with extra-handsome sides. The best slips are those with a fairly
close curl, not too strongly marked. All things being thus considered, you may now set to work.

FIG. 138.—Wavy form often
taken by extra-handsome
wood.

Take an ordinary cramp, as at Fig. 116, and by means of it,
and with a small piece of protecting wood, fasten the strip on the
bench at right angles to the edge (of the bench) ; then take a

small steel plane, whose cutting edge, instead of being plain, is
very finely toothed, and with a few sweeps just remove the
excessive roughness of the strip, then firmly smooth it throughout its entire length with a scraper (Fig. 118), and the first
operation is finished.   Above all things, be most careful that
the edge of the plane project only the very smallest possible,
for, in addition to the thinness of the wood you are working
with, the wood is in itself perhaps the most brittle of all to
work with, and the handsomer the curls in the wood, the
more brittle it is.   The scraper should be used *against* the
direction of the curls ; that is, if the curls (or figure of the
wood) incline towards the right, the cutting edge of the scraper
should be slanted towards the left.   After each sweep of the
scraper, *raise it well* to bring it back for the next sweep, or,
catching the edge, it will snap the strip in two.   Mind and
let neither of these processes go too far ; mind not to thin
your strip too much, for remember that this is by no means
the final smoothing, and if worked too thin at the commencement of the work, the after results will be disastrous ; therefore leave the strip rather rough and stout than otherwise.
Then take three of the strips thus prepared, and with a pencil
draw lines across them, as follows : Across two of them, at a
distance of $5\frac{1}{2}$ inches from one end, and across the third, at a
distance of $7\frac{1}{2}$ inches from one end.   Then, with a firm stroke
of a small fine knife (Fig. 120), cut the strips across at those
lines, and it will be found that you have two pieces $7\frac{1}{2}$ long for
the upper bouts, two pieces $5\frac{1}{2}$ long for the centre bouts, and
two pieces $9\frac{1}{2}$ long for the lower bouts.   These lengths are in
excess of what is absolutely necessary ; but it is better to allow
for accident than to start with your wood too short.   Now cut
eight strips of *linen* (*not* calico) $3\frac{1}{4}$ inches long by $1\frac{1}{2}$ broad,
spread glue on both sides of one end of each strip of maple thus
cut, about $1\frac{1}{2}$ inches down each side, and folding the strips of
linen in the middle, cover one end of each strip with linen, so as
to protect the edges; the shortest (or $5\frac{1}{2}$ inch) strips must thus
be covered at both ends ; for the others, one end will be
sufficient.   The reason of this operation will be demonstrated
further on.

The next operation which must occupy us will be the bending
of the sides ; that is to say, to bend them so far like the part of
the mould on which they are to be fixed, that they will not split
when cramped into it.[1]   First thoroughly heat your bending-iron

---

[1] It has been suggested (*Amateur Work*, vol. i., p. 528, and vol. ii., p. 48)
that the ribs may be bent by steaming the strips of maple, and then cramping
them between blocks of the required shape.   This is the plan recommended in

(Figs. 121 and 122) ; when heated, cramp it on to the bench horizontally, so that the hot broad part and end (A and B) lies over the edge ; sit down opposite to it, and proceed to this most ticklish part of your work with a cool head. The iron, when you commence to bend, must only be just hot enough very slightly to singe a slip of wood when pressed against it (the time when this condition is reached must be tested by periodically trying to bend over it a thin slip of waste wood, kept for the purpose). First, bend the C's, or inner bouts, beginning at the two ends covered with linen : set the end on the part B of the iron, hold it there firmly with a block of wood, at the same time applying very gentle pressure to the other end. It will not begin to bend till it is thoroughly hot through, so do not hurry it by heavy pressure, or it will split (the tyro generally splits several to begin with). Bend it thus very carefully round B (B, Fig. 139), and then bend the other end similarly (C, Fig. 139), then give it the final shape on the broad part, A (D, Fig. 139). Fig. 139 shows the various stages of the bending of the centre bouts. (The linen is, of course, understood to be there, though it does not appear in the figure.

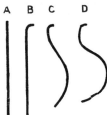

A B C D
FIG. 139.—Different stages of bending the Centre-bouts.

The upper and lower bouts must now be similarly bent, though, of course, it will be appreciated that only the linen-covered ends (which join the corner-blocks) will require the decided bend given by the part B of the iron. Fig. 140 shows the successive stages of the bending of the upper and lower bouts, which are of course similar, except in point of actual size. This done, you must carefully remove with a sharp knife all the projecting linen from the ends. The heat of the iron having scorched the glue, this will be a comparatively easy operation, but in places the linen will still adhere closely, and here you must be most careful not to bring away little pieces of the curls of the wood, which would irretrievably damage the beauty of your sides. The least vestiges of glue and linen must be finally scraped away from both the inside and outside surfaces of the strip with a file, which should be flat on one side and round on the other (Fig. 117),

A B C D
FIG. 140.—Different stages of bending the upper and lower bouts.

H. P. Smith's "The Construction of the Violin" (Syracuse, U.S.A., 1877), but no good workman would *dream* of such an expedient, for, in the first place, it takes ten times as long as the legitimate way, and, in the second, the ribs nearly always warp and twist (as in Fig. 138) after they have been set to the fiddle.

after which you may proceed finally to fit and fix your sides into the mould. This is done as follows: Begin with the lower bouts, taking your leaf of maple, bent as at D, Fig. 140, and fit the top end as nearly as possible to the bend of the corner O, marking it off absolutely square with the T-square, and cutting off the superfluous end with a knife : then proceed to bend it as nearly as possible to exactly the shape of the lower bout (H, on the mould Plate IV.), by means of the hot iron; when this is done, take the cramping-block (H, Plate IV.), and setting it against the inside of the lower bout, so that the cork side presses it closely as far as it extends, cramp it firmly to the outside of the mould by a cramp, Fig. 116, being most careful that the top bend fits exactly, and extends to the end of the corner O.

Then, at the point where the line A (part of the line A B) exactly bisects the bottom curve of the mould, mark the rib in pencil with a T-square, and cut it off exactly square with a sharp knife ; then proceed exactly in the same manner with the left hand lower bout (I), fitting it to the corner P, and cramping it at the curve with the cramping-block (I, Plate IV.). Cut it off at the point A, the same as the other, perfectly square, so that a complete and perfect joint is formed, as close as that of the back and belly. This must most particularly be aimed at, as a perfect joint at the bottom is a sign of good workmanship ; *but* if by some mishap you do not get a good join, do not start fresh with another strip for a new lower bout, unless your material, time, and temper are inexhaustible, for a bad join can be disguised, as will hereafter be shown, with a strip of purfling ; thus adding an ornamentation *ex necessitate rei.* Guarnerius constantly did this, and even the great Stradivari did not disdain to make use of this happy expedient when his master hand failed him at this most critical point. Next proceed with the upper bouts, working in exactly the same way from the corners, Q and R, clamping with the blocks L and M (Plate IV.) respectively ; you need not be particular to a quarter of an inch for the joint of these upper bouts (on the line B), for fitting the neck will cut away the join, be it good, bad, or indifferent. You will have to place cramps at the points O, P, Q, and R, to keep the ends of the sides into the corners O, P, Q, R, placing little slips of wood between the iron arm of the cramp and the wood of the bouts, to protect the latter from being bruised or dented by the pressure, unless, of course, you mean to proceed at once with the work, in which case these last cramps will not be required· Now finally set the lower bouts to shape, and cramp them into the mould, seeing that they are thoroughly freed from all vestige of glue or other mess. When fixed, there must be a slight rim above and below the mould, caused by the superfluous breadth of the slips from which you have made your sides. Now take some slips of paper, about 1½ inches broad, and slip one through at the bottom join of the sides, between the springy lower ends of the bouts and the base of the mould ; glue lightly both sides of the slip, *above* the place where it is held between the sides and the mould, and pull it through from the other side, so that in fact the lower ends of the lower bouts (at the join) are glued to the paper, and the paper to the side of the mould, so that by these secondary means the sides are fast in the mould ; put similarly glued slips of paper between the sides and the mould, at the points s and t (Plate IV.) in a similar manner, and proceed as before to shape, set, and cramp the upper bouts, setting the papers at the top joint and at u and v (Plate IV.). Now proceed to the fixing (in the rough) of the top and bottom blocks. Take two pieces of fine, even-grained pine,[1] planed round the sides and edges till they are both 2 in. long by

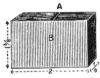

F꞉g. 141.—Top or Bottom Block (in the rough).

⅞ in. broad, 1⅜ deep, the grain setting as in Fig. 141. Now, with a sharp knife and file, shape the side B of the block (Fig. 141), to the very slight curve of the bottom of the sides ; at the join, mark across the top, by means of the line A on the mould, the exact centre of the block A (Fig. 141) ; now glue this on to the sides, exactly in the centre of the base of the mould (*i.e.*, so that the line A on the block exactly coincides with the line A—part of the line A B, Plate IV.), and fix it securely with a clamp. Cut, shape, and fix an exactly similar block at the top of the fiddle in the same way. After each of these operations, take a fine brush, and with a little hot water out of the glue-pot, wash away from your work all traces of superfluous glue. Now proceed to fix the inner bouts, or, as they are technically termed, C's ; these must be most carefully bent to the exact shape of the mould, cutting the ends *square*, and to exactly the right length. The ends must then be cut to a bevel, so as to fit into the corners, *against* the upper ends of the lower bouts, in the manner shown at c, in Fig. 142, which is drawn the actual size of the mould (Plate IV.). When you have got them thus to fit, and cleaned and scraped them thoroughly inside and out, cover the bevel of the ends of the C's with glue, slip

---

[1] Some makers (Stradivari amongst them) frequently used sallow wood for the blocks and linings, as being lighter than deal. There is little, if any, difference between them, and the mode of working is the same. (*Vide* p. 147.)

them in so that the glued ends fit against the lower bouts in the corners, as at C in Fig. 142, and cramp them in with the cramping-blocks, J and K (Plate IV.). Now take a fine slip of wood, and dipping it into the glue, just run it into the corners so as to complete the join, remove the superfluous glue, and set the mould to dry. Bear in mind throughout the operation of setting the sides and blocks, that you must leave a little rim of wood above and below the surfaces of the mould, to be shaved away when levelling the sides to the diameter of the mould, otherwise (if the sides do not reach the surfaces of the mould), they will be found to be too shallow when you come to fix on the back and belly. The next operation is the cutting and fixing of the corner blocks. Take two square-sided pillars of wood

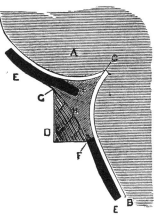

FIG. 142.—Setting of the sides, corner blocks, and side linings in the mould.

$2\frac{3}{4}$ in. long, the one for the lower corners having the ends 1 in. by $\frac{5}{8}$ in., the other for the upper corners having the ends $\frac{6}{8}$ in. by $\frac{5}{8}$ in. This length is just double what is required, and for this reason, that the corners being almost always in *contra-facsimile*, they may be cut to the right shape throughout their length, and sawn in half, which will be a great saving in point of time and work.

' The blocks must be shaped from the square in the manner shown in Fig. 143, the dotted lines showing the two sides before they are cut away with the gouge. The greatest care must be taken to make them fit perfectly throughout their height to the sides, as in Fig. 142, before they are cut in half, and fitted into their respective corners. The lower corner blocks (C, C', Fig. 143) will be cut from the first pillar, and the upper ones (D, D', Fig. 143) from the second. When glued, they must be strongly pressed into the corners, both outwards and upwards, so as to fix them closely both to the upper (or lower) bout and to the centre bout (or C). It is this operation which renders it of so much importance that the ends of the bouts should fit closely into the corners of

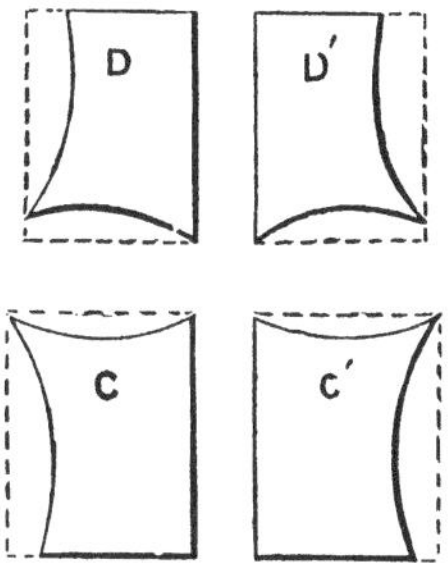

FIG. 143.—Method of shaping the Corner Blocks.

the mould and against one another, as at Fig. 142. If they do not,
this "pressing home" of the corner blocks will force them apart.
When this is done, and the blocks are firmly cramped into their
places, the superfluous glue must be washed off with a brush
and hot water, and the whole mould, with the sides and blocks
thus fitted into it, put away to dry thoroughly. Whilst it is
drying, you may proceed to prepare your side-linings ; the
pine-wood for these should be cut into long slips, $\frac{15}{16}$ inch broad
and $\frac{3}{32}$ thick ; and of these slips you will require for one fiddle
four $9\frac{1}{2}$ inches long (for the lower bouts), four $5\frac{1}{2}$ inches long
(for the inner bouts), and four $7\frac{1}{2}$ inches long (for the upper
bouts). To guard against accidents, it is well to have three or
four extra slips, to take the place of any that may snap in the
bending. Before commencing to bend them, having cut them
roughly to these lengths (which are all in excess of what is
required), let them soak for at least an hour in cold water.
Now, having heated your iron to a fierce heat, bend them to the
shapes they are required to take in the same manner as you
bend your sides, not hurriedly, but quickly, and with decision,
having previously well fixed in your mind the exact bend which
is necessary. The wet wood must rest against the flat side of
the thick part of the iron (A, Figs. 121 and 122) long enough
to be well heated through before commencing to bend, but not
so as to scorch it *too much* (a *little* scorching will not matter
to the linings).

By this time, the corner blocks being thoroughly firm, you
can proceed to render the sides and blocks *very nearly* level with
the surfaces of the mould. Where there is but little of the sides
above the surface, it may be filed away with the flat side of a
file ; but for the blocks, and when there is a good deal of the
sides to file away, you must use the toothed plane. Before
commencing to plane the blocks, the tops and bottoms must be
well wetted with warm water, which will prevent their splitting
away, to further guard against which, the iron teeth of the
plane must only project to an infinitesimal degree. If there is
much of the block to be cut away, you may begin to remove it
with a knife, finishing up with the plane. If the operation of
wetting the tops of the blocks has loosened the glue by which
the sides are fixed (with papers) to the mould, you must secure
the block with a cramp before reducing it.' Throughout this
operation you must not reduce either the sides or the blocks
quite to the level of the surface of the mould. This finishing
touch will not be put until the side linings are fixed, which you
may now proceed to do, beginning with the inner bouts in the
following manner :—First cut out the little slit, as at G, Fig. 142,

by making two deep cuts with the knife, and removing the wood between them with the "lining chisel" (Fig. 123). Take great care not to make this cutting too deep or too wide, testing it in these respects as you cut it by means of a waste slip of lining. When this is achieved, cut off the end of the lining with a cut slanting from the top, as in Fig. 144, which shows the section of the lining A fitted into the block B. Now, in the same way, cut off the other end of the lining, and set it in a similar cutting made in the \oper corner block, and leave it thus till the other linings are fitted. Cut and fit the linings of the upper and lower bouts in a similar manner *against* the corner and top and bottom blocks, as at F, Fig. 142. They are not *let into* the blocks, like the linings of the inner bouts, but the lower ends of the corner blocks are just shaved square with the sides, as at F, Fig. 142, so as to fit the ends of the linings. The ends of the linings are cut with a slight slant, as in Fig. 144, to make them fit well and tight against the blocks. If by any accident the linings become a shade too short, this fault may be rectified by inserting between them and the block a little splinter-wedge of pine to supply the deficiency.

FIG. 144.—Method of setting linings of Centre-bouts into slits cut in corner blocks.

Having fitted both the upper and lower linings all round, the next operation is the gluing and fixing. This must be done very quickly, *especially* if the weather is at all cold, or the glue will worry you by cooling as you work. Begin as before with the C's, or inner bouts, and be careful before beginning that all embracing surfaces (*i.e.*, the surfaces of the sides, and of the linings which are to be glued against them) are perfectly cleaned with a file and scraper. Take a waste slip of lining and thin it at one end to a wedge ; dip this end in the glue, and with it thoroughly glue the inside of the little slits in both corner blocks, quickly coat the inside of the upper lining of the C with glue and set it in its place, pressing it firmly into the slits and against the sides : glue and set the lower lining in the same way, and before the glue has time to set, wash away the super-fluous glue, and cramp the linings to the sides by means of the cramping block, J or K (Plate IV.), placing a slip of paper between the linings and the cramping block. Fix the other C linings in the same manner, and next glue and fix the linings of the upper and lower bouts, which is done in the same way, excepting that if the lengths have been properly proportioned so as to fit tightly no cramping blocks will be necessary, the

superfluous glue being washed away at once and the mould set
to dry. If, however, you distrust your cutting, you may cramp
your linings to the sides in the same way as you cramped the
sides to the mould, interposing (as with the inner bouts) slips of
paper between the linings and the cramping blocks. When
these are quite dry, proceed to render the edges of the sides,
blocks, and linings exactly level with the surfaces of the mould
by means of the toothed plane. When this is done, take a
sharp knife and cut the inner edges of the linings to a bevel,
bevelling off a little more than half the depth of the linings, as
at B, Fig. 145; when this is done, finish them with a file, removing any paper, etc., which may be sticking to the linings and
not removed by the knife. Next shape the blocks to bring them
as at F, Fig. 82. The corner blocks will be cut with the gouge
till they take the shape in the figure (Fig. 142), cutting away all
outside the line H (Fig. 142). The top and bottom blocks must
next be cut to the size set down at page 147. Fig. 181, p. 290,
represents the actual size and shape of the blocks for the mould
(Plate IV.). If there is any difference between the top and
bottom blocks, the top one will be just a shade smaller than the

other. The Guarnerius block is more a segment of a
circle (as at Fig. 104), but as the mould (Plate IV.)
is of the model of Stradivarius, I give a Stradivarian
block (Fig. 181, p. 290). The greatest care must be
taken in cutting both the corner and end blocks
quite parallel with the sides—i.e., that the outline of
the block may be identical at both top and bottom.
They must be finished off with the file, after which
the whole of the inside—i.e., the sides, the linings, and the blocks,
must be thoroughly sand-papered and cleaned, after which the
inside of the mould will present the appearance of Fig. 82, p. 148.

FIG. 145.—Final shape of the linings (section).

The next operation is that of taking the now completed sides
(or ribs) of the fiddle out of the mould to clean and finish the
outer surfaces. You will remember that the ribs are fixed into
the mould with slips of glued paper (p. 233) ; these must now
be loosened in the following manner. Take an ordinary small
table-knife with a fairly narrow blade, and thrust it carefully
through between the sides and the mould close to the points
where the paper is fixed, passing it along wherever the paper
extends. This operation will be accompanied by a series of
the most ominous cracking sounds, which are, however, merely
false alarms, though you must carefully guard against shaving
or splitting off little snips of the sides as you pass the knife
along. Having thus cut the fixings at all the points where glued
paper was put between the sides and the mould, proceed *very*

carefully and gradually to poke the ribs through, and out of the mould, pressing on all the blocks and bouts carefully in succession, having first marked which is the top of the blocks, to serve as a guide, when you come to fixing on the tables.   Now proceed to cleaning the outsides and generally finishing up. Begin by removing (by means of hot water and a brush) any vestiges of the papers which remain glued at the points where the ribs have been fixed in the mould.   Do not be too liberal with the water, and dry the ribs immediately, or they will warp horribly (as *per* Fig. 138).   If any little snips of the curl have been cut out in taking the ribs out of the mould, if possible these very snips, and if not, similar chips, must be glued in again.   If the joint of the corners (at 0, Fig. 142) is not close and tight, the interstice must be filled with glue mixed with chalk, but it is to be hoped that this will not be required. The ends of the corners must now be cut flat and square to the sides (as at C, Fig. 142) by means of a knife and flat file, testing the work with the small square, and, being very careful not to chip off the edges in cutting away the parts that are immediately adjacent to the corners, cut always from the ends to the centre, *not* from the centre to the ends.   The parts inside the C's must now be cleared of all traces of burning or glue with a small chisel and round file, any vestiges of glue all round the outside of the ribs being removed with a flat chisel, after which go carefully and completely round the entire outside with a sharp scraper, and fine glass paper, till they are perfectly clean and smooth as satin.   The sides or ribs of your fiddle are now *finished*, and you must put them away into the mould (into which they will now slip quite easily), out of harm's way, till you are ready for them.   For future purposes you must mark which is the top (or belly side) of the ribs, and which is the bottom ; write therefore, " top " on the top of the blocks, so that when you take them out of the mould there may be no confusion on this point.

" I see Calliope speed her to the place, where my goddess shines,
And after her the other Muses trace, with their violines."
                        (E. SPENSER. " The Shepheard's Calendar." April [1590])

CHAPTER XVI.

THE TABLES : BACK AND BELLY.

Joining the Tables—Planing the Flat Surface—Marking the Outline—Cutting-out—First Gouging—Correcting the Outline—Second Gouging—First Planing—The Sunk Edge—Second Planing—Scraping—Marking the Plane Surfaces for Gouging out Back and Belly.

You may now proceed to prepare the wood for the back and belly in the manner set forth in page 133. You will find the maple intensely difficult to join properly, for when squared and the two halves placed together at the thick sides are held up to the light, no crack showing the light must appear at the join, nor must a fine line of glue appear when the join is finally planed over ; and to produce this perfect fit in curly wood like maple is a very difficult matter to an unpractised hand, and may therefore be relegated to the professional joiner : for it must be noticed that there is only a very small margin to plane away in two halves, each only five inches broad. The belly of soft pine will be found to be easier to join. When joined (as at C, Fig. 77), the under or flat side of the slabs must be so perfectly truly planed that a straight-edge laid

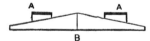

across them in any direction will not show any hollows or inequalities on their surface. For the purpose of producing this result, glue on to the sloping sides two strips of wood as at A, Fig. 146, and plane their surfaces

FIG. 146.—Wood for tables joined, and with steadying wedges for planing the flat surface.

(A, A) even, so that the slab may stand on its pointed surface (so to speak), without wobbling; when both surfaces are planed take your thin plank outline (C, C, C) with the line (A, B) down the centre (Plate IV.), and hold it firmly on the plane side of the slab with the line (A, B) coinciding with the join (B, Fig. 146), which runs down the centre of the slab. Then with a sharp pencil or point mark the outline exactly on the slab ; when this is done on both deal and maple, cut away all the external wood with the bow saw, leaving an edge a *little* beyond the marked outline to allow for finer cutting and subsequent finishing. When both outlines have been cut out, remove the remains of the steadying wedges (A, A, Fig. 146), being careful, in cutting them away, not to injure the sloping sides of this surface of the slab. Now with the gauge (an ordinary small size carpenter's gauge will do) draw a line round the edge of the slab $\frac{5}{16}$ inch from the plane side, and with a flattish gouge cut away the wood down to this line, first at the two ends till the centre of the slab along the line A, B takes the form of the guide represented by the line G, G (Plate IV.) : then cut away very gradually, till along the horizontal lines drawn across the plate the surface takes the form of the guide pieces shown in Plate IV. Cut this surface very carefully, especially on the lines 3, 7, and 8, for a cut of the gouge too deep in a wrong place will spoil your work entirely ; therefore correct your arching by the guides at their respective places at every few cuts that you give with the gouge. Both plates, it is understood, must be submitted to all these operations. The back will be the hardest, especially as the curls of the wood are apt to break out in grooves if you make a cut the wrong way of the grain. The belly will be much easier ; indeed, the difficulty lies in its ease, for it cuts like apple, and the slightest slip of a sharp gouge will do irretrievable damage.

Do not carry this operation too far ; leave the gouge marks distinct in the wood rather than try to chisel them away, leaving all finishing of this sort to the planing, which will be described later on. When this is done, take your plank outline C, C, C (Plate IV.), and set it well in the centre of the slab, fixing it at either end with a little cramp (Fig. 116). You originally cut out your slabs rather roughly, so there will be a little margin round it ; you must now mark with a marking-point the *exact* outline of your plank on to the plane side of your slab, then with a fine, sharp knife remove, absolutely cleanly, all wood *outside* this mark ; this requires much care, for remember you are now cutting the outline of your back and belly *finally*, and as they will appear on the finished violin ; therefore cut both of them exactly to the plank outline, and both being exact to the outline, they will be exact to one another. Remember the plank outline must be cramped face downwards on to the plane surface of the belly slab, and back downwards on to the plane surface of the back slab, for the two to coincide exactly when put face to face.

In marking the outline thus finally, you will see the use of cutting out the position of the sound-post in the plank outline, for of course in marking the back the sound-post will be on the right, and in marking the belly it will be on the left. This is a point which must be attended to, for, as I have said before, in a whole outline taken from a Stradivarius, the two halves will not be found to be in *contra fac-simile* to one another; the difference may be infinitesimal, but none the less appreciable in so fine a work as a fiddle.

It is one of the first worries of the beginner that he splits off pieces of the curves of the bouts whilst doing this cutting, owing to the brittle curls of the wood. When this happens the piece must at once be glued on again (and if neatly done, will not show when the work is finished) in the manner laid down in Chapter XXIII. (Repairs: page 309). When this is finished the edges must again be gauged, this time $\frac{1}{4}$ inch from the plane side of the slab, and then with a knife cut a $\frac{1}{4}$ inch bevel from this line to the roughly arched side, leaving the corners and button thick. When this has been done, and the edges all round both back and belly present a uniform thickness of $\frac{1}{8}$ inch (except the corners and button), take a broad flat gouge and slope the rough arching to the gauge line, extending your slope about an inch from the edge all round, according to the intended model of your fiddle. Do this carefully round back and belly, always leaving the corners and button thickest. For this purpose the back or belly must be cramped on to the edge of the bench, so that half of it overhangs the edge. When you have gouged round one half, turn it round and gouge round the other, being careful to have your gouges very sharp, so as not to have to lean heavily on the work, for fear of separating the centre join, or other calamity. This done, go all over the back and belly with the broad gouge, guiding your work as closely as possible with the arching guides, but not going too far towards smoothing the surface; all gouge marks may be left to the plane to eradicate when the model or arching has been roughly gouged out.

You have now finished with the gouge, and may turn your attention to the first planing. This is done with the toothed oval planes (Figs. 124 and 125), holding the slab with the hand against your body or the bench, going over the gouge marks very carefully, holding the plane so that it cuts in a slanting direction on account of the extremely tender nature of the wood, especially so if it is of a handsome grain or curl. Go on thus till the arching guides (Plate IV.) exactly fit the places on the back and belly indicated on the plate, and the wood is roughly levelled over. Be especially careful in planing to fit the arching guides Nos. 7 and 8 (the entire arching across the centre of the back and belly) to leave plenty of wood, for a bold "breast" is a great beauty in a fiddle.

Throughout the operations of gouging the arching of the

back and belly, you will find it a great advantage if you can compare your work with a true specimen of the great master's work, for then you can check the accuracy of your guide slips, and correct any errors which may creep in in tracing them from the plate. When you have roughly planed the back and belly all over take a smaller plane and plane them pretty smooth (but without altering the shape) for the distance of an inch from the edge. Then take the spring compasses (A, Fig. 126), having one leg just longer than the other, and opening them to $\frac{1}{8}$ inch, set the longer leg against the edge, so that the shorter one just touches the surface of the back or belly $\frac{1}{8}$ inch from the edge like a gauge. Draw in this manner a line all round back and belly $\frac{1}{8}$ of an inch from the edge, being careful to make it steady and even. Now open the compasses to $\frac{5}{12}$ of an inch, and draw a second line inside the first, in a similar manner, $\frac{5}{12}$ from the edge. Now take an ordinary cutting gouge, having a curve represented by Fig. 147, and very carefully cut a little trough or groove right round the back and belly between these two lines, not more than $\frac{1}{20}$ inch or so deep, and being *most cautious* not to cut beyond the *outer* one, which must be left clean and clear. If by any mischance you cut through it, and the thickness of your edge allows it, re-mark the $\frac{1}{8}$ line and gouge a little deeper to save it. When this is done, take a flatter gouge and carefully " melt " the ridge formed by the *inner* line into the arching of the back or belly. Fig. 148 shows the two stages of this grooving, which is meant to begin the graceful raised edges which characterize a well-made fiddle, A representing the groove cut, and B the groove " melted " into the rise of the belly or back. Now go carefully round these new gouge marks with the small oval plane, and bring the entire surface as smooth as you conveniently can with the toothed edge. You must take care in these gouging and planing operations not to alter the rise or arching of your tables as determined by the arching guides to any serious extent. To a certain extent it is of course impossible to avoid altering them, so you must now go all over them again with the guides, getting them as smooth and true as you can with the finest-toothed oval plane. You will most probably find it laid down in any works which go into the subject, that now is the time to purfle the instrument, and without doubt this is frequently done at this stage, but we shall not purfle till the back and belly are glued to the sides ; for though it is *easier* to do it now, by doing it later on we can make it coincide with the sides, and correct any little irregularities of out-line, which we could not do after the purfling is done (*vide* p. 262).

FIG. 147.—Curve of cutting gouge for sinking the edges.

When the last of your planing is done you will be ready to scrape. This is the most difficult and important of the operations necessary to be gone through, for on it depends the entire character and beauty of your instrument ; if it is done carelessly or lazily the marks of the planes and scraper will be left on the tables, visible beneath the varnish ; the rising edge, which you have cultivated so carefully (as in Fig. 148), will be scraped away and destroyed, and in fact, your fiddle will have the appearance of a rough Guarnerius instrument, instead of the work being in keeping with the beautiful Stradivarius patterns we have been working on up to now. However, remember *Labor ipse voluptas omnia vincit.* Let all your scrapers be very keen all round the edges, and working boldly and strongly, and very carefully, scrape the whole back and belly all over, using the round side and corners of the scrapers all round the outline and wherever necessary, so that there are no plane marks, gouge marks, bumps, or scratches anywhere visible on holding the slab sideways to the light. Mark : that it is important to

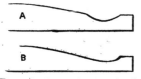

Fig. 148.—Stages of the cutting in sinking the edges.

sit in a good light during this operation—*i.e.*, where the light striking the edge of the back and belly will cast a shadow, and " throw up " any bumps, hollows, or plane-marks.

In this operation you will finally adjust all the curves of the tables, so that the hollows melt into the bumps of the model, and a smooth harmonious whole is the result. The great danger of this process is that a careless or unnoticed sweep of the scraper will scrape down a piece of your carefully-left edges and corners. When by accident you do this, you must re-mark the ⅛-inch gauge line as set forth above, and try to reclaim your error ; but this must not be done unless you have sufficient *thickness* left round the edges by the first and second gougings. When this operation is completed to your own entire satisfaction (or, better still, to the entire satisfaction of some disinterested party), take a wet sponge or brush, and wet the tables all over, back and front, and dry them again at once with a cloth. You will now see for the first time the true magnificence (if it exist) of your wood. The object of this proceeding is to show up any slight defect in your work, which must then be corrected again with the scraper ; and the process must be repeated till the wetting no longer shows any defects on the surfaces of the table. This takes very little time to say, write, and read, but you will find it is the most difficult and important part of your whole work.

Now turn both tables over, and opening the spring compasses (B, Fig. 126) ⅓ of an inch, draw a gauge line all round the plane surfaces of the slabs, as shown in Fig. 149. This serves as a mark beyond which the gouge must not go, being left to include the edge, the sides, and the linings. Then,

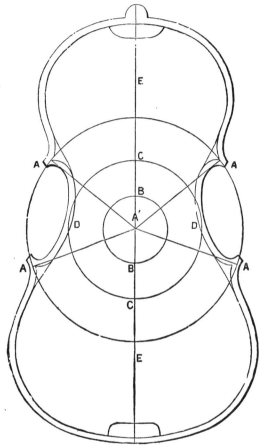

Fig. 149.—Diagram for regulating the thicknesses of the back.

with a pencil, mark across the four corners and at the top and bottom the parts of the tables which will be glued to the blocks (as shown in Fig. 149), marking them fully large for the present; these places must not be touched again by the gouge, but left quite flat. You are now going to commence what may be called the real operation of fiddle-making—*i.e.*, scooping out the back

and belly. For this purpose you must screw a long squared
beam of wood on to the bench, about ten inches from its edge,
and in front of it spread a folded cloth. The latter is to place
the arched surfaces of the tables upon, setting them against
the beam, so as to afford resistance to your gouge. Your
work now divides itself into two sections, the scooping of the
back and the belly—beginning with :

" Magnanimas Mulcet Modulando Musica Mentes.
  Virginibus Vinclum, Vitæ Veneranda Voluptas
  Solamen Senii, Servatrix Sacra Stridentum.
  Incitat Ipsa Iuventutem, Iuvat Ipsa Iocosum,
  Carmine Conciliat Cœlestia Castra Colentem,
  Autorem Autor Amans Alit (κῦδος) Artis Amantes !

CHAPTER XVII.

THE BACK.

Gouging-out—Planing—Scraping—Bevelling the Edge—Fitting on the Ribs —Sizing the Blocks—Peg-holes—Fixing the Ribs— Finishing—The Label— Correcting the Bottom Join—The Tail-pin Hole.

BEGIN by cutting gouge marks roughly right across the inside of the back, about $\frac{1}{8}$ inch deep at the centre line. When this is done, find by means of the compasses the exact centre point between the four corners A, A, A, A, in Fig. 149, which will be found to be A'.[1] At A', therefore, dig in the point of the compasses deep enough to preserve the puncture when you gouge over it (but not deep enough to mark upon the *final* thickness), and opening the compasses $2\frac{5}{16}$ inches, draw the circle C C, and then reducing them to $1\frac{3}{16}$ inches, draw the inner circle B B. The first rough thicknesses will be at A' $\frac{3}{12}$ inch, and at D D $\frac{5}{24}$ inch. These must be gouged carefully, constantly consulting the gauging callipers (Fig. 128), till this graduation is registered by the scale D (Fig. 128) as the callipers travel across from D to D (Fig. 149). You had better gouge a single scoop right across till these thicknesses are obtained, and this gouged line will serve as a guide. The thickness at present at D D will be, in fact, the thickness of the gauged line which, neither now nor in the ensuing processes, must be trespassed upon in the slightest degree. Similar guide lines must now be gouged across the upper and lower bouts, across E E, deepening gradually from the gauge line till the thickness of the table at the centre is $\frac{1}{8}$ inch. You now have three bands (or guide lines) of the (for the present) proper thicknesses across the fiddle ; now using your eye and hand together, gouge away between the guide lines till they only form part of the entire hollowing out. Be careful not to get *deeper than them* anywhere in their vicinity, and *not* to cut into the edge (*i.e.*, outside the gauge line), or into the parts you

---

[1] The *outer* circle connecting the four corners in the figure is merely drawn to prove to the reader that the points A are really equidistant from A'; without it, by an optical delusion, the two *lower* corners seem further from A' than the two upper.

have marked for the blocks. All the wood inside the circle B B must be $\frac{3}{12}$ inch thick ; all within the circle C C $\frac{5}{24}$, and all elsewhere $\frac{1}{8}$, the thickest part being in the centre ; the edges will naturally get cut a *shade* thinner, owing to the lesser quantity of wood ; but to prevent their getting too thin, let the slope from the gauge line to the centre be quite gentle, not an abrupt, downward curve. When this is done fairly smoothly, cut down

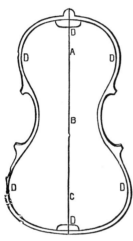

the ridges left by the deep gouge marks, as far as it is safe to do so. But do not go too far with the gouge, it is a bold weapon ; the plane is not so rapid, but much safer. Take a fairly coarse-toothed plane with a convex plate (Fig. 124), and go over the entire inside of the back, smoothing down the ridges left by the gouge, till holding the plate sideways to the light, the only grooves and ridges visible are the little ones left by the plane, and the thicknesses, in this their first stage, are pretty well adjusted. Now take a very sharp round-edged scraper, and proceed strongly to scrape the inside of the back all over, keeping inside the line you gauged round it and the places you marked for the blocks, until the marks of the plane are no longer

FIG. 150.—Final thicknesses of the back.

visible anywhere, and the inside of the back nearly approaches the smoothness of the outside. In this operation you will consult the callipers every moment, finally adjusting the thicknesses till they are as follows: according to Fig. 150, at the point A', $\frac{7}{40}$ inch (*i.e.*, just over $\frac{1}{6}$) ; at the point B, $\frac{1}{5}$; at the point C, just a *shade* thinner than at A ; at the points D, D, $\frac{9}{64}$ (*i.e.*, just over $\frac{1}{8}$). The thicknesses must merge into one another without any bumps, the wood being a shade stronger in the upper than in the lower bouts, and similarly a shade stronger

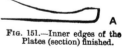

FIG. 151.—Inner edges of the Plates (section) finished.

just where the sound-post will be set ; the edges and parts touching the blocks must be left quite flat (in fact, not touched since the exterior arching was modelled). These, then, are exactly the correct thicknesses for a *new* fiddle-back. When they are properly adjusted, take a good fine biting file, and bevel very slightly round the whole inside of the edge, using a round file where the short curves render it necessary, and a flat one everywhere else ; finish off this little bevel (which must only be just enough to blunt the angle formed by the inside of the edge and the thickness of the edge) with medium sand-paper, so that it presents (in section) the appearance of A, Fig. 151. The margin left in scooping out the back will by this time be pretty clearly defined by the dirt which accumulates on it (never being touched in all the foregoing operations). Now take a keen, flat-edged scraper, and carefully scrape it clean, being cautious not to alter its planeness of surface. Finish the cleaning with a flat file, which must be passed round the edge *very true*, to avoid rounding it in any way. Your back is now finished (except the purfling), and it will be found that it gives a note *about* two tones higher than the belly scooped out and the *f f* holes cut, but without the bar. If you turn to page 153, you will see that the addition of the bass bar to the belly will raise the note a tone, which will establish the proper interval (viz., one tone) between the back and belly. The back is now finished, and ready to glue on to the ribs. You will remember that these are resting finished in their mould ; take them out carefully, for, if they have warped at all, they run a danger of splitting ; and turning them bottom-side upwards, go round them carefully. with a keen flat file, to thoroughly clean them and the blocks.

These last having the edge (as it were) of the grain exposed by their cutting, you must size them in the following manner : Spread a coating of glue all over the ends of the blocks, which will be fixed to the back, and put an iron (a poker will do) into the fire to get red-hot. When the glue has nearly set, apply the iron very " gingerly " to the coating of glue (which must not extend beyond the blocks over the sides and linings), rubbing it lightly, so that all the glue is burnt and caked over the ends of the blocks in a brown mass. Now with a flat file rub off all this burnt mass (but do not file down the blocks), and the tops of the blocks will be found to be no longer rough and porous (as would be natural with wood cut across the grain), but hard and smooth as ivory. Unless this precaution were taken, the single coat of glue with which you fix the back to the sides would sink into the blocks, which in course of time would consequently become unglued. This operation being completed, you must proceed to fit your ribs on to your back, which is done with fiddle-screws (Fig. 129) in the following manner. When you place your ribs on your back you will find that the two do not (or rather do not appear to) coincide at all. This is only the natural effort of the bent wood to regain its equilibrium ; you must therefore place the ribs on the back, and making one corner fit, fix it with a screw (Fig. 129). Turn the back round, and fit and fix the opposite corner in the same manner. Get the four corners of the ribs thus fitted on to the back by placing two screws at each corner, one on each side of the corner. N.B. Never fix a screw *on to* the corner itself, for it will infallibly snap it off. Now fix the top and bottom of the ribs, so as to have a margin equal with that at the corners, by means of iron cramps fixed to the blocks ; the surface of the back and the belly-end of the block must be protected in the ordinary manner, by means of little pieces of wood, from the hard pressure of the iron.

Many, indeed most, of the old makers were in the habit of securing the table to begin with, at top and bottom, by thrusting a bradawl right through the wood of the back into the block, the hole made by which had subsequently to be filled with a peg. Some modern makers also pursue this practice, but it is undoubtedly better to secure it at these points with a cramp, as above described, and then, as to putting in pegs, it may be done (as will be described further on), or not, as the fancy takes

FIG. 152.—Table fitted on to Ribs and fixed with screws.

you. Then proceed to fix the ribs similarly all round by means of as many screws as can be set round them, as in Fig. 152. You will find twenty-six are required, four for each upper bout, three for each inner bout, and six for each lower bout ; but these numbers may vary with the size of the screws. In the figure, for the sake of clearness, the screws are represented too few and too far apart. The object to be attained is the keeping of an overlapping edge of even width all the way round, and you must screw and unscrew, fit and refit, till this is attained.

The ribs being thus fitted to the back without glue, the next thing is to glue and fasten them. For this purpose it will not be necessary to entirely unfix them, but two or three screws may be taken off at a time, and that bit glued and re-fastened before going on. Begin by taking off the top cramp and three screws on each side ; take an old table knife, and dipping it quickly in the glue, insert it between the back and ribs, and run it round as far as it will go, repeating the operation till all you can get at is thoroughly glued ; then, seeing that the ribs are rightly set on the edge, cramp and screw them up again *tight*. Take off three or four adjacent screws, glue that bit and refix it, and so on ; go all round the fiddle a "bout" at a time, taking care to reset the ribs, so as to leave an even edge. Then take a brush, and with hot water (out of the glue pot) thoroughly wash away all traces of glue clinging outside, inside, or on the edges of the ribs or back. Set the whole arrangement to dry for a day Your principal difficulty will be that the hold taken by the screws being rather precarious, whilst you fix one, another will drop off, and so on, and this is damaging both to the temper and the success of the operation. Therefore fix your glued ribs quickly, *but* carefully and surely. When sufficient time has elapsed for the glue to have dried thoroughly, remove the screws, take three qualities of sand-paper (the last being very fine indeed) and thoroughly sand-paper and smooth the entire inside of the ribs and back : remember it will not be pleasant to think that in some centuries to come the repairer will find that the work you have been so careful over outside is slovenly inside. You can now put in your ticket or label. Every violin made ought, to my mind, to be ticketed with the name of its right maker ; for preference in Latin, but of course this is optional. The place for the label is discovered by temporarily putting a belly on, and looking through the left-hand *f* hole ; in this way the most visible place for the label is ascertained, and on this spot it may be glued firmly at once.

Whilst considering the construction of the ribs of the fiddle, I pointed out that if the join at the bottom is not all that might be desired, any deficiency may be hidden by means of a row (or more) of purfling. If the join is *perfect*—*i.e.*, close, straight, and coinciding with the join down the back, so much the better; but if a line of glue marks it, or if it is crooked, or if it is on one side of the join of the back, these faults may be rectified (without being ashamed of the expedient) in the following manner : Take a few inches of ready-made purfling (such as can be bought at a penny a foot at any fiddle-maker's) and cut, with a sharp knife and the lining chisel, a square cut groove, at exactly right angles with the back, on the site of, and broad enough to cover, any fault that may there be found. Cut it a little shallower than the depth of your ready-made purfling, and according to the diameter of the latter, and glue into this groove, one, two, or three strips of purfling, according as the fault you wish to hide may require. These ready-made strips may always, if necessary, be thinned by hammering the sides lightly, or broadened by hammering the top.

This ornamentation, without impairing the fiddle, will effectually hide any fault which is apt to be found at this point. Cut off the ends flush with the belly side of the ribs, wash off all superfluous glue, and when this inlaying is dry, level it down flush with the ribs with a knife or scraper. Now, a shade below the exact centre of this line bore a small hole ($\frac{1}{8}$ inch in diameter) which will serve as the *commencement* of the hole for the tail-pin. This is not *finally* cut till the varnishing is finished, but it is best to *begin* it now, as the belly being off you can guard against the drill splitting away bits of the lower block, which cannot be obviated or corrected when the belly is on. It must not be finished now, or the varnish running into it will make it messy and inconvenient to work with. This hole may be made with the peg-hole cutter, Fig. 184, described on page 300. Your back and sides are now finished, and it remains, therefore, only to glue on the belly, for the body of your violin to be finished " in the white."

> " Arte maternâ rapidos morantem
> Fluminum lapsus, celeresque ventos,
> Blandum et auritas, fidibus canoris
>   Ducere quercus."
>   (*Hor.*, 1, 11.)

CHAPTER XVIII.

THE BELLY.

YOUR pine, or belly slab, is still in the state in which we left it
at the conclusion of Chapter XVI., that is to say, having one
side arched and finished, and the other flat. You will commence by giving its personal appearance the finishing touch, by
marking out on its arched surface the ff holes, which is done
as follows. In p. 155 are given directions for copying any
single, or pair of, ff holes. If the belly from which you are
copying is detached from the instrument, and you have copied
its two ff holes, as described in p. 156, having traced down
your parchment the centre line, or join of the belly, and having
transferred the drawing to a leaf of wood (not more than
$\frac{1}{15}$ or $\frac{1}{20}$ of an inch thick), cut it down the exact centre line with
a sharp knife, so as to produce the model represented in actual
size in Fig. 153. The explanation of this figure is as follows :
It is an actual working size model of an f hole, taken from, and
corresponding with the outline, etc., of the instrument represented
in Plate IV. (In this plate an f hole is drawn ; but only to indicate
which half of the outline represents the belly.) In Fig. 153,
A′, A, A′, represents A B, in the plate, the centre join of the belly.
The line A, A, A, A is the plank model of your f hole as cut out,
and with its flat side set to coincide with the line A′, A′ ; the figure
shows its exact position on the belly, the outline of which is
shown by the dotted outline c, c. A nick is cut in the flat side
of the model, exactly opposite the inner cranny (G) of the f
hole at the point B The belly represented in Plate IV. is
$14\frac{1}{8}$ inches long ; measure from the top, down the centre line
(which should be marked on the plate with pencil for con-
venience and clearness), $7\frac{13}{16}$ inches (or from the bottom, $6\frac{5}{16}$),
and make a little mark. Now set the nick B of Fig. 153 at
this mark, and see that the line A′, A′ lies exactly on the line

A B, drawn on the arching of the belly. The model is on such thin wood, that on pressing it, it will bend and lie close on the

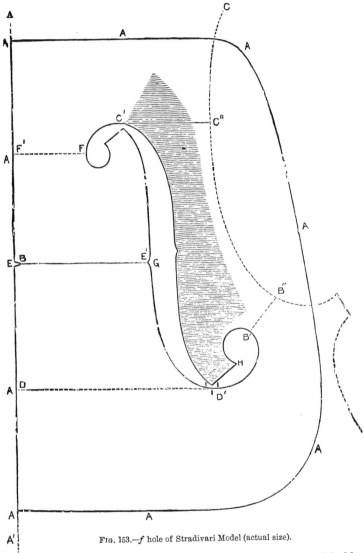

FIG. 153.—*f* hole of Stradivari Model (actual size).

arching of the table. Take a *very fine pointed* pencil, and holding the model firmly on the belly with one hand, trace the inside of the f hole on to the belly with the other ; turn the model over, and repeat the process exactly on the other side for the other f hole, and your ff holes are marked on your belly.

But, if you are not following the model of Plate IV., or if you wish to use some other f hole (say one of those on pp. 73-80) trace it from there, or from the original, with a dirty finger or glove, as described on p. 155, and set and mark it on the belly, according to the relative distances it should hold thereon, and which are planned out by the dotted lines on Fig. 153. You will have to mark (as before) the point B on the centre line A B, opposite which to set the cranny G of the f hole. This you can do, adapting the directions given above by common-sense to the outline you have chosen, or by comparing the fiddle from which you are copying. Its position with regard to the outline and centre join of the fiddle will then be as follows :—

From B' to B'', $\frac{7}{16}$ inch.	From E to E', $1\frac{7}{16}$ inch.
„ C' to C'', 1 „	„ F to F', $1\frac{3}{16}$ „
„ D to D', $2\frac{1}{8}$ „	

These measurements are of course taken from the plate and Fig. 153, but if another model is being worked upon, an intelligent workman will easily adapt them ; the difference being, probably, only in the lengths of the lines D D', E E', and F F'.

The ff holes being marked, now put the finishing touch to the arching of the belly—viz., the sinking noticeable in all well-made fiddles just *outside* the ff holes (*i.e.*, between them and the edge), and indicated on Fig. 153 by the slight shading on the right-hand side. This is a hardly perceptible hollowing, beginning in the lower wing of the f, extending just as far as shown by the shading, and so " melted " into the arching already given to the belly, as not to be noticeable unless looked for. Its depth will be, to a certain extent, regulated by the model you are working on, but will not generally be deeper than the groove you ran round the sides (Fig. 148). It must be begun with a flat gouge, " melted " into the arching with the smallest curved plane, and finished off (like the rest of the belly) with the scraper. Be careful in doing this not to obliterate the marking of the ff holes (except at the inner side of the *lower round* hole of the f, which cannot help being gouged away, but can be at once re-marked), and particularly be careful of the raised edges of the fiddle, which are in considerable danger during this operation. So bear in mind in this, as in all the stages of your work, the motto " *Cavendo tutus.*" When the scraping is finished, you will give your tables a rub all over with medium sand-paper, and then re-mark your *ff* holes, which will have got partially obliterated by the handling of the belly since they were traced. When they are re-marked, punch out their round holes in the following manner :—

Take the two piercers (or *f* hole punches, Fig. 127), and setting the bigger of the two exactly in the centre of the *lower* circle of the *f* hole (which it will not quite fill), and holding exactly underneath it a small block of wood to press against, press the punch firmly into the wood, twisting it at the same time, so as to cut out a little disc of wood. You need not punch right through, but no harm is done if you do ; indeed, the hole going through to the flat side serves as a guide when you begin to scoop out the belly. Repeat the process with the smaller punch for the upper circle of the *f*, and as with the larger piercer punch out the upper holes in the same manner with the smaller. You must be very careful to place it exactly before beginning to cut, for you will find that the smaller punch (c, Fig. 127) has exactly the diameter of the upper circles of the *f* hole, Fig. 153. (The big punch is *just* smaller than the lower circles.) After (and possibly during) this operation you must pick the pieces or discs of wood out of the bore of the punches by means of a sharp point (such as the marking point), being very careful in so doing not to injure the cutting edge of the piercer or punch. (*Vide* page 223.)

Now commence to scoop out the belly, which is begun in the same way as the back, placing the arched side downwards on the cloth, and the edge against the beam ; and you will gouge it in a manner similar to the back, so as to have it ⅛ inch thick *all over*. Be very careful how you cut, for this belly pine is as tender as cheese under the chisel, and before you know where you are, you will find yourself through the plate, and an irremediable injury done. If in an unguarded or absent moment you cut it too thin, you must take one of the thick shavings which fits the gouge mark which has gone too deep, glue it in neatly, closely, and firmly, by means of the apparatus figured on p. 310 (Fig. 191), and in the manner there described, and when it is dry go on with the operation. When this has gone as far as it is safe to go with the gouge, take the sharpest and finest curved oval plane, and plane over the entire inside of the belly most carefully, till all the gouge marks have faded into the plane furrows. You may then cut your *ff* holes, which at present are only punched out as above described. They are cut out with a very fine-bladed knife, which is introduced from underneath, holding the belly with your hand against your body for the purpose. Begin by cutting round the lower circle, so as exactly to conform to the pencil marking which will be *just* cut away : then cut the lower curve of the *f, always cutting against the grain and inwards—i.e., towards the centre join of the plate;* otherwise, you will *infallibly* split off the corner of the " wing " (H in Fig. 153), and such a mishap is almost irremediable. If you *do* have an accident, and can preserve the tiny bit chipped off, glue it on *at once,* wedging it in its place by means of shavings set in the lower circle of the *f.* When you get to the lower point (I, Fig. 153), press the knife strongly, and work it through the narrow ·channel into the long part of the *f,* and proceed as follows :—Cut a groove right down the centre of the *f* with two *carefully guided* but strong cuts of the knife, and pick out the splinter thus loosened. Continue this groove till you go through to the other side, and then, working carefully from underneath as before, cut out all the wood in the long part of the *f,* keeping most carefully to the pencil lines, and being especially cautious when you are cutting in the channel I. The top curve and circle are cut out the same as the lower one, the crannies G are neatly cut out, and the opposite *f* hole is cut out in the same manner. If you chip off a corner (H) beyond hope of repair, or lose the piece, you must remedy it by cutting the angle at I sharper and that at H more obtuse, and making the opposite *f* similar. But it will be a thousand pities if you mar the symmetry of your belly by such a mishap, so guard against it *by always cutting against the grain in the direction* H *to* I, *and never* I *to* H. (Fig. 153.)

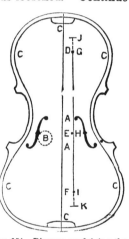

FIG. 154.—Diagram explaining the thicknesses of the belly and the setting of the bar.

The *f f* holes being cut out, they will serve as a further guide in determining the thicknesses ; so with the finest plane and the scraper proceed finally to adjust them *inside* the gauged border-line and block-boundaries, till they are left as follows, according to Fig. 154, which represents the inside view of the belly :—At the centre, A A, it must have a substance of $\frac{9}{64}$ (just over $\frac{1}{8}$ inch) ; it must only just thin off (say $\frac{1}{20}$ less) at the edges marked C, C, C, C, and must be a shade thicker just over the sound-post B, which, it will be noticed, is placed on the *left* in the figure which represents the *underneath* surface of the belly. Finally, adjust these thicknesses by means of sand-paper, and then correct any little faults or roughnesses which may be found round the ff holes, being, of course, cautious not to alter their shape in any way.

You can now shape your bar, and affix it to the belly, first of all marking the place where it is to go, as follows :—It will be placed on the right-hand side of the belly (as you work at the inside). Make three small marks at the exact centre of the belly. 1, at the broadest part of the upper bouts, D ; 2, exactly midway between the crannies of the two ff holes, E ; and, 3, at the broadest parts of the lower bouts, F. If your join is *exactly* in the centre, these marks will be on the join ; but it sometimes happens that it is not *quite* so, in which case the true centres must be marked between the outside edges with compasses, and a line drawn to connect the three marks. Now on the right of these three marks, make three other marks, G, H, I ; the top mark G being $\frac{3}{4}$ inch from the exact centre, D ; the middle one, H, being $\frac{4}{5}$ inch from the centre mark E ; and the lower one, I,

being $\frac{5}{6}$ inch from the centre mark F, and connect them with a pencil line. Now from two points rather to the right of the top and bottom blocks draw the two short lines J, K, I $\frac{11}{16}$ of an inch from the upper and lower edges, and lengthen the line G H I till it touches them. This line, therefore, marks the exact *locale* of the bar which will be glued, with its outer edge just touching it. Take a strip of fine even-grained pine, about 11 inches long, and plane it till it is just $\frac{3}{16}$ inch thick throughout its length, and perfectly straight and parallel.

Fig. 155.—Method of raising the wing *a* of the *f* hole.

Cut it about 1 inch broad, and slope off the two ends on one side, so that it roughly takes the shape of the inside of the belly, and cut it so that its two ends touch the points J and K. Now make a mark on, and draw a line across, this rough bar at the point H (Fig. 154), and mark the top and bottom of the bar to distinguish them. Before commencing to fit the bar, take a slip of wood about 4 inches long, and about $\frac{1}{16}$ thick, and $\frac{1}{3}$ broad ; insert this into the middle of the *f* hole nearest the bar (*i.e.*, the left-hand one looking at the front of the belly), and under the corner, as in Fig. 155, which represents the operation viewed from the outside of the belly. Its object and result will be to press up the " wing," *a*, and press down the lower wing, *b*. The strings will correct this discrepancy by their pressure ; if this precaution were not taken, the pressure of the strings would force the wing *a*, *below* the wing *b*, which would be hideous to the last degree. This precaution gives the belly a *temporary* excess of rise at this point, to which artificial rise the bar is fitted, to maintain it till the greater influence of the strings is exerted. The bar being roughly rounded to shape, it may now be accurately fitted ; for this purpose it is set in the belly, and fixed at its two ends with sound bar clips (Fig. 130). It being thus held, you can hold it sideways, and mark on one side where it must be cut down ; take it off, correct it, and reset it with the clips over and over again, till it adheres closely all over the edge to the belly, throughout its length. Care must be taken each time you set it in the belly, to place the centre mark on the bar, on the point H on the belly (Fig. 154), and also to place the top of the bar at the top of the belly, and *vice versâ.*

This operation of fitting the bar may be done in ten minutes, and it may take hours, for it must be absolutely exact through out its length, so that when glued it seems to be cut out of one solid piece with the belly, and again, it must be at exact righ. angles with the edges of the belly, as in Fig. 83 (p. 149), which will be more difficult to attain, because of the slope of the arch-ing. When, however, being fixed by the clips, you can no longer see a cranny below it at any point, it may be just finished with a flat file and glued into its place—*i.e.,* just on the line G H I (Fig. 154) ; if, by reason of the narrowness of your model, the bar overhangs the top circle of the *f* hole, so as to obstruct it, it must be set throughout its length *and parallel to the line* G H I, a little nearer the centre, so as just to clear the hole of the *f :* if this would involve too great a shift towards the centre, a little scoop may be taken out of the side of the bar so that the hole of the *f* is not obstructed. When glued, it must be fixed in its place by means of three wooden bar cramps (Fig. 131) and left to dry. Whilst gluing in the bar you may as well " size " the belly ends of the blocks with glue, to fill up the pores before gluing on the belly, in the same way as you did before gluing on the back (*q. v.*), *i.e.,* with glue, hot iron, and file. When the gluing of the bar is dry, take a small fine plane and cut it into shape, which, when finished, should be as follows in the middle : (*i.e.,* at the point H, Fig. 154) it should be $\frac{2}{5}$ of an inch deep; therefore plane away till this depth is obtained at H, and the top of the bar is plain and straight; then proceed to finally " shape " it. From the point c (Fig. 156) it must soften off to the belly at the ends, the extreme ends being finished with a knife, not scalloped, but merely softened down to the belly, so as to have about the shape of Fig. 156 ; A shows the finishing of the ends, B the shaping of the edge of the bar not glued to the belly ; this last is obtained by means of a file and sand-paper. When the bar is thus finished, take three squares of glass-paper of progressive fineness (the last being *very* fine), and carefully smooth the whole inside of the belly till it is perfectly soft to the touch. Then take a flat and round file and bevel off the inside edge of the belly in the same way as described for the inside edge of the back (as represented at Fig. 151), then in a manner similar to that there described, clean and smooth the edge you have left round the scooping of the belly, and this having been done, your belly is ready to glue on. For this operation you must increase the glue in the pot to twice its bulk by the addition of water, so as to dilute the glue, and render it much weaker than that with which you "sized" the blocks and fixed on the back. The object of this is that the belly may have to come off some day for repairs, etc., and if it were fixed on with the ordinarily strong glue, this would be an impossibility. Some people, before gluing on their bellies, put curious, historical, or sentimental inscriptions out of sight up in the upper bouts of the fiddle. The old luthiers

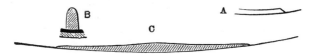

Fig. 156.—Final shaping of the Bass-bar.

were very great at this, and now in taking the bellies off old fiddles, quaint couplets and mottoes are often brought to light. Before applying the glue (which is not done after the belly is fitted, as in the case of the back), set the belly on the ribs with a couple of screws. and look round it to note the points where the sides will require pressing or stretching to shape, for the longer the time that elapses between the gluing on or the back and of the belly, the more will the ribs twist and warp out of shape. When, by this means, you have arrived at an approximate notion of what difficulties you will have to contend with, spread the glue quickly *all over* the top edges of the blocks, sides, and linings, being very careful not to let any run down *inside*, for though any that runs down *outside* may be washed off, any that trespasses inside cannot be removed *after* the belly is on. Having got a buttering of glue spread all round, set the belly on, and screw it fast all round. beginning with the C's, or inner bouts, being most particular to avoid the corners[1] (as in Fig. 157), then fitting the ribs and putting on the other screws and cramps the same as with the back. This

[1] If you do by any chance split a corner, mend it at once according to the directions given for "Repairs" (p. 308).

must be done quickly, but not without care in adjusting the edges, for the glue soon sets; and particularly do not attempt this performance until you have precluded all possibility of draughts or currents of air, which would seriously increase your difficulties; but to counteract any evil which may arise from the premature setting of the glue, the application of the hot water, when you wash the superfluous glue from the sides, will remelt it a little and aid the operation of fixing the belly. When the screws are applied, set a slip of wood in the f hole from one of the screws, to keep down the lower wing and raise the upper one (just as a while ago you set a similar slip from the corner), as shown in Fig. 157. This being done, take a brush and some hot water and wash all round the sides, to remove any superfluous glue, and to re-warm and set that which is spread to keep the belly on. In applying the screws to both back and belly, when fixing them, the head of the screw (A, Fig. 129)

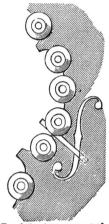

FIG. 157.—Arrangement of screws in fixing belly (to avoid the corners).

must be on the side of the table which is being glued (*not* the moving collar B), otherwise when you wash away the superfluous glue it will get washed into the collar B, and fix it to the screw. Set the belly aside in a warm place to dry, and when quite fast, remove the screws. You will now look round the edges, and wherever they appear to be too broad in proportion, (*i.e.*, too far from the sides), they can be reduced and made equal by means of a sharp knife and file, the corrections being neatly finished with glass-paper.

" The trembling lute some touch, some strain the viol best,
In sets which there were seen, the music wondrous choice,
Some likewise there affect the gamba with the voice."
(M. Drayton, " Polyolbion," Song iv. [1613])

CHAPTER XIX.

PURFLING AND FINISHING THE BODY.

Marking the Purfling—The Pegs—The Purfling—Fitting—Fixing—Raising the Edges and Corners—Final Scraping—Sand-papering—The Rest—Fitting—Fixing—Finishing—Rounding the Edges—Finishing the Body "in the White."

IT is now that you will see the advantage of not having purfled before scooping out the back and belly. If you had done so, your edges must have remained as originally cut, whether quite coincidental with the ribs or not ; but as it is, where for the sake of uniformity you now slightly reduce the edges, the purfling may be made to follow the correction which it will now hide, instead of showing it up, as it would have done if already inlaid. Take the purfling gauge (Fig. 133), and setting the cutter (which must be thoroughly sharp) $\frac{7}{32}$ inch from the rounded part of the stem A, trace a line (not letting the cutter sink deep) all round the tables (back and belly). Then reduce the distance from the cutter to the stem to $\frac{5}{32}$, trace another line round back and belly, which will thus be $\frac{1}{16}$ outside the first. This seems simple enough to say, but you will find it most difficult to preserve a uniform distance from the edge, the stem requiring to be pressed very strongly against the edge, as it travels round, especially on the tender pine of the belly, and it will be most difficult to preserve the second line at an exact distance of $\frac{1}{16}$ from the first ; however, *festina lente*, and patience, and careful perseverance will overcome all this difficulty. Mind and not cut these marks too deep ; they are only to serve as guides for the knife in cutting the groove in which the purfling is laid. The curve of the marking will have been interrupted at the top of the back by the button, and the corners must be re-marked to have the purfling pointed across them in true Stradiuarius style. If you look at any Stradiuarius you will see that at the corners the purfling is *not* finished off in the middle of the corner (as at A, Fig. 158), but pointed up (or down, as the case may be) to the point B, as at c, Fig. 158. This is a small particular, but it is a great point in the purfling of Stradiuarius. To mark this "style," and to complete the tracing of the purfling, prepare a slip of wood exactly similar to the shaded piece on Fig. 158, which is prepared from a Stradiuarius instrument. The *contour* a, a, a, a, represents the completion of the curve at the top of the back, underneath the button, which may be traced by its means. The purfling at the corners is at present as shown by the dotted line at A. The guide slip must be set on the 8 corners, coinciding with the curve as at D, in Fig. 158, but, as there shown, altering the position of the point as at C. The curve of the purfling in the

inner bouts must be brought round to neet this point as at C, so that when finished the tracing of the purfling will be as represented by the double lines D D′, Fig. 158. When these are marked, proceed with a sharp-pointed knife to cut round the two lines of the tracing on back and belly till the purfling is marked by two even, parallel, and cleanly-cut lines $\frac{1}{12}$ of an inch deep. You must be most careful in this operation to guard against letting the knife slip away from the lines, as this will spoil the symmetry of the purfling, and in the purfling it is that the true delicacy of handling and workmanship really shows itself in the construction of the fiddle. When the lines are cut, pick out the wood from between them with the purfling chisel (Fig. 135), being very careful that the lines are cut deep enough at the corners, or you will pick out a piece too much at this point, and spoil its finish. Let the depth be made even and smooth all round the instrument before proceeding further.

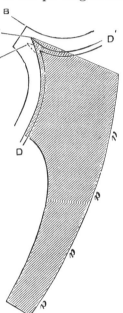

FIG. 158.—Method of purfling in the corners; and outline for marking purfling under the button.

The next step is to put in the pegs; these are the small, round spots of wood let into old fiddles at the top and bottom of the back (*vide* p.164), for the reasons already set forth—namely, to fill the hole made by the bradawl thrust in to secure the back and belly at these points when fitting them to the sides, before the iron cramps were used for this purpose.

You will notice that every Stradiuarius violin has them just so placed in the back, *on* the join, that they are cut in two halves (of which only one is left) by the purfling, as at A, in

Fig. 92. Although these are not absolutely necessary to the fiddle, yet, as you are working on the Strad. model, they impart a finish to your fiddle as a copy. Take a round, sharp-pointed tool (such as the marking-point), and press a hole just where the centre join of the fiddle meets the groove cut for the purfling (as in Fig. 92), so that half the hole is in the groove. Make a similar hole at the bottom to correspond, and also similar ones in the belly at top and bottom, and then cut your four pegs to fit. These are made out of a rod of maple, not highly figured, but of a colour or tone which contrasts with the maple of the back. Cut the rod to a long, round point, like a pencil, cut off the extreme end, and finish it with a file, so that it exactly sticks into the hole you have made ; cut off the point about $\frac{3}{16}$ inch long, and tap it into the hole, so as to stick whilst you fit the rest of the pegs. When all are cut, dip each one into glue, and fix it into its hole with a good smart tap, and leave them to dry thoroughly. When this is accomplished, cut off the projecting ends, so as to make them flush with the back, and cut off as much from the sides of the pegs as projects into the groove cut for the purfling (i.e., half the diameter), which will reduce it, as in Fig. 92. Now take a brush full of water and wet all round the grooves on back and belly, wiping off superfluous moisture with a cloth. This will throw any defects in the uniformity of the grooves into prominence, and this will enable you the better to correct any such irregularities. When this has been done, you will be ready to put in your purfling. Purfling, as I have said before (page 163), is composed of a strip of plane wood between two strips of the same wood stained black (not, as some have supposed, a strip of rosewood between two of ebony). The exceedingly delicate diameter of these strips may be imagined when we reflect that the three glued together and inlaid only present a diameter of $\frac{1}{16}$ inch. Purfling may be bought of any fiddle-maker ; and I should advise the amateur to purchase his purfling ready cut, though I shall tell him how to prepare it for himself. It is sold in two forms ; in separate strips of plain black and white, and also as a sandwich, ready glued together ; the latter is perhaps the easier to work with, but is terribly liable to split, and in putting it in it will be necessary to dip the ends in the hot water of the glue-pot for an instant (not long enough to unglue it) before giving the ends the strong bend necessary at the corners and centre bouts. An experienced fiddle-maker will always prefer to inlay three separated strips together rather than chance a split with the ready-made purfling. If you use the disintegrated purfling of the thorough luthier, it is prepared as follows : Get some long strips of plane veneer in the natural state, and some also stained black, as thin as you can ; cut it, for convenience' sake, into leaves four inches by two feet, and reduce it by means of scraping as nearly as possible to a uniform thickness of $\frac{1}{48}$ inch *at the most.* Now make one edge *absolutely* straight and true (by means of a steel rule and knife), and then cut it up, by the same means, into strips $\frac{1}{12}$ inch broad. When you have got double as much black as white, you can proceed to fit it to the grooves, commencing, as usual, with the c's, or inner bouts. Take three strips (two black and one white), or a piece of sandwich which you judge to be long enough to fit the bout you are working on ; make the ends (at one end) even, and with a sharp knife bevel off the three together, as in Fig. 159. Fit this point close up into the corner shown in Fig. 158, and carrying the strips round the centre bout to the other corner, fit them into the other corner with another bevel, which you must be careful not to make too short, fitting it, in point of fact, much the same as you fitted your ribs into the mould, as described at page 232. Next proceed to fit in another three from the corner either to the centre join, or, right round the upper (or lower) bouts to the opposite corner. If you cut them to the centre join, you must make the point of union very close, square, and, if possible, imperceptible, especially in the back. In the belly you need not care about making so exquisite a job, for the purfling will be cut away at the top in the forma-

FIG. 159.—Purfling. The 3 strips cut to a bevel.

tion of the chamber cut to receive the neck, and will be hidden by the finger-board, and at the bottom by the chamber cut to receive the rest, and will be hidden by the tail-piece. For the same reasons it is often omitted to put the pegs (Fig. 92) into the belly. When you have got the purfling fitted all round both back and belly, you can proceed to glue it. For this purpose the purflings must be taken out, a sandwich (or a set) at a time, the grooves filled with glue, and the sandwich (or three strips) replaced, being most careful to make them fit accurately at the corners, and particularly at the joints at the top and bottom of the back, where the three strips must join those opposite so exactly as to render the join imperceptible (unless of course you have purfled in one long strip from corner to corner). This is best effected by cutting off the ends at the join, slanting downwards from the top edge, just as the linings of the inner bouts were fitted into the corner blocks, as shown in Fig. 144. Mind and use plenty of glue before setting the strips into the grooves ; for remember, it has not only to fix the purflings into the groove, but also, if you use three strips, to permeate between the component strips themselves, to keep them together. It also fills up and disguises any errors or faults in the cutting of the groove, which it is impossible (especially for an amateur) to obviate ; therefore, when the purflings are set in the groove, it is well to run a little glue all round them with a little slip of wood to fill up anywhere where there was not sufficient.

The purflings are tapped into the groove all round with a little hammer to insure their sinking well into it. The superfluous glue is then wiped off with a cloth, and the whole thing is left to dry thoroughly. When this is effected, cut the purflings down level with the surfaces of the back and belly by means of a sharp, flat gouge. The defects (if any) will now be brought into prominence, but cannot be remedied. However, we console ourselves that if slight defects exist in our purfling, they exist also, if carefully looked for, in the works of the finest Cremonese masters. Now take a flat file, and rub right round the tops of the edges (left as in Fig. 151), with a view to cleaning them and removing any slight inequalities which may have invaded them since they were last corrected. Now open the spring compass (A, Fig. 126) $\frac{3}{32}$ of an inch, and draw a line all round the edges of the instrument, open them again $\frac{3}{8}$ inch, and draw a second line round the edge inside, the first, from which it is consequently distant $\frac{7}{24}$. (It will be observed that this operation resembles, in all respects, excepting its measurements, the processes by which we originally sunk the edge, as shown by Fig. 148.) Now take a gouge and sink a trough all round, cutting out the wood (and with it the top of the purfling) about $\frac{1}{24}$ inch deep, being most careful to keep exactly between the lines, and make the hollow quite smooth and even. Lower the wood also at the corners by gouging down between the points of the purfling, so that the sinking round the edge follows the guitar outline of the inside of the fiddle, and throws the corners and edges into that bold relief which is such a beauty in a well-finished fiddle.

When you have gone all round, go all over the ground, bringing the outside and inside edges of the trough exactly true to the marked lines all round. Then take the smallest oval toothed plane (Fig. 125), with the finest and sharpest toothed iron, and plane all round the inside of the groove, so as to melt this trough into the rise of the belly or back (it is, of course, understood that these operations must be repeated on both tables), and bring the edge once more to the curve represented at B, Fig. 148. Now take a sharp scraper and scrape all round where there are

any plane or gouge marks, and, indeed, more or less all over the
tables, so as to bring it as smooth and clean as it was after the
principal scraping set down in Chapter XVI. Let them be
wetted and re-scraped two or three times, to get them beautifully
smooth and soft. They must then be sand-papered three times,
beginning with a medium roughness and ending with the finest.
Rub the sand-paper *up* and *down* the tables the way of the
grain, and just round inside the groove you have sunk round
the edge. Be careful not to rub *on* the edge thus left, or you
will rub it down, especially at the corners, which must be
carefully worked into with a corner of sand-paper, so as not to
encroach upon the edge at all, but at the same time so as to clear
away the roughness and gouge marks which are almost inevitable at these points. Rub all round and up to the edges of
the *f f* holes, but not across them, as it is a great point that the
sharp angles made by the surface of the belly and the cutting
out of the *f f*'s should be preserved. Between each rubbing wet
the surfaces all over with a sponge, and rub them dry directly
with a cloth. When you
give it the first or coarsest
rubbing, go also all round
the sides, which will be
by this time pretty con-
siderably dirty again. You
need, however, only give
the ribs one rubbing now,
and that with the coarsest
of the three papers. Fort

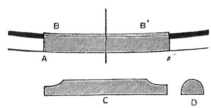

FIG. 160.—The operations of cutting, fitting, and
finishing the Rest.

all these operations it is best to hold the fiddle on a *clean* towel
spread across the knees.

The next operation is the fixing in of the "rest," or piece of
ebony which protects the edge of the fiddle from the pressure
exerted by the loop of the tail-piece, and which is represented in
position at E, Fig. 105 (p. 195). Take the spring compasses (B,
Fig. 126), and opening them ⅔ inch, mark two points (A, A',
Fig. 160) on the lower edge of the fiddle, 1⅓ inches apart ; *i.e.*,
each being measured exactly ⅔ inch from the centre of the lower
bouts. Take as the centre point from which to measure, the joint
(purfled or otherwise) of the two lower bouts, not the centre join
of the belly (if this latter does not coincide with the former—*i.e.*,
it is more important that it should be true to the tail-pin and
centre of the lower bouts than to the join of the belly). Now
with a sharp, thin knife at these two points make two clean cuts
(A, A', Fig. 160) right down to the top of the ribs, but *not* deeper,
so as to cut into the ribs. The cuts must extend on to the

surface just through the purfling, as in Fig. 160, A, A'. Now with a straight-edge and knife connect these two with a straight line, B, B', which will cover part of the purfling. Draw the knife along this till it is as deep as the other two (A, A'), and then the wood comprised by these lines may be cut and picked out with a knife, leaving a little right-angled chamber (formed by the thickness of the belly and the tops of the lower bouts and bottom block) to receive the rest, which may now be cut. If by misadventure in making the cuts, A, A', the edge gets a little split on either side, it must be cut away, and a corresponding slip cut down on the other side, so as to make the cutting, though wider, still true to the centre join of the ribs and the tail-pin. I need not remark that the cutting must be quite square and perpendicular to the top surface of the bottom block. Now take a little slip of ebony, 1⅝ inch long by ⅜ inch broad, and ⅜ inch deep. Make two sides quite square and true to one another, and adjust the length with plane, file, and knife, so that it just fits tightly into the chamber cut, as in Fig. 160. Never mind about cutting it flush with the edge of the fiddle, this will do when it is fixed ; round the upper surface, as at D, Fig. 160, and shape off the ends roughly, as at C, Fig. 160. Put plenty of good glue into the chamber, set the roughly finished rest in it, tap it in fast with a little hammer, so as to fix it, and wipe off the superfluous glue with the brush and warm water, and leave the fiddle to dry. When dry finish it off carefully by cutting it even with the lower edge, and flush with the belly at the bevelled ends, which last must be exact and equal to one another. Round off the top, so that it is about ⅛ inch above the edge of the belly. These operations are done with a sharp knife and flat file; the Rest as finished must then be scraped quite smooth. Now take a set of files, and go right round the edge of both back and belly, making them quite *round* by filing both corners of the edge, till the line from the under to the upper sides of the edge is a perfectly even curve. When this is done, go round the edges thus rounded and smooth off all file marks with sand-paper of a medium fineness, give the ribs a final thorough sand-papering, and the body of your fiddle is finished " in the white," and can be put away out of dust, etc., until the neck and scroll are ready to go on.

CHAPTER XX.

THE NECK AND SCROLL.

The Wood—Preparation—Marking Outline—Cutting-out—Marking and Shaping
out the Neck and Scroll—Roughing out the Volute—Finishing the Volute
—Hollowing the Back of the Head—The Peg-box—Finishing the Head—
The Neck—Fitting the Neck to the Body of the Fiddle—Cutting out the
Chamber—Shaping the Shoulder—Testing the Fit—Fixing—The False
Finger-board — The Button—The Shoulder—Finishing the Neck and
Shoulder—Final Operations.

FIRST proceed to prepare the maple for the neck and scroll.
This is stored in blocks slightly wedge-shaped $10\frac{1}{2}$ inches long,
$2\frac{3}{4}$ inches broad, the depth of the wedge, thinning from 2 to $1\frac{1}{2}$
inches. Plane one side perfectly smooth and even, like the
slabs for the back and belly, then with a small plane and
T-square, square to the planed side the 2-inch (or thicker) edge
of the block. When this is done, and the square is quite true,
take an ordinary cutting or marking gauge, and mark a line
along the thick edge $1\frac{11}{16}$ inches from the planed side. Then
make the other side smooth and square to the planed thick edge
by planing down to the gauged line. This done, you will have
a block $10\frac{1}{2}$ inches long, about $2\frac{1}{2}$ broad, one edge $1\frac{11}{16}$ deep,
squared and planed, the other edge left rough, and your neck
block is prepared for work.

You may now proceed to mark and cut out the neck and
scroll. In Plate IV. is given the outline of a Stradiuarius scroll
corresponding with the outline of the model on which we are
working. In page 159 are given directions for copying any
scroll on to paper. Let a tracing of the scroll given in Plate IV.,
or your own scroll outline, be glued on to a thin plank or leaf
of wood (like the plank outline of the whole fiddle), and cut it
out in the same way very exactly, so that you have, in fact,
Fig. 161 in thin wood. Now all along, or rather round the line
a, a, a of the volute, pierce with a small drill small holes, so that
the form of the scroll is marked on the plank by a perforated
volute, as in Plate IV. Now on the front of this outline make
three little notches at the points A, B, C, Fig. 161, and you have
the complete model for marking the neck and scroll, as at Fig. 85

You will remember that one side of the block prepared for
the neck is smooth and squared, and the other side is left rough.
Now fasten the plank outline of the neck and scroll on to one
smooth face of the block against the squared and planed side of
the block, as in Fig. 161, taking the square D, E, F, G to represent
the block, and G F its squared side, the outline just touching the
edge at the points H, A, B, as in the figure. It is important that
it be flush with the edge at A and B, but at H it may be just a
shade lower, as in the figure, to allow for the cutting.

Now with the marking-point mark the exact outline, marking
a rougher one outside it with a pencil ; now by means of a
square, mark *across* the smooth edge, G F, of the block three
lines at the points A, B, C, Fig. 161, exactly at the notches, A, B, C.

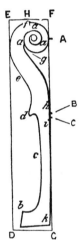

These will serve as a guide where to fix the outline on the other side, which is done by unfasten-
ing it, and fastening it to exactly the same position
by making the notches A, B, C exactly coincide
with the lines marked across the edge, and mark
the outline in the same way with point and
pencil, and thus you have two outlines marked
exactly on either side opposite one another.
Before removing the plank outline from either
side, mark the volute of the scroll by thrusting
a point through each of the drilled holes, a, a, a,
which indicate it on the outline, by which the
volute of perforations in the outline model will
be marked by little dents on the outline drawn
on either side of the block.

Now proceed to cut out the block, following
the outer (or pencil) line of your markings with
the bow-saw, which must be held very upright to
prevent it exceeding or going inside the marking
on the under-side (*i.e.*, the marking other than the
one you are following with the saw). In marking the outline, you
must trace round the line b, c, d, e, f, g, h, Fig. 161, but not along
the line i k, if the plank outline does not exactly follow the
smooth edge.

Fig. 161.—Plank out-
line of Neck and
Scroll (on block).

Finally, you have now, instead of the neck-block, an outline
of the neck and scroll shown by the line b, c, d, e, f, g, h, exactly
like the plank outline you have been marking from ; but instead
of being $\frac{1}{16}$ inch thick, it has the thickness of the whole block,
and instead of having the volute marked by perforated holes,
each side bears the curl marked by small indentations, a, a, a,
in the wood. There will be a slight margin of wood just outside the line made by the marking-point. This must now be

carefully removed, and the surface of the scroll block made perfectly square by means of a chisel and file, till from side to side the block is perfectly plane and square to the sides.

Now proceed to mark the design of your scroll on the back and front of the block. First find the exact centre of the front

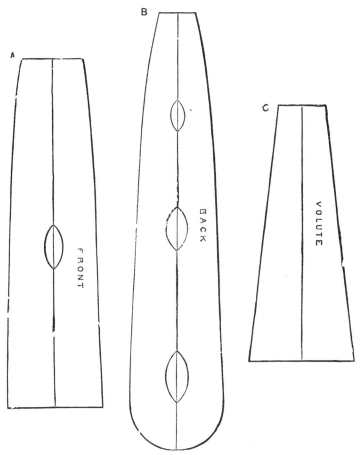

Fig. 162.—Outlines (Zinc) for marking front and back of Scroll (actual size).

and back of the scroll block, on the block outline you have obtained by the foregoing directions, which is $1\frac{11}{16}$ inches across, you will find the centre exactly $\frac{27}{32}$ from each side ; having found it and set a gauge to this distance, mark a centre line right round the neck and scroll, being careful that the side along which you run the gauge is the plane side from which you

squared and planed the two other surfaces. With the aid or
this centre line proceed to mark your scroll by means of a set of
three models, made of pliable zinc or soft brass, taken from
some acknowledged master-violin. The outlines, Fig. 162, are
taken from the Stradiuarius fiddle from which I have taken all
the models with which I have presented my readers, A being
tne front, B the back of the head, and C the front of the volute.
First set the fine end of the model, A, Fig. 162, up under the

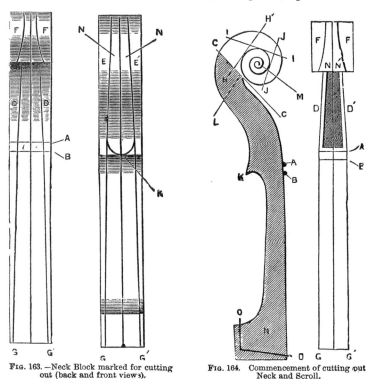

FIG. 163. —Neck Block marked for cutting   FIG. 164.   Commencement of cutting out
        out (back and front views).   Neck and Scroll.

volute on the front of the scroll, so that, as in A, it exactly
coincides with the centre line drawn round the block, as shown
by the line drawn down the front of the model A (Fig. 162),
and the opening in the centre thereof. At present only the
lines A, B (Figs. 163 and 164) are marked on the block ; it
will now be found that the bottom of A, Fig. 162, just reaches
the line A, Fig. 163, so by the model A, Fig. 162, you can mark
the lines D, D´, Fig. 163. Next set the top of the model, B
(Fig. 162), at the top of the scroll block, and similarly mark

the back of the scroll with the lines E, E', as in Fig. 163. Now mark the front of the scroll, setting the model C (Fig. 162) on the centre line, coinciding with the tops of the lines E, E, Fig. 162, and mark the lines F, F'. These being done, you may roughly elongate the lines D, D' and E, E' to G, G' on back and front, as in Fig. 163. Be careful, however, to leave plenty of breadth between G and G', which should be at least $1\frac{3}{8}$ inch apart. Meanwhile, the sides of your neck-block are marked as in Fig. 161, which is enlarged at Fig. 164, the volute (a a a, Fig. 161) being marked by punctures in the wood, as there described ; now draw the line C C' in the position indicated in Fig. 164, on both sides, and with a fine tenon saw cut down to the lines D, D' and E, E' ; be careful not to go beyond either of them on either side, for they are not opposite one another on back and front (*i.e.*, F, F' are much nearer the *sides* of the block than D, D).

Now set the block upside-down in the vice so that about three inches are above the bench, and saw down the lines G, G' to the head, only sawing two or three inches at a time, for the least strain on the head will split off the volute at

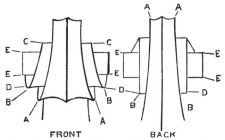

FRONT   BACK

FIG. 165.—Front and back of Volute (Geometrical).

the line C C', turning the head down as you reach the line C C', so as to finish off there neatly. The wood will therefore have been removed along the lines G, G' to C C' so as to present the appearance of Fig. 164. Now prithee be as careful as if you were catching the sparks of a squib in a plate over a powder magazine, and proceed as follows :—Make from the sides to the lines F, F' and E, E', on back and front, the three cuts H H, I I, and J J, Fig. 164, remove the pieces outside these cuts, and the corners left round the outer volute by them, and take care not to cut *beyond any part* of the lines F, F' and E, E' on either side.

You must, at this point, get hold of a good scroll, and copy the obvious shape until, in the rough, you have got the spiral from the cheek of the peg-box to the eye of the scroll M (Fig. 164) perfect, proceeding gingerly with saw and gouges I cannot describe it, words fail me to express the actual cuttings, suffice it to say the model (without which, as a guide, you cannot get on) must be carefully if roughly copied. When the spiral is roughly hewed out, proceed to make the two sides exactly similar to one another, and perfectly true to the centre line, by means of the spring compasses. Fig. 165 represents the geometrical principles of the back and front of a properly cut volute ; if you cannot copy by eye and hand, leave off fiddle-making, for as a luthier you are a failure. Having made the lines of the volute, as viewed back and front in Fig. 165, perfectly straight and parallel to one another, with chisels, gouges, and files, proceed with a flat oval, or oblong plane (Fig. 125 or 136), to plane the cheeks of the peg-box smooth, making them true to the centre line, by means of the spring compass, and adjusting the breadth from your model—copy by the bow compass (Fig. 132). Now, from the model B (Fig. 162), cut out a thin slip of wood, like Fig. 166, by which to regulate the cutting of the chin of the scroll, K (Figs. 163 and 164), which must now be done with a sharp knife and file, so that when viewed sideways it is pronounced and well-angled, as in Fig. 164, and nicely rounded into the lines E, E', as in Fig. 163, and at B, Fig. 162. Next, with a fine-bladed knife,

FIG. 166.—Model for chin of Scroll.

cut out and neatly form the corner under the volute, L (Fig. 164), so that it follows the model on Plate IV. Now open the spring compasses $\frac{1}{16}$ inch, and gauge a line round the sides of the volute from the eye of the scroll M (Fig. 164) to the outer point C of the line C C' in the same figure. This " edge " (as it were) must be left in the subsequent chiselling of the scroll. Taking this line as an outside margin to be left flat, proceed to chisel the scroll, letting the lines which appear perpendicular in Fig. 165 (back), A, A, and B, B, sink in a little towards the heart of the scroll, but keeping the horizontal lines C, C, D, D, E, E, absolutely straight and at right angles to the centre line, and exactly parallel with and opposite one another, for these are the great beauties of the Stradiuarius scroll ; any deviation from, or careless treatment of, these particulars would render the scroll more Guarnerius-like, and unworthy the model we are working on. Now proceed to cut out the grooves down the back of the scroll and around the volute (N, N, Figs. 163 and 164) ; this must be done by fastening the head face downwards into the vice, and grooving it out carefully, taking the depth, etc., from the model you are following. Before commencing to do so, open the spring compass $\frac{1}{16}$ inch, and mark a gauge line round the back and over to the front of the scroll, similar to the one you drew round the sides and volute ; the grooves, N, N, must be sunk between this gauge line and the centre line, which latter must be left strong and clearly defined. One of the great beauties of the Stradiuarius scroll is that these grooves are very well marked and finished, and the outer edges of them are deeper—*i.e.*, the curves are deeper than those rising to the centre ridge (as shown in Fig. 167). This you will see on consulting your copy. These grooves must be equal on both sides of the centre line, and must come right over the scroll and under the volute to the point L (Fig. 164) ; but this last had better be left till the peg-box is cut out, which may now be done, first marking it by opening the marking compass $\frac{3}{16}$ inch, and drawing a line down each side of the front of the scroll and along the line A (Fig. 164), so as to enclose a space as shaded on Fig. 164. N.B.—In case by the chiselling of the chin, the line B is not exactly on a level with the base of the chin, as at Fig. 164, it must be corrected—*i.e.*, the line B (Fig. 164) must be exactly opposite the chin, and the line A brought as before just $\frac{9}{40}$ inch (the breadth of the nut) above it, as in the plate

The peg-box, therefore, being marked as in Fig. 164, proceed to cut it out, beginning with a small gouge, and going on with gouge, knife, and flat chisel, till the peg-box is cleanly and sharply cut, as set down on page 158. The cheeks are a *little* thinner just above the nut than elsewhere, to allow the G and E string to go from their pegs to the nut, clear of the cheeks, and at an equal distance from the others. Finish

FIG. 167.—Cutting of *coulisses* or grooves round the head.

the peg-box by scraping the bottom of it with the flat edge of the chisel, and file the insides of the cheeks, and also the outsides, quite clean and smooth with a flat file. File also the fronts of the cheeks, to have them clean, smooth, and sharp-cornered, as in Fig 167. Your scroll is now therefore cut ; as I warned you before commencing, the description of the process is, perforce, meagre, and you must get a well-cut head as a model, which you must work from more than my directions, which, after all, can only serve as an outline of procedure. The measurements also on page 158 are only approximate ; they vary, of course, with every model ; and in this also you must be guided by common sense and eye, without which you can never make a fiddle, much less its head. This done, finish off the head as near as you can with the chisel, then scrape it well with a scraper, and sand-paper it thoroughly all over the curves and in the corners of the volute. In cutting the grooves on the back, etc., mind and leave the centre ridge prominent and untouched ; the sand-papering, etc., will remove the pencil line from the top of the ridge. To sand-paper the grooves you will find it a good plan to roll a piece of sand-paper round the end of a penholder, and work thus with a cylinder of sand-paper. When thoroughly sand-papered, wet the head all over with ⏜ brush and cold water ; this (as in the case of the back and belly) will throw up any faults, defects of scraping, etc., after which it must be thoroughly re-scraped, if necessary, and re-sand-papered, which operations must be gone through some two or three times. Be most cautious not to alter the character of the head, or spoil its lines by too vicious sand-papering. When this is done, proceed to bevel off the edges of the head, all round the head and volute (but not inside the peg-box), extending the bevel to lines, which should be very carefully and exactly gauged round the corners $\frac{1}{20}$ inch from the edges. Begin this bevelling with the knife, and finish it with a file to make it even, removing the file marks with fine sand-paper (but keep the edges of the bevel sharp). This done, dip the head in water for the last time, and when thoroughly dry polish it up well with finest glass-paper, including the eye of the scroll, which must be perfectly flat. As sand-papering the eye in the ordinary way would almost inevitably result in rounding off its edges, you will find it best to place a piece of sand-paper on the bench, and rub the eye of the scroll flat upon it. Your head is now finished, and it remains only therefore finally to shape the neck and shoulder before setting it upon the body of the violin. For this purpose you will require a neck outline, which, though properly used for splicing heads (an operation described further on), is useful here as well, and so may now be made. It is represented by Fig. 168 (on Plate VI.) actual size, and may therefore be copied in facsimile on a thin leaf of wood. From the line B (Figs. 163 and 164) measure down the centre line, and make a mark at a distance of $5\frac{7}{16}$ inches from B. Now with a square draw a line across the face of the neck (as at G G', Figs. 163 and 164), and laying the neck outline (Fig. 168, Plate VI.) on the side of the neck and scroll, so that its lower point A is on the line drawn across the neck, as above, and its straight edge corresponds throughout its length with the flat side of the neck, mark on the rough shoulder of the neck, as it is at present (N, Fig. 164), the slant and outline of the true shoulder (as at O O, Fig. 164), as determined by the neck outline (Fig. 168, Plate VI.) ; remove all wood well out-side these lines with a fine tenon saw, and with a flat chisel and plane, and slope off the sides of the shoulder till the under surface presents the appearance shown in Fig. 169. This is done as follows : Note the point on the line D D', Fig. 169 (the lower

THE NECK AND SCROLL.

edge of the face of the neck), where the centre line, which extends from the nut throughout its length, ends (at the point A). From the point A, by means of a square laid on D D', draw a centre line A A'. Open the spring compasses $\frac{17}{20}$ inch, and mark on each side of A' the points B, B', and finish the slopes D B, D' B', which must be quite straight, true, and, above all things, plane.

You can now proceed to fix your neck and scroll on the body of the fiddle. With the spring compasses ascertain the exact centre of the belly between the crannies of the two ff holes, and make a small mark; in like manner find and mark the exact centre between the edges of the upper bouts at their broadest part. A flat edge laid along the belly coinciding with these two points, will naturally divide the belly throughout its length into two parts, down its exact centre; by this means mark the exactly central point of the top edge. Now open the spring compasses about the distance c c' (Fig. 169), and mark two points at equal distances on the top edge, from the point you have marked in the centre of the top edge, in the same manner as when you were marking the place on the lower edge in which to fix the rest. At these points make two cuts, extending vertically and horizontally, through the edge as far downwards and inwards as the top and surface of the ribs. In the hollow thus cut,

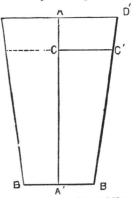

FIG. 169.—Base of Shoulder and Shape of Chamber (actual size).

set the shoulder cut as at Fig. 169, so that the end B B' goes against the button left on the back. If the cuts are not wide enough to allow the end B B' to touch the button, re-cut them a little wider. Be careful, however, not to cut them too wide; though, if by accident it should be so, by planing down the end B B', the neck will go farther back and fill up the space between the cuts.

The neck and shoulder being thus held on to the top of the fiddle, see that it is quite straight, and mark *on the top of the ribs* the lines D B and D' B', with a fine marking-point or the point of a knife. Holding the knife firmly, deepen this mark by drawing the knife down it (being careful not to let it slip on to the belly at the end of the cut) till you have cut quite through the ribs. Now remove the wood between the lines, cutting away equally belly, ribs, and block, till you have hollowed out the chamber (in the same manner as for the " rest "), quite square and clean

cut, ¼ inch deep all over, being so exactly the shape of the
shoulder (Fig. 169), that the latter fits quite tightly into it.
The under surface of the shoulder must be planed until from
the nut (line B, Fig. 164) to the end of the neck (G G′, Fig. 164),
is a distance of exactly 5⁷⁄₁₆ inches. The planing must, however,
not alter the slant determined by the model (Fig. 168).   The
depth of the shoulder will of course vary with the height of the
sides.   The back of the shoulder (O, Fig. 164) must be cut so
as to fit exactly against the button, and, when thus fitted, the
front of the shoulder (O′, Fig. 164) must project exactly ¼ of
an inch above the belly.   Besides fitting exactly, the neck must
be set exactly straight to the axis of the instrument.   This is
tested in three independent ways to ensure perfection, which is
very hard to get.   The neck being fixed in without glue : 1st,
Hold the back of the fiddle, horizontally and lengthways, level
with the eye, so that you see the back join quite straight from the
rise of the arching to the button ; if the neck is on straight, the
centre ridge of the back of the scroll will coincide with and
form a continuation of this line.   2nd, Hold the belly similarly,
so that the mark you made between the crannies of the *f f* holes

FIG. 170.—Wedge for testing setting of Head and Neck.

coincides and forms a line with the
point A, Fig. 169, at the bottom of
the neck. If the neck is straight,
the centre ridge on the front of the
volute of the head will coincide with and continue this line.
3rd, Prepare a wedge 6 inches long, 1 broad, and 2½ inches
high at the broad end (Fig. 170).   Now set the fiddle on its
edges, and slipping the wedge underneath the scroll, note
the point (on the side of the wedge) where the eye of the scroll
first touches it.   Now turn the fiddle over and set it on the edges
of its other side ; repeat the process, and if the scroll touches at
the same point, it stands to reason, that, if your model is regular,
the head and neck must be exactly true to the axis of the
instrument.   This is the best, because the most certain test for
the fiddle-maker.   When a fiddle is very old and knocked about,
the outline has become untrue, and then it fails ; but for the present
it is the best for our purpose.   Having ascertained, therefore, by
these means that your fitting is true, proceed to glue in the neck.
Fill the chamber, and smear the button with good strong glue,
press the neck in as hard as you can with the hand, and
just rapidly repeat your tests, to make assurance doubly sure ;
then, with a strong iron cramp, cramp the shoulder to the
button, protecting the latter with a slip of wood, seeing that
the shoulder is well pressed to the bottom of the chamber.
Apply the screw button of the cramp to the face of the neck,

pressing as hard as you can. (It will be remembered that all this time the *button* has *never* been touched since the outline of the back was cut out, as on p. 240). Wipe off the superfluous glue with warm water, and set the fiddle to dry. The next thing, before shaping down the neck, is to cut and glue on the *false finger-board*, which is a finger-board made of pear or sycamore, or other hard wood, to take the place, *for the present*, of the final ebony finger-board, and to protect the edges of the neck till we are ready to fit up the fiddle. For this purpose we must prepare what is called the finger-board holder, which is a wooden contrivance, shaped as in Fig. 171, in which the finger-board (false or final) is held for working on, and which serves as a guide to the outline and shaping thereof. It is composed of a slip of wood, A, represented by the shaded part, 1 inch thick and $11\frac{1}{8}$ inch long, being $1\frac{5}{16}$ in. broad at B, and $1\frac{11}{16}$ in. broad at C ; it is slightly hollowed down the centre, as shown in section. This is enclosed between two walls, D D, formed of two other strips of wood, high enough to stand $\frac{1}{10}$ inch above A on each side. A piece of wood the shape of A may be pushed into this, and held firmly whilst being worked at, the scooping out allowing of its being inserted curved side downwards.

Fig. 171.—Finger-board Holder

To make the false finger-board, take a piece of wood as aforesaid, of shape of A, Fig. 171, and being 6 in. long, 1 in. broad at the narrowest, and $1\frac{1}{3}$ in. at the broadest end. Set it in the holder and make one side absolutely plane. Turn it over and replace it in the holder, and having reduced it to a thickness of $\frac{1}{5}$ inch, round the top approximately like that of a real ebony finger-board. Now go over the face of the neck of your fiddle with a fine steel plane, so as to render it quite plane and level (but not so as to plane it down), so that the false finger-board lies close upon it. Take a gouge and hollow out a trough along the under (or plane) surface of the false finger-board, so that it will not present too great a glued surface for you to have to force apart when you come to remove it to make way for the permanent one, and smearing what is left of this under surface with glue ; set it on the neck, the narrow end being flush with the lower edge of the peg-box (line A, Fig. 164), when it will be found just to project about $\frac{1}{2}$ inch or a little more over the belly. Fix it with three iron cramps, one just below the chin of the scroll, one in the middle, and one at the button (as in fixing the neck), which latter must be protected by a slip of wood placed between it and the lower arm of the cramp.

When this is quite dry, proceed finally to shape the neck with a sharp knife. First cut the button to the present rough shape of the shoulder, being careful to slant the knife upwards, and not cut down into the back towards the joint, which is a very ugly nature in badly-made fiddles.

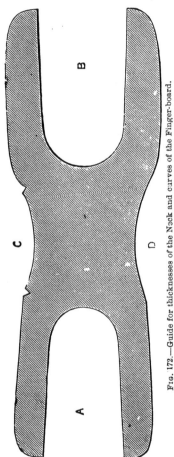

FIG. 172.—Guide for thicknesses of the Neck and curves of the Finger-board.

Now prepare a guide, which is represented in actual size at Fig. 172 (from which it may be prepared by tracing off the outline, and cutting it out on a slip of wood about $\frac{1}{4}$ inch thick); the roughly-hewn neck must be cut away with the knife, being most cautious not to let the knife slip and injure the head, till the end A of Fig. 172 fits over it just below the chin of the scroll, and the end B fits over it just above the shoulder. It is best that at these points the forks of the model (Fig. 172) should, in the first stage of the cutting, barely go over the wood; it will be sufficient to get these diameters approximately right, and leave the perfection of them till the neck approaches the finish; besides, the filing and polishing will still further reduce them. Before beginning to shape the shoulder, cut the top of the button, till the distance between the chin of the scroll and the top of the button is just $4\frac{7}{16}$ inch.

Continue to cut down the neck and shoulder till the guide (Fig. 172) just goes over both neck and false finger-board at the two points above explained. Now with the smallest flat steel plane smooth the sides of the false finger-board, till the line where it joins the neck is only as visible as the join of the back or belly. Having done this, finish off the button, making it as even and circular as possible, and rising well at a right angle (neither more nor less) from the edge of the back. When you have shaped the neck as far as possible with the knife, take a good rasp and obliterate, as far as possible, the marks of the knife, but no more ; then with a pair of files obliterate the rasp marks, using a fine flat one for the neck, and a fine oval one for the shoulder and chin of the scroll.   Bevel off the outer edge of the button just as much as (in fact, to match) the bevel of the edges of the fiddle.   Now, with a scraper, scrape the neck and shoulder as smooth as possible, after which give it a good polishing with coarse sand-paper, and then another with fine. Now go all over the fiddle (especially the sides and edges), with fine sand-paper, to clean off any dirt which may have accumulated since the last rubbing, and having satisfied yourself that the fiddle is as clean and smooth as you can make it, your instrument is finished " in the white," and can at once be varnished preparatory to fitting it up and playing on it.   If it is in the summer time this can be proceeded with at once, as described in Chapter II. ; but if it is in autumn or winter, hang up your fiddle, if possible, in a dry glass case, or in a warm room till the return of the hot weather, and it will be greatly benefited by this seasoning " in the white."   It remains, therefore, only to give instructions for varnishing and bringing up to melody point.

CHAPTER XXL

THE GUARNERIUS MODEL, WITH WHOLE TABLES ON AN INSIDE MOULD.

The Inside Mould and its Accessories—The Cramping Blocks—The Outline—
The *Contre-Moule* or Sides Outline—Tracing the Model—Preparing the
Wood—The Blocks—Fixing—Shaping—The C's—The Lower Bouts—The
Upper Bouts—The Depth of the Ribs—The Side Linings—The Back and
Belly—The *ff* Holes—Taking out the Mould—Finishing the Ribs, Linings,
and Blocks—Fixing on the Belly—The Neck and Scroll.

The Inside Mould and its Accessories.—The first thing, as
before, to decide upon is the model, and, consequently, the mould
on which you are going to build your fiddle. As I gave a mould
of Stradiuarius before, I have now presented my readers in
Plate V. with a mould of Guarnerius.[1] It will be seen that the
construction of this mould is quite different to that of the one
represented by Plate IV. In working with this one we shall fix
on the ribs outside the mould, and the cramping blocks will be
fixed on *outside* the ribs with cramps fixed in the holes A, B, C, D,
E, F. To make a mould of this sort from any fiddle, proceed, as
before, to take the outline on the outline board (Fig. 78), or
otherwise, and having transferred it to paper, and drawn a centre
line down the exact middle, you will have the outline o o o
(Fig. 173). (It will be observed that on the Plate V. o o o
is only a half outline, but this does not matter, as will be seen
further on, for the two sides of the fiddle we are copying are in
exact contra-facsimile.) Now, at a distance of about $\frac{3}{16}$ inch inside
this line, draw very carefully a second line, and you will have the
(whole) outline P P P (Fig. 174). Let this second or inner
outline be traced off and pasted on to a plank of hard ·well-
seasoned wood $\frac{3}{4}$ inch thick. Trace inside it the six places for
the blocks to go—viz., I, J, K, L, M, N, as shown in the plate and in
Fig. 175, and then cut it out most carefully, and you will have
a mould as represented by Fig. 175 (which, however, shows the

---

· The models and outlines of this chapter and of Plate V, are taken in the
min test facsimile from a magnificent Joseph Guarnerius del Gesù of the date
1734 the property of M. Sainton. It is one of the most celebrated and
character stic instruments of this great master's make which exists.

block pieces glued in roughly).   Now take another plank fully
½ inch thick, and cut it exactly similarly to the shape of mould
No. 1, so that when the second is placed over the first it coincides
so exactly as to appear to be only one solid mould 1¼ inches thick.
Cramp them together thus exactly, and boring five screw holes,
U, V, W, X, Y, Plate V., screw them firmly together, so as to
make one solid plank.   The screws must not be long enough to
go *through* on the other side of this double mould, and the heads
must be sunk a good $\frac{1}{12}$ inch below the surface, so that they can
be planed over.   Now plane down the top half, at the upper bouts,
so that the double mould is 1¼ inch thick at the lower bouts, and
$1\frac{5}{32}$ inch at the upper (a difference of just less than $\frac{3}{32}$), which are

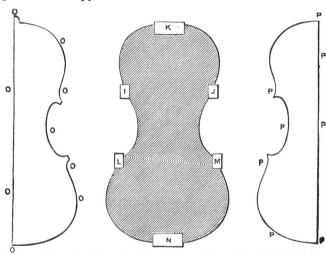

FIG. 173.—Half outline of   FIG. 175.—Inside mould,   FIG. 174.—Half outline
  Tables (back and belly).   with rough blocks fitted.   of Sides.

the right proportions for the ribs of a fiddle.   (*Vide* Chapter VII.
page 145.)   Then bore with a large centre-bit the eight holes
A, B, C, D, E, F, G, H, opposite the inner bouts and the cuttings
made for the blocks as shown in the plate.   Next take a tracing,
like Fig. 174 from your original paper diagram, and paste it on,
a thin leaf of wood, which will give the half outline P P P, by
which you determine and correct the outlines of your blocks (or
if you like, take a *whole* outline from P P P, Plate V., and
correct all your blocks together ; however, a half outline can be
turned over for the blocks on the other side, and ensures their
being in contra-facsimile to the others).   Next take a similar
tracing of the entire outline (the original paper diagram will
do), and mounting it similarly, you have the outline model, O O O,

from which you trace on the slabs the outlines of your back and belly. As before, a half outline (Fig. 173) can be taken, and will serve the same purpose, only it must be turned over on the centre line to trace the other half of the table. Your mould and plank outlines being now complete, the next thing to do is to make your cramping blocks, which are the same as described in Chapter XIV., p. 228, only that they are in this instance made to go outside the mould instead of inside, as was the case when we were working with an outside mould, and are represented in actual size to go with our present mould on Plate V. by the pieces 1 to 8. As before, they are 1½ inches deep, and fit against the

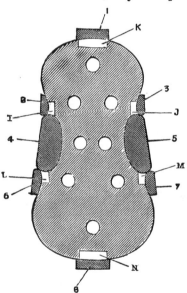

sides, so that the numbers which are inscribed on each cramping block coincide with those drawn on the mould at the points opposite which they go, as in Fig. 176 (which will be fully explained further on). These, therefore, are the operations by which a mould, etc., can be taken from, and for the purpose of copying, any fiddle, and by which those on Plate V. were produced ; so that if my readers are content to make a Guarnerius fiddle, they have only to make their tracings and plank outlines as described, from the plate. From this point I shall assume that we are working on this mould, and write accordingly ; though, as will be seen, the processes can be

FIG. 176.—The Cramping Blocks of Plate V. in position against the mould (blocks finished).

applied to any model, and to avoid repeating my first chapters, where (as is generally the case) the work is identical, I shall merely refer my readers to the pages where they will find the necessary information, should they have forgotten the work they did before. I may also repeat that any of the processes in the following chapters, which differ from the methods before described, may be pursued with any model or outline, and any mould, whether inside or outside. The main points in which our work will differ (beyond the matter of mould) will be in the slab back and the spliced head.

As before, the first thing after deciding on the pattern is the choice of the wood. As we joined our back and belly before, we will now make them in one piece, and a table in one piece may be either " whole " or " slab." If you turn to Fig. 77, p. 134, these cuttings are explained ; for a whole table an exceptionally broad, fine trunk is required, from which is cut a wedge, as at Fig. 77, only twice as broad as that there described, and varying from 2 inches on the thick side to $\frac{1}{2}$ on the thin side. This is re-marked on the end, as in Fig. 177, by the line A B, which is then sawn down, and the wedge C thus cut off is sawn up into as many thin strips, $\frac{1}{12}$ or $\frac{1}{16}$ inch thick, as can be cut, from whence are cut the ribs, which thus match the back in grain, etc., which is a great beauty in a fiddle with a whole back. For a slab back the planks are cut out of the trunk, as at Fig. 77, which style of cutting shows the *grain* of the wood running *round* the back in serpentine ovals, which follow the outline of the fiddle, with the *curls* or *figure* of the wood running across from right to left in greater quantity, but narrower, than they appear on backs cut " on the quarter," whether whole or joined. I have chosen the slab back because it is simpler to work and has a very pretty effect.

The strips for the ribs cut and stored, as on page 135, and the block for the neck, must be selected of a small, close curl, to match

FIG. 177.—Wedge cut for "whole" Back.

and contrast with the back. I shall also assume that you have got a piece of belly pine of sufficient size *and* quality (attributes very difficult to find *together*) to make a belly of good acoustic properties. If you cannot find this, and you cannot get supplied by a good fiddle-maker, make your belly joined as described on page 133, which is much better than to use a single piece whose grain is much wider at one edge of the belly than at the opposite one. (Before rejecting a slab as too narrow *vide* the expedient for increasing the breadth set down on page 290.) These preliminaries having been settled and arranged, let us, gentle reader, start forth again together to make our second fiddle, and may the success which I trust attended our first efforts attend us again now.

The Blocks.—These are the commencement of a fiddle on an inside mould. For them you must take six little rectangular pieces of fine-grained pine, as in Fig. 141, which when set up on edge (*i.e.*, with the grain perpendicular to the bench) have all equally a depth of $1\frac{1}{2}$ inches with the top surfaces, as follows : Two for the top and bottom blocks, $2\frac{1}{8}$ inches by 1 ; two for the upper corners, 1 by 1 ; and two for the lower corners, 1 by $1\frac{1}{8}$. The bottom edge of each must be square to one side, and both ends of the

top and bottom blocks must be squared to the sides thus squared.
Two sides of each corner block must be squared to one another.
Cut down the top and bottom blocks till they just fit nicely (not
too tight or too loose) into the cuts K and N, Plate V., and
Fig. 175, made to receive them.   When fitted, rough the lower
half of the side that goes against the mould, and glue it to the
lower plate of the mould (gluing the side *only*, not the *ends*) so
as to present in section the appearance of Fig. 178, B representing

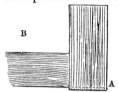

FIG 178.—Section of block
fixed in mould.

the mould, and C the block.   The top and
bottom blocks, when glued, must be cramped
to the mould by iron cramps from the holes
A and H, Plate V.   The corner blocks are
merely fitted to the cuttings I, J, L, and M,
Plate V., and Fig. 175, the lower half of
one side of each roughed and glued, and set
in the cuttings without cramps, in the same
manner as the top and bottom blocks, and the whole is then set
to dry, presenting the appearance of Fig. 175.   It will be seen
that all project just below the mould (as below the dotted line
A, Fig. 178) ; this is so to guard against their not being set
quite flush with the lower surface of the mould.   All below the
lower surface of the mould must now be removed by turning the
whole concern over, wetting the thus presented bottoms of the
blocks, and planing them down with a toothed plane till they are
even, and plane and true to the lower
surface of the mould, so that a straight-
edge moved all over the surface shows
no light and catches on nothing.   Now
with the mould (or ribs outline, Fig.
174, P P P, Plate V.) mark on the top
and bottom of the top and bottom
blocks what wood has to be removed
to make the outline continuous at top
and bottom, and by this means make
the top and bottom blocks even with,
and part of, the outline, as at K, Plate
V., being careful, however, to keep

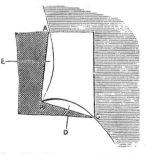

FIG. 179.—Diagram explaining the
cutting of the corner blocks.

them quite true and square to the bottom or flushed edges and
lower surface of the mould.   Now laying the outline again over
the blocks, so that, as before, it coincides exactly with the outline
of the mould, mark with a sharp point the exact shape or outline
of the corners.   Cut away most of the superfluous wood by
(carefully) removing the wood represented by the shaded part of
Fig. 179, *outside* the block, and by cutting down the lines A, B
and B, C.   Next, with a gouge, cut away the remaining wood D

inside the c's, keeping to the lines marked on both ends of the block, so as to have these cuttings quite square to the plane surface of the mould, but leaving the superfluous wood E till the inner bouts are fixed to the blocks and dry, so as to withstand the pressure on the point caused by the gluing of the c's to the blocks. If, by mishap, you cut too much, so that the inside of the corner is *not* square to the mould, the defect must be repaired by cutting a little curved chip from the superfluous wood of another block with a gouge, and gluing it on where the want is found; the block with the added chip can then be recut as originally. The lower corner blocks are carried to the same point in exactly the same way. The next operation is the preparation of :—

The Sides or Ribs, and the fixing of the c's. Select a plank of maple, whose grain matches the slab prepared for the back, and prepare from it enough strips $1\frac{1}{2}$ inches broad and $\frac{1}{12}$ thick, to make two strips $5\frac{3}{4}$ long for the inner bouts or G's, two $7\frac{1}{8}$ long for the upper, and two 10 long for the lower bouts. These must be cut and planed down as described on page 231. They may be further regulated as to thinness by setting the *fillière*[1] to $\frac{1}{20}$ inch, and scraping the strips through like purfling. As before, glue linen on one end of the upper and lower bouts, and on both ends of the c's, which, when dry, must next be bent, fitted, and fixed, proceeding as follows :—Bend the c's, as described on page 232, until they just fit into the inner curves of the mould, and the corner blocks finished as above by the removal of the wood D, Fig. 179. When this object is attained, take a small stick of old soap, and thoroughly soap the *mould* where the c's will press against it, *but not letting the soap touch the blocks.* This is to prevent the ribs from sticking to the mould if by mischance the glue should run anywhere but on the blocks. Next clear all traces of linen and glue off the ends of the c's, and file the whole inner surfaces of them quite clean. (N.B.—The "inner surface of the c" means the *outside* of the *curve—i.e.,* the surface that goes against the edge of the mould.) Now plentifully coat the inside of the blocks (the line D, Fig. 179) with good glue, set the c's in the inner bouts, and fix them with the cramping blocks 4 and 5, Plate V., by means of cramps

[1] The *fillière* is an appliance used in thinning down veneer to make purfling. It consists of a plane iron, which can be adjusted by means of a screw, at any required distance from the polished surface of a steel plate, over which it is held at right angles by a bent arm. It is used thus : If it is required to give a strip of wood an uniform thinness of $\frac{1}{8}$ inch, the blade of the *fillière* need only be "set" at this distance from the plate and the strip carefully and strongly pulled through between the edge of the blade and the plate till the desired uniformity of diameter is obtained. By this means a strip of plane-tree veneer may be evenly reduced to a substance of $\frac{1}{8}$ inch or even less.

set in the holes D and E.   The ends of the c's must be pressed
tight up against the glued blocks, by pushing in between them
and the cramping blocks, at the top and bottom of the latter,
little wedges and chips of wood, so as to ensure a close and firm
contact between the ends of the c's and the inner or glued
surfaces of the corner blocks.   The edges of the c's jutting just
below the lower surface of the mould (in the same way as did
the blocks below the line A, Fig. 178) must, when the glue is
dry, be filed down flush and plane with the lower surfaces of
the mould and blocks.   Lastly, reduce to manageable length
the ends of the c's which project beyond the corners.   The next
operation is the cutting to outline of the outer faces of the
blocks E, Fig. 179, which must be done in the same way as the
inner faces, keeping them quite square to the plane surface of the
mould, blocks, and c's.   In cutting this face you will make the

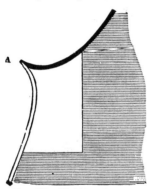

c's work into the outline by cutting
them to a point, as at A in Fig. 180.
When this is safely and correctly accomplished, you can proceed to bend and fit
the upper and lower bouts, beginning
with the latter.   First bend and fit
the ends which fit against the corner
blocks and which are protected with
linen, and then the rest of the strips,
after which you must make the join
at the bottom.   This is done by taking
each lower bout (as fitted) separately,
and, setting it on the mould, mark
on the edge the point where it is
touched by the centre line drawn down

FIG. 180.—Finishing the corner
blocks and joining the ribs.

the mould ; from this mark, by means of a square, draw a line
across the strip, as described on page 233, fit the other lower
bout similarly, and if your marking and cutting have been true
to the centre line of the mould, a perfect join will be the result.
The join being thus made, and the ends of the lower bouts freed
and cleaned from glue, linen, etc., soap the sides of the mould
(carefully avoiding the blocks), and coating the bottom block
and the still exposed surfaces of the lower corner blocks and the
bevel at the ends of the c's with glue, fix the lower bouts to the
mould by means of cramps with the cramping blocks 6, 7, and
8, Plate V., in the same manner and position as you fixed the
c's.   The upper bouts are next fitted in a precisely similar
manner, only that you need not trouble to make a close join at
the top.   Now cut down the projecting pieces of the corners,
and make them square to the mould, as in Fig. 180, by means

of a knife, cutting from the edges to the centre of the strip, for fear of splitting off pieces, and finishing with a file and square Then go round the lower edges of the ribs, which just project (as did the c's) below the lower surface of the mould, and render them flush and level with the lower surface of the mould with a knife and flat file. The next thing is to regulate the height of the ribs, which with this model is at the bottom block $1\frac{1}{4}$ inches (or $14\frac{1}{2}$ lignes French), and at the top block $1\frac{5}{32}$ inches ($13\frac{1}{4}$ l. Fr.). (The French measure is the larger, but I prefer the English, $1\frac{1}{4}$ and $1\frac{5}{32}$.) Set off on the gauge $1\frac{1}{4}$ inches, and from the lower surface of the mould trace this breadth round the lower bouts and c's from upper corner to upper corner. Now reducing the gauge to $1\frac{5}{32}$, trace a line $1\frac{5}{32}$ from the lower surface of the mould, about two inches long, opposite the top block. From the line at $1\frac{7}{24}$ to the line at $1\frac{1}{2}$ the upper edges of the ribs and blocks must gradually decline; therefore begin by wetting the upper surfaces of the blocks (to make them cut easily), and then level the ribs and blocks down to the top surface of the upper plate of the mould [which is already (*vide* p. 283) of the proper thicknesses], so that a straight-edge lies true and flat across the top of the mould. Now, by loosening the screws U, V, W, X, Y, Plate V., take out the upper plate of the mould and proceed to prepare and fit your side-linings to the upper edges of the ribs, precisely as you did before (page 236), first cutting two grooves in the corner blocks, as there set down, in which to fit the linings of the centre bouts. When fitted, proceed to glue and fix them as before described on page 237. It is as well to bend both sets of linings, so that when the mould is taken out you will not have another bending job to do. When they are glued it will be necessary to fix the linings of the c's with lining clips (Fig. 137), two or three being necessary.

If the upper and lower bout linings are well cut they will not require clips, but if a little short they are good as a safeguard, and to make assurance doubly sure. When the linings are fast, cut them to a wedge shape, as shown and described on page 238 .Fig. 145). Next cut the blocks to shape, that is to say, their top halves, which stand above the mould. This is done with a sharp, broad gouge, cutting down but small splinters at a time and breaking them off at the surface of the lower plate of the mould. It was observed on page 238 that the Guarnerius block is different to the Stradivarian, being more curved (as in Fig. 104), the block, Fig. 181, being rather made by rounding off the angles at the ends of the block. The present (or Guarnerian) block (Fig. 104), is shaped so as to be a continuous curve from lining to lining. Then go round the linings and blocks (as cut) with a file and sand-paper, to smooth and soften their inner surfaces, and, as far as you can go at present, the *inside* of the fiddle is finished. Finally, go right round the *outside* of the ribs with a sharp scraper, so as to remove all dirt and inequalities, and make the exterior thoroughly smooth with two degrees of sand-paper, after which, the ribs being, as far as you can go for the present, finished, they can be put away in a drawer or elsewhere out of harm's way till the back is ready to go on.

Back and Belly.—The slabs prepared for these being all in one piece, you will not have to join them. It is, however, very important that the entire slab have a fine even grain all over, not close at one edge and wide at the other, as is the case if the slab has been cut from a small tree. It consequently sometimes happens th it a piece of wood may be excellent across all its breadth, excepting for the last inch or so, which is consequently cut off. In this case, the outline model being placed upon it, the lower bout will overhang one edge (or, in other words, the wood will be too narrow for the model). This may be remedied as follows : Roughly trace the outline on the wood,

FIG. 181.—Stradivarian Block.

marking on the edge the part which is too narrow; you can now, with a bow-saw, cut out a little strip from inside one of the c's, and making both faces plane, glue it edgewise to the edge where the narrowness is apparent. If necessary you can do this on both sides of the slab; the pieces thus added matching exactly in grain, and being well joined, their presence will be undiscernible under the varnish, especially when further hidden by the purfling, and by this means you will be able to utilize a slab of wood acoustically and otherwise desirable, that without this expedient you could only use for a smaller instrument, if at all. Your plates being of the proper size, make one side quite plane, as described on page 240. If you are working a slab (as I am presuming you are), the back plate will be of a nearly even thickness throughout, so can be marked at once ; but if it is to be a "whole" back, it will be a long, thin wedge, as in Fig. 177, and must be cut away on one side as there shown (saving the slips thus got, as I have said before, for the ribs), and the tables prepared for marking, as on page 249 (**Fig.** 146). You can now mark the outlines by means of the model, Fig. 173 (o, o, o, Plate V.), marking one-half of the outline, and then turning over the model and marking the other (unless you have a *whole* outline model). This being done, cut it out as carefully as you possibly can, as before set down (page 240). Then shape the model or arching of the back and belly with gouge, oval planes, and scrapers exactly as before, using the arching models 1A, 2A, 3A, 4A, 5A, Plate V., which are the arching models of the characteristic Guarnerius pattern we are working at, and are the same for both back and belly. (It will be remembered that for Stradiuarius we used different arching models for the back and belly.) The points at which the arching models must fit the tables are shown by the numbers on the short lines across the centre line down the mould. When the rough gouging is done, gauge a line round the edge of the plates (*i.e.*, perpendicular to the plane surface), as described on page 241, $\frac{5}{16}$ from the flat side, and with the gouge and oval planes fine down the rounded surface with the models. Then gauge again another line $\frac{1}{8}$ inch from the flat side, and with a knife pare down the edge (so as to form a bevel on the arched side) to this uniform thickness all round; then with an oval plane, plane round the edge of the arched surfaces so as to melt this bevel into the arching you have already got, still working and correcting with the models. Now with a file, smooth round this outer margin of the arched side, and make a groove and melt it into the arching, as described on page 243. This done, finally get the arching on both plates *exactly* to coincide with the models, and your plates will be ready to scrape. This is done as before described, p. 243, scraping, wetting, and re-scraping until the requisite degree of smoothness and equality has been attained. Now mark the ff holes according to the pattern shown in Plate VI., which represents the pair of ff holes belonging to the Guarnerius fiddle we are now making. Both ff holes, and their position in the belly are shown, as the peculiar character of the fiddle in question is that they are slightly different, and one is higher than the other, all very ugly, doubtless, but very characteristic and interesting. Find the exact centres between the upper, middle, and lower bouts, and connect them with a line as set forth on p. 253. Call this line (on the belly) A B. Make an f hole model by pasting a tracing of the upper figure of Plate VI. on to a leaf of veneer, and cutting out the two ff holes. Now set this model on the belly with the line A B on the model coinciding with the line on the belly, and trace the two ff's as you did before (p. 254). Next punch out the upper and lower holes of the ff's, as prescribed on p. 256, and proceed to gouge out the back and belly to the requisite thicknesses as set down on pp. 248 and 256, planing, scraping, and finishing the edges as before (p. 248), after which the back will be ready to be glued on. Take the mould (round which the sides are set as they were left on p. 290), and setting it on the back, see if the sides fit the back nicely ; if they do, you can clean off the lower edges of the sides, linings, and blocks, and prepare them for the glue as set down on p. 249, and immediately fit on the back and glue it as before described (p. 250). It is not, however, impossible that the sides or the back may have shrunk a little, so that the edges do not appear even when the ribs (on the mould) are set on the back ; in this case take the ribs off the mould by forcing a table-knife between the *glued* sides of the blocks and the mould, and carefully easing off the sides. Be sure that the ribs are well separated from the mould before you slip them off. Sometimes, in spite of the most careful soaping (*vide* p. 287), a drop of glue will adhere to the mould, and the ribs will stick to the mould at that point ; in this case the rib must be carefully prised off with the table-knife before attempting to slip them off the mould. When slipped off, the ribs must be fitted to the back and glued as described on p. 249. This done, the next thing will be to cut the remaining or upper halves of the top and bottom blocks *only* to shape in the same way as the lower halves were, shaping them exactly so as to be *quite* perpendicular to the plane of the fiddle ; then proceed to put in the upper side linings. This is done exactly as the lower ones were, only that at the corner-blocks having only half a block to cut into you must be very cautious, and guide the knife very carefully, to avoid splitting them right down in making the grooves in the corner-blocks to receive the linings of the C's or inner bouts. When these are set, the corner-blocks may be cut to shape like the others, and the linings all round bevelled off, and planed and filed down level with the tops of the ribs ; the insides of the ribs are then thoroughly cleaned with water and sand-paper, all which operations have been described before fully, and do not require repetition. The belly duly finished, as described on p. 260, is then set on the ribs in the manner there described, and the body of the fiddle is then completed by the addition of the purfling, as described on p. 262, so that you have now only to carve the scroll, fit it on a neck, and place it on the fiddle in the manner set down below.

Neck and Scroll.—As the head will first be finished and then spliced on to the neck, we are at present concerned only with the head or scroll, the outline model of which (which should be traced off, pasted on a leaf of wood, and cut out) will be found on **Plate V.** Having selected a block of maple to match your sides and back of the proper length, *i.e.*, $5\frac{1}{2}$ inches, and being 2^1 inches broad, make one *side* quite plane, and then make one *edge* quite plane and quite square to the planed side. Then mark with a gauge on this edge a line $1\frac{11}{16}$ from the true edge, and plane down all wood on the other side in excess of this line, so that you have a squared block $5\frac{1}{2}$ long by $2\frac{1}{2}$ broad by $1\frac{11}{16}$ thick. Mark by the nick A on the two sides of this block the outline of the head in the manner described on page 270, except that there we had a neck to mark as well, whereas here it is cut off just beneath the chin of the scroll. Let this be cut out, keeping very true to the lines on *both* sides as before (p. 270). This done, the scroll is carved exactly as has been already set forth ; but when carved it must be fitted upon a neck, in the manner carefully described on page 312 (Repairs). This done, the fiddle is fitted with a false finger-board (as on page 279), and varnished (*vide* the next chapter) and fitted up as is set down in Chapter XXII., page 297.

This, therefore, completes our second fiddle, with its variations from No. 1. We can now therefore proceed to varnish and fit up the two together ; and how this is to be done is the subject of the next chapter.

---

* Carmina vel cœlo possunt deducere lunam;
Carminibus Circe socios mutavit Ulyssi ;
Frigidus in pratis cantando rumpitur anguis."
(Virg *Ecl.* viii.)

VARNISHING AND FITTING UP.

Staining—Varnishing—Polishing—Fitting the Finger-board—Fixing the Nut—Finishing the Nut and Finger-board with the Neck—Fitting the Pegs—Finishing the Pegs—Fitting and Fixing the Tail-pin—Fitting the Tail-piece and Loop—Setting up the Sound-post—The Strings—Cutting and Fitting the Bridge—Finis !

" ENFIN C'EST UN VIOLON."—Our fiddle is finished "in the white," our varnish has been carefully prepared, and we are ready to lay it on. This operation must not be commenced till the end of May, or the beginning of June at the latest, when we can be sure of a spell of fine hot weather in which to do our work. The fiddle must be carefully washed with clean water all over, so as to remove any dirt which may have accumulated ; the last touches must be put (if required) with sand-paper and file, and the work can proceed at once. Begin by sizing or staining the fiddle all over, bright yellow ; when I say all over, I mean the whole of the body and the shoulder, and the head ; the neck will bo loft, being subsequently varnished as hereafter set down. The best stain may be made as follows : Get some gamboge, as pure and unadulterated as possible, and some pure spirits of wine ; pound up the gamboge and put it into the spirit in a phial for two or three days, shaking it up whenever you think of it—*i.e.*, as often as possible. The absolutely pure gum will be dissolved, leaving all the impurities and insoluble parts at the bottom of the phial, in the form of sediment ; the solution thus formed will be *quite transparent*, of a magnificent *red* colour. Test it by brushing a drop or two on to a piece of wood, when, if it appears a fine yellow colour, it is right, and will do. This solution of gamboge, this coloured sizing, this preliminary stain (call it what you will), must now be carefully laid on, beginning with the head. For this purpose use a camel-hair brush of *the finest quality*, having a diameter of about half an inch ; at a first-class *artists'* colourman's it will cost you from six to eight shillings. Let the brush be well filled with stain (but not over-filled and sopped), and lay it on *quickly* and carefully all over, missing no spot which it will be necessary to

go back to : work as *quickly as possible, never* going over the
same ground twice, nor putting one coat over another, for this
dye sinks in at once, and if you touch a surface with it twice, or
retouch it after it is laid on, it will *infallibly* turn out streaky
and blotchy.   Practise, before touching your fiddle, on a planed
plank of deal, for once the harm is done it cannot be undone.
After doing the scroll, go round the ribs, then all over the back,
then all over the belly (not forgetting the inside of the *f f* holes),
and finally round the *edges*, being careful in brushing round the
edges not to retouch the back, belly, or sides.   This wash will dry
very quickly, and as soon as it is dry lay on your first coat of
varnish, proceeding in exactly the same way, excepting that as
it does not dry in at once you need not be in a hurry, but can go
carefully, backwards and forwards, getting on an *even* coat. as
thin and smooth as possible, *not* clogged under the edges or in
the angles of the scroll.   When this coat is laid on, hang up the
fiddle to dry in the lightest, hottest, dryest, sunniest place you
can ; in the hottest weather it will take at least twenty-four
hours ; in poor weather, or if you have laid the varnish on too
thick, it will take longer.   When it is *quite* dry, go over the
fiddle carefully with a fine knife, removing any blacks, dust,
hairs, flies, etc., etc., which may have stuck to it, and lay on
another coat in the same manner as at first, the neck being
always left bare (by which it may be held), and a spike, stick, or
brush handle being pushed into the hole made to receive the
tail-pin (when it is finished), also to hold it by ; in this way the
varnished fiddle may be freely handled without fear of touching the varnish and leaving marks, which is a fatality most
strenuously to be guarded against.   The fiddle should be hung
up by a string tied tightly round the unvarnished neck, with
a loop in front to hang on a nail ; it must hang quite free, and
so as not to touch anything.   When the second coat is quite
dry, proceed as before to remove every trace of blacks or other
impurities, and after that go over the entire fiddle with a piece
of the very finest sand-paper, *not* hard enough to bring off the
varnish, but just so as to polish the surface thereof, and remove
the fine layer of dust which almost infallibly will adhere to the
varnish in drying.   This done, proceed to lay on two more
coats (the third and fourth) in a precisely similar manner.
These two should consist of a rather deeper-coloured varnish
than the first two, and it will be already noticed that the flaring
yellow of the preliminary wash is becoming tempered and
modified by the varnish, of which it is not necessary to say
anything further in this place.   Go on varnishing in this way,
using a deeper-coloured varnish for each two coats till the fiddle

SCRAPE THE FIRST 7-8 COATS OF VARNISH
DOWN TO THE SURFACE OF THE WOOD

has seven or eight coats, always being careful to remove any dust, blacks, flies, or other impurities which may have stuck to the fiddle before laying on a coat, and between each two coats levelling any lumps or ridges with a piece of the finest sand-paper. After the seventh or eighth coat, take a knife and scrape the varnish off *down to the wood* round the bevelled outline of the scroll, and along the *edges* of the ribs where they meet at the corners, at right angles to the plane of the instrument. These lines must now be covered with black, so that when finished the outline of the scroll (back, front, and volute) and the ends of the bouts (at the corners) will be accentuated by a black line; the proper black with which to do this is the ordinary stick Indian ink, which is to be had of any artists' colour merchant. After this, finish the varnishing by continuing to lay on coat after coat, as thin as possible, and always taking care that one coat is dry, clean, and smooth before laying on another, until the requisite tone and substance are obtained. This will require from twelve to fifteen coats, according to the nature and quality of the wood and varnish.

12-15 COATS

The fiddle is now finished and varnished; it must be hung up for at least a month, if not two or three, to dry *thoroughly* before fitting it up. Personally, I prefer the rich, creamy appearance of the varnish in its present state to the unnatural mirror-like polish which is generally seen on a new fiddle, but if this is desired the varnish must be allowed to dry thoroughly, and after some months carefully polished as below described, till it is smooth as glass. Otherwise, after a month or so the fiddle may be fitted up as is hereafter set down; before doing so, how-ever, it is well to remove the extreme roughness or cakiness which will be present unless the varnish is of a particularly perfect description, by dipping a slip of the finest sand-paper in water and rubbing it quickly over the surface of the belly; the back may remain as it is unless it is particularly lumpy. When the varnish is very thoroughly dry, you can polish it to produce that glassy smoothness which is by some considered a great beauty. Begin by rubbing the surface of the varnish carefully with a rag dipped in finely-powdered pumice-stone, having first dropped a few drops of oil on the surface of the fiddle; this must be done carefully all over the fiddle where varnished till the surface is quite smooth. But be most careful not to bring off the varnish. Then repeat the process with oil and finely-pulverized Tripoli till the surfaces are quit polished; now rub the fiddle smartly all over with an old silk handkerchief till the surface is quite glassy; finally go over the polished surfaces with a fine linen rag and dry Tripoli, by which time the polish will be perfect, and needs only an occasional rub with an old silk hand-kerchief to preserve its mirror-like appearance.

Fitting up.—Now follows the adaptation to your fiddle of those fittings of which I have exhaustively treated in a former chapter; and the first operation is the fitting of the finger-board. At one time it was necessary for violin-makers to make their own finger-boards out of the solid ebony, which was a great labour, but now they may be bought ready-made of first-rate quality, and only require fitting to the fiddle in hand. Their dimensions as thus sold are $10\frac{1}{2}$ inches long, 1 inch broad at the top, $1\frac{19}{24}$ inch at the broad end, and having an uniform thickness down the sides of $\frac{1}{4}$ inch. They are sold properly curved on the upper surface, but their correctness may be checked by means of the neck-guide, Fig. 172; the scallops, c and D, at the sides of the guide representing the top and bottom of the finger-board properly curved. If you are fitting a finger-board to a new fiddle, it is as you left it on page 281, with a false finger-board on it: this must be prised off with an old table-knife; if you are fitting a finger-board to a new neck only, as set forth in Chapter XXIII., this will not be required. Commence by planing the front of the neck quite clear of all glue, pencil marks, or indentations formed by the pressure of the cramp by which it has been fixed to the fiddle. Then at a height of exactly $5\frac{3}{16}$ inches from the ribs (not from the edge of the fiddle) mark a line across the neck, which will be the upper boundary of the finger-board, and consequently the lower boundary of the nut. Now take your finger-board and make the top (or narrow end) exactly square, by means of the "false square" in the ordinary manner; this done, set the finger-board, curved side downwards, in the holder, Fig. 171, in which we made our false finger-board, and with a fine plane make the under surface quite plane and smooth. Now place the upper end on the nut line, and see how we are getting on; a straight-edge laid along the finger-board ought to extend $1\frac{1}{8}$ inch above the belly in the centre between the nicks of the *ff* holes. If it does not do so, the lower end of the face of the neck and the under surface of the finger-board must be planed away until this required height is attained. Now find the exact centre between the nicks of the *ff* holes in the usual way with compasses, and prick a small mark. Assuming that the lower end of the finger-board is truly square to the length (as ascertained by the false square), the two lower corners of the finger-board will be at an equal distance from this mark—*i.e.*, a compass opened from this point to one corner of the finger-board, exactly reaches the other also from the point, and the finger-board must be shifted till this true setting is obtained. On a full-sized fiddle the length from the nut line to this point (the bridge) is just 13 inches; of course in a large or small model this length will vary, so do not mind if you have not got it. The curved lower end of the finger-board is always hollowed out, and the edge thus presented should be a shade thinner than the thickness down the sides.

On the ready-made finger-boards of commerce, this end is generally thick, so it must be reduced to proper proportions by gauging round this lower end to the thickness of the sides with the gauging compasses A, Fig. 126, and cutting out and finishing the hollowing out of the under surface just beyond the line thus gauged; this hollowing is begun with the knife and a small gouge, and finished off neatly and smoothly with a round file, (Fig. 117), a scraper, and sand-paper of various degrees. Now with the toothed plane just plane over, so as slightly to rough the under side of the finger-board where it is to touch the face of the neck itself. Warm the under side of the finger-board well over a lamp, so that it shall not chill the glue directly it is put

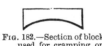

on (for ebony is very cold wood), coat the face of the neck with glue, and quickly rub on the finger-board, so that the top just touches the nut line you drew on the neck, and cramp it in its place by means of a cramping iron, and a block represented in section at Fig. 182, which follows and cramps the curve of the upper surface of the finger-board. Before putting on the other two cramps, see for the last time that the top of the finger-board is level with the nut line, and that the lower corners are even to the point in the centre of the belly. Then set it aside to dry, cramped firmly in its place by three strong cramps.

FIG. 182.—Section of block used for cramping on the Finger-board.

The Nut is the next fitting to be applied, and fills up the interval between the top of the finger-board and the bottom of the peg-box. It is made and fitted as follows: Take a little slip of ebony about 1½ inches long, ½ inch wide, and ¼ inch deep, and make one side and one edge square to one another and smooth, so as to fit exactly against the face of the neck and top of the finger-board; then with a chisel and file get it to the exact thickness required—*i.e.*, the thickness of the space between the top of the finger-board and the edge of the peg-box, which space it must exactly fill; this done, set it in its place and mark the length required—*i.e.*, the top of the finger-board, and cut it with a fine tenon saw *just* over the right length so as *just* to project at the ends. When it exactly fits, set it in its place, and with a pencil, mark on its front the curve of the top of the finger-board, and with a knife cut away the wood above it till it stands about a full $\frac{1}{16}$ inch above the finger-board, following the curve. This done, glue it well, and just stick it into its place, when, if well fitted, it will hold quite tight.

It has been asked me by a correspondent why the nut is a piece separate from the finger-board. It is, of course, that the grain of the finger-board being parallel to the tension of the strings, it could not stand the strain of the strings, but would become dented by them at the upper end; the nut is therefore placed at this point so that the strings on leaving the peg-box encounter only the cross-grained piece of ebony constituting the nut, on which they can make no impression as they would on the soft parallel grain of the finger-board.

Finishing the Nut and Finger-board with the Neck.—Your finger-board and nut are now fixed to the fiddle in the rough. The finger-board probably overlaps the sides of the neck, and must be shaved down till it is even with it, with a knife. If the neck is broader than the finger-board it is too large, and must be cut down level to the sides of the finger-board, and the two together to the right breadth. Then cut the nut down to shape, finishing it with a file, and leaving it rather large. There cannot be laid down any rule for shaping the nut; the only plan is to have another fitted fiddle by your side and copy that. Now take the neck gauge, Fig. 172, and finally regulate the thickness of the neck with the finger-board. The neck must be cut away underneath in little shavings with a knife, until the small end, A, of the guide, Fig. 172, will just go over the neck and finger-board sideways, from the chin to about 1 inch above the shoulder; the large end B of the gauge must come right down to the shoulder. When the proportion has been got, finish the shaping of the chin and shoulder, working by eye from a finished instrument till the right shaping is attained. The work is begun with a knife, but finished and principally done with a rasp or good file; in this operation you will file all the varnish off the chin of the scroll and the shoulder, the neck being revarnished, as laid down further on (p. 318). When with the biting file you have got the right shape, go all over the neck (including, of course, the edges of the finger-board) with a finer file, then finish with a scraper and sand-paper. Now with a file round off the upper edges of the finger-board and the nut at all its angles, as you see it done on a finished fiddle The neck (including the edges of the finger-board) is then thoroughly sand-papered with different finenesses of paper till the requisite smoothness is attained, then varnish and polish it as laid down in the concluding chapter on Repairs (Par.: "Varnishing Repairs"). When this is done, and the varnish is dry, polish it with oil and pumice powder, and then with oil and Tripoli in the same way as the rest of the fiddle was varnished (*vide supra*). Now scrape off all traces of varnish from the edges of the finger-board (being careful in doing so not to remove the varnish of the neck), and polish it and the nut with pumice and Tripoli as before, but rubbing it over first with a slip of the finest sand-

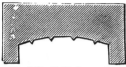

FIG. 183.—Guide for marking string grooves on the Nut.

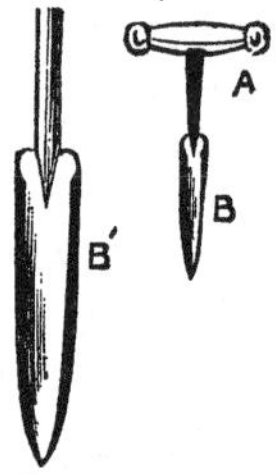

paper and a few drops of oil. The last touch to be given to the nut is the making of the four little grooves which take the strings. The position of these can be measured out from a finished finger-board with compasses, but sometimes a guide is used (represented actual size in Fig. 183), which is made of hard wood or steel, and by which the four points are marked. When they are marked, these little grooves are made with a very small mouse-tail file. Next fit the pegs.

FIG. 184.—Peg-hole Borer.

Fitting the Pegs.—The first things required for this are a borer and finisher for the holes in the peg-box, in which the pegs are to fit. The former is represented at Fig. 184, and consists of a steel rod, with a cross handle like a gimlet or tuning key, A, bearing a tapered cutter, like a cheese-taster, B. The finisher is represented at A, Fig. 185, and consists similarly of a steel rod, bearing a tapered piece, B, which is fluted so as to present all round its circumference a series of sharp edges. With these

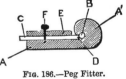

FIG. 186.—Peg Fitter.

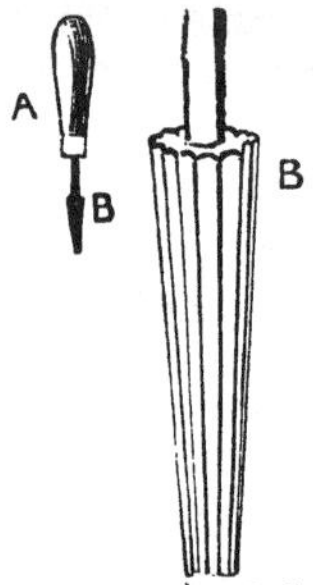

FIG 185.—Peg-hole Finisher.

you will proceed to make the peg-fitter, Fig. 186. This is done as follows : Take a piece of solid hard maple, $2\frac{1}{2}$ inches square, and 5 or 6 inches long, and cut out of it the piece A A', which is in the form of a solid block A, having at one end the high rounded piece A'. In this part (A') at the point B, make a hole just 'arge enough for the *thin end* of the part B of the peg-hole borer (Fig. 184) to fit in ; and, by turning the borer, make a tapered hole through the block A A', at the point B, just large enough to receive the finisher (Fig. 185), up to the top of B, and no further, so that you have a tapered hole B through A', Fig. 186.

C is an ordinary steel plane-iron, which must lie along A, so as just to project into B by means of a narrow passage cut into B at D, on the principle of the pencil-sharpeners into which you put the end of a pencil and turn against a blade. C is kept fast in its place by another slab of maple, E, which holds it fast against A by means of a screw F, which passes through the slab E, and the oblong hole or slot in the plane iron C, into the block A. A moment's thought will make it clear that if a rough peg be put into B, and turned (against C) till it exactly fits into the hole B, it will also exactly fit into any hole made by B, the fluted borer of the boring tool, Fig. 185. You can now, therefore, make the four holes in the peg-box to receive the pegs, two on each side, by beginning them with a drill, and finishing them with the boring tool and finisher. Be careful over this, or you will split away the wood inside the peg-box, or split the head to pieces; the positions of the holes must be, of course, regulated by the model of the scroll, the only things to be regarded being, that the holes on either side must be exactly in the middle, and very exactly opposite one another, and so set relatively to one another that the pegs can be turned easily with the fingers without interfering with one another. Be careful to begin the holes on the proper sides (*i.e.*, the G and D on the left, and the E and A on the right); it is not uncommon for a thoughtless beginner to start wrong. (I did this once : it made me *extremely* angry.) The G and E holes, and the D and A holes, it will be noticed, are closer together than the E and D, so be careful not to commit the error of making the spaces an equal distance all the way up. When the holes are made, remove any roughnesses left round the edges by the finisher with a fine knife, and finish the *insides* of the holes with a piece of fine sand-paper rolled up small. A glance at any well-arranged peg-box will enable you to measure the places of the holes and their relative distances better than pages of explanation ; but Fig. 187 represents the most usual setting, actual size, the letters representing the respective pegs. Now fit the pegs one by one into the peg-fitter, Fig. 186, till they fit exactly into the holes in the peg-box made by the borer and finisher, Figs 184 and 185. By fitting exactly, I mean that they must turn stiffly, but without jerking, in the holes thus made, and the " thumb-pieces " of the pegs must be even with one another when the scroll is held up before the eye, *id est*, one peg must not go in further than another. The ends of the thumb-pieces must be just $\frac{7}{10}$ of an inch from the cheek of the scroll. The ends of the pegs projecting beyond the outer face of the opposite cheek of the peg-box must now be cut off about $\frac{1}{20}$ of an inch beyond the outer face, and this projecting $\frac{1}{20}$ of an inch must be nicely rounded with a file, sand-papered, and may be polished by licking it and rubbing it hard up and down the apron stretched across one's leg. The whole shaft of the peg must then be nicely smoothed with fine sand-paper, and a hole drilled through it rather near the cheek of the peg-box, on the side of the "thumb-piece," or head of the peg. These operations being repeated four times, your set of pegs is fitted. Sometimes it is found that the peg-box is too shallow to allow

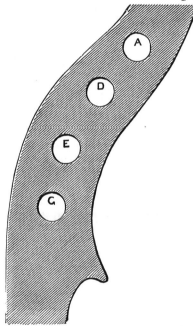

Fig. 187.—Setting of the pegs in the cheeks of the scroll.

the pegs, *with the strings coiled on them,* to turn easily; this has a tendency to smash the head. In this case the peg-box must immediately be deepened with a chisel; it is always as well before leaving the pegs to test each thus, by winding a piece of thick D string round it inside the box, and remedying any defect so found. If the pegs were put in just as they are, they would, of course, stick, and be very stiff to turn; you must, therefore, put them in and turn them round a few times so as to mark them a little where they turn in the cheeks of the peg-box. Then at these points rub them with a piece of soap, and then with whitening. This will make them turn easily, but hold fast when screwed up to pitch. Clean away all trace of this operation inside and outside the peg-box—first with a dry brush, and then with one slightly moistened. Finally, give the thumb-pieces and shafts of the pegs a good rubbing with a slightly-oiled rag, and your pegs are fitted ready to receive the strings.

Fitting the Tail-pin.—Tail-pins are sold everywhere for a few pence, and are very easily fitted into the lower block by enlarging the hole already there with the borer, Fig. 184, and fitting the short shaft of the tail-pin into the hole thus made by means of the peg-fitter, Fig. 186, as if it were a peg. (*Vide* Figs. 104 and 105, p. 195.) It must not, however, be glued in its place till the *very last* moment (when you want to put on the tail-piece by its loop), for the hole is the luthier's peep-hole, through which he can see the whole inside of his fiddle by applying his eye to it. Indeed, it is better not to glue it at all. Merely leave the shaft of the tail-pin as long as you can, fit it nicely, and put it in. It cannot come out of itself; but you can pull it out if you want to, to look inside the fiddle.

The Tail-piece.—These are sold ready-made by all violin-makers, so you will only have to fit it on. Procure a piece of the black gut string used for the F or G of a harp, and let it through the holes made to receive the loop; bring one end well through, and with a spirit-lamp burn the extreme end until it swells up to double its size, flatten it whilst soft and tie round it tightly, just below the swelling, a twist or two of A string, the ends of which must be similarly burnt to prevent its knot slipping. This makes a knob big and strong enough to prevent the loop slipping through the holes in the tail-piece. Now put the loop on the tail-pin, and lengthen it till the wood of the tail-piece *just clears* the " rest," take it off carefully (so as not to slip), mark it, leaving enough to make the knob, which must be made by burning the end and tying a piece of A string round it as before. This done, the tail-piece is fitted.

FIG. 188.—Sound-post Setter (front and side views).

The Sound-post, on the importance of which I have always said so much (p. 149), must next be made from a piece of fine-grained pine, and fitted to the fiddle. It must be perfectly circular, $\frac{7}{32}$ inch in diameter, and in the rough about $2\frac{3}{8}$ inches long. You should have a set of about six or more " trial posts," ranging in length from $2\frac{1}{2}$ inches to $1\frac{3}{4}$ inch, and according to the build of your fiddle, you will, in turn, put in one after another of these graduated " dummies " till you find the one that fits exactly according to the rules laid down on p. 151. When this is found, cut your real sound-post to that length, with a slant at the top and bottom of the post, so as to fit close against the back and belly, following the arching of the model, and set it in its place in the fiddle with the sound-post setter (Fig. 188), on the sharp end of which it is stuck for the purpose of putting it into the instrument. Remember in putting it in that it slants *a little outwards*—*i.e.*, towards the *f* hole, and that the grain of the post goes at right angles to that of the belly. Be very careful not to injure the edges of the *f* hole by notching it with the sound-post setter (Fig. 188) whilst you are putting the post in, for inexperienced hands nearly always do this.

Now put on the strings, selecting them to your instrument (*vide* p. 204) ; but, of course, do not attempt to screw them up till the *final* operation is performed, namely :—

Fitting the Bridge.—This is the last operation of all, and must be carried out with careful regard to the remarks contained on page 161.   First carefully select your bridge ; the first thing is to shave off the surfaces of the little " inverted T," which gives the " kidney " or " heart " shape to the hole cut in the centre.   This must be *shaved* down with a fine knife, so as to be *just* below the levels of the back and front of the bridge, other-wise its delicate points catch in things (*e.g.*, the handkerchief which wipes the fiddle), and it gets snipped off.   Now take an old bridge and prop up the strings with it, setting it against the bottom of the finger-board, and protecting the varnish from its feet with a slip of paper; this enables you to fit the new bridge easier.   The strings are only just tightened enough to hold the bridge up, without pressing on it.   First reduce and shape the feet, so that when put upon the fiddle, and held in a line with the eye, the feet fit closely and absolutely to the arching of the belly ; this is a *most* important essential in the fitting of the bridge.   When they fit *absolutely*, they should be about $\frac{1}{16}$ inch (or less) in their thickest parts; but they will, of course, be thinner towards the centre of the fiddle, because they have to be cut away to suit the arching.   When they are fitted, mark their exact outlines on the varnish with a point, and *scrape away all the varnish* exactly beneath them, so that the feet touch the bare wood of the belly.   By this a better tone is obtained ; and if it is not done the feet will slip on the varnish, tearing it off as they shift about with the constant vibration. Now take the model of the arching of the bridge, Fig. 188A, and mark the proper curve of the bridge at the right height.   This is determined by holding the fiddle (scroll towards you) on a line with the eye, and looking along the finger-board.   The top of the bridge (when finished) should appear to the eye to be about $\frac{1}{4}$ inch above the end of the finger-board at the G, a little less at the E.   (Of course it must be understood through-out the fitting of the bridge that the old dummy bridge always supports the strings when the real one is being manipulated ; and when the latter is put up for a moment the former comes

FIG. 188A.—Guide for cutting the arching of
the Bridge.

down.)   When the arching is properly adjusted, round off with
a file all the corners and edges of the bridge, making the top
quite round, and thinning it gradually to the top from the
" waist " (so to speak) of the bridge ; the whole is finished with
fine sand-paper till it is perfectly smooth.   The niches for the
strings are then made with the " mouse-tail " file you used for
the nicks in the nut, the dummy bridge is taken down, the new
one is put up, the A is screwed up to pitch, the other strings
tuned to the A, and your fiddle is finished.

" Hic fidibus, scriptis claris, hic magnis alumnis,
  Cui par nemo fuit forte, nec ullus erit."
            (*Fr.* Tartini's " Trattato di Musica, etc." [Padua, 1754].)

CHAPTER XXIII.

REPAIRS.

Removing the Belly of the Fiddle—Cracks in the Back or Belly—Cracks in Wings of *ff* Holes—Cracked Corners—Crack at the Joint or Un-gluing of the Tables—Cracked Edges, and Bits Split off the Outline—Crack from the Pressure of the Sound-post—Veneering New Wood into a Fiddle—Loosening of the Belly from the Heat of the Chin or Hand—Split Block—Splicing the Head on to a Neck, and Fitting it on a Fiddle—Varnishing Repairs—CONCLUSION.

It would hardly be right to complete a practical treatise on the fiddle-makers' art without turning for a few moments to the consideration of one of its most important branches—viz., Repairs. Unlimited though the care you take of your fiddle may be, as years of hard work thereon go by, you will be exceptionally fortunate if your instrument, delicate and nervous in temperament as it is, escapes entirely the ravages of time and misfortune, which in a thousand and one forms assail the existence of the productions of Cremona and Mirecourt alike, just as perseveringly as they do that of their masters and makers. If your fiddle is what Gemünder would call " a master-violin," its repairs should only be trusted to a great high-priest of the fiddle-making faculty, just as to our doctor-princes we confide the well-being of a dear child or relation ; but if your violin is not an historical instrument, and you are yourself a fiddle-maker, amateur or otherwise, you will find yourself quite capable of following the below-given directions for ministering to the minor vicissitudes of your instrument. Always repair an injury, or have the injury, whatever it be, repaired, without a moment's delay ; every moment between the accident and the reparation increases the damage.

> " Principiis obsta ; sero medicina paratur,
> Cum mala per longas convaluere moras."

As a first step towards a diagnosis you must be able :—

To Remove the Belly of a Violin.—The back is never removed ; as 1 have pointed out on p. 260, the belly is put on with much thinner glue, and therefore may be easily taken off with a

moderately blunt, short table-knife. It must first be forced
between the belly and the sides, in one of the c's, or inner bouts.
After separating about two or three inches there, go to the curves
of the upper and lower bouts, and when the beginnings have been
made thus, push the knife right round, separating the belly in
a similar manner from the corner and bottom blocks.   When
you get to the neck you will have to make two short cuts (one
on each side) at right angles to the edge, to loosen the table
from the sides of the shoulder, which is here mortised into the
top block *through* the ribs (or sides) and edge.   When it is
thus loosened all round, the belly may be pulled off from under
the finger-board; and the belly being removed, all the ills which
violins are heir to will, if they exist, be exposed to your scrutiny.
You will find it almost impossible to take off a belly without
splitting off little splinters from the under surface of its edges
(especially at the blocks) ; if these are very bad and pronounced,
you must carefully remove them from the sides and blocks to
which they adhere with a sharp knife, and re-glue them into the
belly with a cramp and two slips of deal to protect the surfaces;
but to reduce their production to a minimum the knife must be
held very flat, and pressed close on to the side and blocks on its
journey round the fiddle. And, also, you must not be too fond of
" tinkering up " your violin ; every time you take the belly off
it is bad, so you must never do it unless absolutely forced by the
nature of the evil, for many (indeed most) repairs require no
more disarrangement of the fiddle than merely unstringing.
Having therefore explained to you how to get inside your
instrument, let us turn to the consideration of the actual
remedies which are applied to sick fiddles.

  Cracks in Back or Belly.—These are often sufficiently serious
to render it necessary to take off the belly for the purpose of
getting at them, but generally they may be got at and repaired
with no more disarrangement of the fiddle than merely unstringing it.   In the latter case the crack must merely be encouraged
by pressing the instrument so as to open the crack a little, and a
little thin pure glue run along it. The two sides must be pressed
level, which may be done with a stick of wood inserted in an *f*
hole; and when the superfluous glue is washed away, and the
whole has dried, the damage will be practically invisible. Cracks
which may be mended thus are generally those arising from the
pressure of the bridge, or from cramming music, etc., into the
lid of the case, or from the bow, as described on page 202, and
from a multitude of other causes.

  Cracks in Wing of f-hole.—These, which are represented in
Fig. 189, arise from many contingencies, it being a most delicate

and brittle portion of the instrument. The wing must be lightly pressed down so as to open the crack, a little glue streaked into it, and the crack pressed together by slipping in a little strip of thin wood, fixing it under a screw put on the side, or under the finger-board as in the figure.

Cracked Corners.—The corners of the fiddle frequently get split, as shown in Fig. 189, either (1) by the pressure of some heavy weight, or (2) whilst gluing the tables to the sides, if in putting on the screws the corners are not carefully avoided they will split in this manner. To remedy the defect the extreme end

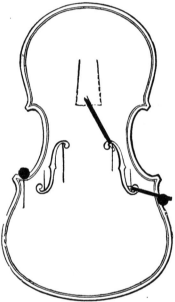

of the corner must be pressed so as to open the crack, a little glue must be streaked in, and a violin screw applied just so as to hold it together as in Fig. 189. A little post just the length of the depth of the sides being set between the upper and lower corners to aid and counteract the pressure of the violin screw.

Crack at Joint, or Ungluing of the Tables.—This is an accident which sometimes occurs, and is the result generally of a severe jar or fall ; the back (or belly) coming apart, often throughout its length, along the centre join of the table. It not unfrequently happens that the bottom block is also split half through by the same mishap ; but this is not discovered till the belly is removed, which is the first step towards a repair of this kind. The belly

FIG. 189.—Cracks in the "wings" of the *ff* holes, and split corner.

being removed, the loosened joint is pressed open, a streak of glue applied throughout its length (and to the split cranny in the block, where this has also suffered), and the two halves of the tables are pressed together by means of cramps and the edge-holders described in the next paragraph. When the wood is very old and tender, it will often be necessary to strengthen the table after such a repair as this by gluing little studs of strong new wood (each about $\frac{1}{4}$ inch square) all along the crack at intervals at about 1 inch or $\frac{3}{4}$ inch. They are made of maple, and the outer surfaces should be nicely bevelled off, the sides glued to the table being quite flat. I think it better to dispense with these if possible, but often the age of the wood renders their application imperative.

Cracked Edges, or Bits Split from the Outline.—The edge which projects beyond the sides of a fiddle, though a great beauty to the instrument, and of the highest importance to preserve the symmetry of the outline, is often damaged by the fiddle falling down, or being forced into or out of a case too small for it, little slips of it getting split off just at the outer curves of the upper and lower bouts, where the edges of the grain are on both sides exposed, as at *a* in B, Fig. 190. The beginner will also be very liable to be troubled by this mishap, when in finally adjusting the *outline* and arching of the back and belly; the knife, chisel, or plane slipping off little chips, as at *a'* in C, Fig. 190; C representing a slab of maple or pine arched and cut out, but not yet scooped. (Both in B and C the pieces *a a'* are not shown, the pieces really chipped off being generally very small.) This chip must be immediately searched for and secured, or if it cannot be found, the edge must be shaved straight and flat, and another small slip of wood glued on. Both the original chip, or the new slip having been glued, it must be fixed to the side, and held there¡ by an edge-holder (or possibly two). This apparatus,

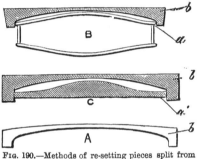

Fig. 190.—Methods of re-setting pieces split from the outline of the fiddle.

which can be cut out of any strip of $\frac{1}{4}$ inch deal in a few moments, is represented alone at A, Fig. 190, applied to an unscooped slab at C, and applied to the edge of a completed fiddle at B in the same figure. The holder itself is in each case lettered *b*; one end of it is placed on the glued chip, and the other end being just shorter than the breadth of the fiddle, it is drawn down the curved edge of the other side till it is firmly set, the outline of the fiddle being thus wedged fast into the holder by its own curvature. When the glue is dry and the holder is removed, the place where the split was will be invisible. If, however, you had lost the chip and had to apply a new slip of wood, the outer surface of the latter must be cut and shaped to conform to the outline of the table.

Crack in Back or Belly resulting from Pressure of Sound-post. —This is a damage often found on old violins, especially on ones of not very excellent make, or which have been ignorantly fitted

with too long a sound-post. The cracks in these cases generally
occur nearly the whole length of the plate, and to repair them
you must proceed as follows : Having taken off the belly, the
full extent of the crack will become visible, and it will be found
that the wood at the point from which the crack seems to start
away on either side has worked thin, so that besides mending the
crack, the wood must here be replaced by careful veneering.
The crack must first be mended by pressing it slightly open, and
running a streak of clear glue down it in the ordinary manner,
with an old knife or thin strip of wood ; when you are sure

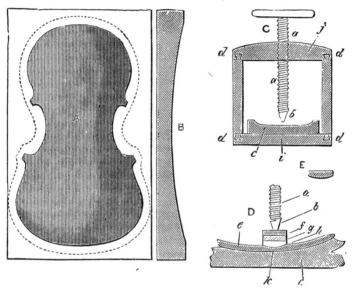

Fig. 191.—Apparatus for strengthening an old table with a veneer of new wood.

that the glue has run well through all along the crack, wipe
away superfluous glue and set the fiddle aside to dry.

When the glue is perfectly dry, you may proceed to veneer in
a plate of wood in the following manner. For this purpose you
will require a mould-plate and press, represented by Fig. 191.
In this figure A represents a mould-plate—i.e., a plate of hard wood
an inch and a half or so thick, *into which is sunk*, or rather out of
which is scooped, the approximate arching of a back or belly ;
B therefore represents a section down the centre of the mould-
plate. You will find that if you cut it round as shown by the
dotted line on A, it will be much easier to work with ; but mind
and cut it well clear of the scooped part. C represents the press
itself. which consists of a lower plate, i, connected by the two

uprights *d d, d d*, with the cross-bar *j*, which is perforated to admit the screw *a a*, which has a broad, smooth end *b*, which can be screwed down on to the mould-plate *c*, which is placed under it as in the figure. The lower plate *i* must be broad enough for the mould-plate *c* to be so moved about that the end *b* can be made to impinge upon it at any point on it, and thus when the table *e* is set in the mould-plate A, and A is set in C (*c* in C and D), any portion of it can be thus pressed as shown at D. This being therefore understood, and the gluing of the long crack dry, you may now veneer in a slab where the table is worked thin (over or under the sound-post) as follows : First cut a slip of brown paper about two inches by one, and glue it on the *outside* of the table where the thinness is to be corrected. Now take an oval and convex plane, with very fine teeth, and thin out the old wood in a little oval patch, as at *k* in D. Next, by means of a chisel, file, plane, and glass-paper, prepare a little oval slab of wood E *exactly* to fit the hollowing *k*, in back or belly (*e*), as the case may be, making it exactly true by rubbing it into the hole with chalk and fine sand.

When this is done, and both surfaces are clean and smooth, place the table into the mould-plate, set the mould-plate in the press, set the piece E into its place, thinly covered with warm strong glue, as at *h* in D, place over it a piece of cork *g* of similar size, place over that a similar piece of ½ inch wood *f*, bring the hollow *k*, with the three strata (of wood, cork, and wood), under the point *b* in the press C, and apply a strong pressure by means of the screw *a*. The wood and cork equalize the pressure of B all over *h*. Mind and make the grain of the new wood match and coincide in direction with that of the table to prevent it being too obvious (for one likes to hide a repair on the *ars est celare artem* principle). When all is dry, remove the table E from the plate *c*, and remove the wood and cork, *f* and *g*, and, with a small fine plane, plane down the new wood *h* till it coincides with, and is of proper thickness for, the table in which it has been set. If you dirty the new surface with your fingers and a little dust, and your new wood has been well chosen, and the repair has been (as the bootmakers say) " neatly executed," the locale of your remedy will be hardly visible, and the fiddle will be greatly improved.

Loosening of the Belly in consequence of the heat of the Hand or Chin.—It being remembered that the belly is put on with glue of a much thinner consistency than that used in putting on the back, it is not surprising that in hot weather, and with players who are troubled with hot hands, or profuse perspiration consequent on nervousness, the belly is apt to become unglued

at the place where the pressure of the chin is applied, and at
the part on the side of the neck where the hand rests, when
playing in the third position.   The first of these contingencies
seldom occur to players who use the appliance known as a
chin-rest, as this contrivance serves in a manner to hold the
belly fast and prevent its becoming unglued.   In either case the
damage is rectified as follows : Take an ordinary old table-
knife, and thrusting it in as if about to take the belly off the
instrument, ascertain the exact extent of the harm done, but be
careful not by this means to increase it.   If you turn to the
directions which have been given for gluing on the belly, you
will find how, the belly being held in position by screws, the
thin glue is applied with the blade of a table-knife, gluing a
piece at a time.   Proceed here precisely similarly, thinning
down the glue with warm water, and using plenty of it.   The
glue which holds the belly on everywhere else, in this operation
takes the place of the screws, but some repairers put on a couple
of screws, one on each side of the loosened part, to prevent the
operation of applying the glue from extending the injury.
Wipe off the superfluous glue as usual, and apply three or four
screws to the part glued, which are taken off when the glue is
dry and your repair is complete.

Split Block.—It sometimes occurs, from accident or careless-
ness, that when the ribs of a fiddle are being worked upon
without either the back or belly attached (as, for instance, new-
made ribs before the tables have been fixed on), the upper or
lower block will split perpendicularly throughout its depth ; in
this case the split being opened, and a sufficiency of good glue
being run in, the two split halves must be squeezed together
with the fingers, and cramped into that position with an iron
cramp and two slips of pine, the cramp being fixed at right
angles to the ribs.

How to Splice a Head upon a Neck and fit same to a Fiddle.
—In making a fiddle on a given model, it is generally the
custom not to make the head in one piece with the neck, but
separate from it, and " spliced " on to it, as is hereinafter
described.   And again, this delicate operation is often required
to be performed on old violins; for it must be remembered that
(as I have said before) on old instruments the original neck is
always too short, consequent on the alteration in the present
pitch, and requires to be replaced by a new neck suited to
modern requirements   And again, as a simple repair, it is one
of the most frequently required and important; for it constantly
happens that from bad choice of wood, or inferior fitting, the neck
sinks forward (so as to make the end of the finger-board too

low), or twists, or inclines to one side, in all of which cases a new neck must be adjusted rather than resort to the clumsy expedients of veneering and refitting the original neck. And this repair or operation is performed as follows : If you are fitting a new neck to an old fiddle, begin by prising off the finger-board and nut with an old table-knife, then cut the head off the old neck close up under the chin, and cut the old neck off the fiddle as close as possible above the shoulder. Thus, whether your head is old or new, you have the head as at A, Figs. 192 and 193, or as on Plate V.

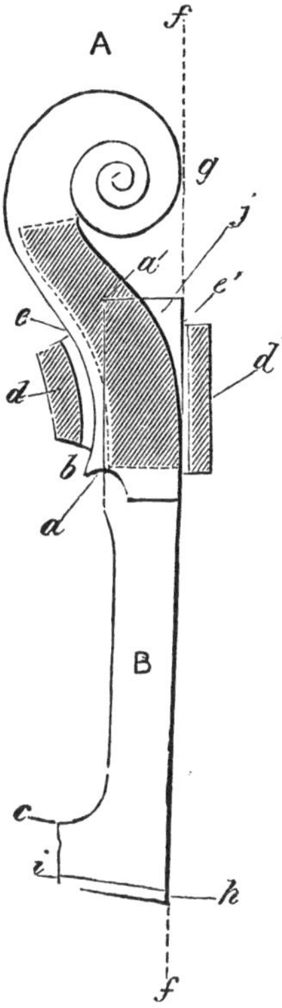

Now take a block for the neck, and prepare and square it as described in page 269. Take the neck model, Fig. 168 (Plate VI.), and cramping it to the plain surface of the block, as described in page 277, with a marking point mark this outline on the block and cut it out. The materials you have therefore to hand are—(i.) the scroll, and (ii.) the rough neck, which is about $7\frac{3}{4}$ inches long, $1\frac{3}{4}$ inch deep at the shoulder, and $1\frac{11}{16}$ inch wide on the face, down the exact centre of the surface of which you must draw a straight line, which will be the line $a\,a'$, Figs. 193, 195, and 196. First prepare the head to receive the splice, as follows: Fig. 194 represents the base of the front of the peg-box (b, Fig. 196). With a fine tenon saw make the two cuts $a\ b$, $a'\ b'$, Fig. 194, as deep as the bottom of the peg-box, perhaps a trifle deeper, as at $a\ a'$, Fig. 192 (the shaded part, Fig. 192, representing the peg-box), and cut out with the saw, knife, and chisel all the part c, Fig. 194, until the chamber thus formed is quite clean and square, the lines $a\ b$, $a'\ b'$, are quite straight, and the points b, b, are sharp and fine as the edge of a knife. The distance of these points (b, b') from one another should be as nearly as possible

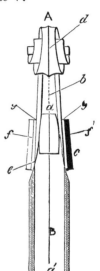

FIG. 192.—Operation of splicing head on to neck (side view).

FIG. 193.—Operation of splicing head on to neck (front view).

1 inch, but of course this depends on the breadth of the model
of the scroll. When this chamber is finished smooth and clean,
you can proceed to prepare the neck (B, Figs. 192, 193, and 196)
with the conical plug, Fig. 195, to fit into this chamber. Take
the breadth between the sides of the peg-box at a, a', Fig. 194,
with a pair of compasses, measure this breadth on a rule, and
divide it exactly by half (so that if the breadth was $\frac{2}{3}$ inch, you
have your compasses open $\frac{1}{3}$ inch). Mark off this distance
$b\ b'$, Fig. 195, on each side of the line $a\ a'$, Fig. 195, which represents the face of the neck block before the plug is cut. Now
take the breadth at $b\ b'$, Fig. 194, and mark off half of it, $c\ c'$,
Fig. 195, on each side of the line $a\ a'$, Fig. 195, and taking the
points $b\ c$, and $b'\ c'$, Fig. 195, as guides, draw on the surface of
Fig. 195 the lines $d\ e$ and $d'\ e'$. Now cut away with a chisel and
plane all the parts $f\ f'$ outside the lines $d\ e$, $d'\ e'$, Fig. 195, and
go on shaving and fitting till the plug (Fig. 195) exactly fits into

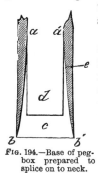

the chamber (Fig. 194) fast
and close all round, as in Figs.
193 and 196. AND N.B., the
distance from b to c, Fig. 192,
is as nearly as possible $4\frac{1}{4}$
inches, the shoulder being in
the rough state. Especial care
must be taken *throughout* this
fitting that the line $a\ a'$, Figs.
193 and 196, is in an exactly
straight line with the centre
ridge d of the front of the
scroll A, Fig. 193 (otherwise,

Fig. 194.—Base of peg-
box prepared to
splice on to neck.

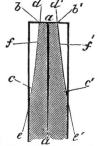

Fig. 195.—Top of neck
prepared to receive
head.

of course, the head will not be straight on the neck). When this
has been done, the next thing is to glue the plug into the chamber,
which is done as follows: Mark on the side of B, Fig. 192, a line
where the point b, Figs. 194 and 196, reaches on it as at e, Fig.
193. This is to know how far to push the plug into the chamber;
for when it is glued the glue acts as a lubricant, and there is
great danger of pushing it too far, and thus splitting off the
cheeks of the scroll. Now glue the sides and bottom of the plug
and the inside of the chamber, and push the plug into its place,
wiping off superfluous glue and cramping it tight into its place
by means of two cramping irons and cramping blocks $f\ f'$,
Fig. 193, which must be protected by cork surfaces $g\ g'$; and
between the cork surfaces and the sides of the scroll must also
be put slips of paper to protect the varnish of the scroll.
Similarly place another cramping iron with cramping blocks at
right angles to the first pair, the blocks being shaped and set

as at *d e*, *d' e'*, Fig. 192, and the whole must be set aside to
dry thoroughly.

When it is dry the first thing is to plane down the face of B,
Figs. 192, 193, and 196, with the plane, fit to receive the
finger-board. First plane it smooth throughout its length, till
at the splice the new wood is just flush with the old, then
(by leaving or planing down the lower end of B, Figs. 192
and 196) the surface B must so be left that a straight-edge,
f f, Fig. 192, *just* clears the centre ridge of the scroll, as at
the point G, Fig. 192, by about $\frac{1}{20}$ of an inch. This last
planing will of course have cut away the marking of the
line *a a'* on the surface B, Fig. 196. A new
centre line must therefore be made by taking
the exact centre of the surface of the block B,
Fig. 196, at the upper *h*, Fig. 196, finding same
with a pair of compasses in the usual way, and
then from the point *h*, Fig. 192, by the point
d, Fig. 193, drawing the new line *a a'* on B,
Fig. 196. Now with the small square laid
on the *side* of B, Fig. 192, mark a point on the
face of B, Fig. 196, *exactly* level with the end of
the chin of the scroll *b*, Fig. 192, and at this
point draw the line *b b'* across B, Fig. 196,
and the line *c c*, $\frac{1}{4}$ inch above it, and prolong
the lines formed by the inner surfaces (*d d*,
Fig. 196) of the cheeks of the peg-box, till
they meet *c c'*, Fig. 196, drawing by eye as
well as possible, thus completing on the face
of the plug the outline of the peg-box. Now
at the three points indicated on the line *a a'*,
on the plug above the line *c c'*, drill three
holes, *j*, Fig. 196, as deep as the bottom of the
peg-box, and as wide as the plug will hold

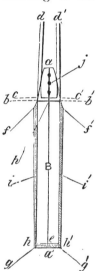

F<small>IG</small>. 196. Operation of
splicing head on to
neck.

(care must be taken not to injure the sides or bottom of the peg-
box, as these holes are only made so as to have less wood to cut
out with the knife and chisel afterwards) [and similarly bore
through the peg-holes already in the head (if it is an old scroll),
as this will remove yet more of the wood] ; the plug B is always
tapered enough to block up the holes of the G and E pegs.
Now proceed to mark the boundaries of the neck on the face
of B, Fig. 196. First on the line *a a'* mark a point *e*, Fig. 196,
exactly $5\frac{1}{2}$ inches from *b b'*, and with a square rule a line,
h h', across B at this point, then, placing the neck model, Fig.
168 (Plate VI.), along the side of B, Fig. 192, so that the shoulder
end (A, Fig. 168) is even with the line *h h*, Fig. 196, draw the

line i, Fig. 192, which gives you the proper " set " of the shoulder base. Repeat this line on the other side, and then carefully with a fine tenon saw and toothed plane cut away all the wood *below* these lines. Now opening the compasses $\frac{1}{2}$ inch, from the point h (on the nut line), Fig. 196, on the line $a\ a'$ (where it is crossed by $b\ b'$), set off $\frac{1}{2}$ inch on each side of h on the line $b\ b'$, which will give us the points $f\ f'$. Again opening the compasses $\frac{11}{16}$ in., set off, and in a similar manner mark two points, $g\ g'$, from the point e on the line $h\ h'$, and connect by means of a fine line the points f and g, and f' and g', Fig. 196. These last two lines give the correct proportions of the neck ready to finish. This is done by cutting away all the wood represented by the shaded parts $i\ i'$, Fig. 196, with a knife and chisel, and then with a knife *roughly* rounding the neck and shoulder to the approximate shape of the finished neck and shoulder, but leaving plenty of wood to cut away and finish when the neck is set on the fiddle; also, be very careful in cutting along close to the lines $f\ g$, $f'\ g'$, not to bring out the curls of the wood with the knife. If this does unfortunately happen, you must at once glue back the chip thus pulled out, and when dry, complete the operation.

Now finish the peg-box by cutting out with knife and small chisel all the part of the plug j (Fig. 196) which fills it up. This is to a great extent already done by the drill holes above mentioned, but the thus honey-combed wood must be carefully chiselled and picked out so as to make a perfect and cleanly-proportioned peg-box, as shown at d, Fig. 194 (and described in page 275). The little wings, j, Fig. 192, left above the curve of the peg-box by this operation must be carefully chiselled down to the old wood e, Fig. 194, and the whole of the interior and front of the new base of the peg-box thus made being neatly finished with a file, the head and neck are finished ready to set on the fiddle. During the whole of the operation of finishing the peg-box, the back of the scroll should be held firmly against the edge of the bench, protected with many folds of cloth to prevent injury to the varnish if it is an old fiddle, or to the carving if it is a new one.

How to set the Head and Neck upon the Body of the Fiddle.— If the fiddle is a new one, the chamber to receive the neck must be cut as described in p. 277 ; if, however, it is an old fiddle to which you are fitting a new neck, the remains of the old shoulder must be cut away to receive the new. Begin by taking a fine tenon saw, and cut *down* the shoulder close to the button, almost as far as the sides; then make another cut at right angles to this one from the front of the shoulder, so as to leave only the base of the original shoulder sticking in the chamber in which it was fitted. This "root," so to speak, must be cut out in small chips, holding the fiddle by the waist between your knees, with its back towards yourself, and carefully chipping out the root of the old shoulder with a small chisel, tapping it with a hammer till the whole of the chamber is cleared out, and is in the condition of the chamber finished in p. 278. Great care must be taken not to chip away pieces of the belly of the fiddle with the first few chips of this operation, an accident which may be obviated by making two little cuts between the root of the old shoulder and the edges of the belly into which it has been let.

When the chamber has been cut, as described in p. 278, or has been cleaned out as above, the base of the shoulder must be carefully cut to fit closely into it, regulating the cutting, which is done with a plane and chisel, by the chamber, and making the slope equal on both sides by means of the false square. The base of the shoulder must be cut away when fitted, till from the *ribs* (not the edge of the fiddle) to the nut (*i.e.*, to the line b b', Fig. 196) the distance is exactly $5\frac{3}{16}$ of an inch. In cutting away the base, great care must be taken not to split pieces off the sides thereof ; and this is obviated by always wetting the ends of the grain before cutting it, and working against the broad edge of the bench. The *back* of the shoulder must be cut to fit closely against the button, and the base must be so cut to fit the chamber, that holding the fiddle horizontally to the eye, the *front* of the shoulder projects just $\frac{1}{4}$ of an inch above the belly, and be exactly even all across—*i.e.*, $\frac{1}{4}$ of an inch above, both at h and h', Fig. 196. The proper " set back " of the neck is attained when a straight-edge perpendicularly laid along the line a a', Figs. 123 and 196, is just $\frac{11}{16}$ of an inch above the belly between the nicks of the $f f$ holes. Now find the exact centre between the $f f$ holes in the ordinary way, with compasses, and make a small point. A straight-edge *must* coincide, with this point, with the base of the line $a a'$ at e, Fig. 196, *and* with the centre ridge of the scroll d, Fig. 193 : if it does this, the neck is set straight ; *also*, place a wedge on a flat surface, and put the fiddle with the neck in position (it should fit tight enough to be able to carry the fiddle about by it, without shifting or coming out) sideways on the table, pushing it to the wedge till the " eye " of the scroll touches the inclined surface of the wedge, at which point on the inclined surface make a mark. Now turn the fiddle over, so as to repeat the process, and if the other " eye " touches the inclined surface at the same mark, the neck is set straight on the fiddle. This supplemental test is not so certain as the first, as sometimes a scroll may have one eye shorter than the other.   Between the chin, b, Fig. 192, and the top of the button, the distance should be just $4\frac{7}{16}$ of an inch, though this will sometimes vary slightly with the model.

All these conditions having been observed, finish the joint with a fine file, glue both shoulder, chamber, and button quickly and plentifully, and cramp the neck in its place with an iron, protecting the button with cramping blocks, as usual.   Before the glue sets, and before the cramp is fixed, see finally that the neck is set straight by the above tests, and set aside the whole when fixed to dry ; when, the operation being completed, we are ready to put on the finger-board, as described in page 297.

Varnishing Repairs.—It stands to reason that the great art and secret of successful repairing is to conceal the fact of a repair having taken place at all ; and the way in which all trace may be effectually hidden is by scientific and artistic varnishing.

We will suppose that a new neck has been fitted to an original head and set in the fiddle, as described above ; the object to be attained is to conceal the fact of its being a new neck by so varnishing and colouring the new wood as to render it indistinguishable from the old, to which it is attached, and to replace the original varnish, which must necessarily have been sand-papered off the old wood immediately contiguous to the join.   In the case of a new neck, this will be at the button, the top of the ribs, and round the chin of the scroll.   The new neck being finished and fitted in the manner that I have described, commence by just washing over the new wood with a slight stain to darken it a little before varnishing.   This stain may be composed of saffron or burnt umber dissolved in water, or of saffron *and* burnt umber mixed (which is better) ; but it must be concocted and applied so as not to make the fiddle neck look either too yellow or too brown.   Then take an ordinary spirit varnish, composed of shellac dissolved in spirits of wine, and varnish all over the new wood and where the original varnish has been removed ; two light coats of this will be sufficient.   Now take a darker spirit varnish (that sold ready made by Messrs. J. Rea and Co., of Wardour Street, under the name of " Violin Varnish," and which is a well-constructed shellac varnish, coloured with a vegetable pigment, and tempered with a tenderer gum, will do very well) and varnish well, so as to deepen in colour the shoulder of the new neck and the chin of the old scroll with the new wood adjacent to it.   You will now want a little powdered dragon's blood and a little burnt umber, mixing these according to the shade required by the rest of the fiddle, with the shellac varnish.   If the fiddle is red in tone, as, for instance, a Vuillaume or Guadagnini, you will require more dragon's blood ; if brown, like a Ruggerius, or old English fiddle, you must deepen your varnish with the burnt umber, till a satisfactory imitation of the rest of the fiddle and scroll is attained. Then take some burnt umber, and making with it a thick brown varnish, tip and touch the new wood lightly with it, especially over the joins where the old and new wood must contrast, so as effectually to disguise the same. When a piece of new wood has simply been let into a fiddle, the process of varnishing the repair is precisely similar, using lighter or darker varnish and pigments, according to the colour of the instrument, the dirt, dents, etc., of the rest of the fiddle being imitated artistically with burnt umber, especially, as before, round the edges of the new wood. I have seen fiddles thus patched and varnished so as to defy the closest scrutiny in searching for traces of the repair.

"I did an idyll on Joachim's fiddle,
    At a classical soirée in June,
  While jolly dogs laughed at themes from Spohr,
    And longed for a popular tune."

Conclusion.

My task is finished.

It is with a genuine regret that I lay down my pen, for as I have gone through in my mind the various processes of fiddle-making, and " made my fiddles o'er again," the deep and absorbing interest which for me attaches itself to all things connected with :—

> " This small, sweet thing,
> Devised in love and fashioned cunningly
> Of wood and strings,"

has made me linger lovingly over the minutiæ of the operations which call its wondrous powers into being.

Until he has pursued the art no one can imagine the fascination of violin-making,—the thousand pains the player never dreams of, the thousand touches the uninitiated eye never appreciates, the exquisite work of the interior which no eyes, save those of the maker and repairer, ever will be privileged to see. These are the things which make the Luthier love the work of his hands, as if it were his own child.

Years ago (it is said) there lived in Bremen a watchmaker, whose fame was universal, for his watches were the most perfect in the world. No one could discover the secret of his pre-eminence. At last he sickened and died, and the secret was revealed, for all his watches stopped one by one :—he had wrought a little of his own Soul into each timepiece, and when he died—they died also !

So it is with the Fiddle-maker: his whole soul is put into his work ; *but* his work does *not* die with him ; it lives, divinely sweet, till sheer old age crumbles it away,—till long after his grandchildren's grandchildren have lived out their allotted threescore years and ten, in blissful ignorance of their ancestor who " made fiddles."

Gentle Reader, *au plaisir de vous revoir :* give me rest now. Let me lay down the goose-quill to take up the gouge, and for a space let me resume again the solution of the problem :—

> "*Given :* A Log of Wood :—*Make :* A Fiddle."

> "Quante han voce la terra, e il cielo, e l'onda,
> Quanti accenti il dolor, la gioia, e l'ira,
> Tutto un concavo legno in grembo accoglie."
> *Felice Romani.*

Appendices.

TO A CHILD VIRTUOSA.

(Reprinted from *The Lute*, September 1884.)

I.

CHILD, when to-night alone upon the stage
  With tiny hands you woke the fev'rish chords
In streams of harmony which might assuage
  Passion, pain, longing, out of reach of words;
When (ev'n as Amphion in the old time played,
  Drawing dead ships which fraught with being seemed)
You wielded the deft bow my life was stayed,
  And I sat tranced, and, as I listened, dreamed.

II.

I see you now as then, child-like and fair,
  Lost in the clouds of harmony you made,
Whilst the light streaming from your sunny hair
  Revealed the dimple by its lurking shade;
And the soft cadence of the theme you breathed
  Well might have made the tortured soul forget!
Raising sweet living memories which wreathed
  With garlands new the ashes of Regret.

III.

I saw you when some other stronger hand
  Imprisons that which lately sped the bow;
(And this ere yet the running of life's sand
  Had marked a decade by its silent flow):
And then—when bow and "croude" are laid aside,
  And children's hands wake fresh those echoes bright,—
Will you remember your life's morning-tide,
  Will memory bear you back, dear, to to-night?

ENVOI.

  Child, thus I dreamed; and suddenly I woke,
  Roused by the thunders of applause which broke
  From all who heard you.—Ah! in the To-be
  Will praise delight you ev'n as now, *m'amie.*

ED. HERON-ALLEN.

APPENDIX A.

GUMS, RESINS, AND OTHER SUBSTANCES USED IN COMPOUNDING VIOLIN VARNISHES.

(a) *Benzoin, Benjamin,* or *Gum Benzoic.* The dried milky juice of the *Lithocarpus Benzoin,* a tree indigenous to Siam and the Indian Archipelago. It arrives in reddish-yellow lumps, the whitest being the best. Benzoin consists of 10 to 14 per cent. of Benzoic acid, and the rest resin. It is used in perfumery and medicine, and is a component of court plaister. It fuses easily, and is soluble in alcohol.

(b) *Saffron.* The dried stigmas of the *Crocus sativus.* An acre will yield 5 lbs. the first, and 24 lbs. the second year, after which it must be renewed. Its value is £2 an ounce.

(c) *Venetian Turpentine* is the most esteemed kind of turpentine, and is a clear pale yellow viscous mass. On distilling it with water the essential oil (or spirits) of turpentine is obtained, which is a colourless volatile oil, soluble in alcohol, ether, and other oils, and is a ready solvent of nearly all resins. The residue left in the retort after distilling is the rosin, or colophony, which is familiar to every violinist.

(d) *Frankincense* is the exudation of the *Epicea pectinata* (silver fir), a gum of a pinkish colour and agreeable odour. The frankincense of the Scriptures was the gum of the *Boswellia thurifera,* now known as olibanum.

(e) *Gum mastic* is the resin of the *Pistacia lentiscus,* from which it oozes in pale yellow tears. If not collected in time, it falls to the ground and becomes impure, and, consequently, it is best in tears. It is soluble in alcohol and oil of turpentine.

(f) *Aloes hepatica* is a species of resin of a liver-brown colour, obtained from several sorts of Aloes, particularly the *Aloe socotrina,* a native of the island of Socotra, whence it is imported into Bombay, where it acquires the name of Bombay aloes.

(g) *Sandal wood.* The name, as here used, signifies the wood of the *Pterocarpus santalinus* (and *not* of the *Santalum Yasi*), which grows in Southern India and Ceylon ; the heart wood is dark red, and so heavy as to sink in water ; it is much used as a dye.

(h) *Dragon's blood* (or Gum Dragon) is a gum obtained from several trees, but principally the *Pterocarpus draco,* a native of South America. It is also obtained from the *Pterocarpus santalinus* (*vide* note *g*), but tne most esteemed kind comes from the *Calamus draco.* It is of a deep reddish-brown colour, very opaque and brittle, smelling like benzoin when burned; it is soluble in alcohol and most oils and turpentine.

(*i*) *Madder* is a colour obtained from the peeled roots of the *Rubia tinctorum*, a shrub grown principally in Holland. The roots are lifted in October or November, the brown epidermis is removed by a process called "*robage*," and the inner part is cut into small pieces and packed off to the countries where it is ground into a fine powder for use.

(*j*) *Logwood* is the dark red heart-wood of the *Hæmatoxylon campechianum*, a tree which grows in Mexico and Central America. The sapwood and bark are peeled off, and the heart-wood is imported in billets. The colour dissolves readily in boiling water.

(*k*) *Brazil wood* is obtained from various species of *Cæsalpina* growing in Brazil. The best is that of the *Cæsalpina echinata* or Pernambuco wood, which is much used for making violin bows. The dark yellowish-red heart-wood is the valuable part.

(*l*) *Cinnabar* (or Vermilion). An ore of mercury, found in crystals, masses, and powder. Chemically it is bisulphuret of mercury.

(*m*) *Orpiment*, a combination of arsenic with sulphur, of a brilliant yellow colour known as king's yellow.

(*n*) *Elemi* is a fragrant resin obtained chiefly from the *Amyris elemifera* of Egypt (whence it arrives wrapped in cane or palm leaves), and from the *Elaphrium elemiferum* of Mexico. It is collected once a day from incisions made in the bark in warm weather, and put into casks. It is at first soft and sticky, but becomes in time hard and brittle. It is usually in greenish-yellow, semi-transparent masses with dark streaks in them, which soften when held in the hand.

(*o*) *Animé*, or hard copal, is the resin which exudes from the *Hymenæa courbaril*, a native of South America. A gum obtained from the *Vateria Indica*, known as gum animé, is very like true copal (only more soluble in alcohol), with which it is frequently confused in commerce.

(*p*) *Copal* is a name given rather indiscriminately to various gums, especially that known as animé (*o*). The best, or Mexican copal, is obtained from a species of *Hymenæa*, but it is also obtained from Africa, India, Madagascar, and Brazil. It arrives in round, tasteless, odourless, lemon-yellow masses; it is readily fusible and inflammable, and though only slightly soluble in alcohol and oil of turpentine naturally, it is readily so when it has been fused. In hardness, as a gum, it ranks next to amber. It is easily soluble in oils of spike and rosemary, and the addition of either of these to alcohol promotes its solubility. It is also soluble in oil of turpentine which has been exposed to the air (*vide* p. 181).

(*q*) *Gum tragacanth* is yielded by the shrub *Astragalus tragacantha*; it occurs in opaque whitish flakes, only partially soluble in water; it grows chiefly in Persia and Asia Minor, and comes to us from Smyrna and Constantinople.

(*r*) *Oil of lavender* is obtained by distilling flowers of lavender with water; the variety used chiefly for varnishes is called oil of spike, and is obtained from the *Lavandula latifolia*, or *spica*.

(*s*) *Cyprian turpentine* is that variety yielded by the *Pistacia lentiscus*. It is inferior to the Venice turpentine.

(*t*) *Gum lac* is the product of an insect (the *Coccus lacca*) which lives on the twigs of various trees (such as *Butea, Ficus, Croton*, etc), which it gradually covers with a resinous coating which contains their dead bodies, eggs, and a purple colouring matter which they secrete. The eggs germinate inside the resinous covering drawn from the trees by the parent insect, and the insects eat their way through and continue to build up the coating of resin (or gum lac), which often becomes as thick as half an inch, being honeycombed by the dead bodies of succeeding generations. When well covered, the twigs are gathered by natives and soaked and kneaded in hot water, which operation dissolves the colouring matter, and purifies the mass from the dead bodies of the insects. It is then put into coarse bags and melted before a fire till it oozes out over sticks on which it dries and forms shell-lac ; what falls through the sticks is called tear-lac, and plate or tablet-lac. Stick-lac is the twigs just as they are gathered, shipped with all impurities. That which is shaken to the ground from the trees by wind, etc., is collected, and called seed-lac. It is of various shades of colour, from clear orange to opaque liver-colour. It comes principally from South-Eastern Asia, and is imported at the rate of about 1,500 tons annually.

(*u*) *Sandarach* (so-called) is a brittle, yellowish, transparent resin imported from North Africa, where it exudes from the bark of the *Callitris quadrivalvis*. It is more soluble in oil of turpentine than alcohol, and in excess renders the varnish soft and brittle. *True* sandarach is got from the common juniper, and is the same as juniper gum (*vide* p. 175, Note [1]).

(*v*) *Amber* is the fossil gum, probably of an extinct coniferous tree, found generally in conjunction with coal, in lumps or tears of a yellow or opaque colour. It burns brightly, and is rather brittle. It melts at 550° Fahr. It is found principally on the shores of the Baltic, cast up by the sea, gathered in nets, and dug up. It is also sometimes found on the east coast of England. It is partially soluble in alcohol, and totally in chloroform.

(*w*) *Asphalt* is a kind of bituminous pitch, obtained chiefly from Trinidad, though it is also found in many other parts of the world. An artificial asphalt is obtained from the residue left in the retort after the evolution of coal-gas. It resembles pitch, but does not soil the fingers; it is sparingly soluble in alcohol, but more so in oil of turpentine, ether, and naphtha.

(*x*) *Gum arabic* is obtained from the *Acacia arabica* and *vera*, both natives of North Africa and Eastern Asia, whence it is imported to us from Barbary and Turkey. It varies in colour from straw-yellow to deep red.

(*y*) *Gamboge* is the gum resin of the *Cambogia guttifera* of the East Indies. It is a thick yellow juice, which reaches us in pipes, cylinders, and masses, of which the two former are the purest. The best comes from Siam.

(*z*) *Myrrh* is the resin of the *Balsamodendron myrrha*, a native of Arabia and Abyssinia. It exudes from the tree in thick yellow drops, which harden and darken on exposure to the air. It reaches us in tears and lumps, varying from yellow to reddish-brown. It is brittle and waxy, with a balsamic smell, and an aromatic and bitter taste.

(*a a*) *Opoponax* is obtained by puncturing the roots of the *Pastinaca opoponax*, a kind of parsnip, indigenous to Southern Europe. Except as a perfume, this gum is not now much used.

(*b b*) *Copaïba* (or *Copaïva*) is the volatile oil flowing from trees of the species *Copaifera* growing in tropical South America. It is principally used as a medicine.

APPENDIX B.

THE PRESERVATION OF THE INSTRUMENT.

MANY and various are the suggestions made to, and the duties imposed upon, amateurs, with a view to keeping their fiddles in good condition and playing order. Although it is certain that a violinist who does not take care of, and do everything conducive to the welfare of, his violin, can never expect to make a good performer, many of the operations set down in the books are ridiculous and unnecessary, such, for instance, as the practice recommended by Otto, of rubbing the strings from nut to bridge, with a piece of silk moistened with almond oil, before putting the instrument away, after playing on it, and rubbing them dry again with a linen rag before again using it. It is always hopeless to expect owners of new fiddles to pay that attention to bran new instruments that they bestow upon their already dilapidated and time-worn masterpieces of Cremona, partly because they do not consider them worth it, and partly because they like to see them looking old and service-marked. It would be a great boon to future generations if amateurs would preserve their new fiddles in all their pristine "spick and span" beauty, and this object may be obtained by following and adhering to the following rules.

The violin should, after being played on, be dusted free from all impurities and accumulated rosin dust, with a soft silk handkerchief, for rosin dust, if allowed to remain in a white layer, is apt to check the vibrations of the belly, to say nothing of its unsightly appearance. It should be then wrapped in a silk handkerchief, and laid in a baize or velvet-lined case, and not tied up in a bag, or hung on a nail, as is the fate of many fiddles, especially tenors, though there is no doubt about it, that if a new fiddle can always be kept lying out of the case in some safe place, in a well-ventilated and warm room, where it will not be knocked about or run a risk of draughts, it will mature and mellow very much quicker than if shut up from the first in a case. An additional protection is gained by a quilted satin " fiddle blanket " cut to fit the case, which " blanket " affords much scope for ingenuity and beauty of design in the embroidery work of our sisters and others (especially others). The case should not be set on the floor under a piano, as it usually is, because there is nearly always a draught along the floor, and the fiddle must *never*, if possible, be in a draught, but it must be put on a shelf or table three or four feet from the ground, in a *dry* warm place, and in fine weather (if practicable) the case should be left open, and the fiddle unwrapped for a few hours every day. This goes far towards mellowing the tone, and preserving the instrument. It must be remembered that the close, dried pores of an old violin are extremely susceptible to damp, for they open, and absorb the moisture of the atmosphere, and this has a tendency to loosen the joints by melting the glue.

The fiddle should not be subjected to sudden changes of temperature ; the tone of a delicate instrument may for a time be completely spoilt by carrying it through the open air to a concert room, by reason of the sudden contraction of the instrument from the cold and subsequent expansion from the heat of the room, which have the effect of throwing the instrument out of its harmonic equilibrium, and thus rendering the tone harsh. Again ; the pores of the wood being full of cold air, the sudden transition to a warm atmosphere turns this cold air into steam or perspiration, and, as a consequence, the strings (especially the D) lose their tone and become nazal. Periodically it is good to pour a handful of barley slightly warmed in at one of the *ff* holes, a process which cleans out the inside effectually, removing the coating of fine dust which would otherwise retard the thorough seasoning of the wood. The strings should always be kept stretched up to pitch : the practice observed by some players of relaxing the strings after playing (with a view to economy in the matter of strings) is absolute ruination to the instrument in the matter of tone, for the equilibrium being constantly disturbed, the fiddle never gets thoroughly settled and free in its vibrations.

In addition to this, you should watch your fiddle as if it were a delicate child—*i.e.*, whenever you play on it, you should look it over to see if anything is going wrong (*vide* p. 306). Never let a want of repair go on till it makes itself apparent in the tone; therefore, examine the bridge to see that it is quite perpendicular ; if not, press it forward or back as the case may require. See that the sound-post is also quite straight up, and that the neck ı not sunk forward a little, as it sometimes will when a new neck has been set on the instrument, or the fiddle has not long left the maker's hands. This will also sometimes happen when a fiddle is suddenly carried from a warm into a cold temperature, the glue being by this means loosened, as above mentioned. This becomes apparent by the strings appearing too high above the finger-board, and consequently an awkwardness being experienced when playing in the high shifts. When this happens, the only thing to do is to have a new neck put on by a good workman ; some players get over the difficulty by lowering the bridge, but this is always a dangerous and unsatisfactory expedient (*vide* p. 161). See that the belly has not become unglued on the left of the tail-piece, as is sometimes the case consequent upon the heat of the chin, or on the right of the shoulder, which sometimes results from a hot hand playing in the third and higher positions. By tapping the fiddle lightly round the edges, any contingency of this description becomes immediately apparent by the sound. If by any mischance the sound-post falls down, or the fiddle gets unglued at any of the blocks, relax all the strings at once ; it is better to put up with the temporary disturbance of the instrument thus occasioned, than to risk the deleterious strain otherwise put upon the belly.

I have said, never let a want of repair go too long, but, on the other hand, do not be too anxious to have your fiddle tinkered about; remember that as with the human subject amputation is the very last resort to be tried when all other remedies are hopeless, so with the fiddle. To take off the belly is a *most* serious thing, and to meddle with the bar, or scoop out the wood, worse still ; therefore, never suffer your fiddle to undergo these operations unless every other means has failed, never have the belly taken off except in the case of a bad crack, a loosening of a block (and even then it may be dispensed with sometimes [*vide*, p. 307]), or unless the obstinate ghastliness of the tone tells you there is some serious internal complaint torturing your darling. On the same principle, never shift about the bridge and sound-post yourself (irresistible as is the tendency to do so when the tone goes wrong) ; confide all such matters to some high-priest of the art of *lutherie*, whom you can trust with the well-being of your instrument.

By attending to these things a good fiddle can be kept in perfect order for an indefinite length of time. The above directions may seem to the reader to be unnecessarily minute and "faddy," but as a matter of fact, the points I have set down to be attended to ought not to require setting down at all, but are instinctively observed by any fiddler who really *worships* his fiddle as (alas !) a fiddler always does sooner or later. By attention to the above-mentioned particulars, your instrument is kept in good temper and tone, and you are saved the *awful* expense of first-class fiddle repairing.

APPENDIX C.

THE BIBLIOGRAPHY OF THE VIOLIN.

THE following catalogue of works on the violin cannot, I know, pretend to anything like *completeness*, but I think I am justified in saying that it is the largest list hitherto published, of works exclusively devoted to the history, theory, construction of, and miscellanea connected with, the Violin. It aims at being no more than a transcript of the catalogue of my violin-library, a library which, for some years past, I have grudged neither time nor expense to make as complete as possible, and I shall esteem it a great favour if any of my readers, who know of any works not included in the following list, will send me a note of their title, etc., so that I may, with this valuable help, still further complete this bibliography. I have arranged the titles in chronological order in preference to alphabetical, for I think the former is the more interesting arrangement for students of the literature of the violin, and I have placed the authors' names in an index of the names contained in this and the following appendices in front of the index to this volume, so that any author's work may be found at once, without necessarily knowing the date thereof, or searching through the whole list. So as further to aid my readers in their search, I have divided the principal countries from one another, a plan which unfortunately shows me my poverty as regards the violin-literature of some of the nations. I have been obliged, by want of space, to exclude magazine articles, extracts from other works, patent specifications, and many other matters connected with the violin which must necessarily have interested those whom such things concern: at some future date, however, I propose to embody all these in a complete analytical bibliography of the violin in the form of a separate volume. In the meantime, I present my readers with the following catalogue, which has been hitherto jealously guarded from prying eyes, and which comprises the titles of many works never before referred to in any work on the instrument.

ENGLISH WORKS

1. HAMILTON, *J. A.* Hamilton's Catechism for the Violin. London, n.d. : *R. Cocks & Co.* 12mo. The fifth edition appeared in 1848. The fifteenth edition (n.d.) has an appendix by John Bishop, and appeared about 1883.

2. FÉTIS, *François Joseph.* Biographical Notice of Nicolo Paganini. Followed by an analysis of his compositions, and preceded by a sketch of the history of the violin. Translated by Wellington Guernsey. London, n.d. : *Schott & Co.* 8vo. (*Vide* No. 26.)

3. ΜΟΥΣΙΚΗ-ΙΑΤΡΕΙΑ ; or a Fiddle the best Doctor. London, 1775 : *Kearsley.*
4. JOUSSE, *J* . Theory and Practice of the Violin. London, 1811.
5. MACDONALD, *John.* A Treatise Explanatory of the Principles constituting the Practice and Theory of the Violoncello. London, 1811. *Appendix* 1815. *Folio.*
6. ANONYMOUS. The Lay of the Poor Fiddler, a Parody on the Lay of the Last Minstrel. With notes and illustrations : by an admirer of Walter Scott. London, 1814 : *Crosby.* 8vo.
7. MACDONALD, *John.* A Treatise on the Harmonic System, arising from the vibrations of the aliquot divisions of strings, etc., etc. Giving an easy and familiar adaptation of the whole to the purposes of composition and of instrumental music, and more particularly to the practice of the violin, tenor, violoncello, and double-bass, on all the strings in every compass of these instruments by every practical mode of execution, etc. London, 1822. *Printed for the Author. Folio.*
8. IMBERT DE LAPHALÈQUE, G. Some Account of the Celebrated Violinist Nicolo Paganini. Translated from the French of *G. I. de L.*, with additional notes. London, 1830 : *Chappell, etc.* Large 8vo. (a translation of No. 83).
9. ANONYMOUS. Practical Rules for producing Harmonic Notes on the Violin, etc. Bury St. Edmund's and London, 1831 : *Cramer.*
10. OTTO, *Jacob Augustus.* Treatise on the Construction, Preservation, Repairs, and Improvement of the Violin, and all bow instruments, together with a Dissertation on the most Eminent Makers, pointing out the surest marks by which a genuine instrument may be distinguished. Translated from the German, with notes and additions by Thomas Fardeley, professor of languages, Leeds. London: *Longmans.* Leeds: *J. Cross,* 1833. Large 8vo. (vide No. 16, to which it is greatly inferior). (Translation of No. 130.)
11. DUBOURG, *George.* The Violin. Being an account of that leading instrument and its most eminent professors, from its earliest date to the present time, including hints to amateurs, anecdotes, etc. London, 1836 : *Hy. Colburn.* Small 8vo.
Second Edition. London, 1837 : *Hy. Colburn.* Small 8vo.
Third Edition. London, n.d. (1850): *R. Cocks.* Small 8vo.
Fourth Edition. Revised and considerably enlarged, 1852 : *R. Cocks.* 8vo.
Fifth Edition. Newly revised and enlarged by John Bishop, of Cheltenham, 1878 : *R. Cocks.* 8vo.
12. MACKINTOSH, . Remarks on the Construction of, and Materials employed in, the Manufacture of Violins. Dublin, 1837 : 8vo Pamphlet.
13. ANONYMOUS. The Handbook of the Violin, its Theory and

Practice. London, 1843: *H. G. Clarke.* Small 16mo Pamphlet.

14. ANONYMOUS. Handbook of the Violin. London, 1845: *Whit-taker.* Small 16mo Pamphlet.

15. JAMES, *E* . Camillo Sivori. A Sketch of his Life, Talent, Travels, and Successes. London, 1845: *P. Rolandi.* Large 8vo Pamphlet.

16. OTTO, *Jacob Augustus.* A Treatise on the Structure and Preservation of the Violin and all other Bow Instruments. Together with an account of the most celebrated makers, and of the genuine characteristics of their instruments. Translated from the original, with additions and illustrations by John Bishop, of Cheltenham. London, 1848: *R. Cocks & Co.* Large 8vo.
   Second Edition, 1860; *Larger* or *Third Edition,* 1875: *R. Cocks & Co.* Small 8vo (translation of No. 130).

17. PAINE, *John.* A Treatise on the Violin. Showing how to ascertain the true degrees of time, and an exact method of bowing, exemplified by various examples in each degree; likewise the easiest method of keeping correctly in tune, with directions in shifting and transposition; interspersed with entertaining poetry and anecdotes in a dialogue between a master and his pupil. London, n.d. *Published for the Author.* Three or four editions prior to 1850. 8vo.

18. PURDY, *George.* A Few Words on the Violin. Being the result of thirty years' experience as a teacher of that instrument. London, 1858: *W. G. Goulbourn, imp.* 8vo.

19. SANDYS, *William,* and FORSTER, *Simon Andrew.* The History of the Violin and other Instruments played on with the Bow, from the remotest times to the present. Also an account of the principal makers, English and Foreign, with numerous illustrations. London, 1864: *J. R. Smith, Addison & Lucas.* Large 8vo.

20. FÉTIS, *François Joseph.* Notice of Anthony Stradivari the celebrated Violin-maker, known by the name of Stradivarius. Preceded by Historical and Critical Researches on the Origin and Transformations of Bow Instruments, and followed by a Theoretical Analysis of the Bow, and remarks on Francis Tourte, the author of its final improvements, by F. J. Fétis, etc. Translated (with the permission of the author) by John Bishop, of Cheltenham. London, 1864: *R. Cocks.* Large 8vo (translation of No. 95).

21. PEARCE, *Joseph, jun.* Violins and Violin-makers. Biographcial dictionary of the great Italian artistes, their followers and imitators to the present time, with essays on important subjects connected with the violin. London, 1866: *Long-mans.* Sheffield: *J. Pearce.* 8vo.

22. ADYE, *Willet.* Musical Notes. I. The Great Composers. II

Violinists and the Violin. III. The Violin and its History. London, 1869 : *R. Bentley.* 8vo.

23. **Davidson,** *Peter.* The Violin. A concise exposition of the general principles of construction, theoretically and practically treated, including the important researches of Savart and an epitome of the lives of the most eminent Artists, and an alphabetical list of violin-makers. Illustrated with lithographic vignette, and numerous woodcuts. Glasgow : *Porteous.* London : *Pitman.* Edinburgh, Aberdeen, etc., 1871. Small 8vo.

Second Edition (?).

Third Edition (?).

Fourth Edition. The Violin. Its construction theoretically and practically treated, etc., etc. London : *F. Pitman.* Edinburgh, Glasgow, Dundee, 1881. Small 8vo.

24. **Reade,** *Charles.* A Lost Art Revived. Cremona Violins and Varnish. Four letters descriptive of those exhibited in 1873 (*sic*, should be 1872) at the South Kensington Museum, also giving the data for producing the true varnishes used by the great Cremona makers. Reprinted from the *Pall Mall Gazette* by George H. M. Muntz, Birchfield. Gloucester, 1873 : *John Bellows.* Large 8vo Pamphlet.

25. **Barnard,** *Charles.* Camilla, a Tale of a Violin. Being the artist life of Camilla Urso. Boston, U.S.A., n.d. (1874): *Loring.* 8vo.

26. **Fétis,** *François Joseph.* Biographical Notice of Nicolo Paganini. With an analysis of his compositions and a sketch of the history of the violin by F. J. Fétis. With portrait and wood engravings. London, *Second Edition* of No. 2, n.d. (1876): *Schott & Co.* 8vo (translation of No. 90).

27. **Goffrie,** *Charles.* The Violin. A condensed history of the violin, its perfection and its famous makers. Importance of bridge and sound-post arrangement. Philadelphia, U.S.A., 1876 : *G. André & Co.* 8vo Pamphlet.

27a. **Smith, H. P.** The Construction of the Violin. Gives full and complete Directions, by the aid of which any Amateur Mechanic can construct a perfect Violin. Syracuse, U.S.A., n.d. (1877): *J. Roblee.*

28. **Schebek,** *Dr. Edmund.* The Violin Manufacture in Italy and its German Origin. An historical sketch. Translated from the German by Walter E. Lawson. Reprinted from *The Musical Standard.* London, 1877 : *W. Reeves.* Large 8vo Pamphlet (translation of No. 145).

29. **Phipson,** *Dr. Thomas Lamb.* Biographical Sketches and Anecdotes of Celebrated Violinists. London, 1877 : *R. Bentley.* 8vo.

30. [**Fothergill,** *Jessie.*] The First Violin. A novel. London, 1878 : *R. Bentley.* 3 vols., 8vo.

31. **Frederic,** *Henrietta.* The Enchanted Violin. A comedy in two acts, for male characters. London, 1879 : *Washbourne.*

32. BROADHOUSE, *John.* Facts about Fiddles. Violins old and new. Reprinted from *The Musical Standard.* London, n.d. (1879): *W. Reeves.* 8vo Pamphlet.
Second Edition, enlarged, n.d. (1882), *ib.*

33. PORTER, *Thomas.* How to Choose a Violin. With directions for keeping the instrument in order and for repairing and improving faulty instruments. London, n.d. (1879): *F. Pitman.* 8vo Pamphlet.

34. COURVOISIER, *Karl.* The Technics of Violin-playing. Edited and translated by H. E. Krehbiel, of the Cincinnati College. London, n.d. (1880): *W. Reeves.* 8vo (translation of No. 149 ; *vide also* No. 144).

35. ANONYMOUS. The Singular Life and Surprising Adventures of Joseph Thompson, known by the name of Fiddler Thompson, of Halifax, etc. Wakefield, n.d. (1880): *W. Nicholson.* 16mo (*vide* note ², p. 12).

36. ANONYMOUS. The Blind Fiddler. By the author of Wee Hunchie, etc. Edinburgh, n.d. (1880): *Religious Tract Society of Scotland.* 12mo.

37. THOMAS, *Bertha.* The Violin Player. A Novel. London, 1880: *R. Bentley.* 3 vols., 8vo.

38. [NICHOLSON, *J.*] Designs and Plans for the Construction and Arrangement of the New Model Violin. London, 1880: *H. K. Lewis, imp.* Large folio.

39. HART, *George.* The Violin, its Famous Makers and their Imitators. With numerous wood engravings from photographs of the works of Stradivarius, Guarnerius, Amati, and others. London, 1875: *Dulau & Schott.* Large post 4to, small post 8vo, pp. xxiv. and 352.
Second Edition, greatly enlarged, 1884.
Popular Edition, 1880, pp. vi. and 310.

40. GEMÜNDER, *George.* George Gemünder's Progress in Violin-Making. With interesting facts concerning the art and its critics in general. Astoria, New York, 1881. *Published by the Author.* 8vo.

41. [HONEYMAN, *W.*] The Violin: How to Master it. By a professional player. Editor of *Köhler's Repository.* Edinburgh: *E.Köhler.* London, *Jarrold,* n.d. (1881). 8vo. Six or seven editions already published.

42. HART, *George.* The Violin and its Music. With several engraved portraits on steel of eminent violinists, whose style both in playing and in composition may be regarded as representative. London, 1881 : *Dulau & Schott.* Large post 4to, small post 8vo.

43. MITCHELL, *C   H   .* How to Hold a Violin and Bow. With instructions in bowing. London, *First Edition,* 18—; *Second Edition,* 1882: *F. Pitman.* 8vo Pamphlet.

44. READE, *Charles.* Jack of all Trades. A matter of fact romance.

London, 1882: *Chatto & Windus.* (The biography of J. F. Lott; *vide* page 84.)

45. HERON-ALLEN, *Edward.* Opuscula Fidicularum. No. 1. The Ancestry of the Violin. Being a discourse delivered at the Freemasons' Tavern, on Friday, June 2nd, 1882, to the Sette of Odd Volumes. Part I. The Origin of the Violin. Part II. The Welsh Crwth. London, 1882. Printed for the Author by *Mitchell & Hughes.* 8vo Pamphlet (*vide* note [1], p. 29, and note [1], p. 67).

46. CHANOT, *Georges.* Hodges *v.* Chanot. Criticisms and Remarks on the Great Violin Case, March 1882. London, 1882: *Mitchell & Hughes.* Large 8vo Pamphlet.

47. ENGEL, *Carl.* Researches into the Early History of the Violin Family. London, 1883: *Novello, Ewer, & Co.* 8vo (*vide* note [1], p. 67).

48. FLEMING, *James M* . Old Violins and their Makers. Including some references to those of modern times, with facsimiles of tickets, sound-holes, etc. London, 1883. *L. Upcott Gill.*

49. HERON-ALLEN, *Edward.* De Fidiculis Opusculum II. Hodges against Chanot. Being the history of a celebrated case, collected from the newspapers and from personal observation and annotated. Part I. Biographical. Part II. The Cause of Action. Part III. The Trial. Part IV. The Opinions of the Press. London, 1883. Printed for the Author by *Mitchell & Hughes.* 8vo Pamphlet.

50. FERRIS, *George J.* Sketches of Great Pianists and Great Violinists, Biographical and Anecdotal, with account of the Violin and Early Violinists. London, 1884: *W. Reeves.* 8vo.

Note.—I have headed the above list with two works (Nos. 1 and 2) whose dates of publication I have not been able to ascertain. Nos. 3, 6, 30, 31, 35, 36, 37, and 44 I have inserted (though unconnected with the history, theory, or practice of the violin), as likely to be of interest to those sufficiently concerned with the instrument to make them take an interest in any literature of the violin. In excluding all mere instruction books I doubted for some time whether to insert the works of Christopher Simpson: (i) "The Division Violist; or, an Introduction to the Playing upon a Ground" (London, 1659: *W. Godbid,* folio), and (ii) "The Division Viol; or, the Art of Playing *extempore* upon a Ground" (London, 1667: *H. Brome,* folio); so I have compromised by noting them here. Having mentioned Charles Reade's "Jack of all Trades" (No. 44) I ought, perhaps, to have noted the anonymous novel "Charles Auchester" (London, 1879: *Chapman & Hall*), which is said to be a biography of Herr Joachim, all the characters in the book being intended to represent well-known musical celebrities (Mendelssohn, Sterndale-Bennett, Sainton, Moscheles, Ferd. David, etc.), though the portraits are somewhat indistinct.

ITALIAN WORKS.

50A. ZANNETTI, *Gasparo.* Il Scolaro, di G. Z. per imperare a suonare di violino ed altri stromenti. Milan, 1645.

51. FANZAGO, *Francesco.* Orazione del Signor Abate Francesco Fanzago, Padovano, delle lodi di Giuseppe Tartini, Recitata nella Chiesa de' R.R. Serviti in Padova li 31 di Marzo l'anno 1770. Con varie note, illustrata, e con un breve Compendio della Vita del Medesimo. Padua, 1770: *Conzatti.* 4to.

52. TARTINI, *Giuseppe.* Lettera del defonto Signor Giuseppe Tartini alla Signora Maddalena Lombardini inserviente ad una importante lezione per i Suonatori di Violino. Londra, 1771. *Second (translation) Title.* A letter from the late Signor Tartini to Signora Maddalena Lombardini (now Signora Sirmen), published as an important lesson to performers on the violin, translated by Dr. Burney. London, 1771 : *R. Bremner. Second Edition,* do., 1779. Large 8vo (*vide* No. 126).

53. BAGATELLA, *Antonio.* Regole per la Costruzione de' Violini, Viole, Violoncelli, et Violoni. Memoria presentata all' Accademia di Scienzi, Lettere, ed Arti di Padova, al Concorso del premio dell' Arti dell' anno MDCCLXXXII. Padova, 1786 : *A spese dell' Accademia.* 8vo (*vide* No. 128).

54. [THURN AND TAXIS, *Prince of.*] Risposta di un animo al celebre Signor Rousseau circa il suo sentimento in proposito d'alcune proposizioni del Sig. G. Tartini. Venice, 1789. 8vo Pamphlet.

55. RANGONI, *Giovanni Battista.* Essai sur le goût de la Musique avec le caractère des trois célèbres joueurs de Violon, Messieurs Nardini, Lolli, et Pugnani. Livourne, 1790 : *T. Masi.* In French and Italian. *Second Title:* Saggio sul gusto della Musica col carattere di tre celebri sonatori di Violino, i signori Nardini, Lolli, e Pugnani. Livorno, 1790 : *T. Masi.*

56. VALLOTTI, *Francesco Antonio.* Elogi di Giuseppe Tartini, primo Violonista nella Capella del' Santo di Padova. Padua, 1792 : *Conzatti.* 12mo.

57. LEONI DI PIENZA, *A Raimondo.* Elogio di Pietro Nardini, celebratissimo professore di Violini. Florence, 1793 : *Cambiagi.* 8vo.

58. ANTOLINI, *Francesco.* Osservazzioni su due Violini esposti nelle sale dell' I. R. Palazzo di Brera uno de' quali di forma non communa. Milan, 1832 : *L. di G. Perola.* 8vo Pamphlet.

59. PANCALDI, *Carlo.* Progresso Italiano nella Costruzione del Violino operato da Antonio Gibertini da Parma, Cenno Artistico. Palermo, 1845 : *Tipografia Maddalena.* Small 8vo Pamphlet.

60. CONESTABILE, *Giancarlo.* Vita di Nicolo Paganini da Genova, Scritta ed Illustrata di *G. C.* Perugia, 1851: *V. Bartelli.* 8vo.

61. REGLI, *Francesco.* Storia del Violino in Piemonte, intitolata A. S. M. Vittorio Emanuele II., Re d'Italia. Turin, 1863: *Enrico Dalmazzo.* Large 8vo.

62. LOMBARDINI, *Paolo.* Cenni sulla celebre scuola Cremonese degli stromenti ad arco, non che sui lavori e sulla famiglia del sommo Antonio Stradivari. Cremona, 1872 : *Tipografia dalla Noce.* Large 8vo.

63. RINALDI, *Benedetto-Gioffredo.* Classica Fabbricazione di Violini in Piemonte. Turin, 1873 : *Rinaldi.* Large 8vo Pamphlet.

64. VALDRIGHI, *Luigi Francesco.* D'un arpa e di un Violino e Violoncello intagliati da D. Galli. (Museo Estense.) Modena, 1878 ; *Tip Moneti e Mamias.* 8vo.

65. VALDRIGHI, *Luigi Francesco.* Liuteria Modenese antica e moderna con Catalogo di Liutari. Modena, 1878 : *Toschi.* 8vo.

66. CONSILI, *D* . Il Poggia-Violino, invenzione meccanica brevettata applicata al Violino : brevi cenni sulla utilitata di essa sotto il rapporto del arte in Italiano e Tedesco. Bologna, 1879 : *Tip. soc. Azzoquidi.* Large 8vo. - Three pamphlets of 12 pp. each, bound together, one in Italian, one in French, and one in German.

67. VALDRIGHI, *Luigi Francesco.* Musurgiana No. 4. Il Violoncellista Tonelli e suor' Maria Illuminata corista ed organista delle clarisse di carpi nel Secolo XVIII. Modena, 1880 : *G. T. Vincenzi e Nep.* Large 8vo Pamphlet.

68. VALDRIGHI, *Luigi Francesco.* Musurgiana No. 9. Strumenti ad arco Rinforzati. Modena, 1881 : *Tipografia Legale,* Large 8vo Pamphlet.

69. WALDEN, *E. Dworzak von.* Il Violino ossia Analisi del suo Meccanismo. Naples, 1883 : *F. Furcheim.*

69A. VALDRIGHI, *Luigi Francesco.* Nomocheliurgografia, antica e moderna ossia elenco di Fabbricatori di Strumenti armonici, etc. Modena, 1884 : *Società Tipografia.*

Note.—It is a fact not without a certain significance that so few books should have reached this country from that to which the instrument owes its invention and highest development. It may be that I am particularly poor in the Italian literature of the subject.

FRENCH WORKS.

70. ROUSSEAU, *Jean.* Traité de la Viole qui contient, Une Dissertation Curieuse sur son origine, Une Démonstration générale de son Manche, etc. Paris, 1687 : *Chr. Ballard.* 8vo.

71. LEBLANC, *Hubert.* Défense de la basse de Viole contre les Entreprises du Violon et les pretensions du Violoncelle. Amsterdam, 1740 : *P. Mortier.* 16mo.

72. TERRASSON, *A* . Dissertation Historique sur la Vielle. Paris, 1741.

73. DOMENJOUD, *Jean Baptiste.* De la préférence des vis aux chevilles pour les instruments de musique ; et un essai sur la manière de changer l'A-mi-la en tendant ou détendant toutes les cordes à la fois sans détruire l'harmonie ; ce qui donne lieu à des manches d'une forme nouvelle, beaucoup plus commodes que les anciens. Paris, 1757 : *Thiboust.* 8vo.

74. BRIJON, *E   R   .* Réflexions sur la musique et la vraie manière de l'exécuter sur le Violon. Paris, 1763. 4to

75. LECLAIR, *Jean Marie.* Tablature idéale du Violon, jugée par feu M. le Clair l'aîné être la véritable. Paris, 1766. 8vo.

76. EYMAR, *A   M   .* Anecdotes sur Viotti; précédé de quelques réflexions sur l'expression en musique. ' Milan, n.d. (1801) : *Zeno.* 8vo.

77. BAUD,   et GOSSEC, *François Joseph.* Observations sur les cordes à instruments de musique tant de Boyau que de Soie, suivi d'une lettre du citoyen Gossec au citoyen Baud, du rapport du citoyen Gossec à l'Institut National sur les cordes de soie du citoyen Baud, et de l'extrait du procès-verbal de l'Institut National relatif à ce rapport. Versailles, 1803 *P. D. Pierres.* 8vo.

78. SIBIRE, *L'Abbé.* La Chelonomie, ou le Parfait Luthier. Paris, 1806. *chez l'Auteur* et *Millet.* 8vo. *Second Edition.* Brussels, 1823 : *Weissenbruch.* 8vo.

79. FAYOLLE, *François.* Notices sur Corelli, Tartini, Pugnani, Gavinies, et Viotti. Paris, 1810. *E. Dentu.* 12mo (*vide* No. 152).

80. CHANOT, *François.* Institut de France. Académie Royale des Beaux Arts. Rapport fait à l'Académie des Beaux Arts dans la Séance du 3 Avril 1819 au nom de la Section de Musique sur les nouveaux instruments de musique (violons, altos, violoncelles et contre-basses), suivant la facture brevetée de *M. Chanot,* Officier au Corps du Génie maritime, inséré au Moniteur. Paris, 1819. 4to, 4 pp.

81. SAVART, *Félix.* Mémoire sur la Construction des Instruments à Cordes et à Archet. Suivi du Rapport qui en a été fait aux deux Académies des Sciences et des Beaux Arts. Paris, n.d. (1819) : *Roret.* 8vo.

82. BAILLOT, *Pierre François Marie de Sales.* Notice sur J. B. Viotti, né en 1775 à Fontanetto en Piémont, mort à Londres le 3 Mars, 1824. Paris, 1825. 8vo.

83. IMBERT DE LAPHALÉQUE, *G   .* Notice sur le célèbre Violoniste N. Paganini. Paris, 1830: *Guyot.* 8vo (*vide* No. 8).

84. FAYOLLE, *François.* Paganini et Beriot; ou Avis aux Jeunes Artistes qui se destinent à l'enseignement du Violon. Paris, 1831 : *M. Legouest.* 8vo Pamphlet.

85. ANDERS, *G   E   .* Nicolo Paganini, sa Vie, sa Personne; et quelques mots sur son secret. Paris, 1831 : *Delaunay.* 12mo.

86 MAUGIN, *J   C   .* Manuel du Luthier, contenant 1° la construction intérieure et extérieure des Instruments à archet, tels que Violons, Altos, Basses et Contrebasses; 2° la construction de la guitarre; 5° (*sic*) la confection de l'Archet. Ouvrage orné de figures. Paris, 1834 : *Roret.* 12mo.

87. DESMARAIS, *Cyprien*. Archéologie du Violon. Déscription d'un Violon Historique et Monumental. Paris, 1836 : *Dentu & Sapia*. Large 8vo Pamphlet.

88. ST. GEORGE and LEUVEN, *H* . Le Luthier de Vienne, opéra comique en 1 acte. Paris, 1836.

89. DELHASSE, *Félix Joseph*. Henri Vieuxtemps. Erratum de la "Biographie Universelle des Musiciens" par M. Fétis. Brussels, 1844 : *Wouters*. Large 8vo Pamphlet.

90. FÉTIS, *François Joseph*. Notice Biographique sur Nicolo Paganini, suivi de l'Analyse de ses Ouvrages et précédé d'une esquisse de l'histoire du Violon. Paris, 1851 : *Schœnenberger*. Large 8vo (*vide* Nos. 2 and 26).

91. BENEDIT, *G* . C. Sivori. Extrait du *Sémaphore* du 7 Mars, 1854. Marseilles, 1854 : *Barlatier-Feissat*. Large 8vo Pamphlet.

92. MIEL, *Edmd. François Antoine Marie*. Notice Historique sur J. B. Viotti. (Extrait de la Biographie Universelle de M. F. J. Fétis, T. II., p. 49). Paris, 1856 : *Everat*.

93. FOURGEAUD, *Alexandre*. Les Violons de Dalayrac. Paris, 1856 : *J. Leclerc*. Large 8vo Pamphlet.

94. [YOUSSOUPOW (*or* JOUSOUPOF), *Prince.*] Luthomonographie Historique et Raisonnée. Essai sur l'Histoire du Violon et sur les ouvrages des Anciens Luthiers Célèbres du temps de la Renaissance, par un Amateur. Frankfort S/M., 1856 : *Ch. Jugel*. Large 8vo.

95. FÉTIS, *François Joseph*. Antoine Stradivari. Luthier Célèbre, connu sous le nom de Stradivarius, précédé de Recherches Historiques et Critiques sur l'origine et les transformations des Instruments à archet, et suivi d'Analyses Théoriques sur l'Archet et sur François Tourte, Auteur de ses derniers perfectionnements. Paris, 1856 ; *Vuillaume*. Large 8vo (*vide* No. 20).

96. DESFOSSEZ, *A* . Henri Wieniawski. I. Education. II. Premières tournées artistiques en Russie, en Allemagne, en Belgique, et en Hollande. III. Parallèle entre Paganini et Wieniawski. IV. Conclusion, le Passé, le Présent, et l'Avenir. Esquisse. La Haye, 1856 : *Belinfante*. Large 8vo Pamphlet.

97. MAILAND, *Eugène*. Bibliothèque des Professions Industrielles et Agricoles. Série G., No. 17. Découverte des Anciens Vernis Italiens, employés pour les instruments à Cordes et à Archet. Paris, 1859 : *E. Lacroix*. 8vo.
Second Edition. Paris, 1874 : *E. Lacroix*. 8vo.

98. SAUZAY, *Eugène*. À Monsieur Ingres. Haydn, Mozart, Beethoven, Étude sur le Quatuor. Paris, 1861 : *chez l'Auteur*. Large 8vo.

99. BURBURE, *Léon de*. Recherches sur les Factures de Clavecins et les Luthiers d'Anvers depuis le XVI⁰ siècle jusqu'au XIX⁰. Paris, 1863. 8vo.

100. THOINAN, *Ernest* (pseudonym of *Antoine Ernest* ROQUET). Maugars, Célèbre Joueur de Viole, musicien du Cardinal Richelieu, etc. Sa biographie suivie de sa réponse faite à un curieux sur le sentiment de la musique d'Italie. Paris, 1865 : *Claudin.* Square 8vo.

101. GALLAY, *Jules.* Les Instruments à Archet à l'Exposition Universelle de 1867. Paris, 1867 : *Jouaust.* 8vo.

102. RENIER, *J   S   .* L'Enfance de Vieuxtemps. (Extrait de l'Annuaire de la Société libre d'émulation de Liége). Liége, 1867. One leaf, small 8vo.

103. BOISTEL,   . Société de Statistiques des Sciences et des Arts de Grénoble. Rapport sur le Vernis inventé par M. Victor Grivel. Grénoble, 1867 : *F. Allier.* 8vo.

104. GRIVEL, *Victor.* Vernis des Anciens Luthiers d'Italie, perdu depuis le milieu du XVIIIe siècle, retrouvé par V. Grivel, Artiste à Grénoble. Grénoble, 1867 ; *F. Allier.* 8vo.

105. RICHELME, *Marius.* Études et Observations sur la Lutherie Ancienne et Moderne. Marseilles, 1868 : *F. Canquoin.* 8vo.

106. MAUGIN, *J   C*   et MAIGNE, *W*   . Nouveau Manuel Complet du Luthier. Contenant la construction intérieure et extérieure des instruments à archet, tels que le Violon, l'Alto, la Basse et la Contre-basse, ainsi que celle de la Guitare ; et traitant de la fabrication des Cordes Harmoniques employées par le luthier et de la fabrication des diverses cordes dites à boyaux, employées dans l'Industrie. Ouvrage accompagné de Planches. Paris, 1869 : *Roret.* 12mo. *Second Edition* of No. 86.

107. GALLAY, *Jules.* Les Luthiers Italiens aux XVIIe et XVIIIe siècles. Nouvelle édition du Parfait Luthier de l'Abbé Sibire, suivie de Notes sur les Maîtres des Diverses Écoles. Paris, 1869 : *Académie des Bibliophiles* (*vide* No. 78).

108. GALLAY, *Jules.* Les Instruments des Écoles Italiennes. Catalogue précédé d'une Introduction et suivi de notes sur les principaux maîtres. Paris, 1872 : *Gand et Bernardel.* 8vo.

109. BAILLOT, *Pierre Marie François de Sales.* Observations relatives aux Concours de Violon du Conservatoire de Musique. Oeuvre Posthume. Paris, 1872 : *Firmin Didot.* 8vo.

110. POUGIN, *Arthur.* Notice sur Rode, Violoniste Français. Paris, 1874 : *Pottier de Laleine.*

111. BENTZON, *Théodore.* Le Violon de Job. Paris, 1875 : M. Lévy. 8vo.

112. PLASSIARD, *J   A   .* Des Cordes du Violon. Lille, 1876 : *Danel.*

113. VIDAL, *Antoine.* Les Instruments à Archet, les Faiseurs, les Joueurs d'Instruments, leur Histoire sur le Continent Européen. Suivi d'un Catalogue générale de la Musique de Chambre. Orné de planches gravées à l'eau forte par Frédéric Hillemacher. Paris, 1876 · *J. Claye.* 3 vols., 4to. Édition de Luxe.

114. FLEURY, *Jules* (CHAMPFLEURY). Le Violcn de Faïence. Dessins en couleur par M. Émile Renard de la manufacture de Sèvres, eaux-fortes, par M. J. Adeline. Paris, 1877: *E. Dentu.* 8vo. Édition de Grand Luxe.

115. FANART, *L   S*   . Rapport lu à l'Académie Nationale de Reims dans sa séance publique du 3 Août, 1876, sur les Violons de M. Émile Menesson, Luthier à Reims. Reims, 1877; *Second Edition, Gepy.*

116. VIDAL, *Antoine.* Les Vielles Corporations de Paris. La Chapelle St. Julien des Menestriers et les Menestriers de Paris. Paris, 1878: *Quantin.* 4to. (A reprint of Chaps. I.-VI. of Part II. of No. 113, *i.e.*, Vol. I., p. 289 to end, and Vol. II., pp. 1-51, with Plates 47, 49, 50, 52, 53. 55).

117. THOINAN, *Ernest* (vide No. 100). Louis Constantin, Roi des Violons, avec un fac-simile de brevet de maître joueur d'instruments de la Ville de Paris. Paris, 1878: *Baur.*

118. PLASSIARD, *J   A*   . Des Cordes Harmoniques en général et spécialement de celles des instruments à Archet. Paris, 1880: *Thibouville-Lamy.* Mirecourt, 1880: *Chassel.* 8vo.

119. HUET, *Félix.* Étude sur les différentes Écoles de Violon depuis Corelli jusqu'à Baillot. Précédée d'un examen sur l'art de jouer des instruments à archet au XVIIe siècle. Chalons-sur-Marne, 1880: *F. Thouille.* Large 8vo.

120. GRÉVILLE, *Henry.* Un Violon Russe. 2 vols. Paris, 1880, *Tenth Edition*: *E. Plon.* 8vo.

121. CORMON, ——, and GRANGÉ, *E*   . Le Violon de Père Dimanche. Pièce en trois actes, etc. Représentée pour la première fois à Paris sur le Théâtre des Folies Dramatiques le 31 Octobre, 1854. Paris, 1881: *Tresse.* Large 8vo.

122. COPPÉE, *François.* Le Luthier de Cremone. With explanatory Notes, Historical, Biographical, etc., by Alphonse Mariette. London, 1880: *Dulau & Co.* 12mo.

123. SIMOUTRE, *N   E*   . Aux Amateurs du Violon. Historique, Construction, Réparation et Conservation de cet Instrument. Bâle, 1883: *G. A. Bonfantini.* 8vo.

Note.—No. 70 is the oldest work on bow instruments known, and like No. 71 is of very great rarity ; Nos. 88, 121 and 122 being dramatic works, and Nos. 93, 111, 114, and 120 being romances have, perhaps, ɪ ɔ serious place in this bibliography, but I insert them as likely to be of interest to my readers.

GERMAN WORKS.

124. REICHARDT, *Johann Friedrich.* Ueber die Pflichten des Ripien-Violinisten. Berlin und Leipzig, 1776: *G. J. Decker.*

125. [TAUBER, *Carl von.*] Ueber meine Violine (a poem). Vienna, 1780: *J. Edlin.*

126. TARTINI, *Giuseppe.* Brief an Magdalen Lombardini. Hanover, 1786. (*Vide* No. 52.)

127. HILLER, *Johann Adam.* Anweisung zum Violinspielen für Schulen und zum Selbstunterrichte, etc. Leipzig, n.d. (1792) : *Breitkopf und Härtel.*

128. BAGATELLA, *Antonio.* Ueber den Bau der Violine, Bratsche, Violoncell, und Violons. Translation of No, 53 by J. O. H. Schaum. Leipzig, n.d. (1806) : *Kuhnel.* 8vo.

129. OTTO, *Jacob Augustus.* Ueber den Bau und die Erhaltung der Geige und aller Bogeninstrumente. Nebst einer Uebersicht der vorzüglichsten Künstler und der sichersten Kennzeichen ihrer Arbeiten. Halle und Leipzig, 1817. 8vo.

130. OTTO, *Jacob Augustus.* Ueber den Bau der Bogeninstrumente und über die Arbeiten der vorzüglicnsten Instrumentenmacher, zur Belehrung für Musiker. Nebst Andeutung zur Erhaltung der Violine in gutem Zustande. Jena, 1828 : *Bran. Second Edition of* No. 129.

131. WETTENGEL, *Gustav Adolph.* Neuer Schauplatz der Künste und Handwerke: Band 37. Vollständiges theoretisch-praktisches, auf dem Grundsatze der Akustik begründetes, etc., Lehrbuch der Anfertigung und Reparatur aller noch jetzt gebräuchlichen Gattungen von italienischen und deutschen Geigen, etc. Mit sechzehn lithographirten Tafeln. Ilmenau, 1828 : *B. F. Voigt.* (*Vide* No. 142.)

132. HARRYS, *Georg.* Paganini in seinem Reisewagen und Zimmer, in seinen redseligen Stunden, in gesellschaftlichen Zirkeln, und seinen Concerten. Aus dem Reisejournal von *G. H.* Brunswick, 1830 : *F. Vieweg.* 12mo.

133. SCHÜTZ, *Friedrich Carl Julius.* Leben, Charakter, und Kunst N. Paganini's, eine Skizze. Ilmenau, 1830 : *Voigt.* 8vo.

134. SCHOTTKY, *Julius Max.* Paganini's Leben and Treiben als Künstler und als Mensch, mit unpartheiischer Berücksichtigung der Meinungen seiner Anhänger und Gegner. Prag, 1830 : *J. G. Calve.* 8vo.

135. VINELA, *Ludolf.* Paganini's Leben und Charakter nach Schottky dargestellt. Hamburg, n.d. 8vo. (A condensation of No. 134.)

136. BACHMANN, *Otto.* Theoretisch - praktisches Handbuch des Geigenbaues, oder Anweisung italienische, und deutsche Violinen, Bratschen, Violoncellos, Violons zu verfertigen, . . . etc., für Geigenmacher und alle diejenigen, welche das Geschäft derselben erlernen wollen. Mit 4 Tafeln Abbildungen. Quedlinburg und Leipzig, 1835 : *G. Basse.*

137. BIOW, *Henri.* Ole Bull, eine biographische Skizze. Hamburg, 1838 : *J. O. S. Witt.*

138. SPOHR, *Louis.* Louis Spohr's Selbstbiographie. Cassel und Göttingen, 1860 : *H. Wiegand & Co.* 8vo.

139. ABELE, *Hyacinth.* Die Violine. Ihre Geschichte und ihr Bau.

Nach Quellen dargestellt (Mit lithographirten Abbildungen
und einer musikalischen Beilage). Neuberg, A/D., 1864 :
A. Prechter. Small 8vo.
Zweite vermehrte und verbesserte Auflage. *Ib.* 1874 : *ib.* 8vo.

140. SCHUBERT, *F   L*   . Die Violine. Ihr Wesen, ihre
Bedeutung und Behandlung als Solo- und Orchester-
Instrument. Leipzig, 1865 : *Merseburger.* 8vo.

141. DIEHL, *Nicolaus Louis.* Die Geigenmacher der Alten Italieni-
schen Schule. Eine Uebersicht aller bekannten italienischen
Geigenmacher der alten Schule, Charakteristic ihrer
Arbeiten, getreue Abbildungen von den hervorragendsten
unter ihnen gebrauchten Zetteln in den Instrumenten, nebst
einer vorausgehenden Abhandlung über den Ursprung der
Geige. Hamburg, *First Edition* [?] ; *Second Edition,* 1866 ;
Third Edition, 1877. *J. F. Richter,* 12mo.

142. WETTENGEL, *Gustav Adolph.* G. A. W.'s, weil Violinbogen-
machers zu Markneukirchen, Lehrbuch der Geigen- und
Bogenmacherkunst ; oder theoretisch-praktische Anweisung
zur Anfertigung und Reparatur der verschiedenen Arten
Geigen und Bogen, etc. Mit einem Atlas enthaltend 10
Folio Tafeln. Weimar, 1869 : *B. F. Voigt.* (New Edition
of No. 131.)

143. WASIELEWSKI, *Joseph Wilhelm von.* Die Violine und ihre
Meister. Leipzig, 1869 : *Breitkopf und Härtel.* Large
8vo. *Second Edition, ib.,* 1883.

144. COURVOISIER, *Carl.* Die Grundlage der Violin-Technik. Frankfort, S/M., 1873. 8vo (*vide* No. 34).

145. SCHEBEK, *Dr. Edmund.* Der Geigenbau in Italien und sein
deutscher Ursprung. Eine historische Skizze. Prag, 1874 :
Bohemia-Actien-Gesellschaft. Large 8vo (*vide* No. 28).

146. WASIELEWSKI, *Joseph Wilhelm von.* Die Violine im XVII.
Jahrhundert und die Anfänge der Instrumentalcomposi
tion. Bonn, 1874 : *M. Cohen.* 8vo.

147. RITTER, *Hermann.* Die Viola Alta. Ihre Geschichte, ihre
Bedeutung und die Principien ihres Baues. Heidelberg,
1876 : *G. Weiss.* 4to.
Second Edition. Die Geschichte der Viola Alta und die Grundsätze ihres Baues. Zweite vermehrte und verbesserte
Auflage. Mit 5 in den Text gedruckten und 2 Tafeln Abbildungen. Leipzig, 1877 : *J. J. Weber.* 8vo (*vide* No. 150).

147a. NIEDERHEITMANN, *Friedrich.* Die Meister der Geigenbaukunst
in Italien und Tyrol. Vienna,: *F. Schreiber.* Hamburg :
Aug. Cranz., 1876. 12mo.

148. NIEDERHEITMANN, *Friedrich.* Cremona. Eine Charakteristik der
Italienischen Geigenbauer und ihrer Instrumente. Leipzig, 1877 : *Carl Merseburger.* 8vo.

149. COURVOISIER, *Carl.* Die Violin-technik. Cöln, 1878 : *P. J
Tonger.* 8vo (*vide* No. 34).

150. ADEMA, *E* . Hermann Ritter und seine Viola Alta. Gesammelte Aufsätze. Supplement zu H. Ritter's Buch, Die Geschichte der Viola Alta und die Grundsätze ihres Baues. Würzburg, 1881 : *A. Stüber*. 8vo (*vide* No. 147).

151. RÜHLMANN, *Julius.* Die Geschichte der Bogeninstrumente; insbesondere derjenigen des heutigen Streichquartettes von den frühesten Anfängen an bis auf die heutige Zeit. Eine Monographie. Herausgegeben von dessen Sohn, Dr. Richard Rühlmann. Mit in den Text eingedruckten Holzstichen und einem ATLAS von XIII. Tafeln. Brunswick, 1882. Large 8vo. Atlas, oblong 8vo.

Note.—Though fewer in number, the German works are, as a rule, much more serious and thorough than the English or French. No. 151 particularly, I consider to be, with the exception of Vidal's work (No. 113), the best work written on the Violin. I possess also one Swedish work on the Violin, a translation of No. 79.

152. ANONYMOUS. Om Violinens Ursprung jemte Biografiska Anteckningar ofra Corelli, Tartini, Gavinies, Pugnani, och Viotti. Med Porträtter. Stockholm, 1811. *Carl Delén.* 8vo.

This concludes this Bibliography of the Violin; it may be that there exist, in some cases, subsequent or prior editions to those I have given. I can only ask those of my readers who know of any such, or of any works on the violin not put down in the above list, to do me the very great favour of sending me particulars of them. I need hardly say that a very large proportion of the above works are out of print and extremely difficult to obtain. Mr. B. Quaritch, of 15, Piccadilly, London, W., has, however, got me most of them, and I have no doubt that by applying to him a large number of them might be obtained.

APPENDIX D.

A CATALOGUE OF VIOLIN SCHOOLS AND INSTRUCTION BOOKS.

THE following table, like the Bibliography (Appendix C.), cannot, of course, pretend to anything like completeness, much less so in fact than the Bibliography, for we must remember that the number of violin tutors which have been written in every language is practically unlimited, whilst from their very nature they are less heard of, less taken care of, and sooner lost sight of, than any class of musical publication. I have therefore contented myself with giving a list of those "Méthodes du Violon," which have been sufficiently authoritative to have lasted till to-day in use among violinists, and of those sufficiently well known to have had their existences recorded in any of the best musical books of reference. Another great difficulty which I have had to encounter has been the circumstance that hardly any music is ever dated, so that in a majority of cases it is impossible to give the date of publication of a violin school unless it is to be found in some *catalogue-raisonné*, or in some reference work, such as the " Biographie Universelle des Musiciens et Bibliographie Générale de la musique" of M. Fétis (Paris, 1860 to 1865, *2nd Edn.* Supplément et Complément, Paris, 1881), or the " Bibliographie Musicale de la France et de l'Etranger" (Paris, 1822, *Niogret*). Where by reference to such books, I have been able to date a *méthode*, I have done so, and all such as I have been able to date I have placed in chronological order in the first section of this catalogue ; all such as I have been unable to date I have placed alphabetically in the second section thereof. Finally I have included no books, or sets, of studies or exercises (for they are, of course, innumerable), that is to say, I have only named violin schools in which the examples are interspersed with letter-press and illustrations, being, in point of fact, complete directions for the acquisition of *technique* upon the violin, (presumably) without a master. Thus this list of *méthodes* becomes practically a supplement to Appendix C., and might be headed " A Bibliography of Works on the Technique of the Violin," and as such it might be said that Nos. 1, 4, 5, 7, 9, 13, 14, 18, 34, 41, 43, 50A, 52, 69, 70, 74, 75, 124, 144, 149, in Appendix C., should be here included ; but I placed them there because they are principally printed instructions, with very few musical examples, whereas here we have works which are principally musical examples to which the printed instructions are practically subordinate. For this reason, seeing that music may be said to be a cosmopolitan language, I have not divided the following works under the heads of their various nationalities.

SECTION I.

VIOLIN SCHOOLS IN ORDER OF DATE.

N.B.—Except where otherwise mentioned, the size of the following works is always understood to be music-size.

1. *Gerle*, H.　Musica Teusch (*sic*) auf die Instrument die Grossen unnd (*sic*) kleynen Geygen auch Lautten, etc. Nürnberg, 1532. *Second Edition*, 1546.
2. *Simpson*, C.　The Division Violist, or an introduction to the playing upon a ground, divided into two parts. London, 1659: *W. Godbid*. Fol.
3. *Simpson*, C.　The Division Viol, or the Art of Playing *ex tempore* upon a ground, divided into three parts. *Second Edition* of No. 2. London, 1667 : *H. Brome*. Fol.

4. *Geminiani*, F. Art of Playing the Violin. London, 1740.
5. *Geminiani*, F. The Entire New and Complete Tutor for the Violin, containing the easiest and best methods for learning to obtain a proficiency. London, n.d. (1800): *J. Preston.*
6. *Mozart*, L. Versuch einer gründlichen Violinschule. Augsburg, 1756.
7. *Anonymous.* The Complete Tutor for the Violin, containing the best and easiest Instructions for Learners to obtain a Proficiency, etc. London, n.d. (1765): *Thompson & Son.* Obl.
8. *Mozart*, L. Gründliche Violinschule. Augsburg, 1770: *Lotter,* 4to.
   Méthode raisonnée de Violon, par L. Mozart. Translated by V. Rœser. Paris, 1770. *Boyer.*
   Second Edition, Paris, 1801: *Ch. Pleyel.*
9. *Geminiani*, F. The Art of Playing on the Violin, containing all the rules necessary to attain to a perfection on that Instrument, etc. Op. IX. London, n.d. (1740). *Second Edition,* 1791: *Bremner.*
10. *Saint-Sevin*, J. B. Principes de Violon. Bordeaux, 1772. 4to.
11. *Löhlein*, G. S. Anweisung zum Violinspielen mit praktischen Beyspielen und zur Uebung mit 24 kleinen Duetten erkläret. Leipzig, 1774. *Second Edition,* 1781. *Third Edition,* 1797. *F. Frommann.* Obl.
12. *Bailleux*, A. Méthode raisonnée pour apprendre à jouer du Violon, avec le doigté de cet Instrument, et les différens agrémens dont il est susceptible. Paris, 1798. *Second Edition,* 1779.
13. *Milandre (?).* Méthode facile pour la Viole d'Amour. Paris, 1782. 4to.
14. *Corrette*, M. L'Art de se perfectionner sur le Violon. Paris, 1783.
16. *Leone (?).* Méthode raisonnée pour passer du Violon à la Mandoline. Paris, 1783.
16. *Bornet (aîné).* Nouvelle Méthode du Violon et de la Musique. Paris, 1788.
17. *Bedard*, J. B. Méthode de Violon, courte et intelligible. Paris, 1800; *Leduc.*
18. *Cartier*, J. B. L'Art du Violon, ou Division des écoles, servant de complément à la Méthode de Violon du Conservatoire. Paris, 1801.
19. *Baillot*, P., *Rode*, P., et *Kreutzer*, R. Méthode de Violon. Paris, 1803; *Ozi.* English Edition, translated by J. A. Hamilton London, n.d.
20. *Hering*, C. T. Praktische Violinenschule nach einer neuen, leichten und zweckmässigen Stufenfolge. Leipzig, 1810; *G. Fleischer.*
21. *Billiard (?).* Méthode de Violon. Paris, 1817.

22. *Baillot*, P.   L'Art du Violon.   Nouvelle Méthode, dediée à ses
     Élèves.   Paris, n.d. (1835): *Imprimerie du Conservatoire.*
23. *West*, W.   The Art of Playing the Violin on a new Principle by
     which the progress of the learner is greatly facilitated.
     London, n.d. (1840) : *B. S. Williams.* Obl.
24. *Bates*, J.   Bates' Complete Preceptor for the Violin, containing
     the easiest and most modern methods for learning to obtain
     proficiency.   London, n.d. (1845): *T. Bates.* Obl.
25. *Gühr*, C.   L'Art de Jouer du Violon de Paganini; appendices à
     toutes les méthodes qui ont paru jusqu'à ce jour avec un
     Traité de sons harmoniques simples et doubles.   Paris, n.d.
     (1845); *Schönenberger.* English Edition translated by Jas.
     Clarke.   London, n.d. : *R. Cocks.*
26. *Anonymous.*   The Violin Preceptor, or Pocket Guide to the Art
     of Playing the Violin.   Glasgow, 1846 : *W. Hamilton,* obl.
27. *Spohr*, L.   Violinschule von Louis Spohr mit erläuternden
     Kupfertafeln.   Vienna, n.d. (1830): *T. Haslinger.*
     Louis Spohr's Grand Violin School from the original
     German, dedicated to Professors of the Violin by the
     Translator, C. Rudolphus.   London, n.d. (1850) : *Wessel & Co.*
     Spohr's Violin School, Revised and Edited with additional
     Text, by Henry Holmes, the translation from the German
     by Florence Marshall.   London, n.d. (1878): *Boosey & Co.*
28. *Campagnoli*, B.   Nouvelle Méthode de la Méchanique progres-
     sive du jeu du Violon divisée en 5 parties et distribuée en
     132 Leçons progressives pour deux Violons, et 118 Études
     pour un Violon seul.   Hanover, n.d. : *Bachmann,* 2nd
     Edition.   Leipzig, n.d. (1870): *Breitkopf und Härtel.*
     English Edition, translated by John Bishop, of Cheltenham.
     London, n.d. (1856): *R. Cocks & Co.*
29. *Beriot*, C. A. de.   Méthode de Violon en trois parties.   Paris,
     n.d. (1855) : *chez l'Auteur.*
30. *David*, F.   Violinschule von Ferdinand David.   Leipzig, n.d.
     (1864): *Breitkopf und Härtel. Second Edition,* 1874.
31. *Tours*, B.   "Novello's Music Primers."   Edited by Dr. Stainer ;
     No. 17, The Violin.   London, n.d. (1874): *Novello.* 4to.
32. *Papini*, G.   Le Mécanisme du jeune Violoniste.   Cours com-
     plet et progressif en forme de méthode pour le violon, divisé
     en quatre parties.   London, n.d. (1883) : *F. W. Chanot,* 4to.
33. *Mason's* Violin Tutor.   An easy and simple method for learning
     this popular instrument.   London, n.d. (1883).   Obl.
34. *Otto Langley's* New Violin Tutor.   London, n.d. (1884): *Rivière
     & Hawkes.*

SECTION II.

UNDATED MÉTHODES IN ALPHABETICAL ORDER

35. *Anonymous.*   The Art of Playing the Violin without a Master.

An improved and complete Tutor for the instrument, etc. Glasgow, n.d. : *Cameron & Ferguson*. Small 4to.

36. *Anonymous*. The Art of Playing the Violin, with a New Scale showing how to stop every Note, Flat or Sharp exactly, and where the Shifts of the Hands should be made, etc. London, n.d. 8vo.

37. *Aday (Père)*. Nouvelle Méthode de Violon, contenant les principes détaillés de cet instrument, etc. Lyons, n.d.: *Cartoux*

38. *Alard, D.* École du Violon. Méthode complète et progressive à l'usage du Conservatoire de Paris. Mayence, n.d. : *Schott & Co.*

39. *Campagnoli, B.* L'Art d'inventer à l'improviste des fantaisies et cadences pour le Violon. Leipsic, n.d.: *Breitkopf und Härtel.*

40. *Chevesailles (?)*. Petite Méthode de Violon. Paris, n.d.

41. *Dancla, C.* Méthode élémentaire et progressive de Violon. Paris, n.d.
L'École des cinq Positions. Paris, n.d.
L'École de l'Archet. Paris, n.d.

42. *Dupierge, F. T. A.* Méthode de Violon. Paris, n.d. : *Frère.*

43. *Farmer, H.* The New Violin School, wherein the Art of Bowing and Fingering that Instrument is explained in a series of exercises and scales. London, n.d. : *Brewer & Co.*

44, *Frey, J.* Méthode de Violon. Paris, n.d.

45. *Froehlich (?)*. Méthode de Violon. Bonn., n.d.: *Simrok* (4th Edn.).

46. *Garaudé, A. de.* Méthode de Violon, contenant un abrégé des principes de musique adaptés à cet instrument, les règles générales de la tenue et du doigté du Violon, etc. Paris, n.d. : *for the Author.*

47. *Gebauer, M.* Principes Élémentaires de la Musique. Positions et Gammes de Violon. Leipsic, n.d.

48. *Hamilton, J. A.* A Complete and Easy Course of Instruction for the Violin. London, n.d.

49. *Henry, B.* Méthode de Violon, contenant . . ·. la tenue de cet instrument et de l'archet, des exercises pour bien placer les doigts, etc., etc. Paris, n.d. : *Boildieu & Imbault.*

50. *Hermann, F.* Violin-Schule. Leipzig, n.d.

51. *Hone, J.* Méthode de Violon. London, n.d.

52. *Klier, J. B.* Methodo Elementa Theorico e Pratico para rebeca. Lisbon, n.d.

53. *Lachnith, L. W.* Exercises sur les quatre cordes du Violon ; ou Méthode simple et facile pour appendre les premiers principes de cet instrument. Paris, n.d. : *Dufaut & Dubois.*

54. *Lottin, D.* Principes élémentaires de musique et de Violon. Paris, n.d. : *Leduc.*

55. *Marque, A.* Grand Method for the Violin, revised by Saint-Jacome. London, n.d.

56. *Mazas, J. F.* Méthode de Violon, suivie d'un traité des sons harmoniques, etc. Paris, n.d. : *Frey.*

57. *Paiey*, C. A.   An Elementary Treatise on the Art of Playing the Violin, with Scales, etc.   London, n.d.

58. *Præger*, H.   Elementary and Practical Violin School.   In three parts.   London, n.d.

59. *Ries*, H.   Violin School.   London, n.d.

60. *Sanderson*, J.   The Study of the Bow, etc., Exercises in Fingering and Bowing.   London, n.d.: *Longmans*.

61. *Schall*, O.   Études de l'archet et du doigté, ou cinquante-huit exemples mêlés de caprices pour le violon.   **Paris** : *Ch. Pleyel.*   Hamburg : *Bœhm*, n.d.

62. *Waud*, W. W.   Instruction book for the Violin, etc.   London, n.d. : *W. Waud.*

Note.—The dates of the *Méthodes* in Section II. may be approximately ascertained by reference to any biographical dictionary (such as Fétis or Grove), which will give us the time at which the composer lived. No. 1 is inserted (perhaps without right of *entrée*) as being the earliest instruction book I have been able to find for stringed instruments. Nos. 2 and 3 again, are schools for the viol da gamba, but I have included them on account of their interest in connection with this subject. No. 13 is interesting also, being an instruction book for the violin proper, but retaining the old name. The earliest violin-tutor I have being able to find, dates from 1654, but as it is only a section of a musical work, I have not been able to include it in the above catalogue, but I have, on account of its fascinating interest, set it out almost in its entirety as Appendix E.

APPENDIX E.

AN HISTORIC VIOLIN SCHOOL.

WHEN one looks through the magnificent "Méthodes du Violon," which are published to-day at prices which bring them within the reach of the humblest student of the violin ; when one ransacks the stores of Violin-lore, historical, technical, and practical, contained in the pages of the violin schools of De Beriot, of Berthold Tours, of Ferdinand David, and of many others, my mind often reverts to the days when an instruction book for the "new-fangled fiddle" was a matter of rare expense ; to days when the masters of the Italian schools of violin-making were in full vigour, before the violin had established itself as the first instrument in the orchestra ; and when, as Anthony à Wood tells us, "gentlemen played three, four, and five partes with viols, and that they esteemed a violin to be an instrument only belonging to a common fidler, and could not endure that it should come among them for feare of making their meetings to be vaine and fidling." [1] I have before me the fourteenth edition (published in

---

[1] Anthony à Wood, Autobiography in MS. in Ashmolean Library at Oxford written 1653.   Published at Oxford in 1772.

1700) of a work first published in 1654 [1] by John Playford, stationer
bookseller, musicseller and publisher, "at his shop in the Inner
Temple, near the Church door," entitled, "An Introduction to the
Skill of Musick, in Three Books."

The second book consists of "Instructions and Lessons for the
Treble, Tenor, and *Bass-viols*, and also for the TREBLE VIOLIN,"
the latter section (which occupies pp. 91—110) being of great
interest to the violin-player of to-day, and headed by a curious and
interesting, if rather fanciful, representation of "the treble violin,"
and the bow with which it was played, the latter being particularly
worthy the notice of musical archæologists. The writer commences
his discourse as follows :—

"The *Treble Violin* is a cheerful and sprightly Instrument, and
much practised of late, some by *Book*, and some without ; which of
these two is the best way, may easily be resolved : To learn to play
by *Rote* or *Ear*, without Book, is the way never to play more than
what may be gain'd by hearing another Play, which may soon be
forgot ; but on the contrary, he which learns and Practises by Book,
according to the *Gamut* (which is the *True Rule* for Musick) fails
not after he comes to be perfect in those *Rules*, which guide him to
Play more than ever he was Taught or Heard, and also to play his
part in consort, which the other can never be capable of.

" *Directions for tuning the* VIOLIN.

"The *Violin* is usually strung with four Strings and Tuned by
Fifths. For the more plain and easie understanding of it, and
stopping all *Notes* in their right *Places*, and *Tune*, 'twill be necessary,
that there be plac'd on the *Neck* or *Finger-board* of your *Violin*, six
Frets, as 'tis on a *Viol* : This (tho' 'tis not usual, yet) is the best and
easiest way for a *Beginner*, who has a bad Ear, for those *Frets*
are a certain and direct *Rule* to guide him to stop all his *Notes* in
exact Tune ; where as, those which learn without, seldom have at
first so good an Ear, as to stop all *Notes* in perfect *Tune*. Therefore
for the better understanding thereof, in this following *Example* is
assign'd to those six *Frets* on the *Finger-board*, six Letters of the
Alphabet in their order : The first *Fret* is *b*, the second *c*, the third
d, the fourth *e*, the fifth *f*, and the sixth *g ; a* is not assigned to any
Fret, but is the string open."

Then follows a diagram of the finger-board fretted from the open
strings to the sixth semitone (B♭ on the 1st string), and the names
given to the four strings are : The *Treble*, the *Small Mean*, the *Great
Mean*, and the *Bass*. The author then gives, " *The* scale *of* MUSICK
on the Four Strings of the TREBLE VIOLIN, *expressed by* LETTERS
and NOTES.

[1] Of this edition only one copy is known ; it was sold at the dispersion of
the library of the late Dr. Rimbault in 1877, for ten guineas. (*Vide* Note [1], p. 55.)

"This *Example* doth direct the Places of all the *Notes*, flat and sharp, each *Note* being plac'd under the *Letter*, according to their several *Stops* upon each *String* distinctly, beginning at the lowest *Note* on the *Bass*, or *Fourth String*, and ascending up to the highest on the *Treble*, or *First String* according to the *Scale* or *Gamut* :[1]   In which you may also observe, that the *Lessons* for the *Violin* by *Letters*, are prick'd on *four Lines* according to the *four* general *Strings*, but *Lessons* by *Notes* are prick'd upon *five Lines*, as appears in the Example above.

"For the *Tuning* of the *Violin* is usually by *Fifths*, that is, five Notes distance betwixt each *String ;* which according to the *Scale* or *Gamut*, the *Bass*, or *fourth String* is called *G-sol-re-ut ;* the *third* or *Great Mean*, *D-la-sol-re ;* the *second* or *Small Mean*, A-la-mi-re ; the *first* or *Treble*, *E-la ;* as in the following Example.'

Then follows an ordinary table of the notes on each string, intituled " *Example of* the Tuning, *as the five Notes ascend on each of the four Strings, beginning on the* Bass *or* Fourth String." After which follows a paragraph which will strike the modern violinist as, to say the least of it, original.

" Also, for a Beginner to Tune by *Eighths*, will be easier than by *Fifths*, if his *Violin* be *fretted ;* to begin which, he must wind up his *first*, or *Treble String* as high as it will bear, then stop it in *f*," (*i.e.*, the 5th fret) " and Tune his *second* an *Eighth* below it ; then *stop* the *second* in *f*, and Tune the *third* an *Eighth* under it ; then *stop* the *third* in *f*, and tune the *fourth* an *Eighth* below that ; and so your *Strings* will be in perfect Tune."

Then follows an " *Example of Tuning by* Fifths *and Eighths* " and " *Another* Scale *for the* VIOLIN, *Directing the Places of the* Notes *on each String, and the* Stops *by each Finger*." After which the author continues :—

" Having thus given you the *Tuning* of the *Treble-Violin*, it will be necessary here to set down the *Tuning* of the *Tenor* and *Bass-Violins*, being both used in Consort.

The *Tenor* or *Mean* is a larger *Violin* than the *Treble*, and is Tuned *five notes* lower than it : The *Cliff* is sometimes put on the middle, and sometimes on the second *Line*."

We have then tables of the open strings of the Viola as it is now tuned, and of the Violoncello, the first string being G instead of A,

---

[1] Down to the seventeenth century the shift on the violin was unknown, the players of those times confining themselves to the first position. M. l'Abbé Sibire tells us that the sole departure therefrom, which they seldom allowed themselves to attempt, was the extension of the little finger to C on the first string. This was looked upon as a great and marvellous feat, so much so, that when the audience knew it was coming they would murmur aloud, as the terrible moment arrived, " Gare l'Ut " ! and player and listeners were in a fever of excitement. If the unlucky virtuoso failed to strike the *Ut* pure, a storm of disapproval would make him bitterly repent his temerity ; but if successful, a whirlwind of applause greeted this striking exhibition of his powers.—L'Abbé Sibire, " La Chelonomia ou le Parfait Luthier " (Paris, 1806.)   *Vide* Note [2], p. viii., preface.

the other three respectively C, F, and B the lowest note. The principles of the *Treble Violin* then conclude as follows :—

" Thus I have (after the plainest methods could be set down) given you several *Rules* and *Directions* for the *Treble-Violin* by way of *Freting*, which I have known used by Eminent Teachers on this Instrument, as the most facile and easie to Initiate their Scholars ; and also *Directions* for Pricking down Lessons in *Letters :* Yet I do not approve of this way of Playing by *Letters*, save only as a Guide to Young Practitioners, to bring them the more readily to know all the Stops and places of the *Notes*, both *flat* and *sharp*, and being perfect therein, to lay the Use of *Letters* aside, and keep to their Practice by *Notes* and *Rules* of the *Gamut* only : For this Reason, I have added some few Lessons both ways, that after you can play them by *Letters*, you may play the same by *Notes*."

At the foot is placed the following note :—" *Those that desire more Lessons for this Instrument, I refer to the First and Second Parts of* Apollo's Banquet, *containing the Newest Tunes for the* Violin, *with the most usual* French *Dances used at Court and Dancing-Schools:* (sic) *And also in the* Dancing-Master ; *Both which are now doing in the New* Tied-Note, with additions being both more compleat than ever."

Some General Rules *for the* Treble-Violin.

" *First*, The *Violin* is usually play'd above-hand, the *Neck* thereof being held by the left Hand, the lower Part must be rested on the left Breast, a little below the Shoulder. The *Bow* is held in the right Hand, between the ends of the Thumb and the 3 Fingers, the Thumb being stay'd upon the Hair at the Nut, and the 3 Fingers resting upon the Wood. Your *Bow* being thus fix'd, you are first to draw an *even Stroak* over each *String* severally, making each *String* yield a clear and distinct sound.

" *Secondly*, For the posture of your left Hand, place your Thumb on the back of the Neck, opposite to your Fore-Finder, (sic) so will your Fingers have the more liberty to move up and down on the several Stops.

" *Thirdly*, for true **Fingering**, observe these *Directions ;* (which will appear more easie to your Understanding, if in your first Practice you have your *Violin* Fretted, as is before mention'd :) That where you skip a *Fret* or *stop*, there to leave a *Finger*, for every *Stop* is but half a Tone or Note ; for from *b* to *c*, is but half a note, but from *b* to *d*, is a whole note ; (!) therefore the leaving of a *Finger* is necessary, to be in readiness when half notes happen, which is by *Flats* and *Sharps*.

" *Fourthly*, When you have any high Notes which reach lower than your usual *Frets*, or *Stops*, there you are to shift your *Fingers ;* if there be but two Notes, then the first is stopp'd with the second *Finger*, and the rest by the next Fingers.[1]

---

[1] It, will strike the reader that this is, to say the least of it, a *concise* method of explaining the whole science of shifting.

"*Fifthly*, in the moving your *Bow* up and down, observe this *Rule*: When you see an *even Number* of *Quavers* and *Semiquavers*, as 2, 4, 6, or 8, tied together, your Bow must move up, tho it was up at the Note immediately before; but if you have an *odd Number*, as 3, 5, or 7 (which happens very often by reason of a *Prick'd Note*, or an *odd Quaver-Rest*), there your *Bow* must be drawn downwards at the first *Note*.(!)

"*Lastly*, In the Practice of any *Lesson*, play it slow at first, and by often Practice, it will bring your Hand to a more swift motion.

"As for the several *Graces* and *Flourishes* that are used, (*Viz. Shakes*, *Backfalls*, and *Double Relishes*) this following TABLE will be some help to your Practice; for there is, first, the *Note* plain; and after, the *Grace* express'd by *Notes* at length."

This "Violin-School" then concludes with "*A Table of Graces proper to the Viol or Violin*," which include "*A Beat, A Back-fall, A Double Back-fall, Elevation, A Springer, A Cadent, A Back-fall Shaked, A close Shake, a Shaked Beat*," and "*A Double Relish*."

A sort of Appendix consists of "*Short* TUNES *for the* TREBLE VIOLIN *by Letters and Notes*," and "*Some* TUNES *of the most usual* PSALMS *Broken for the* VIOLIN," and completes this Historic Violin-school. I think it cannot fail to interest the Violinist of to-day, and to convince the most inveterate *laudator temporis acti*, that in the matter of musical instruction, we have at any rate cause to be thankful that we do not live in the "good old days," when at a music meeting at Oxford, at which Thomas Baltzar (or Baltzarini) exhibited his marvellous feat, the whole shift,[1] Professor Wilson stooped down to see whether he terminated *in hoofs!*

---

[1] Thomas Baltzar, born at Lübeck in 1630, came to England in 1655, and is said to have been the first who taught the use of the whole shift. He had in consequence a reputation only equalled by that of Paganini.

In former days we had the *Viol in*,
    Ere the true instrument had come about;
But now we say since *this* all ears doth win,
    The *Violin* hath put the *Viol out*."
                          (*Old Epigram* 17th century.)

Indices.

"Et est completus per Eduardum Heron-Allen die secundo Novembris, Anno Domini m.d.ccc.lxxxiiij., pro quo sit Deus Gloriosus cum Matre Ejus Gloriosa, benedictus in sæcula sæculorum.   Amen."

(BIBL. ABUND. MS. 430.)

INDEX OF AUTHORS
NAMED IN APPENDICES C AND D.

THE letters after the names in the following index refer to the Appendix (C or D) in which the Author's works occur ; in some instances they occur in both (*e.g.*, "Baillot"). Tho numbers refer to the chronological order of the works, preserved throughout the Appendices where possible.

GENERAL INDEX.

In the following Index the names of Authors to whose works reference is made in this volume are printed in *italics*, to the end that the Index may be so complete as possible, and include both Subject and Bibliographical Indices.

Moulds

1, 2, 3, 4, 5, 7, 8, 9, 10, 11, 12, Models for the Arching of Back and Belly: H, I, J, K, L, M, Cramping Blocks belonging to Mould.

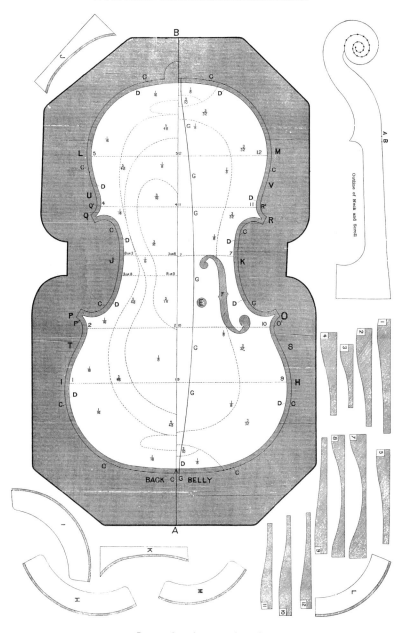

Image has been reduced.
Enlarge by 338% for actual size.

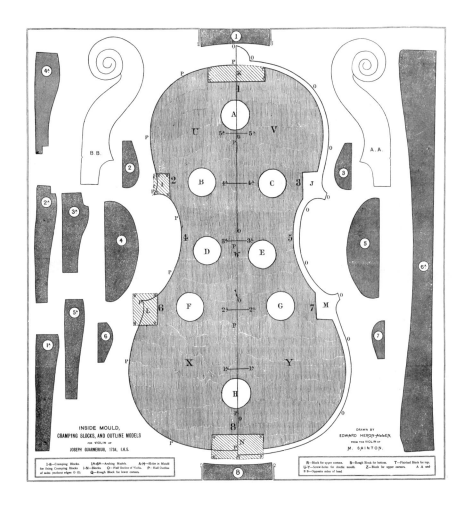

INSIDE MOULD,
CRAMPING BLOCKS, AND OUTLINE MODELS
FOR VIOLIN OF
JOSEPH GUARNERIUS, 1734, I.H.S.

DRAWN BY
EDWARD HERON-ALLEN,
FROM THE VIOLIN OF
M. SAINTON.

I–B—Cramping Blocks.   1A–6A—Arching Models.   A–H—Holes in Mould
for fixing Cramping Blocks   I–N—Blocks.   O—Half Outline of Violin.
of sides (without edges O O).   Q—Rough Block for lower corners.   P—Half Outline

R—Block for upper corners.   S—Rough Block for bottom.   T—Finished Block for top.
U–Y—Screw-holes for double mould.   Z—Block for upper corners.   A A and
B B—Opposite sides of head

Image has been reduced.
Enlarge by 336% for actual size.

PLATE VI.

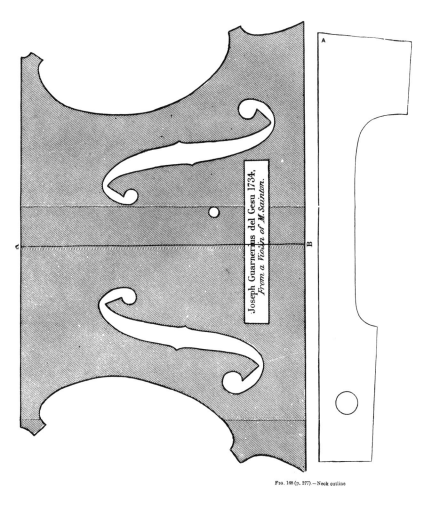

Joseph Guarnerius del Gesù 1734.
From a Violin of M. Sainton.

Fig. 168 (p. 277).—Neck outline

Image has been reduced.
Enlarge by 165% for actual size.

A CATALOG OF SELECTED
DOVER BOOKS
IN ALL FIELDS OF INTEREST

A CATALOG OF SELECTED DOVER
BOOKS IN ALL FIELDS OF INTEREST

CONCERNING THE SPIRITUAL IN ART, Wassily Kandinsky. Pioneering work by father of abstract art. Thoughts on color theory, nature of art. Analysis of earlier masters. 12 illustrations. 80pp. of text. 5⅜ x 8½. 23411-8

ANIMALS: 1,419 Copyright-Free Illustrations of Mammals, Birds, Fish, Insects, etc., Jim Harter (ed.). Clear wood engravings present, in extremely lifelike poses, over 1,000 species of animals. One of the most extensive pictorial sourcebooks of its kind. Captions. Index. 284pp. 9 x 12. 23766-4

CELTIC ART: The Methods of Construction, George Bain. Simple geometric techniques for making Celtic interlacements, spirals, Kells-type initials, animals, humans, etc. Over 500 illustrations. 160pp. 9 x 12. (Available in U.S. only.) 22923-8

AN ATLAS OF ANATOMY FOR ARTISTS, Fritz Schider. Most thorough reference work on art anatomy in the world. Hundreds of illustrations, including selections from works by Vesalius, Leonardo, Goya, Ingres, Michelangelo, others. 593 illustrations. 192pp. 7⅛ x 10¼. 20241-0

CELTIC HAND STROKE-BY-STROKE (Irish Half-Uncial from "The Book of Kells"): An Arthur Baker Calligraphy Manual, Arthur Baker. Complete guide to creating each letter of the alphabet in distinctive Celtic manner. Covers hand position, strokes, pens, inks, paper, more. Illustrated. 48pp. 8¼ x 11. 24336-2

EASY ORIGAMI, John Montroll. Charming collection of 32 projects (hat, cup, pelican, piano, swan, many more) specially designed for the novice origami hobbyist. Clearly illustrated easy-to-follow instructions insure that even beginning papercrafters will achieve successful results. 48pp. 8¼ x 11. 27298-2

THE COMPLETE BOOK OF BIRDHOUSE CONSTRUCTION FOR WOOD-WORKERS, Scott D. Campbell. Detailed instructions, illustrations, tables. Also data on bird habitat and instinct patterns. Bibliography. 3 tables. 63 illustrations in 15 figures. 48pp. 5¼ x 8½. 24407-5

BLOOMINGDALE'S ILLUSTRATED 1886 CATALOG: Fashions, Dry Goods and Housewares, Bloomingdale Brothers. Famed merchants' extremely rare catalog depicting about 1,700 products: clothing, housewares, firearms, dry goods, jewelry, more. Invaluable for dating, identifying vintage items. Also, copyright-free graphics for artists, designers. Co-published with Henry Ford Museum & Greenfield Village. 160pp. 8¼ x 11. 25780-0

HISTORIC COSTUME IN PICTURES, Braun & Schneider. Over 1,450 costumed figures in clearly detailed engravings–from dawn of civilization to end of 19th century. Captions. Many folk costumes. 256pp. 8⅜ x 11¾. 23150-X

STICKLEY CRAFTSMAN FURNITURE CATALOGS, Gustav Stickley and L. & J. G. Stickley. Beautiful, functional furniture in two authentic catalogs from 1910. 594 illustrations, including 277 photos, show settles, rockers, armchairs, reclining chairs, bookcases, desks, tables. 183pp. 6½ x 9¼.   23838-5

AMERICAN LOCOMOTIVES IN HISTORIC PHOTOGRAPHS: 1858 to 1949, Ron Ziel (ed.). A rare collection of 126 meticulously detailed official photographs, called "builder portraits," of American locomotives that majestically chronicle the rise of steam locomotive power in America. Introduction. Detailed captions. xi+ 129pp. 9 x 12.   27393-8

AMERICA'S LIGHTHOUSES: An Illustrated History, Francis Ross Holland, Jr. Delightfully written, profusely illustrated fact-filled survey of over 200 American light-houses since 1716. History, anecdotes, technological advances, more. 240pp. 8 x 10¾.
25576-X

TOWARDS A NEW ARCHITECTURE, Le Corbusier. Pioneering manifesto by founder of "International School." Technical and aesthetic theories, views of industry, eco-nomics, relation of form to function, "mass-production split" and much more. Profusely illustrated. 320pp. 6⅛ x 9¼. (Available in U.S. only.)   25023-7

HOW THE OTHER HALF LIVES, Jacob Riis. Famous journalistic record, expos-ing poverty and degradation of New York slums around 1900, by major social reformer. 100 striking and influential photographs. 233pp. 10 x 7⅞.   22012-5

FRUIT KEY AND TWIG KEY TO TREES AND SHRUBS, William M. Harlow. One of the handiest and most widely used identification aids. Fruit key covers 120 deciduous and evergreen species; twig key 160 deciduous species. Easily used. Over 300 photographs. 126pp. 5⅜ x 8½.   20511-8

COMMON BIRD SONGS, Dr. Donald J. Borror. Songs of 60 most common U.S. birds: robins, sparrows, cardinals, bluejays, finches, more–arranged in order of increasing complexity. Up to 9 variations of songs of each species.
Cassette and manual 99911-4

ORCHIDS AS HOUSE PLANTS, Rebecca Tyson Northen. Grow cattleyas and many other kinds of orchids–in a window, in a case, or under artificial light. 63 illus-trations. 148pp. 5⅜ x 8½.   23261-1

MONSTER MAZES, Dave Phillips. Masterful mazes at four levels of difficulty. Avoid deadly perils and evil creatures to find magical treasures. Solutions for all 32 exciting illustrated puzzles. 48pp. 8¼ x 11.   26005-4

MOZART'S DON GIOVANNI (DOVER OPERA LIBRETTO SERIES), Wolfgang Amadeus Mozart. Introduced and translated by Ellen H. Bleiler. Standard Italian libretto, with complete English translation. Convenient and thoroughly portable–an ideal companion for reading along with a recording or the performance itself. Introduction. List of characters. Plot summary. 121pp. 5¼ x 8½.   24944-1

TECHNICAL MANUAL AND DICTIONARY OF CLASSICAL BALLET, Gail Grant. Defines, explains, comments on steps, movements, poses and concepts. 15-page pictorial section. Basic book for student, viewer. 127pp. 5⅜ x 8½.   21843-0

THE CLARINET AND CLARINET PLAYING, David Pino. Lively, comprehensive work features suggestions about technique, musicianship, and musical interpretation, as well as guidelines for teaching, making your own reeds, and preparing for public performance. Includes an intriguing look at clarinet history. "A godsend," *The Clarinet,* Journal of the International Clarinet Society. Appendixes. 7 illus. 320pp. 5⅜ x 8½. 40270-3

HOLLYWOOD GLAMOR PORTRAITS, John Kobal (ed.). 145 photos from 1926-49. Harlow, Gable, Bogart, Bacall; 94 stars in all. Full background on photographers, technical aspects. 160pp. 8⅜ x 11¼. 23352-9

THE ANNOTATED CASEY AT THE BAT: A Collection of Ballads about the Mighty Casey/Third, Revised Edition, Martin Gardner (ed.). Amusing sequels and parodies of one of America's best-loved poems: Casey's Revenge, Why Casey Whiffed, Casey's Sister at the Bat, others. 256pp. 5⅜ x 8½. 28598-7

THE RAVEN AND OTHER FAVORITE POEMS, Edgar Allan Poe. Over 40 of the author's most memorable poems: "The Bells," "Ulalume," "Israfel," "To Helen," "The Conqueror Worm," "Eldorado," "Annabel Lee," many more. Alphabetic lists of titles and first lines. 64pp. 5³⁄₁₆ x 8¼. 26685-0

PERSONAL MEMOIRS OF U. S. GRANT, Ulysses Simpson Grant. Intelligent, deeply moving firsthand account of Civil War campaigns, considered by many the finest military memoirs ever written. Includes letters, historic photographs, maps and more. 528pp. 6⅛ x 9¼. 28587-1

ANCIENT EGYPTIAN MATERIALS AND INDUSTRIES, A. Lucas and J. Harris. Fascinating, comprehensive, thoroughly documented text describes this ancient civilization's vast resources and the processes that incorporated them in daily life, including the use of animal products, building materials, cosmetics, perfumes and incense, fibers, glazed ware, glass and its manufacture, materials used in the mummification process, and much more. 544pp. 6⅛ x 9¼. (Available in U.S. only.) 40446-3

RUSSIAN STORIES/RUSSKIE RASSKAZY: A Dual-Language Book, edited by Gleb Struve. Twelve tales by such masters as Chekhov, Tolstoy, Dostoevsky, Pushkin, others. Excellent word-for-word English translations on facing pages, plus teaching and study aids, Russian/English vocabulary, biographical/critical introductions, more. 416pp. 5⅜ x 8½. 26244-8

PHILADELPHIA THEN AND NOW: 60 Sites Photographed in the Past and Present, Kenneth Finkel and Susan Oyama. Rare photographs of City Hall, Logan Square, Independence Hall, Betsy Ross House, other landmarks juxtaposed with contemporary views. Captures changing face of historic city. Introduction. Captions. 128pp. 8¼ x 11. 25790-8

AIA ARCHITECTURAL GUIDE TO NASSAU AND SUFFOLK COUNTIES, LONG ISLAND, The American Institute of Architects, Long Island Chapter, and the Society for the Preservation of Long Island Antiquities. Comprehensive, well-researched and generously illustrated volume brings to life over three centuries of Long Island's great architectural heritage. More than 240 photographs with authoritative, extensively detailed captions. 176pp. 8¼ x 11. 26946-9

NORTH AMERICAN INDIAN LIFE: Customs and Traditions of 23 Tribes, Elsie Clews Parsons (ed.). 27 fictionalized essays by noted anthropologists examine religion, customs, government, additional facets of life among the Winnebago, Crow, Zuni, Eskimo, other tribes. 480pp. 6⅛ x 9¼. 27377-6

CATALOG OF DOVER BOOKS

FRANK LLOYD WRIGHT'S DANA HOUSE, Donald Hoffmann. Pictorial essay of residential masterpiece with over 160 interior and exterior photos, plans, elevations, sketches and studies. 128pp. 9¼ x 10¾. 29120-0

THE MALE AND FEMALE FIGURE IN MOTION: 60 Classic Photographic Sequences, Eadweard Muybridge. 60 true-action photographs of men and women walking, running, climbing, bending, turning, etc., reproduced from rare 19th-century masterpiece. vi + 121pp. 9 x 12. 24745-7

1001 QUESTIONS ANSWERED ABOUT THE SEASHORE, N. J. Berrill and Jacquelyn Berrill. Queries answered about dolphins, sea snails, sponges, starfish, fishes, shore birds, many others. Covers appearance, breeding, growth, feeding, much more. 305pp. 5¼ x 8¼. 23366-9

ATTRACTING BIRDS TO YOUR YARD, William J. Weber. Easy-to-follow guide offers advice on how to attract the greatest diversity of birds: birdhouses, feeders, water and waterers, much more. 96pp. 5³⁄₁₆ x 8¼. 28927-3

MEDICINAL AND OTHER USES OF NORTH AMERICAN PLANTS: A Historical Survey with Special Reference to the Eastern Indian Tribes, Charlotte Erichsen-Brown. Chronological historical citations document 500 years of usage of plants, trees, shrubs native to eastern Canada, northeastern U.S. Also complete identifying information. 343 illustrations. 544pp. 6½ x 9¼. 25951-X

STORYBOOK MAZES, Dave Phillips. 23 stories and mazes on two-page spreads: Wizard of Oz, Treasure Island, Robin Hood, etc. Solutions. 64pp. 8¼ x 11. 23628-5

AMERICAN NEGRO SONGS: 230 Folk Songs and Spirituals, Religious and Secular, John W. Work. This authoritative study traces the African influences of songs sung and played by black Americans at work, in church, and as entertainment. The author discusses the lyric significance of such songs as "Swing Low, Sweet Chariot," "John Henry," and others and offers the words and music for 230 songs. Bibliography. Index of Song Titles. 272pp. 6½ x 9¼. 40271-1

MOVIE-STAR PORTRAITS OF THE FORTIES, John Kobal (ed.). 163 glamor, studio photos of 106 stars of the 1940s: Rita Hayworth, Ava Gardner, Marlon Brando, Clark Gable, many more. 176pp. 8⅜ x 11¼. 23546-7

BENCHLEY LOST AND FOUND, Robert Benchley. Finest humor from early 30s, about pet peeves, child psychologists, post office and others. Mostly unavailable elsewhere. 73 illustrations by Peter Arno and others. 183pp. 5⅜ x 8½. 22410-4

YEKL and THE IMPORTED BRIDEGROOM AND OTHER STORIES OF YIDDISH NEW YORK, Abraham Cahan. Film Hester Street based on *Yekl* (1896). Novel, other stories among first about Jewish immigrants on N.Y.'s East Side. 240pp. 5⅜ x 8½. 22427-9

SELECTED POEMS, Walt Whitman. Generous sampling from *Leaves of Grass.* Twenty-four poems include "I Hear America Singing," "Song of the Open Road," "I Sing the Body Electric," "When Lilacs Last in the Dooryard Bloom'd," "O Captain! My Captain!"–all reprinted from an authoritative edition. Lists of titles and first lines. 128pp. 5³⁄₁₆ x 8¼. 26878-0

THE BEST TALES OF HOFFMANN, E. T. A. Hoffmann. 10 of Hoffmann's most important stories: "Nutcracker and the King of Mice," "The Golden Flowerpot," etc. 458pp. 5⅜ x 8½. 21793-0

FROM FETISH TO GOD IN ANCIENT EGYPT, E. A. Wallis Budge. Rich detailed survey of Egyptian conception of "God" and gods, magic, cult of animals, Osiris, more. Also, superb English translations of hymns and legends. 240 illustrations. 545pp. 5⅜ x 8½. 25803-3

FRENCH STORIES/CONTES FRANÇAIS: A Dual-Language Book, Wallace Fowlie. Ten stories by French masters, Voltaire to Camus: "Micromegas" by Voltaire; "The Atheist's Mass" by Balzac; "Minuet" by de Maupassant; "The Guest" by Camus, six more. Excellent English translations on facing pages. Also French-English vocabulary list, exercises, more. 352pp. 5⅜ x 8½. 26443-2

CHICAGO AT THE TURN OF THE CENTURY IN PHOTOGRAPHS: 122 Historic Views from the Collections of the Chicago Historical Society, Larry A. Viskochil. Rare large-format prints offer detailed views of City Hall, State Street, the Loop, Hull House, Union Station, many other landmarks, circa 1904-1913. Introduction. Captions. Maps. 144pp. 9⅜ x 12¼. 24656-6

OLD BROOKLYN IN EARLY PHOTOGRAPHS, 1865-1929, William Lee Younger. Luna Park, Gravesend race track, construction of Grand Army Plaza, moving of Hotel Brighton, etc. 157 previously unpublished photographs. 165pp. 8⅞ x 11¾. 23587-4

THE MYTHS OF THE NORTH AMERICAN INDIANS, Lewis Spence. Rich anthology of the myths and legends of the Algonquins, Iroquois, Pawnees and Sioux, prefaced by an extensive historical and ethnological commentary. 36 illustrations. 480pp. 5⅜ x 8½. 25967-6

AN ENCYCLOPEDIA OF BATTLES: Accounts of Over 1,560 Battles from 1479 B.C. to the Present, David Eggenberger. Essential details of every major battle in recorded history from the first battle of Megiddo in 1479 B.C. to Grenada in 1984. List of Battle Maps. New Appendix covering the years 1967-1984. Index. 99 illustrations. 544pp. 6½ x 9¼. 24913-1

SAILING ALONE AROUND THE WORLD, Captain Joshua Slocum. First man to sail around the world, alone, in small boat. One of great feats of seamanship told in delightful manner. 67 illustrations. 294pp. 5⅜ x 8½. 20326-3

ANARCHISM AND OTHER ESSAYS, Emma Goldman. Powerful, penetrating, prophetic essays on direct action, role of minorities, prison reform, puritan hypocrisy, violence, etc. 271pp. 5⅜ x 8½. 22484-8

MYTHS OF THE HINDUS AND BUDDHISTS, Ananda K. Coomaraswamy and Sister Nivedita. Great stories of the epics; deeds of Krishna, Shiva, taken from puranas, Vedas, folk tales; etc. 32 illustrations. 400pp. 5⅜ x 8½. 21759-0

THE TRAUMA OF BIRTH, Otto Rank. Rank's controversial thesis that anxiety neurosis is caused by profound psychological trauma which occurs at birth. 256pp. 5⅜ x 8½. 27974-X

A THEOLOGICO-POLITICAL TREATISE, Benedict Spinoza. Also contains unfinished Political Treatise. Great classic on religious liberty, theory of government on common consent. R. Elwes translation. Total of 421pp. 5⅜ x 8½. 20249-6

CATALOG OF DOVER BOOKS

MY BONDAGE AND MY FREEDOM, Frederick Douglass. Born a slave, Douglass became outspoken force in antislavery movement. The best of Douglass' autobiographies. Graphic description of slave life. 464pp. 5⅜ x 8½. 22457-0

FOLLOWING THE EQUATOR: A Journey Around the World, Mark Twain. Fascinating humorous account of 1897 voyage to Hawaii, Australia, India, New Zealand, etc. Ironic, bemused reports on peoples, customs, climate, flora and fauna, politics, much more. 197 illustrations. 720pp. 5⅜ x 8½. 26113-1

THE PEOPLE CALLED SHAKERS, Edward D. Andrews. Definitive study of Shakers: origins, beliefs, practices, dances, social organization, furniture and crafts, etc. 33 illustrations. 351pp. 5⅜ x 8½. 21081-2

THE MYTHS OF GREECE AND ROME, H. A. Guerber. A classic of mythology, generously illustrated, long prized for its simple, graphic, accurate retelling of the principal myths of Greece and Rome, and for its commentary on their origins and significance. With 64 illustrations by Michelangelo, Raphael, Titian, Rubens, Canova, Bernini and others. 480pp. 5⅜ x 8½. 27584-1

PSYCHOLOGY OF MUSIC, Carl E. Seashore. Classic work discusses music as a medium from psychological viewpoint. Clear treatment of physical acoustics, auditory apparatus, sound perception, development of musical skills, nature of musical feeling, host of other topics. 88 figures. 408pp. 5⅜ x 8½. 21851-1

THE PHILOSOPHY OF HISTORY, Georg W. Hegel. Great classic of Western thought develops concept that history is not chance but rational process, the evolution of freedom. 457pp. 5⅜ x 8½. 20112-0

THE BOOK OF TEA, Kakuzo Okakura. Minor classic of the Orient: entertaining, charming explanation, interpretation of traditional Japanese culture in terms of tea ceremony. 94pp. 5⅜ x 8½. 20070-1

LIFE IN ANCIENT EGYPT, Adolf Erman. Fullest, most thorough, detailed older account with much not in more recent books, domestic life, religion, magic, medicine, commerce, much more. Many illustrations reproduce tomb paintings, carvings, hieroglyphs, etc. 597pp. 5⅜ x 8½. 22632-8

SUNDIALS, Their Theory and Construction, Albert Waugh. Far and away the best, most thorough coverage of ideas, mathematics concerned, types, construction, adjusting anywhere. Simple, nontechnical treatment allows even children to build several of these dials. Over 100 illustrations. 230pp. 5⅜ x 8½. 22947-5

THEORETICAL HYDRODYNAMICS, L. M. Milne-Thomson. Classic exposition of the mathematical theory of fluid motion, applicable to both hydrodynamics and aerodynamics. Over 600 exercises. 768pp. 6⅛ x 9¼. 68970-0

SONGS OF EXPERIENCE: Facsimile Reproduction with 26 Plates in Full Color, William Blake. 26 full-color plates from a rare 1826 edition. Includes "The Tyger," "London," "Holy Thursday," and other poems. Printed text of poems. 48pp. 5¼ x 7. 24636-1

OLD-TIME VIGNETTES IN FULL COLOR, Carol Belanger Grafton (ed.). Over 390 charming, often sentimental illustrations, selected from archives of Victorian graphics–pretty women posing, children playing, food, flowers, kittens and puppies, smiling cherubs, birds and butterflies, much more. All copyright-free. 48pp. 9¼ x 12¼. 27269-9

PERSPECTIVE FOR ARTISTS, Rex Vicat Cole. Depth, perspective of sky and sea, shadows, much more, not usually covered. 391 diagrams, 81 reproductions of drawings and paintings. 279pp. 5⅜ x 8½. 22487-2

DRAWING THE LIVING FIGURE, Joseph Sheppard. Innovative approach to artistic anatomy focuses on specifics of surface anatomy, rather than muscles and bones. Over 170 drawings of live models in front, back and side views, and in widely varying poses. Accompanying diagrams. 177 illustrations. Introduction. Index. 144pp. 8⅜ x11¼. 26723-7

GOTHIC AND OLD ENGLISH ALPHABETS: 100 Complete Fonts, Dan X. Solo. Add power, elegance to posters, signs, other graphics with 100 stunning copyright-free alphabets: Blackstone, Dolbey, Germania, 97 more–including many lower-case, numerals, punctuation marks. 104pp. 8⅛ x 11. 24695-7

HOW TO DO BEADWORK, Mary White. Fundamental book on craft from simple projects to five-bead chains and woven works. 106 illustrations. 142pp. 5⅜ x 8. 20697-1

THE BOOK OF WOOD CARVING, Charles Marshall Sayers. Finest book for beginners discusses fundamentals and offers 34 designs. "Absolutely first rate . . . well thought out and well executed."–E. J. Tangerman. 118pp. 7¾ x 10⅝. 23654-4

ILLUSTRATED CATALOG OF CIVIL WAR MILITARY GOODS: Union Army Weapons, Insignia, Uniform Accessories, and Other Equipment, Schuyler, Hartley, and Graham. Rare, profusely illustrated 1846 catalog includes Union Army uniform and dress regulations, arms and ammunition, coats, insignia, flags, swords, rifles, etc. 226 illustrations. 160pp. 9 x 12. 24939-5

WOMEN'S FASHIONS OF THE EARLY 1900s: An Unabridged Republication of "New York Fashions, 1909," National Cloak & Suit Co. Rare catalog of mail-order fashions documents women's and children's clothing styles shortly after the turn of the century. Captions offer full descriptions, prices. Invaluable resource for fashion, costume historians. Approximately 725 illustrations. 128pp. 8⅜ x 11¼. 27276-1

THE 1912 AND 1915 GUSTAV STICKLEY FURNITURE CATALOGS, Gustav Stickley. With over 200 detailed illustrations and descriptions, these two catalogs are essential reading and reference materials and identification guides for Stickley furniture. Captions cite materials, dimensions and prices. 112pp. 6½ x 9¼. 26676-1

EARLY AMERICAN LOCOMOTIVES, John H. White, Jr. Finest locomotive engravings from early 19th century: historical (1804–74), main-line (after 1870), special, foreign, etc. 147 plates. 142pp. 11⅜ x 8¼. 22772-3

THE TALL SHIPS OF TODAY IN PHOTOGRAPHS, Frank O. Braynard. Lavishly illustrated tribute to nearly 100 majestic contemporary sailing vessels: Amerigo Vespucci, Clearwater, Constitution, Eagle, Mayflower, Sea Cloud, Victory, many more. Authoritative captions provide statistics, background on each ship. 190 black-and-white photographs and illustrations. Introduction. 128pp. 8⅞ x 11¾. 27163-3

LITTLE BOOK OF EARLY AMERICAN CRAFTS AND TRADES, Peter Stockham (ed.). 1807 children's book explains crafts and trades: baker, hatter, cooper, potter, and many others. 23 copperplate illustrations. 140pp. 4⅝ x 6.   23336-7

VICTORIAN FASHIONS AND COSTUMES FROM HARPER'S BAZAR, 1867–1898, Stella Blum (ed.). Day costumes, evening wear, sports clothes, shoes, hats, other accessories in over 1,000 detailed engravings. 320pp. 9⅜ x 12¼.   22990-4

GUSTAV STICKLEY, THE CRAFTSMAN, Mary Ann Smith. Superb study surveys broad scope of Stickley's achievement, especially in architecture. Design philosophy, rise and fall of the Craftsman empire, descriptions and floor plans for many Craftsman houses, more. 86 black-and-white halftones. 31 line illustrations. Introduction 208pp. 6½ x 9¼.   27210-9

THE LONG ISLAND RAIL ROAD IN EARLY PHOTOGRAPHS, Ron Ziel. Over 220 rare photos, informative text document origin (1844) and development of rail service on Long Island. Vintage views of early trains, locomotives, stations, passengers, crews, much more. Captions. 8⅞ x 11¾.   26301-0

VOYAGE OF THE LIBERDADE, Joshua Slocum. Great 19th-century mariner's thrilling, first-hand account of the wreck of his ship off South America, the 35-foot boat he built from the wreckage, and its remarkable voyage home. 128pp. 5⅜ x 8½.
40022-0

TEN BOOKS ON ARCHITECTURE, Vitruvius. The most important book ever written on architecture. Early Roman aesthetics, technology, classical orders, site selection, all other aspects. Morgan translation. 331pp. 5⅜ x 8½.   20645-9

THE HUMAN FIGURE IN MOTION, Eadweard Muybridge. More than 4,500 stopped-action photos, in action series, showing undraped men, women, children jumping, lying down, throwing, sitting, wrestling, carrying, etc. 390pp. 7⅞ x 10⅝.
20204-6 Clothbd.

TREES OF THE EASTERN AND CENTRAL UNITED STATES AND CANADA, William M. Harlow. Best one-volume guide to 140 trees. Full descriptions, woodlore, range, etc. Over 600 illustrations. Handy size. 288pp. 4½ x 6⅜.   20395-6

SONGS OF WESTERN BIRDS, Dr. Donald J. Borror. Complete song and call repertoire of 60 western species, including flycatchers, juncoes, cactus wrens, many more–includes fully illustrated booklet.   Cassette and manual 99913-0

GROWING AND USING HERBS AND SPICES, Milo Miloradovich. Versatile handbook provides all the information needed for cultivation and use of all the herbs and spices available in North America. 4 illustrations. Index. Glossary. 236pp. 5⅜ x 8½.
25058-X

BIG BOOK OF MAZES AND LABYRINTHS, Walter Shepherd. 50 mazes and labyrinths in all–classical, solid, ripple, and more–in one great volume. Perfect inexpensive puzzler for clever youngsters. Full solutions. 112pp. 8⅛ x 11.   22951-3

PIANO TUNING, J. Cree Fischer. Clearest, best book for beginner, amateur. Simple repairs, raising dropped notes, tuning by easy method of flattened fifths. No previous skills needed. 4 illustrations. 201pp. 5⅜ x 8½. 23267-0

HINTS TO SINGERS, Lillian Nordica. Selecting the right teacher, developing confidence, overcoming stage fright, and many other important skills receive thoughtful discussion in this indispensible guide, written by a world-famous diva of four decades' experience. 96pp. 5⅜ x 8½. 40094-8

THE COMPLETE NONSENSE OF EDWARD LEAR, Edward Lear. All nonsense limericks, zany alphabets, Owl and Pussycat, songs, nonsense botany, etc., illustrated by Lear. Total of 320pp. 5⅜ x 8½. (Available in U.S. only.) 20167-8

VICTORIAN PARLOUR POETRY: An Annotated Anthology, Michael R. Turner. 117 gems by Longfellow, Tennyson, Browning, many lesser-known poets. "The Village Blacksmith," "Curfew Must Not Ring Tonight," "Only a Baby Small," dozens more, often difficult to find elsewhere. Index of poets, titles, first lines. xxiii + 325pp. 5⅜ x 8¼. 27044-0

DUBLINERS, James Joyce. Fifteen stories offer vivid, tightly focused observations of the lives of Dublin's poorer classes. At least one, "The Dead," is considered a masterpiece. Reprinted complete and unabridged from standard edition. 160pp. 5³⁄₁₆ x 8¼. 26870-5

GREAT WEIRD TALES: 14 Stories by Lovecraft, Blackwood, Machen and Others, S. T. Joshi (ed.). 14 spellbinding tales, including "The Sin Eater," by Fiona McLeod, "The Eye Above the Mantel," by Frank Belknap Long, as well as renowned works by R. H. Barlow, Lord Dunsany, Arthur Machen, W. C. Morrow and eight other masters of the genre. 256pp. 5⅜ x 8½. (Available in U.S. only.) 40436-6

THE BOOK OF THE SACRED MAGIC OF ABRAMELIN THE MAGE, translated by S. MacGregor Mathers. Medieval manuscript of ceremonial magic. Basic document in Aleister Crowley, Golden Dawn groups. 268pp. 5⅜ x 8½. 23211-5

NEW RUSSIAN-ENGLISH AND ENGLISH-RUSSIAN DICTIONARY, M. A. O'Brien. This is a remarkably handy Russian dictionary, containing a surprising amount of information, including over 70,000 entries. 366pp. 4½ x 6⅛. 20208-9

HISTORIC HOMES OF THE AMERICAN PRESIDENTS, Second, Revised Edition, Irvin Haas. A traveler's guide to American Presidential homes, most open to the public, depicting and describing homes occupied by every American President from George Washington to George Bush. With visiting hours, admission charges, travel routes. 175 photographs. Index. 160pp. 8¼ x 11. 26751-2

NEW YORK IN THE FORTIES, Andreas Feininger. 162 brilliant photographs by the well-known photographer, formerly with *Life* magazine. Commuters, shoppers, Times Square at night, much else from city at its peak. Captions by John von Hartz. 181pp. 9¼ x 10¾. 23585-8

INDIAN SIGN LANGUAGE, William Tomkins. Over 525 signs developed by Sioux and other tribes. Written instructions and diagrams. Also 290 pictographs. 111pp. 6⅛ x 9¼. 22029-X

ANATOMY: A Complete Guide for Artists, Joseph Sheppard. A master of figure drawing shows artists how to render human anatomy convincingly. Over 460 illustrations. 224pp. 8⅜ x 11¼. 27279-6

MEDIEVAL CALLIGRAPHY: Its History and Technique, Marc Drogin. Spirited history, comprehensive instruction manual covers 13 styles (ca. 4th century through 15th). Excellent photographs; directions for duplicating medieval techniques with modern tools. 224pp. 8⅜ x 11¼. 26142-5

DRIED FLOWERS: How to Prepare Them, Sarah Whitlock and Martha Rankin. Complete instructions on how to use silica gel, meal and borax, perlite aggregate, sand and borax, glycerine and water to create attractive permanent flower arrangements. 12 illustrations. 32pp. 5⅜ x 8½. 21802-3

EASY-TO-MAKE BIRD FEEDERS FOR WOODWORKERS, Scott D. Campbell. Detailed, simple-to-use guide for designing, constructing, caring for and using feeders. Text, illustrations for 12 classic and contemporary designs. 96pp. 5⅜ x 8½. 25847-5

SCOTTISH WONDER TALES FROM MYTH AND LEGEND, Donald A. Mackenzie. 16 lively tales tell of giants rumbling down mountainsides, of a magic wand that turns stone pillars into warriors, of gods and goddesses, evil hags, powerful forces and more. 240pp. 5⅜ x 8½. 29677-6

THE HISTORY OF UNDERCLOTHES, C. Willett Cunnington and Phyllis Cunnington. Fascinating, well-documented survey covering six centuries of English undergarments, enhanced with over 100 illustrations: 12th-century laced-up bodice, footed long drawers (1795), 19th-century bustles, 19th-century corsets for men, Victorian "bust improvers," much more. 272pp. 5⅝ x 8¼. 27124-2

ARTS AND CRAFTS FURNITURE: The Complete Brooks Catalog of 1912, Brooks Manufacturing Co. Photos and detailed descriptions of more than 150 now very collectible furniture designs from the Arts and Crafts movement depict davenports, settees, buffets, desks, tables, chairs, bedsteads, dressers and more, all built of solid, quarter-sawed oak. Invaluable for students and enthusiasts of antiques, Americana and the decorative arts. 80pp. 6½ x 9¼. 27471-3

WILBUR AND ORVILLE: A Biography of the Wright Brothers, Fred Howard. Definitive, crisply written study tells the full story of the brothers' lives and work. A vividly written biography, unparalleled in scope and color, that also captures the spirit of an extraordinary era. 560pp. 6⅛ x 9¼. 40297-5

THE ARTS OF THE SAILOR: Knotting, Splicing and Ropework, Hervey Garrett Smith. Indispensable shipboard reference covers tools, basic knots and useful hitches; handsewing and canvas work, more. Over 100 illustrations. Delightful reading for sea lovers. 256pp. 5⅜ x 8½. 26440-8

FRANK LLOYD WRIGHT'S FALLINGWATER: The House and Its History, Second, Revised Edition, Donald Hoffmann. A total revision–both in text and illustrations–of the standard document on Fallingwater, the boldest, most personal architectural statement of Wright's mature years, updated with valuable new material from the recently opened Frank Lloyd Wright Archives. "Fascinating"–*The New York Times*. 116 illustrations. 128pp. 9¼ x 10¾. 27430-6

PHOTOGRAPHIC SKETCHBOOK OF THE CIVIL WAR, Alexander Gardner. 100 photos taken on field during the Civil War. Famous shots of Manassas Harper's Ferry, Lincoln, Richmond, slave pens, etc. 244pp. 10⅝ x 8¼. 22731-6

FIVE ACRES AND INDEPENDENCE, Maurice G. Kains. Great back-to-the-land classic explains basics of self-sufficient farming. The one book to get. 95 illustrations. 397pp. 5⅜ x 8½. 20974-1

SONGS OF EASTERN BIRDS, Dr. Donald J. Borror. Songs and calls of 60 species most common to eastern U.S.: warblers, woodpeckers, flycatchers, thrushes, larks, many more in high-quality recording. Cassette and manual 99912-2

A MODERN HERBAL, Margaret Grieve. Much the fullest, most exact, most useful compilation of herbal material. Gigantic alphabetical encyclopedia, from aconite to zedoary, gives botanical information, medical properties, folklore, economic uses, much else. Indispensable to serious reader. 161 illustrations. 888pp. 6½ x 9¼. 2-vol. set. (Available in U.S. only.) Vol. I: 22798-7
Vol. II: 22799-5

HIDDEN TREASURE MAZE BOOK, Dave Phillips. Solve 34 challenging mazes accompanied by heroic tales of adventure. Evil dragons, people-eating plants, blood-thirsty giants, many more dangerous adversaries lurk at every twist and turn. 34 mazes, stories, solutions. 48pp. 8¼ x 11. 24566-7

LETTERS OF W. A. MOZART, Wolfgang A. Mozart. Remarkable letters show bawdy wit, humor, imagination, musical insights, contemporary musical world; includes some letters from Leopold Mozart. 276pp. 5⅜ x 8½. 22859-2

BASIC PRINCIPLES OF CLASSICAL BALLET, Agrippina Vaganova. Great Russian theoretician, teacher explains methods for teaching classical ballet. 118 illustrations. 175pp. 5⅜ x 8½. 22036-2

THE JUMPING FROG, Mark Twain. Revenge edition. The original story of The Celebrated Jumping Frog of Calaveras County, a hapless French translation, and Twain's hilarious "retranslation" from the French. 12 illustrations. 66pp. 5⅜ x 8½. 22686-7

BEST REMEMBERED POEMS, Martin Gardner (ed.). The 126 poems in this superb collection of 19th- and 20th-century British and American verse range from Shelley's "To a Skylark" to the impassioned "Renascence" of Edna St. Vincent Millay and to Edward Lear's whimsical "The Owl and the Pussycat." 224pp. 5⅜ x 8½. 27165-X

COMPLETE SONNETS, William Shakespeare. Over 150 exquisite poems deal with love, friendship, the tyranny of time, beauty's evanescence, death and other themes in language of remarkable power, precision and beauty. Glossary of archaic terms. 80pp. 5$\frac{3}{16}$ x 8¼. 26686-9

THE BATTLES THAT CHANGED HISTORY, Fletcher Pratt. Eminent historian profiles 16 crucial conflicts, ancient to modern, that changed the course of civilization. 352pp. 5⅜ x 8½. 41129-X

THE WIT AND HUMOR OF OSCAR WILDE, Alvin Redman (ed.). More than 1,000 ripostes, paradoxes, wisecracks: Work is the curse of the drinking classes; I can resist everything except temptation; etc. 258pp. 5⅜ x 8½. 20602-5

SHAKESPEARE LEXICON AND QUOTATION DICTIONARY, Alexander Schmidt. Full definitions, locations, shades of meaning in every word in plays and poems. More than 50,000 exact quotations. 1,485pp. 6½ x 9¼. 2-vol. set.
Vol. 1: 22726-X
Vol. 2: 22727-8

SELECTED POEMS, Emily Dickinson. Over 100 best-known, best-loved poems by one of America's foremost poets, reprinted from authoritative early editions. No comparable edition at this price. Index of first lines. 64pp. 5³⁄₁₆ x 8¼. 26466-1

THE INSIDIOUS DR. FU-MANCHU, Sax Rohmer. The first of the popular mystery series introduces a pair of English detectives to their archnemesis, the diabolical Dr. Fu-Manchu. Flavorful atmosphere, fast-paced action, and colorful characters enliven this classic of the genre. 208pp. 5³⁄₁₆ x 8¼. 29898-1

THE MALLEUS MALEFICARUM OF KRAMER AND SPRENGER, translated by Montague Summers. Full text of most important witchhunter's "bible," used by both Catholics and Protestants. 278pp. 6⅝ x 10. 22802-9

SPANISH STORIES/CUENTOS ESPAÑOLES: A Dual-Language Book, Angel Flores (ed.). Unique format offers 13 great stories in Spanish by Cervantes, Borges, others. Faithful English translations on facing pages. 352pp. 5⅜ x 8½. 25399-6

GARDEN CITY, LONG ISLAND, IN EARLY PHOTOGRAPHS, 1869–1919, Mildred H. Smith. Handsome treasury of 118 vintage pictures, accompanied by carefully researched captions, document the Garden City Hotel fire (1899), the Vanderbilt Cup Race (1908), the first airmail flight departing from the Nassau Boulevard Aerodrome (1911), and much more. 96pp. 8⅞ x 11¾. 40669-5

OLD QUEENS, N.Y., IN EARLY PHOTOGRAPHS, Vincent F. Seyfried and William Asadorian. Over 160 rare photographs of Maspeth, Jamaica, Jackson Heights, and other areas. Vintage views of DeWitt Clinton mansion, 1939 World's Fair and more. Captions. 192pp. 8⅞ x 11. 26358-4

CAPTURED BY THE INDIANS: 15 Firsthand Accounts, 1750-1870, Frederick Drimmer. Astounding true historical accounts of grisly torture, bloody conflicts, relentless pursuits, miraculous escapes and more, by people who lived to tell the tale. 384pp. 5⅜ x 8½. 24901-8

THE WORLD'S GREAT SPEECHES (Fourth Enlarged Edition), Lewis Copeland, Lawrence W. Lamm, and Stephen J. McKenna. Nearly 300 speeches provide public speakers with a wealth of updated quotes and inspiration–from Pericles' funeral oration and William Jennings Bryan's "Cross of Gold Speech" to Malcolm X's powerful words on the Black Revolution and Earl of Spenser's tribute to his sister, Diana, Princess of Wales. 944pp. 5⅜ x 8⅜. 40903-1

THE BOOK OF THE SWORD, Sir Richard F. Burton. Great Victorian scholar/adventurer's eloquent, erudite history of the "queen of weapons"–from prehistory to early Roman Empire. Evolution and development of early swords, variations (sabre, broadsword, cutlass, scimitar, etc.), much more. 336pp. 6⅛ x 9¼. 25434-8

CATALOG OF DOVER BOOKS

AUTOBIOGRAPHY: The Story of My Experiments with Truth, Mohandas K. Gandhi. Boyhood, legal studies, purification, the growth of the Satyagraha (nonviolent protest) movement. Critical, inspiring work of the man responsible for the freedom of India. 480pp. 5⅜ x 8½. (Available in U.S. only.) 24593-4

CELTIC MYTHS AND LEGENDS, T. W. Rolleston. Masterful retelling of Irish and Welsh stories and tales. Cuchulain, King Arthur, Deirdre, the Grail, many more. First paperback edition. 58 full-page illustrations. 512pp. 5⅜ x 8½. 26507-2

THE PRINCIPLES OF PSYCHOLOGY, William James. Famous long course complete, unabridged. Stream of thought, time perception, memory, experimental methods; great work decades ahead of its time. 94 figures. 1,391pp. 5⅜ x 8½. 2-vol. set. Vol. I: 20381-6 Vol. II: 20382-4

THE WORLD AS WILL AND REPRESENTATION, Arthur Schopenhauer. Definitive English translation of Schopenhauer's life work, correcting more than 1,000 errors, omissions in earlier translations. Translated by E. F. J. Payne. Total of 1,269pp. 5⅜ x 8½. 2-vol. set. Vol. 1: 21761-2 Vol. 2: 21762-0

MAGIC AND MYSTERY IN TIBET, Madame Alexandra David-Neel. Experiences among lamas, magicians, sages, sorcerers, Bonpa wizards. A true psychic discovery. 32 illustrations. 321pp. 5⅜ x 8½. (Available in U.S. only.) 22682-4

THE EGYPTIAN BOOK OF THE DEAD, E. A. Wallis Budge. Complete reproduction of Ani's papyrus, finest ever found. Full hieroglyphic text, interlinear transliteration, word-for-word translation, smooth translation. 533pp. 6½ x 9¼. 21866-X

MATHEMATICS FOR THE NONMATHEMATICIAN, Morris Kline. Detailed, college-level treatment of mathematics in cultural and historical context, with numerous exercises. Recommended Reading Lists. Tables. Numerous figures. 641pp. 5⅜ x 8½. 24823-2

PROBABILISTIC METHODS IN THE THEORY OF STRUCTURES, Isaac Elishakoff. Well-written introduction covers the elements of the theory of probability from two or more random variables, the reliability of such multivariable structures, the theory of random function, Monte Carlo methods of treating problems incapable of exact solution, and more. Examples. 502pp. 5⅜ x 8½. 40691-1

THE RIME OF THE ANCIENT MARINER, Gustave Doré, S. T. Coleridge. Doré's finest work; 34 plates capture moods, subtleties of poem. Flawless full-size reproductions printed on facing pages with authoritative text of poem. "Beautiful. Simply beautiful."–*Publisher's Weekly.* 77pp. 9¼ x 12. 22305-1

NORTH AMERICAN INDIAN DESIGNS FOR ARTISTS AND CRAFTSPEOPLE, Eva Wilson. Over 360 authentic copyright-free designs adapted from Navajo blankets, Hopi pottery, Sioux buffalo hides, more. Geometrics, symbolic figures, plant and animal motifs, etc. 128pp. 8⅜ x 11. (Not for sale in the United Kingdom.) 25341-4

SCULPTURE: Principles and Practice, Louis Slobodkin. Step-by-step approach to clay, plaster, metals, stone; classical and modern. 253 drawings, photos. 255pp. 8⅛ x 11. 22960-2

THE INFLUENCE OF SEA POWER UPON HISTORY, 1660–1783, A. T. Mahan. Influential classic of naval history and tactics still used as text in war colleges. First paperback edition. 4 maps. 24 battle plans. 640pp. 5⅜ x 8½. 25509-3

THE STORY OF THE TITANIC AS TOLD BY ITS SURVIVORS, Jack Winocour (ed.). What it was really like. Panic, despair, shocking inefficiency, and a little heroism. More thrilling than any fictional account. 26 illustrations. 320pp. 5⅜ x 8½. 20610-6

FAIRY AND FOLK TALES OF THE IRISH PEASANTRY, William Butler Yeats (ed.). Treasury of 64 tales from the twilight world of Celtic myth and legend: "The Soul Cages," "The Kildare Pooka," "King O'Toole and his Goose," many more. Introduction and Notes by W. B. Yeats. 352pp. 5⅜ x 8½. 26941-8

BUDDHIST MAHAYANA TEXTS, E. B. Cowell and others (eds.). Superb, accurate translations of basic documents in Mahayana Buddhism, highly important in history of religions. The Buddha-karita of Asvaghosha, Larger Sukhavativyuha, more. 448pp. 5⅜ x 8½. 25552-2

ONE TWO THREE . . . INFINITY: Facts and Speculations of Science, George Gamow. Great physicist's fascinating, readable overview of contemporary science: number theory, relativity, fourth dimension, entropy, genes, atomic structure, much more. 128 illustrations. Index. 352pp. 5⅜ x 8½. 25664-2

EXPERIMENTATION AND MEASUREMENT, W. J. Youden. Introductory manual explains laws of measurement in simple terms and offers tips for achieving accuracy and minimizing errors. Mathematics of measurement, use of instruments, experimenting with machines. 1994 edition. Foreword. Preface. Introduction. Epilogue. Selected Readings. Glossary. Index. Tables and figures. 128pp. 5⅜ x 8½. 40451-X

DALÍ ON MODERN ART: The Cuckolds of Antiquated Modern Art, Salvador Dalí. Influential painter skewers modern art and its practitioners. Outrageous evaluations of Picasso, Cézanne, Turner, more. 15 renderings of paintings discussed. 44 calligraphic decorations by Dalí. 96pp. 5⅜ x 8½. (Available in U.S. only.) 29220-7

ANTIQUE PLAYING CARDS: A Pictorial History, Henry René D'Allemagne. Over 900 elaborate, decorative images from rare playing cards (14th–20th centuries): Bacchus, death, dancing dogs, hunting scenes, royal coats of arms, players cheating, much more. 96pp. 9¼ x 12¼. 29265-7

MAKING FURNITURE MASTERPIECES: 30 Projects with Measured Drawings, Franklin H. Gottshall. Step-by-step instructions, illustrations for constructing handsome, useful pieces, among them a Sheraton desk, Chippendale chair, Spanish desk, Queen Anne table and a William and Mary dressing mirror. 224pp. 8⅛ x 11¼. 29338-6

THE FOSSIL BOOK: A Record of Prehistoric Life, Patricia V. Rich et al. Profusely illustrated definitive guide covers everything from single-celled organisms and dinosaurs to birds and mammals and the interplay between climate and man. Over 1,500 illustrations. 760pp. 7½ x 10⅛. 29371-8

Paperbound unless otherwise indicated. Available at your book dealer, online at **www.doverpublications.com**, or by writing to Dept. GI, Dover Publications, Inc., 31 East 2nd Street, Mineola, NY 11501. For current price information or for free catalogues (please indicate field of interest), write to Dover Publications or log on to **www.doverpublications.com** and see every Dover book in print. Dover publishes more than 500 books each year on science, elementary and advanced mathematics, biology, music, art, literary history, social sciences, and other areas.